CRISIS RESPONSE

CRISIS RESPONSE

INSIDE

STORIES ON

MANAGING

IMAGE

UNDER

SIEGE

Jack A. Gottschalk, editor

DETROIT • WASHINGTON D.C. • LONDON

Crisis Response:
Inside Stories on Managing Image Under Siege

Published by **Visible Ink Press**™
a division of Gale Research Inc.
835 Penobscot Building
Detroit, MI 48226-4094

Visible Ink Press™ is a trademark of Gale Research Inc.

Art Director: Cynthia Baldwin
Cover and Page Design: Mark C. Howell
My Lai Map Illustrations: George Dzahristos

Cover photo of *Maid of the Seas* cockpit (top):AP/Wide World Photos
Cover photo of *Exxon Valdez* (center): UPI/Bettmann Newsphotos
Cover photo of Three Mile Island (bottom): UPI/Bettmann Newsphotos

ISBN 0-8103-9130-9

Contents

Consumer Troubles

Human Tragedies

Appendix

Foreword

Kurt P. Stocker
Chief Corporate Relations Officer, Continental Bank Corporation

I have always believed that some things can't be taught in a classroom or learned from a textbook, among them wrestling, flying a 747, scuba diving, and handling a crisis. As it turns out, that belief didn't stop Northwestern's Medill School of Journalism from asking me to teach a graduate class in crisis communications management, or Jack Gottschalk from creating *Crisis Response: Inside Stories on Managing Image Under Siege.*

Those who came to the class expecting to find some grand, unified theory on handling a crisis were probably disappointed, and those who come to this book expecting to find a universal outline, a set of telling homilies, or a convenient checklist of crisis dos and don'ts will probably be disappointed as well. The aim of advanced management of this complex topic hasn't been to develop a broad theory of crisis communications, but to identify patterns, principles, and a way of thinking that can help put those principles into action.

The phrase *way of thinking* is important. There may be some theory in this book, but it's in here much the same way the theory of aerodynamics is in the mind of a pilot who loses an engine at 35,000 feet. What counts isn't what's in the text, or even what the last pilot did or didn't do, but how well this pilot's thinking — guided by experience and extensive simulation — helps him or her grasp and respond to the problem on this plane, in these circumstances. Theories, models, and methodologies can help us prepare for a crisis, but once the engine's lost, how we think is all that matters.

In fact, as case after case in *Crisis Response* shows, the right response to a crisis for one organization may be the exact opposite of the right response for another in what seem to be similar circumstances. Look at Johnson & Johnson's handling of Tylenol capsule tampering and Gerber's reaction to accusations of glass in their baby food. Johnson & Johnson immediately removed its product from the market; Gerber fought to keep its product on the shelf. Both companies did the right thing. Compare McDonald's reaction to the shooting in San Ysidro and the actions of Luby's Cafeterias following a similar incident in Texas. McDonald's closed and bulldozed its restaurant. Luby's, with public support, kept its open. Again, each company handled its situation correctly.

Given these complexities, how do you teach crisis communications the "easy way" without putting a product, a company, or a life at risk? The best analogy, again, is the way airlines teach pilots to fly 747s, without risk to real passengers or the expense of taking a plane out of service. You go to the basement of a building and teach through simulation, programming all the things that have gone wrong in past accidents and some other things that could, teaching a pilot how to deal with them. This is not rote learning. It's learning to think in an emergency, since the next crisis may not be covered in the program. This method works for pilots, and it worked for Professor Clarke Caywood and me at Medill last fall. We used these accounts and an interactive case-study approach to teaching crisis communications. [See the Appendix for details.]

There is much to be learned from the professionals who lived the crises described in these chapters, some of whom visited our basement at Northwestern. There is also some less obvious learning to be gained by reading between the lines: understanding we gained by researching many of the cases and talking to participants on both sides of the controversies and some observers on the sidelines.

We learned, for example, that all the statistics and surveys that say that 70 or 80 or 90 percent of *Fortune* 500 companies have crisis plans are somewhat misleading. Most companies have business-resumption or operations plans. Most do not have adequate crisis communications plans, including many cited in this text.

We also learned that few companies really understand when a crisis has actually begun, much less when one is beginning. We all know that the first few hours and the first few decisions in a crisis determine the outcome. If you can't recognize a crisis early on, those hours, decisions, and the day, are lost.

Further, we learned that in many cases the real crisis potential of a set of events was camouflaged by time pressures or by a blind spot at headquarters. Too often, decisions were made to prevent lawsuits, while a company's products or reputation took a beating in the market. Too often, the communicator's counsel was ignored until the situation was out of anyone's control. At that point, a conservative legal approach was often useless.

This book tries to capture the reality and the cost of crises without trying to provide simplistic solutions to all situations. There are basics in this business, and they are valuable. There are theories and processes that can help us prepare for crises, and they are essential. There are specialized approaches to specific industries, and they are vital issues. But it is experience and case studies — learning to fly in the basement without live passengers on board — that really help carry the day.

Kurt P. Stocker is chief corporate relations officer for Continental Bank Corporation, responsible for the company's marketing/public relations, community relations, internal communications, corporate advertising, industry and financial communications, and legislative relations. He is also an adjunct professor at Northwestern University. Prior to joining Continental Bank, he was senior vice-president of corporate communications for United Airlines and senior vice-president of the Chicago office of Hill and Knowlton.

Introduction

Jack Gottschalk

In 1882, in response to a question about public safety, New York Central railroad tycoon William H. Vanderbilt exclaimed: "The public be damned!"

In 1948, Eddie Rickenbacker, then president of Eastern Air Lines, was asked about passenger complaints concerning dirty airplanes. He reportedly said: "We get paid to fly these people … not to coddle them." This attitude, of course, did nothing to help Eastern's image of poor aircraft maintenance and its reputation of flying in conditions that would ground even seagulls.

It is comforting to believe that modern executives, both in the public and private sectors, have come a long way from the attitudes exhibited by Vanderbilt and Rickenbacker.

But many haven't.

Many public officials still run for cover when things go wrong. Likewise, many private sector executives, who often pride themselves on being a different breed from people in public management, share the same unhappy behavior characteristic.

In short, public departments and agencies, private sector organizations, and (sometimes) even entire industries, often react to crisis by pulling the wagons into a tight circle, saying as little as possible, and waiting for the smoke of inquiry or anger to blow over so that they can return to business as usual.

In *Crisis Response: Inside Stories on Managing Image Under Siege*, we examine the ways in which organizations, at least some of them, managed their responsi-

Response, Planning, Execution, and Truth

bility of reacting to the legitimate informational needs of the media and, thus, the public. This does not mean the attempted management of the media, but management of the way in which the organization, facing a major crisis, communicated.

And we have, quite deliberately, looked at the word "crisis" in a very general way.

While it might, at first glance, seem that a crisis connotes a brief, violent incident, that is not always true. When, for example, an organization faces bankruptcy and, perhaps, its ultimate survival, such a crisis is just as severe as one in which a factory disappears with a roar and a cloud of smoke. Crises vary from person to company to government body, of course, but the end result may well be the same.

Planning — being prepared for when a crisis occurs — is given a lot of attention in these pages.

In case after case, it becomes clear that planning for a crisis, in terms of successful media relations, is absolutely vital. But planning must be coupled with effective execution when the crisis occurs. And effective execution requires the *total* support of top management whether in the public or the private sector, whether in profit or not-for-profit organizations.

Planning cannot be simply viewed by top management as just another method of executive staff training. Unfortunately, that is sometimes the case.

Finally, there is the basic requirement that management tell the truth. There are people in management, both in government and in the private sector, who have trouble with that requirement. The best planning and the best execution in the world mean nothing when management lies.

The eyewitnesses and observers of the crises analyzed in here make no claim that these incidents were managed in the best possible way. There are *always* lessons to be learned from any experience.

The fact, however, that we were able to put this book together is a positive sign that some managements *do* recognize the need to prepare for, and execute, public relations responses when facing the demands of the media in a crisis. The accounts presented here, we believe, are both interesting and informative.

Unfortunately, while creating this book, we ran into some negative and disturbing incidents.

Corporate Resistance There are several crisis management incidents that would have been valuable to examine, but the respective corporate managements involved, for whatever reasons, refused to participate.

Their unwillingness to cooperate was particularly disturbing given the fact that this work is not — and they knew it — an investigative report. Each organization missed an opportunity to discuss its respective crisis from its point of view.

Occidental Petroleum, for example, was given such an opportunity with regard to its involvement with the infamous Love Canal. This area, near Niagara Falls, New York, was used as a toxic dumping site from 1947 to 1952 by Hooker Chemicals and Plastics Corporation, a subsidiary of Occidental Petroleum. The company sold the poisoned area to the Niagara Falls Board of Education in 1953. In 1976, the toxic wastes began to take their toll on life and property and the name Love Canal became a symbol of environmental pollution. Hooker Chemical refused to accept any liability for the damages, of whatever kind, created by their use of the canal as a toxic sewer.

Perrier, the bottler of a mineral water that was recalled in February 1990 when benzene was detected in some of its bottles, was another company that chose not to provide a chapter on how it handled the public relations aspects of that recall.

Dow Corning, the company that concealed complaints from medical doctors about its silicone gel breast implants, refused to talk here about how it attempted to deal with the media during that crisis, thereby missing a chance to defend itself against its critics.

Even the City of Chicago, which was applauded by many for its communications efforts during the April 1992 flood that paralyzed the city and cost an estimated one billion dollars, refused to present a case history of how it reacted in the face of that crisis. It is unfortunate that this city administration would not discuss an event about which it should be justly proud.

And these are just a few. The fact that any late-20th-century private or public sector management would turn down a chance to provide information about how it planned for, and managed, any crisis that has been subjected to historical analysis is not just unbelievable, it is chilling. An organization's credibility can suffer major and sometimes irreparable damage as a result.

If, after all, a management will not discuss a subject with which the public is already familiar, can we believe it at all, anytime?

And, in a broader and far more important sense, one must consider what other things that may be detrimental to our health and safety are being hidden in corporate or government vaults, file cabinets, and security-shrouded executive offices.

But, as noted earlier, there is a bright side.

Formulating the Book In determining which crises to include, I talked to people in the public relations business — friends, associates, long-time colleagues. I or those I talked to knew someone (or knew someone who knew someone…!) who had worked with a public or private firm during a crisis. Some PR people agreed to write about their experience during the crisis, while others introduced me to people within the actual organization who agreed to provide a first-hand account. Very public incidents were soon joined by lesser known, but equally important and interesting, episodes.

Laying Out the Book *Crisis Response* is grouped into three broad subject categories: **Business Calamities**, **Consumer Troubles**, and **Human Tragedies**. An appendix and a general index conclude the book. Here's what you'll find in the following pages.

Business Calamities In "The Fall of Drexel Burnham Lambert," **Angela Z. Dailey**, DBL's former senior vice-president, provides an insider's story on that company's efforts to survive a federal government investigation into securities fraud violations. Former public relations vice-president **William P. Mullane, Jr.** discusses how his company dealt with "The AT&T Network Breakdown" in January 1990. In "Mobil and the Oil Embargo," former public affairs vice-president **Herb Schmertz** takes us back to the oil crisis of the mid-1970s and discusses how one oil company not only got through it, but successfully influenced public and governmental opinion.

Continental Airlines vice-president of public affairs **Art Kent** flashes back to the 1990 bankruptcy announcement in "Continental Announces Chapter 11." In "Capping Phillips's Bravo," **James A. Fyock**, former director of public relations, reviews how that company dealt with a well blowout that spewed a 200-foot-high jet of crude oil into the North Sea. **John P. Scanlon**, a partner at Sawyer Miller Group, looks at how a major television network handled its own involvement in a high-profile libel trial: "General Westmoreland versus CBS."

In "Oil Wars: Pennzoil versus Texaco," Pennzoil's vice-president of administrative affairs, **Thomas C. Powell**, reviews the 1985 litigation between these two oil giants, which made mergers and acquisitions soap opera material and ultimately asked, When is a deal a deal? "Meltdown on Three Mile Island," written by **Richard C. Hyde**, executive vice-president in the corporate counseling division at Hill and Knowlton USA, details how Three Mile Island personnel dealt with the near nuclear power plant meltdown in March 1979. In "Anatomy of a Crisis," **Ron Rogers** provides guidelines for formulating strategy decisions as a crisis unfolds.

Consumer Troubles Geduldig Communications Management president **Alfred Geduldig** shows how a condom manufacturer, Ansell-Americas, dealt with a defective batch of condoms as well as bad publicity over one product's effectiveness in "Condom Crises." In "A Red Herring in the Chicken Coop," Fleishman-Hillard, Inc. vice-president **Jane E. Redicker** discusses the poultry industry's attempts to fight off what it felt was unfair publicity on salmonella and the safety of its poultry. In "Villains and Victims of Product Tampering," **L. James Lovejoy**, former director of communications, Gerber Products Company, talks about how that firm handled what turned out to be unsubstantiated claims of broken glass in its baby food jars.

James E. Lukaszewski, chairman of The Lukaszewski Group, writes the "The *Exxon Valdez* Paradox," an analysis of Exxon's handling of the great oil spill, which resulted in environmental peril in Alaska. Hill and Knowlton, Inc. executive vice-president **Christopher P. A. Komisarjevsky** examines product liability lawsuits in "Trial by Media." In "Repealing Gibson's Law," Fleishman-Hillard, Inc. senior vice-president **Peter S. McCue** introduces the notion that for every study presented, there's another study that can refute it. He addresses the question, How do consumers deal with this abundance of information and the resulting confusion?

In "Disaster at Lockerbie," **Raymond J. O'Rourke**, executive vice-president and director of crisis communications at Burson-Marsteller, looks at how international terrorism marked disaster for airline passengers and a small Scottish town — and ultimately had a hand in the demise of Pan American World Airways. **George S. Lowman**, director of communications at GATX Corporation, reviews "The Calnev Pipeline Fire," when a runaway train derailed in a San Bernadino, California, neighborhood and ruptured an underground gas pipeline causing a fire, destruction, and casualties. A partner in public affairs at Arnold Consultants, **Richard H. Truitt** talks about how a New York City stock brokerage firm reacted to "The Wall Street Murder." **Human Tragedies**

In "Death of the Asbestos Industry," **Matthew M. Swetonic**, former director of environmental affairs for Johns-Manville Corporation, explains how asbestos transformed from "magic mineral" to dangerous substance. McDonald's Corporation senior vice-president **Richard G. Starmann** writes in "Tragedy at McDonald's" how this fast-food firm communicated with the press and the community following a mass shooting at its San Ysidro, California, restaurant. Retired Major General **Winant Sidle** goes back to the 1960s in talking about one of the worst atrocities in U.S. military history — "Massacre at My Lai."

In "United Airlines Prepares for the Worst," former manager of external communications **Robert A. Doughty** discusses how United Airlines prepared for crisis — and then acted on those plans when accidents actually occurred. **Jackson B. Browning**, retired vice-president of health, safety, and environmental programs at Union Carbide, looks at how that corporation handled the tragic gas leak that killed thousands in India in "Union Carbide: Disaster at Bhopal." **Larry M. Speakes** gives two eyewitness accounts of crises in "From the White House to Wall Street": the government's handling of the *Challenger* tragedy when he was President Ronald Reagan's chief spokesman; and the business approach to the "Black Monday" stock market crash in October 1987 when he was Merrill Lynch's senior vice-president of communications. **Douglas G. Hearle**, former vice-chairman at Hill and Knowlton, provides basic suggestions in "Planning for Crisis."

In the book's appendix, Northwestern University professor of business communications **Clarke Caywood** and Continental Bank Corporation chief corporate relations officer **Kurt P. Stocker** present "The Ultimate Crisis Plan," an outline on crisis preparedness.

Acknowledgments
My personal and sincere thanks go to the aforementioned authors whose time and effort went a long way in creating the chapters that comprise this book.

In addition, the following graduate students in Caywood and Stocker's Corporate Public Relations class at Northwestern University contributed to the "Ultimate Crisis Plan": Mary Schmitt (plan manager), Cindy Blikre, Elizabeth Bunta, Kathy Krebs, Amy Levinthal, Rhonda Luniak, Maggie Shea, Rhonda Strauss, Becky Teets, Lisa Van Den Berge, and Natasha Wilson.

There are others who helped keep the book process in motion and for that my thanks go to Bill Bruns, Debbie Evans, Tom Failla, Craig Fisher, Terry Hemeyer, Sheldon Woodbury, and a lot of other people who, while unnamed here, made contributions that did not go unappreciated.

On the production end, Gina Renée Gross provided copyediting services, Theresa Murray indexed the book, and Marco Di Vita at The Graphix Group supplied typesetting.

Finally, my thanks to the people who helped turn this book from an idea to a reality. Doug Hearle is one of those people. My agent, John Willig, is another. There were a number of people on the staff at Gale Research Inc., but without question, my closest and continuing contacts were with Greg Michael and Larry Baker. I thank them as well as Visible Ink Press staffers Martin Connors, Julie Winklepleck, and Cheryl McDonald for their continuing help and encouragement.

Jack A. Gottschalk is an attorney and public affairs consultant. He has been involved in PR and corporate communication for more than 15 years. He formerly held corporate marketing and PR posts with Textron Inc. and Sherwin-Williams Inc. From 1981 to 1989, he served as a member of the New Jersey Supreme Court Committee on Relations with the Media. He also was an assistant prosecutor and public affairs officer in the Essex County, New Jersey prosecutor's office.

Mr. Gottschalk holds an M.A. in international relations from Salve Regina University, an M.S. in management from The American College, and a law degree from the University of Baltimore. He also did graduate work at Columbia University. In 1970, he received a direct appointment as a captain in the U.S. Army Reserve, based on his background in journalism and public information.

Gottschalk is an adjunct professor of management and marketing at Fairleigh Dickinson University, and was a guest lecturer on crisis PR at Northwestern's Medill School of Journalism. He is the host of a cable television show, "Legally Speaking." He is also the author of several books, including Promoting Your Professional Practice *(1991),* Managing a Law Firm for Survival *(1991), and* Marketing/Public Relations for Lawyers *(1990).*

Photo Credits

Photographs appearing in *Crisis Response* were received from the following sources:

AP/Wide World Photos: pp. v and 7, 36, 48, 75, 88, 102, 115, 127, 196, 217, 236, vi and 265, 298, 334, 337, 346, 347, 361, 372, 400; Courtesy of William P. Mullane, Jr.: pp. 18; UPI/Bettmann: pp. 64, vii and 312, 389; Courtesy of Ansell-Americas: pp. 146; Courtesy of WAGA-TV, Atlanta, Georgia: pp. 164; Courtesy of *Daily News:* 178; Reuters/Bettmann: pp. 202, 254, 257, 378; Courtesy of *O'Dwyer PR Services Report:* 205; UPI/Bettmann Newsphotos: 208; Keith Meyers/NYT Pictures: pp. 278; The Bettmann Archive: pp. 390.

BUSINESS CALAMITIES

The Fall of Drexel Burnham Lambert

Angela Z. Dailey
Former Senior Vice-President, Drexel Burnham Lambert

This is an insider's story of Drexel Burnham Lambert's efforts to survive a two-and-a-half-year investigation by the government into securities fraud violations that began with the indictment of prominent investment banker Dennis Levine in May 1986.

Overview

During this period the firm was investigated by the Securities and Exchange Commission, the U.S. Attorney, and the Justice Department, who spent an unprecedented amount of money — estimated at more than $2.5 million — and thousands of staff hours trying to prove their case. The investigation placed increasing pressure on the firm and its star employee, Michael Milken, a trader in high-yielding securities in the firm's Beverly Hills office.

Finally confronted with the threat of a RICO indictment (the 1970 racketeer-influenced and corrupt organizations law), CEO Fred Joseph, with board of director approval, plead the firm guilty in December 1988 to six counts of mail and securities fraud and agreed to pay a $650 million fine. Ironically it would be the settlement that would bring about the firm's demise. The firm made public statements that it could survive the fine. However even for a very rich organization, the unprecedented fine made management desperate to find ways to streamline the firm. It chose to sell its retail network; a decision that would directly result in laying off more than half of its 10,000 employees. They felt betrayed by management and even among those who remained, management lost its credibility. Morale plummeted and a little more than 12 months later, the firm again under pressure from the government, filed for bankruptcy protection.

The years during the investigation were a challenging period and a very difficult one for everyone at Drexel Burnham. Management approached the challenge as it did business issues to be managed, and for a while the firm was able to function well, maintain morale, and continue a strong business flow. What was surprising was not that the firm finally collapsed, but rather that it was able to survive for such a sustained period.

The case of Drexel Burnham still remains very controversial — some see the demise as the result of a vendetta of the government and others see the ending as just desserts for a firm rife with greed and symbolizing the ills of the 1980s. However, lessons can be learned from the communications strategies and programs that held the firm together when by all objective measures it should have folded.

Life before Wartime   When I joined the firm in 1972, it was simply Burnham and Company, a medium-sized brokerage firm with 1,200 employees. Its history dated back to 1935 when one of the legends in the securities business, I.W. Burnham II, founded the firm with $100,000 in borrowed capital and one partner. He remained in charge of the firm until the mid-1970s, when a more aggressive management took over.

The firm grew steadily over the decades into a full-service securities firm with branches in major cities across the country. In 1973 a merger with Drexel Firestone brought the firm prestige in investment banking circles, and a then obscure trader in junk bonds — Mike Milken. In 1976 a merger with Lambert Brussels brought the firm additional capital and an international connection.

Fred Joseph, who would lead the firm through the government's investigation as CEO, joined Drexel Burnham in the early 1970s. He was charged with building the firm's corporate finance effort. He knew that it would be very difficult — if not impossible — to challenge firms such as Goldman Sachs and Morgan Stanley to work with America's Fortune 500 companies. This left working with smaller companies to finance their needs. In the late 1970s an innovative idea was hatched between the corporate finance department in New York and the high-yield — a.k.a. junk — department in Beverly Hills. The investment bankers would issue high yield bonds for mid-sized companies excluded from the investment grade bond market and the traders in California would place and trade those securities.

Prior to Drexel Burnham offering these new issue high-yield bonds, very little activity occurred in new issue bonds rated below investment grade. This area continued to grow and by the mid-1980s was responsible for most of the firm's very significant profits. In 1985 Drexel Burnham brought another innovation to the capital markets — high-yield bonds began to be used to finance takeovers, challenging the power and authority of corporate management. Theoretically, no company was too big to be secure from so-called raiders who could get financing from Drexel Burnham. At this point, the firm's troubles really began.

Problems with corporate America, problems with Washington. Our firm was not very popular on or off Wall Street. However, company morale was at its peak. The controversial image did not hurt recruiting efforts. In 1985 more than 5,000 applications were received for 50 openings in the corporate finance department.

The high profits from investment banking and trading operations helped to expand the firm into virtually all areas of finance. In 1986, there were 10,000 employees in the firm, with investment banking and high-yield accounting for only about 500. It was a great place to work — entrepreneurial and less political than most of the other firms on Wall Street.

When I joined in 1972 *I was* the communications department. The communications department grew to more than 20 before the investigation (we would number 40 during the crisis). We had an aggressive, proactive marketing communications effort on all fronts: public relations, advertising, issues management, and employee communications. The staff was young, ambitious, and bright. We were on a crusade along with the rest of the firm to let the world know of our accomplishments and continue to grow the firm into one of Wall Street's best. I thought I had the best job in America.

On May 12, 1986, around 3:30 in the afternoon, I was in a routine staff meeting when my two phone lines lit up simultaneously. On one line was Fred Bleakley, who was then the deputy editor of the *New York Times* business section, and on the other line was Fred Joseph. Both were calling to let me know that one of our recently hired merger and acquisition stars, Dennis Levine, had been indicted in the biggest insider trading case in the history of financial markets. Levine would plead guilty to securities fraud and through his plea bargaining would start the chain of events that eventually led to the collapse of Drexel Burnham Lambert as well as the ruin of many careers.

The Unraveling

The firm had no early warning of the case against Levine. Our CEO was called by the SEC just minutes before news of the indictment came over the wire services. Levine was until then an obscure investment banker. Atypical of Wall Street investment bankers, he had a public education and little to distinguish himself academically. But he was shrewd and very ambitious and was able to make it big in terms of compensation through smart moves from one firm to another. At the time of the indictment he was making a seven-figure salary while still in his early

30s. His illegal activities were uncovered by an anonymous letter sent to the compliance department at Merrill Lynch which concerned a pattern of trading that looked a little too lucky. A determined New York district attorney doggedly tracked down leads that finally lead to Levine. Confronted with the evidence, Levine caved in almost immediately and started talking in an attempt to lessen his sentence.

We had no crisis plan in place at the time of Levine's indictment and indeed we had no idea what being the center of real controversy means. We formed a mini-crisis team consisting of Vice Chairman James Balog (my boss), Fred Joseph, and myself. A strategy was developed to distance ourselves from Levine and his crimes, which in fact had been perpetrated while he was employed at two other Wall Street firms as well as while he was at Drexel Burnham. The facts of that case were such that it would have been impossible for Drexel Burnham and its management to have uncovered Levine's activity. We got through that crisis and, in the words of one of our management, did "better than we deserved."

Beginning of the Creeping Crisis

But our problems did not end with Levine. Over that summer in 1986, we received our initiation to "creeping" crisis. After dealing with Levine, we were right in the middle of what was called "The Yuppie Five" investigation — a group of recent Ivy League graduates working in arbitrage departments and trading on inside information. One of the gang was on our arbitrage desk. Our next crisis was the indictment of an employee who had embezzled funds while at one of Wall Street's most pristine institutions — Morgan Bank. I heard about that news from Eric Berg, a reporter for the *New York Times*, who pulled me out of a meeting (with our CEO) to inform me of the coming indictment. Again our management was totally in the dark on the illegal activities of one of its employees. In fact I was asked to call this man and ask him if there was any substance to the charge. I called and left a message but he never called back.

I will admit that we were beginning to worry that all the money we were making and paying to attract top talent on Wall Street was making us a magnet for the greedy employee. However, by August 1986, we thought that our problems had passed. In fact, they were just about to begin.

Late in the afternoon of Friday, November 14, 1986, I was out of the office at a seminar learning about market research techniques when I got a call from our senior public relations staff member, Martha Goldstein, informing me that firm client Ivan Boesky had been indicted on insider trading charges that dwarfed the Levine case. Boesky plead guilty to charges and began cooperating with the federal government, further expanding the insider trading scandal.

Interesting, but what did that have to do with us? Martha, an insightful and seasoned professional, seemed agitated. My own reaction was to think what's the big deal — Ivan Boesky was a client of virtually every firm on Wall Street — what does this have to do with us? Martha's instincts were right and I was wrong. Over that weekend I would find out that this event was in fact tied to Drexel Burnham.

Later that same day, I got a call from Dan Hertzberg, who was a reporter at the *Wall Street Journal.* He told me that my firm had been served with subpoenas at the same time that Boesky was indicted — this was not a good sign. It meant that the government saw information possessed by Drexel as central to its broadening of the insider trading case. I tracked down our chairman and CEO and it was decided that we should not comment. On that following Monday a front page story appeared in the *Wall Street Journal* indicating that Drexel Burnham and Mike Milken were at the center of the government's investigation. This sent shock waves throughout our firm and Wall Street.

During the Drexel Burnham Lambert crisis, junk bond wizard Michael Milken beams as he enters federal court.

The Boesky indictment triggered our crisis management efforts. Over the next two years, we would unfortunately have the opportunity to elevate these to an art form.

Strategic Issues The strategic issues were very basic: franchise protection and survival. Junk bonds were the firm's major source of revenues — without this franchise Drexel Burnham would find it difficult (if not impossible) to survive — certainly in its current form supporting a network of international branches and 10,000 employees. Many very serious questions were raised: Would our clients stick with us? Would our major asset, our own employees, walk out the door and join our competitors where less obstacles existed to doing business? Management was quick to face the realities and act swiftly.

As soon as the Boesky indictment hit we organized to handle the crisis. Joseph took charge and formed his crisis team, or War Council as it would become known. On the team there were top members of management: Joseph Vitanza, president; Richard Wright, chief finance officer; Haig Casparian, chief legal counsel; Richard Capalbo, executive vice-president, marketing; Mary Jo Jacobi, vice-president, government affairs; a representative of Mike Milken's West Coast operation; outside PR counsel; and myself. As chief of staff, Fred McCarthy was named to keep us on track. This group, which would evolve into 15 members including more outside consultants and crisis managers, would meet every morning at 9:45 for the next two years. At these meetings all of us were updated as to the current status of the investigation and planned how to communicate with various constituents. The members of the group gave the status of their current businesses and action plans to keep business moving as usual.

Our firm had long held brainstorming or creativity sessions with Cavas Gobai, a guru on that subject from MIT. We called our first weekend session in December 1986 to set priorities. Two themes emerged at that meeting that we would communicate throughout the investigation — first, that the firm's business remain strong despite the pressures of the investigation and second, that the contribution of high-yield financing (a.k.a. junk bonds) to the American economy was kept intact. The objectives were to move public opinion to feel favorably toward the organization, maintain morale, and minimize the impact on our business. As the investigation progressed, we became more focused on these themes and research showed the communications became stronger and more effective.

Employees — The Critical Constituent Group During this period, we developed many communications strategies and programs to enable all our audiences to deal with the unfolding events. We had programs for clients, banks who lent the firm billions of dollars overnight to finance huge inventories of securities, regulators, and, of course, the press. However, I'm going to focus on the programming developed for the audience that we identified as our key constituent group — *employees.* We realized early on that here is where the communications battle to impact public opinion would be won or lost. Employee attitudes and dispositions would influence other key audiences — clients, regulators, lenders, and the press.

I remember that when the Levine crisis hit, I suggested (after coming up for air from the hundreds of press calls received) that we get information out to our employees. I was overruled. I was told that we had more important things to spend time on. In the intervening months, management got religion.

Interestingly, when crisis hits there is a rush to communicate, but it's externally. If employees make the list it's usually an afterthought. Firsthand, I can tell you that this is a mistake. When employee morale is up you can fight back. When it's not up everything stands still. Employees don't work, productivity slides precipitously, and defections start. Unfortunately, management saw both sides of this. It took a crisis of the magnitude we faced to make me appreciate and understand the importance of internal communication.

Probably the most important thing I learned from our crisis was to understand who I was communicating with and why. Most of the communication should be aimed at your allies because you need to give them reasons to stick with you, defend you, and influence others. Don't waste valuable resources trying to gain the support of enemies; simply understand that there are those who philosophically or morally will never support you. Identify your allies and focus there.

Analysis: Eight Lessons

An enormous amount of energy was committed to program development and we unfortunately had a long time to test and see what worked and what didn't. Based on these experiences, the following are what I consider to be the key principles in communicating to employees during crisis.

- Don't Trust Your Instincts

- Preempt the Bad News

- Keep the Leader Visible

- Make Employees Insiders

- Be Creative

- Make Employees Part of the Solution

- Communicate the Positive

- Don't Take Loyalists for Granted

Don't Trust Your Instincts

Let research form the basis of strategy and program development. Find out what your employees are thinking. Do they understand what's happening? How do they feel about management's handling of the situation? What are their primary concerns? Do they have the facts to relate to customers and their families? Don't fall into the trap of guessing what they need or the trap of having top management answer these questions.

Focus groups are an efficient way to provide the information you need to address concerns and develop strategies to keep the staff united. We used them extensively for the duration of the investigation. These sessions were conducted by our advertising agency, Chiat/Day/Mojo, a firm known well for its creativity, but also very strong in research. The woman who worked with us, Heather Harris, was able to gain the confidence of our employees and her work was critical to us in program development. Typically these groups consisted of eight to ten employees — some at very senior levels in the organization.

Early on we found out that employees, especially lower level staff, were concerned about the firm maintaining its flow of business and their job security. Part of our strategy was to reinforce that despite the investigation our clients were behind us and it was business as usual. We ran ads to this effect and used our internal publications to highlight business successes and frankly discuss the impact of the investigations on revenues.

As the investigation continued, the information from the groups became more and more sensitive. In the beginning we gave presentations on the findings to the War Council. Toward the end of the fight, we presented the information in private session to our CEO. To his credit he listened and acted to sometimes very negative and critical input. One example occurred after hearings held before Representative John Dingell's committee in Washington. It was revealed that the high-yield department had established a series of partnerships to invest in high-yield securities. According to the committee, this occurred sometimes at the expense of clients. Other trading departments at our firm were not permitted to invest in securities that it traded; it was viewed as a conflict of interest and did not pass the "smell test." Not only was the high-yield department investing in securities that it traded, but from Fred Joseph's testimony it seemed that management was not aware that this was going on. Joseph appeared to be unprepared and ill-advised by counsel.

The heads of other trading desks were up in arms over this revelation. This was not a money issue; they felt betrayed and used the focus groups to get the depth of their feeling back to management. Upon hearing how strongly they felt, Joseph chose to address the issue directly with them over a special dinner and institute tighter controls. And so the issue passed, another taking its place in terms of priorities to be handled.

As soon as you know bad news will become public in the press, get it out to your employees together with your response. It is much better that employees hear bad news from management's perspective than read it first in the newspaper. If necessary, employees can warn clients or regulators. By giving employees the facts to respond to questions about what's happening, you create an army to help you fight back. In addition, telling your troops the news before they read it will have a very interesting effect; it will become old news by the time it appears in the press.

Preempt the Bad News

Various techniques were used to reach employees quickly. Drexeline, a firm-wide voice communications system, was used extensively. Whenever we needed to get out news quickly, Joseph got on Drexeline and gave frank information to employees. Despite the fact that some employees passed information given in confidence to the press, we continued with these messages. We made the decision that these betrayals would not stop us from communicating.

Memos were hand delivered and faxed to key executives. If it was particularly ominous news, our CEO called a meeting of his senior staff and had them relate it to their staffs and external constituents. Prior to the investigation (as part of a management training program), we had established a select group that could be called together within 20 minutes to hear news. We first tried to communicate by putting together a conference call with the 60 people. But this proved to be impractical; it was easier for us to use a team from the human resource department to call the participants and get them quickly to a meeting. Those not located in New York were conferenced in by phone.

We also had what we called a Morning Alert System in order to get a jump on news that we did not have advance notice was appearing in the press. During the beginning of the crisis, I had my first child. I returned to work very quickly and at one of our War Council meetings in March 1987, I volunteered to get up and check the major newspapers at 5:00 A.M. — I was up anyway with the baby. If there was any news that was surprising and shocking, I would call Fred Joseph at 6:00 A.M. and we would decide what to do. If it was serious enough, we had a chain-calling procedure in place to alert our executive committee and had a memo on employees' desks by 8:00 A.M.

Wall Street starts its day early and nothing is more demoralizing to employees than to hear from clients or competitors that there is a news item that they have not seen and have no information on. By keeping them informed we held up the morale. I made many such calls during the subsequent two years. Fortunately, both of us are morning people and despite the hour, the conversations were cordial. Nevertheless, this is not an auspicious way to start the day!

Keep the Leader Visible

Employees need to know that the situation is being managed. The internal spokesperson (preferably the chairperson or CEO) should stay very visible to employees during the crisis. He or she will have to walk a fine line between cheerleading to keep up morale, and painting too rosy a picture that causes him or her to lose credibility.

Despite all the pressures that the investigation placed on management, Joseph made it a priority to stay in close touch with employees. He did this through regular luncheon meetings open to all employees, meetings with senior staff, monthly messages in our two internal publications, his talks over Drexeline, memos, and letters. In our focus groups, we had consistent praise for his efforts. The decision of management to divest the firm's retail network — a reversal of the previous policy of "sticking together" — was the watershed event that destroyed management credibility and caused communications to falter.

Make Employees Insiders

Give employees as much information as you can about the crisis and how management is dealing with it. Just remember that you cannot deal confidentially with any group. The information you give out will become public. However, if you are creative there is much you can give to the troops without putting the company at risk. For example, you can preempt bad news; give previews of ads; reveal strategic initiatives of a nonconfidential nature; and have them meet with and hear from the crisis team.

A big effort was made to explain to our employees the strategy behind our TV ads. Even with this very public form of communication, our employees were our first priority. Advertising is a very expensive way to communicate, but remember the issue — survival.

Chiat/Day was responsible for creating a landmark campaign for an investment bank. In very human terms its ads demonstrated how yield bonds were helping the economy. For example, there was the ad about Kinder Care Day Care Centers that were financed by junk bonds; the story of missed opportunities for companies that were unable to obtain financing; and the story of the playgrounds in California that would have closed without issuing high-yield bonds.

For one of the commercials, we held a lottery to pick 25 employees to appear as extras. Then we used the winners to produce a promotion tape on the making of the commercial. The employees who participated were thrilled; one employee literally cooed in the tape, "To finally win something — to represent such a great firm as Drexel Burnham was like a dream come true."

The ads were a big boost to morale internally. We made sure that our employees were given previews of new ads and had a schedule of when they would be appearing. Research internally and externally told us that the ads worked. That is, until the fall of 1988 when the noise level on the investigation was so loud that nothing was going to help our cause. On September 7, the SEC accused Drexel Burnham, Milken, and five others of insider trading, stock manipulation, and assisting in tax-law violations.

One of the most embarrassing war stories that I can recall was related to the preview of our advertising. When we were ready to launch our advertising campaign in the fall of 1987, we had Joseph do a tape where he explained the strategy behind the advertising and what we hoped to accomplish with the campaign. His five-minute appearance was followed by the two first commercials produced. We sent copies of the tapes to all our 50 branches and asked that the offices show the tape on a specific day after the close of the markets. We were viewing the tape at headquarters, when I got a frantic call from my secretary, Nettie Buonomo, who told me that we had gotten calls from three of our offices informing us that the tape was great — but that after the commercials were finished our offices were being treated to a Spanish language porno film! We never paid the bill from the duplicating company.

There are many ways to communicate beyond memos and meetings. For example, ads and video tapes can be produced solely for internal distribution; special events can be used to provide information and keep up morale.

Be Creative

One of the most creative programs we developed was a employee education program on the high-yield market. Our objective was to make employees proud of their roles in developing that market and to give them the ammunition to fight the myths surrounding junk bonds. We ran a week-long "event" with the theme, "Junk Bonds Keep America Fit." We had clients talk about their companies, bankers explain financing techniques, a "Fun Run", a raffle with prizes from client companies, and a direct mail package distributed to all employees. By the end of the week, bond ratings were being discussed on lunch lines. I still remember this effort with great pride — the communications department worked beautifully as a team. Our advertising director, the very talented Elizabeth Tower, thought of the theme and organized the employee race, "The Fun Run." Our promotion manager organized the raffle. Everybody helped out and, despite the heavy work loads already being handled, the event went off faultlessly. We now had 10,000 advocates for high-yield bonds.

Another creative and very successful part of our program were the ads developed solely for employees. To celebrate a tradition of marking the founding of the firm, in April 1987 we ran an ad that listed the names of all 10,000 employees. It was the brainchild of a team at Chiat/Day. The ad was a proofreading nightmare, but was the biggest single employee morale booster we executed. When the firm was closing down its offices after the bankruptcy in 1990, some employees still had that ad hanging behind their desks with their own names circled. What was interesting was the impact that the ad made externally. In every external focus group we held, that ad was also mentioned — sometimes with the "compliment" that all 10,000 employees couldn't be crooks!

In terms of pure fun, the highlight of our internal communications was a music video created by Broad Street Productions entitled "When the Going Gets Tough, Drexel Gets Going." Called a "riotous video" by *USA Today*, it starred our employees, ranging from our founder, I.W. Burnham, and our chairman, to the clerks in various operations. Employees mouthed the words while pretending to boogie and play the saxophone. Employee "stars" were juxtaposed with Michael Douglas, Kathleen Turner, and Danny DiVito. The employees loved it! We had requests from hundreds of employees for copies. I still smile and get a lump in my throat when I see the eight-minute tape and the spirit, loyalty, attractiveness, and vibrancy of the employees.

Make Employees Part of the Solution   Elicit ideas on how to manage the crisis from a broad spectrum of employees. Good ideas are not restricted to top management and consultants. Have each manager prepare a plan on how he or she will deal with the respective constituent groups. Organize brainstorming sessions to encourage cross fertilization of ideas and actions.

We periodically headed creativity sessions on how to better handle the crisis and develop strategies and programs to deal with the latest news. For example, when we received galleys of *The Predator's Ball* by Connie Brock, we decided that action needed to be taken to prove to the employees that many of the events recounted in the book were not entirely accurate. Central to the book were the happenings at the high-yield bond conference held in Beverly Hills each year to introduce the issuers of high-yield securities to the buyers. The book sensational-ized the conference. Part of the strategy developed at one of these sessions was to send a group of employees who were not conference participants to the meet-ings and bring the facts back to their fellow employees.

Sometimes programs developed to deal with the crisis at hand, which ended up being good for business. Over 40 senior level officers, representing a cross sec-tion of the firm, were organized to give speeches around the country. We wrote the speeches for them, and booked their appearances. This ad hoc speaker bureau was a credit to the organization. The business leads that generated were an unexpected pleasant result. Each year a special lunch was held to thank the participants.

Communicate the Positive

Don't allow a siege mentality to overcome the organization. This does nothing for morale nor does it provide facts to fight back. Publicize small victories as well as major ones. Distribute positive articles and well wishes from clients and others.

The news coverage on Drexel Burnham and the investigation was overwhelmingly negative, but we had our share of support from the media. One striking contrast was the *Wall Street Journal* news coverage versus the perspective of its editorial page. The news department at the *Journal* took the lead in running with rumors and leaks. This coverage was devastating to us. Nothing we did — from meeting with the editors to giving open access to reporters — would stop what we felt was unfair treatment. However, the editorial page of that paper was one of the most supportive. And there were many other reporters and publications who took issue with the concept of the trial by the press and guilty until proved innocent and supported us with opinion articles and commentaries.

We ran ads to present the positive actions of the company. Since Drexel Burnham was synonymous with junk bonds, we developed a series of ads on its contribu-tion to job creation and the quality of life in America. One of the most popular ads educated the readers on the role of high-yield bonds in financing America's growth companies. It pointed out that out of the 25,000 companies in America with sales of over $25 million, only about 600 are investment grade. The rest if they were to issue debt would be rated "junk" bond. Another showed the geographic distribution of investment grade companies — there are some states without any investment grade companies within their borders. Reprints were used extensively in a direct marketing effort to all our audiences including Washington and the press.

Don't Take Loyalists for Granted

Acknowledge employee support and say thank you. We did this in many ways. Special ads were produced and employees thanked in interoffice memos and letters sent to homes. We made several tee shirt companies rich with 10,000 shirt orders. These "little" things meant a lot.

Aftermath

Some proof that the programs worked:

We had very few defections of critical employees over the two-year period. This loyalty remained despite the fact that many employees were intensely recruited by competitors.

Clients stuck by us. This is a credit to the management and the sales team who stayed loyal and upbeat despite the fact that just about every day we were beaten up and vilified in the press.

Teamwork and morale was maintained. Even after Drexel Burnham plead guilty to the SEC's felony charges in January 1989, our employees lead the selling effort of $25 billion of RJR Nabisco bonds, the biggest transaction in Wall Street history.

We lost many battles during our crisis and ultimately lost the war, but we did win the hearts and minds of employees. They were a great group and deserved better.

Prior to founding The DAI Communications Group, Angela Z. Dailey was senior vice-president and member of the board of directors of Drexel Burnham Lambert. Ms. Dailey has extensive experience in all areas of corporate communications and a unique expertise in crisis management. As head of communications during Drexel Burnham's three-year investigation by the government, she provided leadership with both the strategy and implementation of the firm's crisis management efforts. The advertising and employee communications programs were nationally recognized as innovative and effective. She now works with companies on both internal and external communications strategies and programming.

The AT&T Network

Breakdown

William P. Mullane, Jr.
Former Vice-President, Public Relations, AT&T

Monday, January 15, 1990, was Martin Luther King Day, a partial holiday. But **Overview** not for the people of AT&T public relations. For them it was a day that will always stand out in the history of public relations at the company. It was the day the long distance network, the company's premier symbol of reliability and the backbone that linked people throughout the world in a matter of seconds, failed completely. It was the first time in the company's century-plus history that such a calamity had occurred. The nine hours from the time the network failed until it was restored and the days that followed put the years of public relations "fire drills" to their sternest test. This is the story of that incident.

It was a relatively quiet Monday afternoon, a good time to work on some adminis- **Communications** trative duties. I was sitting in my office with an associate, Elaine Logan, dis- **Breakdown** cussing her performance during the preceding year.

About 2:30 P.M., Corporate Information Director Walter G. Murphy stuck his head in the door and reported that there "may be a problem with the network" and left. Moments later he was back to report that indeed there was network trouble and it appeared to be serious. Within seconds, the phone rang. It was Victor A. Pelson, an AT&T group executive responsible for, among other things, the AT&T Network Services Organization, the group that operates and maintains the world-wide AT&T long distance network. He reported that there was severe network trouble and that he wanted me to come immediately (if not sooner) to the Network Operations Center (NOC) in Bedminster, New Jersey, eight miles from my Basking Ridge, New Jersey, office.

My discussion with Logan ended abruptly. I threw some material into my brief-case and headed for the garage and the 10-minute drive down Interstate 287 to Bedminster. As I raced into the NOC there were three public relations colleagues already there — Tom Frazee, Carol Albright, and Jim Messenger. They were on the public relations team responsible for serving the Network Services Organization.

Elsewhere around the nation, public relations people began fielding calls from the media and, in some instances, began calling the media to alert them to the fact that the network was in trouble; that AT&T would keep them posted; and that anything they could do to curtail calling would be appreciated.

Screen video wall monitoring AT&T's telecommunications network at its Network Operations Center in Bedminster, N.J.

At the NOC, my first task was to try to get information on the nature of the fail-ure. It was obvious from looking at the 75 screens that dominated one wall of the Center that something was drastically wrong. Normally a few colored lines indi-cate individual circuits in trouble and additional information tells how calls are being rerouted. In this instance, the screens were awash in a rainbow of colors, all indicating disaster.

AT&T's network that boasts of allowing its customers to reach anyone anywhere at anytime of the day or night wasn't living up to its reputation. Fortunately, it was a partial holiday. Nonetheless, the Network Services people pride themselves on seeking 100 percent call completion — and this was not the case on January 15, 1990.

James Nelson, an NOC manager, said later it was a situation that never before had been encountered. There had been cable cuts; regional failures; fires that knocked out offices. But never had the entire network gone "belly up." And nobody was sure what had happened. Was it sabotage? Hackers? Was it software? What happened?

To find the answer as quickly as possible, teams of AT&T Bell Laboratories engineers and technicians were assembled in Columbus, Ohio, and Naperville, Illinois (a Chicago suburb), to begin trying to fathom what went wrong. They were in constant contact with the NOC in Bedminster and with AT&T Network Services people elsewhere in the Bedminster complex.

Explaining to the Nation

Key AT&T senior executives, led by Pelson and the top echelon of the Network Services and AT&T Bell Laboratories network organizations, were analyzing data on the floor of the NOC trying to determine what "fixes" they could put in the network.

About 4:00 P.M., it became apparent that we weren't going to fix the problem quickly and that it was important that the waiting nation get some information on what was happening. In earlier consultations with Murphy and Media Relations Director A. J. "Herb" Linnen in Washington, we had agreed to avoid making appearances on television because of the dearth of information. At this point, it was agreed that we would be responsive to media requests — though the operating people didn't support the idea — and would tell reporters that the network had failed; that we didn't know what was wrong; that we were working as fast as we could to fix it; and that we would keep them posted.

Although the network was in deep trouble, some calls did continue to get through. But that was fewer than half (about 35 million) of the calls placed during the nine hours the network was down. Other callers were getting a rapid busy signal or a recorded message telling them that due to network trouble their calls could not go through. Unaffected by the failure were private-line services, used primarily by business and government.

A couple of hours after arriving at the NOC, I received a call from Murphy and other colleagues in Basking Ridge. They wanted me to get authorization to provide our customers with the access codes of our long distance competitors. AT&T long distance operators did not have that information as it normally didn't make sense to help the competitors. But it did make extremely good sense in this instance. However, the executives, primarily concerned with getting the network back in operation, rejected the suggestion. A couple of hours later, the issue was raised again and, with strong urging from public relations, the senior managers agreed that we should provide our competitors' access codes if asked. The codes were quickly transmitted to all AT&T long distance operator locations. Marilyn Laurie, AT&T senior vice-president, public relations, who had been in Massachusetts that day and came to the NOC upon her return, was instrumental in getting this decision made.

It became clear about 6:00 P.M., after a series of tests and a process of elimination, that it wasn't sabotage and it wasn't a hacker, though some hackers called AT&T that day claiming credit for the failure and continued to spread that propaganda to the media in the days and weeks that followed.

Diagnosing the Problem

The real culprit appeared to be software. We began telling the media that "we believe" the problem was related to software in a new signaling system that was being installed throughout the long distance network. A signaling system is a data network that connects long distance switching machines and overlays the regular network that transmits customers' voices, carrying calling information such as the calling and called numbers.

As the evening wore on and the railing along the entrance to the NOC became littered with pizza boxes (purchased by public relations), coffee cups, and soft drink cans, we discussed various options to bring the network back into service. One dire possibility, if all else failed, was to shut the entire network down about 2:00 A.M. or 3:00 A.M. Eastern time and then start to resurrect it, switching machine by switching machine. AT&T has 114 of these machines in its network. Fortunately, that didn't have to be tried.

Another public relations problem arose when television crews wanted to visit the site of the initial software failure. It was agreed by one and all that the last thing needed that night was an invasion by the television crews into the location, which happened to be in lower Manhattan. What had been discovered after various network conditions were replicated and solutions attempted was that a software flaw had been triggered in one machine and had spread very rapidly throughout the 113 other machines. In effect, the switching systems were telling one another, "I'm out of service, don't send me any messages."

Once they had isolated the problem, Network Services and Bell Labs technicians tried ways of going around it. Backup links to the signaling system were taken out of service, easing the message load on the affected processors. By about 9:45 P.M., there was some clearing of the congested lines on the maps in the NOC. Slowly, more lines began to disappear and, by 10:30 P.M., there remained only a few pesky disruptions in the Midwest. As time for the late news approached, I urged the operating people in attendance to support an announcement that service had been restored. They were reluctant, but a longtime associate, Craig Gipple, a Network Services vice-president who had stayed around in the event he could help, assured me that the repairs had been made. With that knowledge, I prodded others to give me the green light, which they finally did. Had they not agreed, I was prepared to make the decision on my own to release the information that the nightmare had ended.

But there was PR work to be done. Call-backs to media were required. *USA Today* was scheduled to run one of its polls the following morning that included 900 numbers for readers to call to cast their ballots. The paper had advised us, if the network were back in operation by midnight, to just call and inform the production staff so it could include the number in the next day's papers. That was done. Other media were called. Customer contact people were called and advised that we were back in service.

Coordinating the Explanation

There remained the problem of explaining what had occurred in a coordinated fashion. We had taken the initiative by telling the press that we had a problem and by keeping them posted throughout the nine hours. We had told them when we decided to allow our operators to provide customers with the access codes of our competitors. We had provided spokespeople to appear on camera. But that wouldn't be enough.

As Gipple and I stood talking well after midnight, I said it was important that the chairman get out front early the next day and apologize for the failure. Our very reputation was at stake. We couldn't let much time elapse.

At 7:00 A.M. the following morning, Chairman Robert E. Allen and other top officers, including Laurie, met to analyze what they knew at that juncture. Earlier, Laurie had met with Murphy and me to discuss our public relations strategy and we had suggested a press conference be held at 11:00 A.M. at the NOC. We also urged that Allen be the spokesperson and that he take ownership of the problem.

At the executive meeting, the first orders of business were an analysis of what had happened to cause the network breakdown and what steps could be taken — quickly — to ensure the future reliability of the network. Then the discussion turned to customer issues and public relations.

"No one questioned that we ought to meet with the press," Allen later recalled. "And it was important that we do it at the NOC to show we had nothing to hide."

It also was agreed by the executives that morning that some kind of gesture would be needed to compensate customers in some measure for the inconvenience they had suffered. "We had to demonstrate to our customers that we were concerned," Laurie said. It also was agreed that an advertisement in the form of a letter to customers from Allen would be developed.

The meeting adjourned, but by that time the heavy morning calling period had begun. And the network was operating as if nothing had gone wrong.

But there was some other calling that had to be done.

Satisfying the Thirst for Info
The media were clamoring for more information and we had to tell them about the press conference. The NOC in Bedminster is 40 miles from New York City, where the bulk of the media to be invited were located. So calls quickly went out from a team of media relations people to the media. They were invited to the NOC and told that Bob Allen would be the spokesperson. They also were advised that they could gather at the AT&T headquarters building in New York City and the AT&T media relations office in Washington, D.C., where there would be video and two-way audio links (we hoped). Meanwhile, remarks were drafted for Allen. They were based largely on comments he had made earlier in the morning during the meeting of top executives.

An announcement with press conference details was issued over a commercial wire service. Included in it were satellite coordinates that broadcasters around the country could use to pull down the signal. A 900 number, with an 800 backup number, was provided so reporters outside the New York area could listen to the press conference.

An advisory was sent to AT&T public relations field locations where herculean work had gone on for the previous 18 hours. Because the press conference was scheduled for 11:00 A.M. Eastern time, there was no time to alert reporters on the West Coast. A videotape of the press conference was rebroadcast three times later in the day over the company's internal network. Television footage that an AT&T camera crew had shot the night before at the NOC was offered to television stations via satellite.

Just before the press conference, two key decisions were made. AT&T's 800 service carries a service guarantee if a customer's service is disrupted. Technically, the guarantee didn't cover total network failures. It was applied anyway, in keeping with the company's policy of total customer satisfaction. Also, Allen was able to describe a "special day of discounted calling which would be some small compensation to all our customers, whether they be businesses or consumers." Details remained to be worked out.

At 11:00 A.M., the NOC was jammed with television crews and newspaper reporters. The New York and Washington offices were full as well.

> *As you know, we had a major service disruption Monday. We didn't live up to our own standards of quality. We didn't live up to our customers' standards of quality. It's as simple as that. That's not acceptable to our customers. That's not acceptable to me.*

Those were Allen's opening words. And he went on from there. When asked who was to blame, Allen said, "As far as customers are concerned, I did it ... and that's why I'm here."

The questions from the press were fair. Reporters were reasonable in their expectations and appreciated being able to speak with the chairman quickly. Allen later commented on the media's good behavior, to which Laurie replied, "That's because we had been standing at the barricades giving them facts the day and night before. There was no reason for them to attack."

The network's performance continued on an even keel. The media's interest continued as well. Technical writers and those versed in computers and software were seeking all manner of esoterica. Electronic coverage tapered off after Wednesday, when AT&T executives appeared on two morning news shows and Allen appeared on the "MacNeil-Lehrer Newshour."

As he arrived home following the "MacNeil-Lehrer" appearance, Allen's phone was ringing. He answered and it was James Burke, retired chairman of Johnson & Johnson who had been at the center of that company's Tylenol story. He was calling to compliment Allen on the masterful way he handled the network outage. That's a mighty strong accolade from someone who has been down the same road.

Game Plan

When the first calls came January 15, public relations knew it had a huge crisis on its hands. It was obvious we had to move swiftly to fill the information gap. We had to acknowledge the problem, assume responsibility, volunteer the facts, minimize speculation, and correct inaccurate information. The "hacker" issue was the major one addressed.

Laurie noted, "In crisis communications, the game is won or lost in the first 24 hours. And the best way to be prepared for a crisis is to have a professional staff and the trust of top management."

On January 15, 1990, AT&T public relations had both. That was no different than any other time in the history of public relations at the company. Alexander Graham Bell may have invented the telephone, but it was Theodore N. Vail who invented the Bell Telephone System. It was Vail who remarked some 90 years ago that if the company didn't tell the truth about itself, someone else surely would. That has been the credo of public relations at AT&T through the years.

In the wake of the network failure any number of people asked me and others at AT&T who was in the "meetings" that must have been held when AT&T decided to go public, hold a press conference, or take other initiatives. The answer quite simply, except for the decision on the compensation to customers, was nobody. The decisions were generated within the public relations division and carried out as we normally carry out our duties. We have that level of respect and authority in the company.

Certainly, you can't report that the network is back in operation without learning the facts from the technical experts. Nor can you have a press conference if the chairman doesn't agree to it. But the impetus for these actions came from the public relations environment without a bevy of endless meetings with scores of people around a long table in a sterile room. The network failure was handled in a relatively straightforward manner, following practices that have been in place for a number of years.

No plan is perfect. As this was the first time the network ever had experienced a total failure, AT&T public relations had trouble communicating with its own offices. We had direct tie lines to some locations, for example, New York City. But we had to use the network to reach key media experts in Washington, Atlanta, Chicago, Dallas, San Francisco, Los Angeles, and Miami. In some instances, once communication was established, the line was simply left open. Other times, it was strictly hit or miss.

Someone observed that it must have been a slow news day as radio was all over the story. But it truly was radio's type of story. It had far-ranging impact and was a minute-to-minute situation. Television also covered it heavily. It was the lead story on the Monday night "NBC Nightly News." CNN covered it exhaustively. In fact, a few minutes into Allen's press conference, his image appeared on the screen in the Network Operating Center, where CNN is monitored for breaking news events.

As the volume of media calls climbed and the available news was limited, members of the media relations support staff were pressed into service to read the current statement to the person calling and advise the reporter or editor that it was all we had to say at the moment and would call him or her later Monday evening.

In addition to the handling of media calls and queries, the public relations division had a number of other responsibilities.

The employees were another key audience. They took great pride in the network. **What Worked** It was part of their culture. They wanted to know what was going on and what had happened. A key tool in communicating with employees was AT&T Newsline, an audio report that is updated regularly when there is a breaking story. During the week of January 15, Newsline received 52,000 calls.

Two weeks before the incident, *AT&T Today* had come on line. It is a daily electronic newsletter containing news about the company, industry news items, and letters to the editor. It is piggybacked on existing company data networks. Although only a couple of weeks old, at least 10,000 employees saw *Today* the day following the network breakdown. Many of them printed out the report and shared it with fellow employees. (*AT&T Today* now reaches more than 100,000 employees on a variety of networks and an additional 50,000 or more in printed copies of the day's report.)

An all-employee bulletin was issued early on Tuesday. It was distributed in hard copy in New Jersey locations and sent electronically to all other AT&T locations for copying and distribution. Management distributed another bulletin in the middle of the week and, on Friday, it distributed a letter to all employees from Allen. The letter was a strategic effort by public relations to put the week in context.

"This experience holds powerful lessons for all of us," Allen wrote. "It demonstrates how much people depend on us.... I want January 15, 1990, to stand in all our minds. Not simply as a bad memory. I want it to mark day one of a new resolve to be the epitome of quality." In addition to desk-to-desk distribution, the letter was enlarged and displayed in company cafeterias and elevator lobbies.

Public relations provided major support to the Business Sales division, the organization responsible for reaching AT&T's key business customers. Monday afternoon, shortly after the network went down, the first communique was issued to the sales force via AT&T Mail, the company's electronic messaging service. Several hundred branch sales managers were able to access the advisory through corporate data network facilities not linked to the public telephone network.

Another database system, designed for various AT&T marketing organizations, also was used to reach sales people. The initial advisory offered a synopsis of the problem and provided a statement that could be used in talking to customers. Calls to customers were intense, beginning Tuesday morning. A dozen advisories were issued during the week to the sales force. AT&T Network Systems, which sells switching and transmission systems to telephone companies, made personal calls on its customers. Even Chairman Allen got into the act, making 15 to 20 calls to key customers. Other senior officers did the same. The customers appreciated being contacted and generally were sympathetic to the company's situation.

What Didn't
The major complaint among customers was the failure of AT&T to provide them with the access codes of the competitors. Even Allen admitted he wished we had moved more quickly on that issue.

As the drumbeat of complaints about the access code issue continued, the company seriously considered changing the company policy, considering there are as many as 700 different codes customers can dial. Laurie argued strongly for changing policy and sought a quick solution. A new policy was agreed upon and the nation learned about it in a news release on Monday, January 22.

The new policy instructs operators to give out access codes within minutes after it has been determined that a serious service disruption exists and it can't be quickly repaired. In practice, the operators are equipped only with the codes for the major national long distance carriers, not all 700.

Making the Most of Customer Relations
The compensation to customers — a day of discount calling February 14, Valentine's Day — was detailed in an ad that ran on January 19 in 25 newspapers and in news releases distributed to the media. Spurred by the company's board of directors (which met as scheduled on January 17), the company moved quickly to get that news to the public.

In the ad, addressed "Dear AT&T Customer," Allen apologized for the service disruption and provided details of the "special day of calling discounts." The letter concluded as follows: "For more than 100 years, we've built our reputation on superior quality, reliability and technological innovation. Our goal is to ensure that you always regard us that way."

With the announcement of the discount day and the change in company practice on releasing access codes of competitors, media coverage slacked off. But there still was Valentine's Day and the media paid attention to that event. *Business*

Week printed the AT&T access code so MCI and Sprint customers could "take advantage" of what it called "a sweetheart deal."

The network handled 124 million calls on Valentine's Day, about 13 percent more than on a normal business day. And it did it flawlessly. Today the AT&T network routinely handles 130 million calls a day.

Early Advantages

Public relations objectives in the first hours after the incident and in the days and weeks that followed were quite simple: minimize the damage; correct misstatements and misinformation; and underline the long record of reliability in the worldwide network. (AT&T has had two major network problems since that date, both affecting telephone calling in the Northeast; neither was a failure on a nationwide level.)

AT&T had a couple of strong assets going for it. The media relations people knew the media and knew who to call to get the story handled expeditiously. Local and network television stations had copies of "B roll" footage that AT&T had supplied earlier, which contained scenes from the NOC.

We called media we hadn't heard from to alert them to the network problem, thus quickly eliminating any charges that the company was trying to hide something.

The media coverage was voluminous. The Associated Press updated its story five times Monday afternoon and evening and had at least three different leads or "write-throughs" on Tuesday.

Television covered the news story Monday afternoon and evening and on the Tuesday morning news shows. It covered the press conference on the Tuesday evening news programs; got experts from the company and in the computer business to appear on the Wednesday morning news programs; and had additional spokespeople on Wednesday night.

All of the weekly newsmagazines covered it, as did the telecommunications and computer trade press.

According to PR Data, a tracking firm that analyzes news coverage of AT&T from selected media, the story produced some 850 clips in those media it covers in about 30 major markets. Only a quarter of those were negative. The remainder were neutral in that they included our message. Under the circumstances, I'd call that a pretty good example of fair coverage in a bad situation.

The reputation of AT&T public relations was, if anything, enhanced by its performance in this crisis. Allen was lavish in his praise of the public relations organization as were other senior officers and a number of public relations executives outside the business who called Laurie to commend her on a job well done.

Emerging with Reputation Intact

Looking back on the experience, I come away with the feeling that we gave it all we could. How many of the actions we took would we have changed? What was the fallout? Who were the winners and losers?

The issue that gave us the most serious concern was the failure to release the access codes for major long distance competitors. We should have done that earlier and that's the bad news. The good news is that it never will happen again as procedures are in place to quickly take that step in the event of network trouble.

We also need improved internal communications among the media relations people around the country. That, too, has been addressed and appears to be solved.

The actions the technical staff and the public relations people took during those nine hours followed long-established patterns. Though neither ever had experienced a total network failure, the procedures and practices utilized in earlier, less far-reaching service disruptions served the customers and the business very well.

As I said on a television interview an hour or so before the problem was corrected, "We want every one of those calls to go through and it is toward that objective that everyone is working."

Winners, if anyone can be called winners in a situation of this nature, would have to include the media relations people who kept the press well "fed" with information for the entire evening and throughout the couple of days that followed. Others are the public relations people throughout the division who pitched in and helped out, either filling in for those working exclusively on the problem or just working extra hard to do their jobs better. A special kudo goes to the public relations people supporting the national sales force and the Network Services division for their efforts to communicate with key constituencies.

AT&T surveyed business and residence users in the days following the incident. Most business customers who were in focus group sessions that were conducted on both coasts said they actually learned of the problem only after getting home and hearing about it on the news. Nearly all cited the company for being "honest and aboveboard." A few weeks after the incident, a survey conducted by Business Research Group in Newton, Massachusetts, and reported in *Business Week*, found that nearly all of the 198 corporate telecommunications managers questioned planned to keep their AT&T service.

More than 1,000 customers responded to a telephone survey and nearly nine out of 10 indicated that the problem had not changed their image of AT&T.

AT&T commissioned its own research on the brand reputation. It showed a sharp decline in the week after the incident. But six weeks later, ratings had returned to their pre-January 15 highs.

In the days and weeks immediately following January 15, some 130 letters addressed directly to the chairman had been received. The overwhelming majority of them were from residence customers expressing positive comments about the way AT&T — and he in particular — had handled the crisis. Each letter was read by the chairman, answered and personally signed by him.

One writer, a Wall Street businessman, said in what proved to be typical of the letters received by Allen.

> *I wish to commend you on your quick response to the computer foul-up last week. Your press conferences were most impressive and the way you handled your critics was very admirable. As a businessman and a stockholder, I must say you made me very proud of Corporate America.*

One newspaper publisher wrote the chairman a "fan letter" in which he said, "I think the hardest thing to do in any of our businesses is to handle some sudden adversity with candor and grace. It seems to me that's exactly what you did and I very much admire you for it."

One writer urged Allen not to "feel too bad about your little software bug. AT&T still has the best service of any vendor."

Notes appended to two other letters prove that people don't necessarily see things the same way. Both writers obviously had seen Allen on television. One, from a clothing store owner, offered compliments to Allen's tailor. The other wrote, "Never, never wear that gray suit again on TV."

Aftermath

Key public relations people moved into action on that fateful afternoon, following unwritten, but well-known, procedures that are used in all circumstances. Today they don't simply follow their instincts. They also have the advantage of a step-by-step crisis action plan.

The problem with the AT&T long distance network was in computer software. This led many in the media to comment on the vulnerability of the U.S. infrastructure that more and more was becoming dependent on software, not hardware. This has been a recurring theme in the media and, every time the subject is carried, the AT&T network disruption of January 15, 1990, is mentioned. The two subsequent network problems were not software related. One was an accidentally severed cable. The other was related to a malfunction of an alarm system in a switching building that had gone from commercial power to its own backup power.

The importance of software and new technology in today's business world underscores the need for public relations people who are well-schooled in technology and can talk about it with reporters and editors who have broad backgrounds in subjects that were unheard of 20 years ago.

Knowledge, however, is wasted if people can't use it because of strict "no comment" rules from higher management. The major failing of public relations today is its failure to do what it is paid to do — take those steps that are necessary to enhance and protect the reputation of the company, product, or organization. Management long has wanted problems to take care of themselves. That is not possible in today's era of wide media scrutiny of just about anybody and anything.

We have been blessed with a very open management system at AT&T where public relations sits at the decision-making table, is respected for its views and, best of all, is listened to. That was the case on January 15, 1990, and it has been the case any number of times before and since.

Do screwups occur? Absolutely. We wouldn't be human if we didn't stub our toes from time to time. My philosophy always has been to (a) make sure employees know what's happening before you tell the public and (b) be totally honest in telling your story publicly. That doesn't mean we are required to answer every question a reporter or editor asks. We don't. But we also are aboveboard in telling people that we aren't going to answer that question. We also don't grant every interview request, cooperate on every story being worked on, or acquiesce to every "photo opportunity."

We are tireless in our efforts to make sure we are prompt in responding to the media. It is a goal in AT&T media relations to return every media call within an hour. You may be able to say nothing more than "we're working on your request" but at least the person who called knows that you are working to answer the question. If you're not going to cooperate on a particular story or request, it's important to say so immediately.

When we have bad news, we try to get it out quickly — on our terms — and then work feverishly on damage control to minimize the negative impact of the action the company has taken. More times than not it works.

Following these practices, which had been in place for decades, enabled the public relations team at AT&T to cope with the network failure of January 15, 1990, and, in so coping, to emerge with our public relations reputation, if anything, enhanced.

William P. Mullane, Jr., retired in 1992 after more than 31 years with AT&T and Illinois Bell. He was a public relations officer for 16 years, serving six chairmen of the board and working on a number of major stories, including the announcement of the breakup of the Bell System; the death of then-chairman James E. Olson; the onset of competition in the long distance and telephone equipment businesses; and the network failure of January 15, 1990. He is a past president of the New York chapter of the Society of Professional Journalists, and a member of the Foreign Press Association and the Arthur W. Page Society. Mullane is married and resides in Chatham, New Jersey, where he now is president of Bill Mullane Communications.

Mobil and the
Oil Embargo

Herb Schmertz
Former Vice-President for Public Affairs, Mobil Corporation

This story covers the public affairs efforts of Mobil Oil Corporation during the height of the first energy crisis, beginning in 1973 when war broke out in the Middle East. In fact, the energy crisis had no neat ending, but continued for several years, buffeted by international events and political opportunism. However, by the mid-1970s, when this chapter ends, Mobil's public affairs campaign had effectively influenced the national debate on energy.

Overview

The oil embargo of 1973–74 posed a major crisis for Mobil and for the entire oil industry. It was set off by a chain of events in the Middle East. On October 8, 1973, war broke out between Israel and several of its Arab neighbors. When the U.S. rushed in additional military aid to Israel, the Arabs retaliated by placing an embargo on shipments of oil to the U.S. and several other nations. Over the next three months, the Organization of Petroleum Exporting Countries (OPEC) twice raised the price of oil while curtailing production of the free world's oil supplies. The crisis abated in March 1974, when the embargo was lifted and production restored. But the era of ample low-cost energy had ended, and permanent damage was done to the credibility of the energy industries. In order to regain our credibility, Mobil would need extraordinary skills of persuasion and argument. We would need to speak out and fight back. And that, in essence, is what Mobil did.

Added to the formidable task of finding, producing, refining, shipping, and marketing petroleum products would be the challenge of how best to protect the Mobil name and our autonomy as a corporation. Mobil's greatest concern was that Congress would pass legislation that would nationalize the oil industry or regulate us so that we would be unable to function effectively or efficiently. Bills proposing the breakup of the major oil companies — by "horizontal" or "vertical" divestiture — clogged the congressional agenda during this period. Though none of the bills were passed, a climate of hostility persisted throughout the energy crisis. It affected Mobil's recruiting, shareholder relations, employee morale, and our relations with government officials and the press.

To rebuild a positive image, we used some tools that were predictable: print ads, television commercials, press releases, an executive speakers' bureau, congressional testimony, access to think tanks, even National Town Meetings. We approached these tools in a rather creative manner. While we were fighting this war for credibility, we still sponsored public television programs, art exhibitions, literary prizes, and other projects that had previously won us friends and might continue to do so.

Outspoken Mobil   Long before 1973, when the energy crisis became front page news, Mobil had begun the process, under CEO Rawleigh Warner, Jr., of giving our company a distinctive, multifaceted personality — one that was outspoken, even controversial, while being responsive to the needs and concerns of American society. At the same time we were changing our logo and the look of our service stations, we adopted a new corporate voice that would make itself heard in the most cacophonous of times. We showed that we cared about other institutions in our society by supporting public television's landmark children's series, "Sesame Street," and introducing the long-running dramatic series, "Masterpiece Theatre." And we showed that we cared about critical issues — relating to energy, the economy, the environment, and social well-being — by running the first regular advocacy ads on the op-ed page of the *New York Times*. These print ads, which eventually ran in dozens of newspapers and magazines nationwide, were sometimes bold, sometimes unpredictable, sometimes witty — and increasingly controversial. In an industry known for its caution and virtual anonymity, we became distinctive by speaking out.

The first op-ed, on October 19, 1970, ran with the headline, "America Has the World's Best Highways and the World's Worst Mass Transit." It continued: "We hope this ad moves people...." In this ad, we took the lead among oil companies in calling for a National Master Transportation Program that would include both adequate highways and adequate public transportation. This was an unusual view for an oil company but, as we pointed out in the ad, "We don't believe the gasoline consumed by a car idling in a traffic jam ... is the best possible use of America's limited petroleum resources."

We tried to make people smile — and read on — by catchy headlines like "Growth Is Not a Four-Letter Word" and "More Power to the People." But our goals were quite serious: We hoped to influence public thinking on issues that were becoming increasingly divisive and emotional.

More than a year before the war in the Middle East and the ensuing embargo, we ran ads calling for a national energy policy, warning of a natural gas shortage, and arguing for the need to link economic and energy growth to solve social problems.

One op-ed that deserves special mention is "The U.S. Stake in Middle East Peace," which in June 1973 pleaded for a peaceful settlement of outstanding Middle East issues. Did anyone listen? Plenty of people complained. We received a storm of letters demanding that we spell out what we thought was an "equitable" solution of the Middle Eastern situation. Senator Frank Church of Idaho went further, accusing us of currying favor with the Saudi Arabian government.

Four months later, the onset of the war — and the oil embargo — proved that we had been right in our warnings. Indeed, the Middle East was a volatile area; and the shortages we had predicted became all too real. Sadly, we were prophets without honor. We did not get credit for our warnings.

The embargo of 1973–74 caught the media unaware. Those reporters assigned to energy coverage caved in to rumor, innuendo, and suspicion, while rejecting the ordered and logical explanations of the oil industry. Mobil, therefore, set out to play an active role in their education. And nothing tested this role more than the shortage-spawned "tanker myth," which came on the heels of the embargo.

Tankers, Tankers, Everywhere

The rumors seem to have begun in New York. Early in December 1973, a man in Montauk, Long Island, called the *New York Times* to report what he believed was an unusual number of oil tankers offshore. Around the same time, a Staten Island man called the *Newark Star-Ledger* to say that he had seen some tankers in New York's lower harbor. The implication in both of these reports was that the tankers, which belonged to the major oil companies, were waiting for oil prices to rise before discharging their cargoes.

Both newspapers checked the report with the port captain and the Coast Guard. They were informed that the flow of tankers was normal for that time of year, and that in view of the gasoline shortage, there were, if anything, too few ships. With no corroborating evidence, there was, of course, no story.

But the rumors continued. All through December, newspapers, wire services, and radio and TV news desks took calls from people who insisted that they had seen

This sign at an Edison, N.J., gas station in 1974 expresses frustration brought on by the oil embargo.

or heard of "fleets of oil tankers" standing in harbors or lurking offshore. As the stories mushroomed, the Coast Guard continued to find no significant increase in traffic, and no holdup of the regular flow of oil.

The story was simply untrue — and, in fact, it rested on a faulty premise. There was nothing to be gained by delayed unloading of the oil. On the contrary, since it was expensive to keep a tanker at sea, we would have had an economic motivation to speed up the deliveries.

But rumor and innuendo overwhelmed logic and economics. Suddenly stories of tankers — and even "thousands" of barges — were circulating around the country. Finally, on December 29, the *New York Times* ran a front-page story that gave credence to the rumors. Its reasoning was that it had an "authoritative source" in New Jersey Governor Brendan Byrne, who had told the *Times* that "the tankers were out there waiting for their price."

Five days later, Federal Energy Administrator William F. Simon issued a strong statement on the subject of the mythical tankers: "Such reports are unfounded in fact and do not reflect an accurate understanding of petroleum pricing regulations." In retrospect, we ought to have protested when the *Times* failed to give Simon's denial the same front page prominence it had given the rumors a week earlier. Since the denial was not as exciting as the rumors, it was printed on page 13.

No one had been able to prove there was anything unusual about the tankers that were offshore, and yet reports about them proliferated on radio and TV. Denials counted for nothing, even when expressed by someone as respected as Senator Jacob Javits of New York, who told WABC-TV that "we can't kid ourselves by laying the energy crisis at the doors of the oil companies."

And that's just where the blame was being put. The tanker myth was a symptom of the hysteria that was gripping the country. Both Congress (for political reasons) and the public (for emotional reasons) wanted a scapegoat to explain why the U.S. was being held hostage by the Arab states. Since the oil companies profited from soaring crude prices, we were vulnerable to attack. In response, we defended our record — and our profits. But how could we prove the absence of tankers?

At one point, I became so frustrated that I told a reporter, off the record, that the tankers really were out there, but they were not carrying any oil. Instead, I said, they were filled to the brim with money. But because we were making so much money from the oil crisis, the banks could not store it all. When I finished my story, it took the reporter a while before he realized that I was kidding him. That is how irrational — and how opportunistic — the situation had become.

At first, we responded to the crisis routinely, sending periodic statements to the press denying the rumor, and distributing Simon's statement, together with our own, to all of our shareholders, dealers, distributors, and major customers. But this was not enough, and we knew it.

Instead, since we could not get the press to cover the tanker story fairly, we commissioned the story ourselves. We found a reputable free-lance investigative reporter named Peter Celliers and gave him free rein to track down the reports and to determine for himself whether they were true. Celliers' article, which traced the origin of the tanker rumors and exonerated the oil industry, was published in the American Society of Newspaper Editors' *Bulletin*. We, of course, reprinted the article and got some attention for it. In retrospect, however, I think our response was too timid, too corporate — and too rational.

We were faced with an irrational situation that demanded an irrational solution. I think we should have been more aggressive. For example, what if we had hired a helicopter and invited prominent politicians and journalists to fly over the harbor and *show* us the mythical tankers? Or what if we'd offered a million dollars to anyone who could *prove* their existence?

By the time we made our response, it was too little and too late. Unless you confront rumors quickly and boldly, they may assume a life of their own — a life that persists long after the event. In fact, the tanker myth surfaced two years later in a documentary on WNBC-TV.

Our Musings Are Heard

While we had developed an active PR and advertising program to get our message across, we had to be quite resourceful in combating our critics during this period. For example, early in 1974 journalist Tom Wicker wrote an angry column in the *Times* that attacked the oil industry in general, and our advocacy ads in particular. We responded in our normal op-ed space with "Musings of an Oil Person" — a column by one of our staff writers that was typeset to look like it was done on a typewriter. While seemingly "musing" to himself over the plight of being a PR pro in an unpopular industry, he managed to rebut Wicker's criticisms and to humanize Mobil's side of the argument:

> *Have to take risk of moving Tom Wicker to nausea over the*
> *"...pious, self-serving, devious, mealy-mouthed, self-exculpating,*
> *holier-than-thou, positively sickening oil company advertisements*
> *in which these international behemoths depict themselves as*
> *poverty-stricken paragons of virtue embattled against a greedy*
> *and ignorant world"…. Tom turns a nice phrase, but doesn't he*

know we're frustrated in trying to get information to the public....
Hate to be on the defensive all the time.... What do we tell the guy
who's boiling mad at us — in our station or some other company's
— after waiting two hours for the privilege of paying $1.10 for two
gallons of gas?

This column is a good example of how a personal, almost wistful voice was effective in rebutting a vituperative critic. Other "musings" over the years have been ideal ways for us to express indignation, confusion, or anger.

An Open Letter to the U.S. Congress

Our personal voice served us well when we took out ads in the hometown papers of all members of Congress to remind them and the public that gasoline shortages were a major national concern. We wanted to make a couple of key points: one, that the oil companies had not cooked up the shortages; and two, that the voters had a voice in correcting the shortages by complaining to their representatives and senators about our national energy policy.

Entitled "An Open Letter on the Gasoline Shortage," the ad was addressed to the appropriate member, and began:

We are publishing this letter in your hometown newspaper, and in
those of the other members of Congress, because we want you and
your constituents to have the facts about the gasoline shortage as
we see them. We are doing this because many people are being
misled by the absolute nonsense, totally unsupported charges,
and outright lies being spread around by a variety of people.

Outspoken? Yes. Confrontational? You bet. In this "open letter" we wanted to remind the public that the lawmakers must be made accountable for energy policy and other issues of national concern.

Talking Back to the Television Set

On March 20, 1974, in the midst of the energy crisis, ABC broadcast a documentary entitled *Oil: The Policy Crisis.* Two days before it aired, ABC invited Mobil to comment on the program, which the network described as "basically a primer on oil, designed to help Americans understand a highly charged and difficult problem." Viewing the show, we found 32 inaccuracies or examples of unfairness. Much of the documentary focused on events dating back 50 years and more, including historical film clips of John D. Rockefeller, the Teapot Dome Scandal, and wooden derricks and "gushers," all of which were fundamentally irrelevant to the stated purpose of the program.

While using the clips to portray an image that was damaging to the industry, the documentary failed to confront many of the current world forces driving up the price and threatening supplies of oil. The program failed to include the history of government price controls on natural gas; the moratorium on drilling off Santa Barbara, California, and the severe limitation on offshore leasing generally since 1969; the surge in petroleum consumption due to increased use of power options on automobiles; and the imposition of auto-emission controls. The documentary made only a passing mention of the Arab oil embargo, and no mention at all of the recent cutback in Arab production. How could it purport to cover the energy crisis without discussing the U.S.'s politically hazardous reliance on foreign oil?

We immediately saw the futility of taking our case to the network. At best, someone at ABC would listen, nod, and wait for us to go away. Nothing would change. Instead, we filed a brief with the National News Council, a private watchdog of national news media, asking it to investigate our complaint that ABC's documentary was inaccurate and shoddily researched. In our 22-page analysis of the documentary, we called attention — and responded — to each of the 32 unfair or misleading statements in it.

In making our complaint to the National News Council, we issued a press release detailing some of the specific aspects of the program we found objectionable and why. The controversy generated considerable coverage in the print media, including the *Wall Street Journal*, which labeled the program "an hour-long editorial."

While the National News Council did not see fit to investigate our specific complaints, it issued a statement saying that the documentary "could, and did, select certain facts that pointed in one direction and omit others that pointed elsewhere." The network, the Council said, was guilty of leading viewers to assume that the program was "striving conscientiously for balance and fairness," and should not have contended that the documentary was "executed from every conceivable point of view."

Although we did not win a full victory, we felt we had succeeded in calling public attention to the unfairness of the ABC documentary. Furthermore, our critics were now forewarned that we would continue to speak out against unfair accusations from the media, the public, or even the government.

In this dialogue, we were denied access to the one medium on which we might most effectively have made our voice heard: television advertising. I do not mean product advertising, which in fact we had suspended at the time of the embargo. Instead, we sought to run paid ads in which we would express our views, much as we had done in the op-ed program. Expressing these views on television was critical for Mobil since the networks covered our industry (and all news) in such a shallow and sometimes hostile way. At best, the networks offered a headline service; at worst, as newscaster Walter Cronkite once said about television news, they were guilty of "the inadvertent and perhaps inevitable distortion that results through the hyper-compression we all are forced to exert to fit one hundred pounds of news into the one-pound sack that we are given to fill each night."

When we prepared commercials asking the public how it felt about offshore drilling, two of the three networks refused to run them. CBS argued that the commercial "deals with a controversial issue of public importance and does not fall within our 'goods and services' limitation for commercial acceptance." We argued that the networks' decision infringed upon our freedom of speech, and ran print ads that showed the commercials frame by frame and quoted the networks' reasons for using or not using the commercials.

Fighting mad? You bet. So were many people who read our ad. We received over 2,000 replies to it, and the respondents overwhelmingly favored our right to express our viewpoint on the air. These letters were a clear indication that the public wanted the facts, and supported our basic tenet that we, as corporate citizens with a special expertise in energy matters, should be given the opportunity to express our views in the marketplace of ideas.

We even offered to pay for rebuttal ads if Mobil could get across its own message, but the networks insisted that the pros and cons of energy were in the hands of their own journalists.

Blitzing the Media While we did not get our commercials on two of the major networks, we were successful in getting many of our points across by placing Mobil executives on television. We organized media blitzes in which they crisscrossed the country, appearing on television and meeting the press, with heavy backup support by public relations. The first two blitzes included visits to 90 newspapers and 450 radio and TV news shows. For the third blitz, 23 senior Mobil managers visited 29 cities in 21 states, calling on 30 newspapers and appearing on 69 television shows and on 68 radio programs. The interviews focused on Mobil's proposals for a national energy plan, on bills in Congress that threatened to divest the oil companies of some of their assets, and on America's shrinking energy supplies. This exposure helped to put a human face on our company and to counter some of the negative coverage of our industry.

The National Town Meeting One of our main objectives during this period of dealing with the media relations issue was to be involved in the dialogue about energy, the economy, the environment, and other key social and political issues. We found one effective way to be included in the marketplace of ideas when we sponsored a series of open forums on contemporary issues at the Kennedy Center in Washington, D.C. We called them National Town Meetings — invoking a traditional forum for the exchange of opinions — and adopted a format in which two prominent guests debated an important issue of public policy.

To avoid conflict of interest, we agreed that none of the meetings would cover oil or energy policy. Instead, by our commitment to honest dialogue, we argued for a more open approach to discussions of energy issues. We reinforced our commitment to debating the issues in a public and open manner by including prominent political officials, leaders of constituency groups, and members of the press.

I think the meetings also helped to establish us as an intellectually responsible company that might legitimately have a role in shaping the national agenda. And since the meetings often became newsmaking events in themselves, they attracted favorable media attention for us, the sponsors.

"Observations"

The National Town Meetings, like our advocacy advertising and many of our public affairs programs, were targeted to opinion leaders in government, the media, industry, and academia. While this was unquestionably an important audience in our struggle for credibility, we realized that we had put too strict a definition on who exactly constituted an opinion leader. The demographics of many of our programs, particularly the op-ed program, caused us to ignore other important sectors of the population. Our op-eds were not reaching a vast number of people who cared about issues like energy supply and security — and who might exert influence on their elected officials.

Other than running ads in all of their hometown papers, how might we reach our intended audience? *Parade*, the Sunday newspaper supplement magazine, had the right kind of circulation for us, and yet we felt the op-ed format did not suit it. We therefore came up with a different kind of ad that was more in keeping with *Parade*'s format. Called "Observations," it consisted of a series of short takes — breezily written items, woodcuts, cartoons, witty sayings — with the same editorial themes as our op-ed ads. For example, adjacent to a woodcut of a windmill, we ran an item headed "Good News Blues." It went on:

> *"All I know is just what I read in the papers," cracked humorist Will Rogers back in the 1920s. Today, some things that you don't read in newspapers, or see on network TV news, are what you ought to know — especially about energy, a field where reporters*

too often go tilting at windmills. Well, as a top journalist put it, "Bad news sells better."

At its peak, Observations reached about half of the households in America through 500 different newspapers. In readership scores, Observations far exceeded the average scores of other half-page black-and-white ads. Observations often did better than big four-color ads and occasionally even out-ran the editorial columns of the magazine. Furthermore, our survey indicated that the column really influenced people on public policy issues that we saw as important. We also received lots of letters from Observations readers, many of whom said that the column played a vital role in balancing the information they received from government and the media.

In 1976 we got more corroboration for our advocacy advertising when the Harris Organization conducted a poll to learn how the American public viewed 40 major corporations, including seven oil companies. Although the oil companies in general fared poorly, the people surveyed thought more highly of Mobil than of the competition. In their view, Mobil was "committed to free enterprise," "seriously concerned about the energy problems," and "working for good government." In fact, the public perceived Mobil as the industry pacesetter on 19 of the 21 public policy issues that were mentioned in the survey. Obviously, our advocacy ads were a major factor in our favor.

Moreover, although we had not done any product advertising for nearly three years, the public rated the quality of our products and services higher than the other oil companies in the survey. I think that is evidence that while we may have been selling ideas, there were also some bottom-line benefits from our public affairs program.

The Misinformation War No matter how effective you are in running your company and presenting your message to the public, you remain vulnerable to damaging criticism, even if it is capricious or wrong-headed. When you are under attack, you realize that there is no such thing as a one-day story. Information, especially erroneous information, stays in the computer forever. This makes it easy for irresponsible journalists to regurgitate all the negatives that have accumulated over the years.

By 1974 we thought we had dispelled the tanker myth. No such luck. In 1976 when WNBC-TV began a week-long series called "The Great Gasoline War," the first episode recycled that old story about the tankers waiting off the coast until there was a price rise. The series contained other distortions and errors, including some we had not heard before. But especially after our experience with the

ABC oil documentary, we were quick to respond — and to target many of our criticisms to Liz Trotta, the WNBC reporter who narrated the series.

Over the weekend after the series aired, we prepared a full-page ad headed, "Whatever Happened to Fair Play?" which ran in the *New York Times*, the *New York Daily News*, and the eastern edition of the *Wall Street Journal*. In the ad, we described the WNBC series as "inaccurate, unfair, and a disservice to the people." We took issue with its value as news, calling it "a parade of warmed-over distortions, half-truths, and downright untruths marching across the screen like an army of tired ghosts — ghosts we thought had been laid to rest years ago." We backed up our rhetoric with specifics, documenting 17 "hatchet jobs," with a small drawing of a hatchet next to each of the distortions.

As soon as the ad was ready, we sent a copy of it to each of the NBC affiliates that was planning to run the series. While we will never know for sure, it is certainly possible that this mailing had something to do with the fact that no other station in the country aired the series.

We also asked WNBC to let us purchase half an hour of time in order to present additional information that we felt was pertinent to the many issues raised by their series. They turned us down. Instead, they invited a company spokesperson to appear live on their news show. (We had already turned down an opportunity to appear on the documentary, because we suspected that the interview would be chopped up and would result in a brief segment that had little to do with the points we wanted to make.) "Since you fear editing of your statements," the news director wrote, "I am offering to allow you to make a short statement followed by questions by Ms. Trotta."

But we had already heard a sampling of Trotta's questions, and we did not feel the need to have her questioning us. If anything, she should be "allowed" to make a statement, and then we should ask her questions. That, at any rate, was our private response. In our press release, we called the station's offer "patently unfair because it would be impossible for Mobil to compress its response into a short statement of a few minutes in reply to five nights of one-sided editorializing totaling some 36 minutes."

This episode helped to confirm some lessons we had drawn from our handling of the energy crisis:

Lessons Learned

- First, you have to find creative and unusual ways to communicate with the public if the media will not carry your story — especially when your story involves criticism of it.

- Second, the best way to deal with erroneous information is to embarrass the journalist professionally by bringing his or her mistakes to the public's attention.

- Third, if you do your job well, you can get the last word with print journalists and the electronic media.

Aftermath We became increasingly aware that our message was getting across. Two persuasive cases, in particular, seemed to indicated that we were managing crisis successfully.

In 1977 Opinion Research Corporation conducted an independent survey in which it found that print, TV, and radio editors regarded Mobil more favorably than they did the other oil companies. Furthermore, ORC found that the oil industry improved its relations with the news media during 1976, and it cited Mobil's public relations efforts as a major reason for that improvement.

In 1980 we did our own survey comparing the *New York Times* editorials to those in Mobil's op-ed ads since the series' inception. Whereas the *Times* originally disagreed with us on many key energy issues, our survey found that the paper had changed to positions similar to Mobil's on at least seven of these issues. While we cannot assume any direct correlations between Mobil's ads and the *Times'* turnabouts, we feel there is enough circumstantial evidence to suggest that by speaking out, Mobil has been a key factor affecting the *Times'* decisions.

By 1981 the *Times* wrote: "The Mobil Oil Corporation has made its mark in the advertising world as a tough street fighter that has pioneered an aggressive style of advertising in explaining oil industry profits, pricing, and policy decisions. Public relations experts have generally given Mobil high marks for its techniques."

In retrospect, I think our greatest PR achievements were:

- Making reporters think twice about saying something inaccurate about us.

- Having an impact on the debate on energy issues and legislation.

- Over time, influencing a sizable portion of the U.S. and showing its citizens that what they heard was inaccurate.

On the negative side, when you go into a confrontational campaign, you get a lot of people mad at you. I think that is something you have to accept — and even welcome. But we felt we had the facts on our side, and eventually we would get a fair hearing. And that's just what we did.

Herbert Schmertz is president of The Schmertz Company, a public and government affairs counseling and advertising company founded in 1988, with offices in New York City and Washington, D.C. In 1966 Mr. Schmertz joined Mobil Oil Corporation and enjoyed a healthy career with them, becoming vice-president for public affairs. His portfolio included corporate public relations, domestic and international government relations (including Mobil's Washington government relations office), and investor relations. In 1983 President Reagan appointed Mr. Schmertz a member of the President's Advisory Commission on Public Diplomacy. Mr. Schmertz is coauthor of the novel Takeover *and author of* Good-bye to the Low Profile.

Continental
Announces
Chapter 11

Art Kent
Vice-President, Public Affairs, Continental Airlines

Overview

Twenty-five years in broadcast journalism are over. A new job is needed. PR? Why not?

Six weeks of interviews with Continental Airlines are concluding and everything seems to be going well: "Now you have to have a meeting with Frank!" says a senior vice-president.

"Frank who?"

Wars? Yes. Revolution? Yes. Politics? Yes. Presidential trips? Yes. The Middle East? Yes. The CIA? Yes — covered them all. But Frank Lorenzo, the Peck's bad boy of the airline industry? Never heard of him. First impressions are usually right: "I never want to play poker with this guy; his face doesn't show a thing." But he hired me. I was part of the glamorous world of airlines. I had loved sitting in airports, people watching. But now, I was on the inside. I had been admitted to the secret fraternity. Okay, so it isn't brain surgery, but it is pretty exciting.

Four months later: It was 5:30 A.M. The security detail at Texas Air/Continental Chairman Frank Lorenzo's house woke me up to say there was a network camera crew camped outside, hoping for an interview on the latest set of machinists union accusations as Frank was leaving for work. I ended up driving him to his office in my car. On the way he said, "How would you like to move from the airline

Frank Lorenzo on courthouse steps after announcing the bankruptcy of Eastern Airlines.

to the holding company (Texas Air, at that time)? We're going to put Eastern Airlines into Chapter 11 in three days."

Here we go again! Chapter 11? What's that? Three days?

For a neophyte in the PR field, those first 18 months with Continental/Texas Air were a crash course in crisis communications. Everything was a crisis, heightened by a hostile press and public, and a major union-driven campaign to focus blame for business failure on one man: Frank Lorenzo.

Key lessons were to be learned. Foremost among them was the fact that no major business crisis (and Chapter 11 is certainly a crisis) can be adequately dealt with when the person responsible for communications is excluded until the last moment. Second, you need help. Lots of it! You need a dedicated, committed organization of your own. The rest you can hire. And third, you need input from, and the cooperation of, every part of the organization.

Case in point: Continental's December 1990 filing for protection under Chapter 11 of the Bankruptcy Code.

Toward the fall of 1990, air travel was falling off as the world waited for what became the Persian Gulf War, and the recession started to have a chilling effect on American business. The cost of jet fuel was climbing at an alarming rate, every penny more per gallon costing Continental a million dollars; and the company was already staggering under a huge mountain of debt incurred while Lorenzo was acquiring other airlines, by capital spending, and for facilities refurbishment. Enormous interest payments were looming on the horizon. We couldn't handle all these factors combined.

Crash Course

The CEO at that time, a 36-year veteran of Delta named Hollis Harris, who had been brought in after Lorenzo sold his interests to Scandanavian Airlines Systems (SAS), understood that communications had to be a consideration in major company actions. Now I knew what was coming before it got here, but not as far out in front as I might have wished.

Luckily, I had a small, incredibly hard-working staff. In addition to three secretaries, two people handled charitable giving and community involvement; three people dealt with media, wrote press releases and speeches, and oversaw the in-flight magazine; three handled internal communications such as the company newspaper; and three constituted our video department, which produced training films, sales pieces, and periodic video reports to our employees.

We also had the services of local PR agencies in our major domestic locations: Newark, Cleveland, Denver, and Seattle; as well as in London, Paris, Honolulu, Sydney, and Tokyo. Carl Byoir and Associates, an agency spun off from Hill and Knowlton to handle the Continental account, was our "national" agency of record.

It sounds like a lot of people. It wasn't. Remember, Continental was a $5.5 billion company operating an airline and various subsidiaries (a computerized reservations service, airline catering company, etc.) in more than 200 locations worldwide, and with more than 40,000 employees.

When Harris told me we were going to file for bankruptcy, he agreed we needed outside help. Sensitive to the attitude of our largest single shareholder, SAS, he made it pretty clear that rather than the agencies already on retainer, we should use Daniel J. Edelman to handle the Chapter 11 filing. I was not pleased.

Flashback In another case of Frank Lorenzo playing his cards very close to the vest, he had called me on a Sunday to tell me we would be meeting in New York *the following day* with the unnamed people *to whom he had sold his controlling interest in Continental!* After a briefing on Monday, when I learned the buyer was SAS, I walked into a meeting on Tuesday to find that SAS had hired Edelman to represent its interests *four months previously!* They, of course, were fully prepared, and naturally everything spun toward SAS. On my side I had the hurriedly assembled team of Bob Dillenschneider of Hill and Knowlton, Doug Hearle of Carl Byoir, and Steve Anreder, one of the smartest financial PR people I know. We went to PR war. Forty-eight acrimonious hours later, a balanced announcement was made, though battle scars remained.

Pleased or not, I contacted Edelman's vice-chairman, Michael Morley. He assigned Jim Cox, executive vice-president and head of their Houston office, to the project. To say I got lucky is a classic understatement. Cox is a dynamic man with significant experience and knowledge in corporate bankruptcies, and very easy to work with.

As usually happens in big companies, we called a meeting. It was the first of many that were held in the ensuing frantic days. Crowded into the small corporate communications conference room, away from the executive offices, were Continental's chief operating officer, the executive vice-presidents of administration and marketing, the senior vice-president of human resources, the chief legal officer, and four key members of my staff. The executive vice-president of administration had recently joined the company, coming from Delta with Harris. When asked if he had any comment during the meeting, he allowed as how he didn't have anything to say but he was glad he had not yet sold his house in Atlanta. The circle was deliberately small, the meeting confidential, and notes were carefully protected.

Define the Critical Issues. There really is only one issue. Simply stated, filing for Chapter 11 protection cannot be seen to change a thing! Sure, a company goes into Chapter 11 because, for some reason, it can't pay its bills. And in most cases, all those bills it owed up until the moment it files are not going to get paid, at least not until the company comes out of bankruptcy.

Immediate Tasks

List Your Audiences. In our case, this included employees, shareholders, Wall Street analysts, travel agents, government agencies, and the public, through the press.

Seek Support from Your Audiences.

- Employee attitude is reflected in the product and therefore the customer's propensity to buy travel. Employees must understand why the action is being taken, believe the company will survive, and believe their jobs are secure.

- Company shareholders have to be reached with the company's message. After all, they own it.

- Wall Street analysts, *always* available for an opinion, set the tone for press coverage and, of course, have great influence on how stock will behave.

- Travel agents sell some 80 percent of Continental's tickets. If they are not convinced Continental will be around and their commissions will be paid, they won't sell tickets.

- Airlines are licensed and supervised by various government agencies. They must know what is happening. Congress, which can change the rules, has to be reassured as well. State and local governments everywhere a company operates need their worries alleviated about service, employment, fee and tax income, and future commitment.

- Through the press, the public has to be convinced that a Chapter 11 filing does not mean a company is going away; in an airline's case, the public must be assured that the planes are flying.

Our creditors, of course, would see the filing in a very different light. But since they have a vested interest in seeing the company survive (if it doesn't, they don't get their money), they will support efforts to convince all the audiences that the hallmark is "business as usual."

And that was to be the basic motto that underlaid everything we did: Business as usual.

Preparing the Release Blitz

Our target was Monday, December 3, the date of a meeting of our board of directors, five days away. The filing was to be in Wilmington, Delaware, where the company was incorporated. Because of approval and duplication requirements, we really only had four days to get ready! In continual consultation with key senior management, work began to draft all the communications we would need on the day of filing.

To preserve confidentiality, much of the work was done by Cox's Edelman team, who worked around the clock at Edelman's offices in a different part of town. Only a very few of my staff members were involved at the outset, the circle widening as we reached critical points along the way. Initially, some hard feelings surfaced in my group, centering around not only being left out, but perhaps over the issue of trust. These feelings faded fast as the pace picked up and everyone got involved.

In Edelman's conference room, computers jammed the large center table and other tables that were moved in. Stacks of paper littered the floor. Easels held pads of newsprint with lists of what had been written, what was still to do, and when it was all due. A coffee pot in the corner ran continuously. Empty take-out food containers overflowed the wastebaskets, and the few of us who smoked made up for everyone else who didn't.

The list of documents to be written was long: the basic, national press release; tailored releases for each of our domestic hub cities, plus Honolulu and Guam; a sidebar piece on what Chapter 11 is; a sidebar on the company's debt load and the impact of fuel costs; a fact sheet on the airline; a comparison between the airline's 1983 bankruptcy filing and this one, which would include the holding company and all of its subsidiaries; a graphic representation of the debt and fuel issues; a piece that explained that business as usual meant that all our planes would be flying, tickets would be honored, and full service would continue uninterrupted; a special piece for mailgram distribution to travel agents emphasizing that their pre-petition commissions would be paid, and a second version in case we could not do that; a special piece that was distributed to all employees on the day of filing; a script for an employee video done by the CEO, explaining the "first day orders"; and a detailed question and answer recap.

The last two were critical. First day orders are orders of the bankruptcy court that are requested at the time of filing. In our case, the order, if granted, would allow the company to pay pre-petition travel agency commissions, protect so-called interline agreements that allow other airlines to honor each other's tickets and baggage, refund tickets whether purchased before or after the filing, and maintain employee salaries and benefits. It was the keystone of our "business as usual" motto.

The question-and-answer sheet, 16 pages long, was broken up into sections dealing with management-related questions, questions concerning financial and legal issues, consumer-related matters, employee-related issues, industry, trade, and traveler-related questions, and a special section dealing with matters relating to SAS's recent acquisition of Lorenzo's controlling stake in the company. It was the most-used document of all, the answers having been preapproved by the senior executives and advisors involved.

Employee communications were carefully planned. Stories that highlighted the scope of the crisis and what the rising cost of fuel was doing to our balance sheet had already been in our company newspaper. The employees therefore had some knowledge that the company was in worse financial shape than they had thought.

**Reassuring
Employees**

Similar themes had been included in the CEO's weekly voice mail to employees. When Harris assumed the job, we created an 800 number in our company voice mail system and told everyone about it. Every week, he recorded a message to the employees that they accessed at their convenience. It became our most valuable employee communications tool, especially for an organization as far flung and working on such disparate schedules as an airline. It is still in use today.

We selected officers of the company to be dispatched to major company locations to hold employee meetings and to act as local representatives. A special news bulletin was to be distributed through the company's worldwide teletype system. A special telex and voice mail alert system was established so that local management would be available for conference calls, know the bulletin was coming, and be ready to show the video, which was to be distributed on the day following the announcement.

Since the officers to be sent out were not spokespeople by choice or experience, a media training session was set up for the day before the filing. Without explanation, the officers were summoned to Houston, briefed, sworn to secrecy, and put through three-hour sessions run by Jack Reynolds, a former NBC News correspondent and long-time colleague of mine. The officers hand-carried the specially tailored releases, the accompanying press kit materials, and the question-and-answer sheets to all the major locations.

Covert Operations A location for a press conference had to be secured, under a false name, together with lighting and audio services. This was critical to preserve confidentiality. A two-way phone bridge was needed so reporters in other cities could participate in the press conference. A separate location was needed and arrangements made for a satellite media tour. This may not sound like much, but a station alert system, two-way communications, satellite time, camera crews, and other technology have to be booked, and in some cases paid for, in advance.

The senior vice-president of human resources was assigned to meet with all the company officers on the day of filing and brief them fully. Those officers not in Houston would take part via conference call.

The executive vice-president of marketing was assigned to record a special message for travel agents on an 800 number, which also had to be established. Another 800 number was set up so that travel agents could call in and get their questions answered.

The chief operating officer was assigned to call the administrator of the Federal Aviation Administration (FAA); my chief assistant would brief our PR people overseas, and the local PR agencies in the United States. Since they, too, would become creditors, we could not tell them what was coming and take advantage of their services. They would have to be brought in at the last moment. In the end, I am happy to say, they all stayed with us, and have remained valued associates to this day.

Certain officers of the company were detailed to call civic leaders in the key cities. The vice-president of investor relations drew up a list of key analysts to call. The vice-president of government relations drew up a list of key congressional leaders and staff to call.

Finally, a special message was prepared to be loaded into the computer terminal of every reservations agent in the airline. When the general public heard we had filed bankruptcy, their first question would be, What happens to my trip next month? Then the 800 number for Continental would be dialed. The message would tell the reservation clerks what to say. It was used a lot!

The Friday before the board meeting, all the various communications pieces had been drafted, redrafted, changed by the lawyers (God bless 'em), copied, and the press kits compiled and readied to be dispatched. Our video department, brought in at the last moment, had laid out the employee video and gathered "B-roll" for the video news release (VNR). The VNR pictures had been shipped off to a production house in New York. (Our guys had enough to do just to edit the employee video and get 400 copies made and distributed.) Harris had gone through his media training, recorded the sound bite for the VNR to be released on Monday, recorded his message to our employees on videotape, and gone through a press conference rehearsal.

Of course, last-minute changes were made to the releases. The combination company/Edelman team worked through the night making the changes, making the copies, working out the distribution problems, drinking coffee, and eating cold pizza.

There is a rule in doing corporate PR: The top executives of a company *all* have to make a change in a release. They also do not have the foggiest idea of what is involved when you make changes at the very last minute.

I was not looking forward to the big day. I remembered when we had announced the Eastern Airlines bankruptcy in New York. It was my first press conference as a PR pro. I confidently walked into the hotel, up to the podium, and faced thirteen camera crews, several hundred reporters, and seemingly five million still photographers. I looked at them fondly — after all, they had been my colleagues for 20 years. Not any more! The mob scene became so bad that the New York Police Department dispatched several vans of officers from their Patrol Bureau Standby Force to control the crowd. At least I verified why we in television had believed all still photographers should be stood up against a wall, and shot. They *do* like to get up in front ... close in front!

Flashback II

But this was different. We were dealing with Wilmington, Delaware, not New York. There are not a lot of large hotels in Wilmington with facilities for press conferences. You need lots of telephone lines and a management that is used to weird goings-on, like they are in New York. We picked the Radisson. My secretary moved in on Friday, November 30.

We asked the local telephone company to string extra lines into our command center, which was really the 9x12 foot living room of my suite, and into the room where we would hold our press conference. My secretary assembled computers, telephone modems, and facsimile and copying machines from a local supply house. All this sudden, unexplained activity started to make the hotel management nervous.

That same day, we reserved the lines for the telephone bridge for Monday's press conference. Final versions of releases, messages, and all the other communications were reviewed one last time at Houston headquarters. On Saturday, December 1, Harris recorded his video messages in Houston. The press kits were produced.

On Sunday, the kits were shipped and hand-carried to the various hubs and major operating locations.

The press had been watching us fairly closely. We knew if a bunch of senior people suddenly all flew on passes on a Continental airplane to Philadelphia, the nearest city we served, someone would wonder. So we had Edelman purchase regular airline tickets. (It was nice to see that we were treated every bit as well as if we had been flying in our corporate roles.)

Wilmington offered no television studios for satellite media tours, so we found a satellite truck that would come into town. When the folks from MediaLink parked their truck in back of the hotel and nonchalantly began to string cable into the building, the management *really* got nervous.

We had registered under a phony company name, using cash or an Edelman credit card. So, I finally had a meeting with the hotel manager. He came into our suite, glanced around at all the equipment and all the people on telephones and looked *very* worried. I handed him my business card, swore him to secrecy, and made up a lot of empty threats if he revealed our intentions. I don't know what he had thought we were up to, but the look of relief that flooded his face when I told him the truth was almost comical. They were wonderful folks at the Radisson.

Putting into effect the old adage that the first wire story controls what is written for the majority of the story, we arranged to deliver press releases to the various New York wire service headquarters at the appropriate moment.

We also had ready an innocuous release to be used in the event of a premature media inquiry. Then the lawyers insisted on a last-minute change in the release copy. They found it at four in the morning! We frantically rewrote the basic release and all the separate releases for the various cities. The bulk of the press kits were to be distributed in New York, Houston, and Washington. The changed versions were sent there by modem, reprinted on location, and all the press kits changed. In the other cities the officer spokespeople were telefaxed the changed page, and instructed to have new copies made and inserted in their press kits before they handed them out.

Thankfully the guy responsible for Guam had waited in Honolulu, just in case. Nobody slept that night. On December 3, the board blessed the filing, the lawyers went to the courthouse, and the judge signed all the first day orders.

Pushing the Button   In our hastily arranged control room at the Radisson Hotel at 7:30 A.M., we figuratively "pushed the button." Messengers, already in place at the news agencies in New York and Washington, heard their beepers go off and walked inside to deliver our press kits. Another group was dispatched to the offices of the key analysts. The tactic worked. The second paragraph of every wire story that moved that morning contained the "business as usual" message.

In Houston, managers, already alerted via telex messages, were briefed via conference calls. Key travel agents were called. The chief operating officer and the executive vice-president of administration briefed all the company's officers. A 24-hour command center was opened in the headquarters building, staffed by human resources, benefits, operations, and law department staffers. It was shut down after two days. The feared rush of problems never materialized.

Corporate communications staff fed the press release via the PR Newswire, released the special statement that would be put into every reservation clerk's computer, sent out the telex bulletin to every company location worldwide, and began a 24-hour work schedule. (It, too, was canceled after two days.)

Harris called the secretary of transportation. My chief assistant held a conference call with our domestic and overseas PR agencies, finally breaking the news to them, and dispatched them to the major airports to assist the officer spokespeople who had been sent out.

In Wilmington, Harris fed his voice mail into the system and, at 11:00 A.M., walked into a small ballroom in the hotel, read a prepared statement, and took questions. Considering where we were, and how difficult it was for the press to get there on time, the press conference was well attended. Thankfully, it was a far cry from my New York experience 19 months earlier, although the still photographers were almost as pushy.

At 3:00 P.M., Harris walked into a small room in the hotel. The bed had been pushed aside, a camera was in the middle of the room, pointed at a single chair. Wires were everywhere, lights made it unbearably hot, and the place was jammed with people. He sat down, put an earpiece into his ear, and stared into the camera. A card was held up so that he would know the names of the local TV anchors and reporters who would be talking into his ear. For three hours he did virtually the same interview with a succession of TV stations all across the country.

That evening we went to Washington, D.C., where he appeared on the "Today" show Tuesday morning.

Lessons Learned

- Never forget that you have 30 minutes to get your point of view to the wires. Once that first story moves, if you failed, you will play catch-up forever.

- Never forget that more than 70 percent of the American people get all or most of their news from television ... and that really means CNN and local news. Harris spent those three hours staring into that camera lens, doing one-on-ones with CNN and local anchors all across the country, because it was the best way to communicate with the most people.

- The network morning shows reach more viewers than their evening newscasts. Unfortunately, they compete with one another in a way that can best be described as "take no prisoners." Network careers are made or broken by which show gets the big interview first. We had really fouled up the "Today" show several months before, so I gave them first crack at Harris. ABC and CBS tried all the tricks, made all the usual threats, and finally pronounced the ultimate punishment by declining the interview.

- Unless you have the world's largest in-house PR staff, you need outside help. Not only to provide the arms, legs, typewriters, and logistics, but also another set of minds that can look at the situation objectively, and provide a vehicle for the confidentiality that is so crucial.

- Most of all, you need the full cooperation of the top management of the company. Many businesspeople are still stuck in the mind-set that says all you have to do is issue a press release, carefully worded, thoroughly massaged by the lawyers who consider it a legal document and not a press release, and everything will be fine. There is an innate fear of television because you cannot be assured that *exactly* what you want to say will make its way onto the screen, and businesspeople are used to being in control.

- Recent history is replete with PR disasters brought on by an unwillingness to aggressively communicate up front. The boss has to trust you and believe you know what you are doing. But it does help to have an outside consultant validate your proposals ... we all know that outside consultants always know more than the inside people.

Aftermath

Finally, did it work? Yes, measured by two criteria. The loss of revenue expected in the aftermath of our Chapter 11 filing was dramatically lower than feared. And when two other airlines filed for bankruptcy after we did, they did exactly what we had done; they used the same methods, the same tools, even some of the same press release language, word for word.

As these words are written, Continental Airlines is still under Chapter 11 protection. The end is in sight. I hope by the time this is read, our bankruptcy will be history.

One Last Flashback

On Saturday, October 20, 1990, on a ranch near Intercontinental Airport in Houston, the annual company picnic was held. The sun was shining. The oppressive Houston summer heat had abated. Music came over loudspeakers, interspersed with announcements for the next softball game, or which areas had the shortest line for beer. More than 20,000 Continental employees, spouses, and children showed up, as did many of the officers of the company.

At least for me, and I believe for others, it was a humbling experience. These were not people who made decisions in an ivory tower, thinking of the "big picture." These were people, in some cases, making minimum wage; in many cases not much more.

They laughed, ate, drank, put their kids on rides, talked with their friends, and made new ones. *They* were the company, not us. Those images have not left the minds of many of us, and I am convinced that a lot of decisions made since that day were affected. If all goes well, those 20,000 people will be at another company picnic soon, and so will the officers of the company. But this time there won't be bad days in their futures.

Art Kent is vice-president, public affairs, Continental Airlines and Continental Airlines Holdings, Inc., based in Houston, Texas. Before joining Continental, Mr. Kent had a distinguished career as a broadcast journalist with NBC News, where he worked as a bureau chief, a Middle East correspondent, a national security affairs correspondent in Washington, D.C., and a vice-president, news operations and satellites.

Capping
Phillips's Bravo

James A. Fyock
Former Director of Public Relations, Phillips Petroleum Company

Overview

At approximately 10:00 P.M., Friday, April 22, 1977, a production well of Phillips Petroleum Company blew out during a routine well-maintenance operation. The well, Bravo 14, part of Phillips's Ekofisk field in the North Sea, spewed a 200-foot-high jet of crude oil into the sea at a rate of 16,000 to 18,000 barrels a day. Despite high winds and rough seas, the 112 workers aboard the platform were evacuated by work boats. By early Monday, an oil slick, 12 by 15 miles, had built up northeast of the platform. Within 36 hours, the blowout, which threatened fisheries and the environment around the North Sea littoral, attracted a press corps of more than 100 reporters. After several attempts, the well was successfully capped and shut in on April 30. By that time, as much as 200,000 barrels of oil had spilled into the North Sea.

Innovator in Offshore Drilling

In 1977 Phillips Petroleum Company was ranked 22d in *Fortune* magazine's listing of America's top 500 industrial companies. A significant factor contributing to that ranking was the oil production from Phillips's North Sea oil and gas fields, particularly those in the Norwegian sector.

As one of the early bidders on leases in the North Sea, Phillips drilled several "dry holes" before hitting it big. In fact, the company was very close to abandoning its test well drilling when it struck what is referred to in the oil business as "a dinosaur" at Ekofisk. It was the Norwegian authorities' refusal to release Phillips from its drilling commitment that resulted in the "one more try" that made the big discovery.

In developing the Ekofisk field, Phillips engineers pushed the technology envelope for offshore oil field exploration and production. To accommodate production facilities and to store current production until an undersea pipeline could be built, the company designed and built a giant one-million-barrel concrete storage tank and oil tanker loading facility. Designed to float when empty, the tank was towed 180 miles out to sea and set down on the seabed within a few feet of its intended location.

Phillips used the several acres on top of the tank, which was about 60 feet above sea level, as its production center. Phillips developed the field by establishing a number of production platforms, each of which housed 10 or 15 wells. Some of the platforms were connected to Ekofisk Center by catwalks. The Bravo platform, housing 15 wells, was connected to Ekofisk Center. By the time of the blowout, the top of the tank could have qualified as one of the most intensively developed pieces of real estate on earth, and the entire Ekofisk operation was producing hundreds of thousands of barrels of oil a day.

Another innovation by Phillips was the development of gas injection technology: natural gas produced concurrently with oil production is injected back into producing wells and not flared. A gas pipeline was later constructed linking the field with the European gas grid at Emden, Germany. Additionally, an oil pipeline was constructed to connect the field to storage and refining facilities at Teeside in England.

At the time the Bravo platform's 15 producing oil wells accounted for a substantial part of the total production from Ekofisk. Ekofisk, in turn, accounted for a substantial part of Phillips's total production and was regarded by the financial community as a key factor in the value placed on the company's equities.

For Phillips, the prospect of a blowout of a well at its Ekofisk field could be an unmitigated disaster. The relatively small loss of production would be insignificant, but the potential for environmental damage and the loss of confidence by the financial community could have serious consequences for the company and its shareholders.

Blowout On Friday evening, April 22, 1977, a crew was performing a routine workover of a well on the Bravo platform. During such a procedure, heavy drilling mud is pumped into the well to neutralize down-hole pressure while the well is being worked on. At approximately 9:00 P.M., mud began to flow from tubing at the top of the well. Measures taken by the workover crew to halt the flow were ineffective and by 9:45 P.M. the well was out of control.

A plume of oil and gas thundered into the sky. As much as a thousand barrels of oil were being spilled each hour into the sea around the platform. High pressure natural gas mixed with the oil needed only a spark to set off a monumental fire and possible explosion. As a precaution, Phillips took immediate steps to spray the platform continuously with sea water from tenders and nearby fireboats.

The men on the platform quickly abandoned the rig and were taken by workboats to safety. The workers were so well-drilled and rehearsed in emergency procedures that not a single injury occurred. Nonetheless, word of the disaster spread quickly and within 36 hours reporters and television crew members had converged on Phillips's Norway headquarters in Stavanger.

Some of the public relations implications of the blowout were immediately apparent. Some were not. Oil spilling into the sea in the heart of such a vital fisheries area threatened an important North Sea industry. The time of year made the potential fisheries consequences even more severe since fish eggs were hatching into fry. The spill threatened the entire North Sea littoral. Uppermost in the public's mind were visions of black, viscous waves of oil killing sea life and fouling shorelines.

Implications and PR Response

Neither Phillips nor the Norwegian government was prepared to handle the onslaught of news people from ten countries that descended on the small Norwegian coastal city of Stavanger. Reliable sources were initially so scarce and facts so unavailable that reporters were interviewing each other — on the basis of pure speculation and rumor. Of course, the action was 160 miles at sea.

Reporters were totally frustrated by the lack of information. For television reporters it was doubly frustrating — no pictures available to go with their words. To make matters even worse, from the media's perspective, the Norwegian Navy threw up a blockade around the site that kept enterprising reporters who had chartered small boats or planes away from the site.

Phillips's headquarters in Stavanger was primarily a production management facility staffed with petroleum engineers and other production personnel. Phillips's Norway executives, while possessing outstanding technical qualifications, had little or no experience in handling the media. The Norwegian authorities, under whose jurisdiction the blowout fell, were equally inexperienced in handling such a large press corps.

News of the blowout arrived at Phillips's corporate headquarters in Bartlesville, Oklahoma, late in the evening of April 22. Within a matter of hours, a Phillips jet with engineering and production experts on board was dispatched to Norway. En route the plane stopped briefly in Houston to pick up Asgar (Boots) Hansen and Richard (Coots) Hatteberg, two of the best and most experienced blowout fighters from the Red Adair Company, a well-known oil-well fire fighting firm.

The group arrived in Stavanger at 2:00 P.M. on Saturday, April 23, and immediately began an assessment of the situation. Working late into the night, the group formulated their plan and prepared to fly out to the platform early the next day.

Phillips's Bravo 14 well blows oil into the sky.

Early Sunday, April 24, a five-man group comprised of Phillips and Adair experts landed on the Bravo platform. They were able to stay on the platform for only about 20 minutes, but were able to make their on-site assessment, after which they returned to Ekofisk Center. Hansen and Hatteberg immediately began to assemble and check out the equipment they would need to cap the blowout.

Call to Action   Back in Bartlesville early Saturday morning, I was getting ready to build a brick patio when the phone rang. It was my boss, Tom Boyd, manager of public relations, who said he needed to see me at once and was coming directly to my house. On arrival, Boyd gave me a quick rundown on what little the company knew and said, "Get your bag packed, get to Stavanger as quickly as you can, and get a handle on the public relations situation."

This was just like being back in the army: I had a mission-type order to proceed to a distant location and do what I had to do to get the job done. I was filled with a sense of adventure, excitement, and even anticipation, but was also struck by the magnitude of the task before me.

Within hours I was on my way. Before departing I called my friend, public relations consultant Sid Gross, in New York to see if he could go with me and be part of the PR team. Sid readily agreed and said he'd meet me at Kennedy Airport shortly before our flight time at 7:00 P.M. that evening.

At Kennedy Airport, we discussed the situation and agreed that we would need to set up regular briefings for the media and, above all, keep the matter in perspective. The best way to do this was to keep the facts flowing to the media in a timely manner.

On the first leg of the flight to Norway, we reviewed what little information was available and discussed in general terms the necessary actions needed once we arrived. We had little, if any, appreciation of the physical layout of the port of Stavanger or whether a suitable site was available for use as a media center. Notwithstanding this, we did have a good appreciation of the fact that we would need to do all we could to help the media cover the story.

We arrived at London's Heathrow Airport early Sunday morning on April 24. On the connecting SAS flight to Stavanger, we recognized the *New York Times'* reporter R. W. (Johnny) Apple, Jr. It proved to be a fortuitous stroke of luck. Apple had recently taken over as the *Times'* bureau chief in London. Always one to be where the action was, Apple chose to cover the blowout story himself. Gross and I took the opportunity to introduce ourselves and to offer our assistance once we got to Stavanger and had a chance to get our collective feet on the ground.

Apple pumped us for what little we knew. He then regaled us with stories of other disasters he had covered, particularly those where PR people had stood in the way of reporters getting to the facts. We were both sure that he had embellished the stories to put us on the defensive. By the time we arrived in Stavanger with a few scotches under our belts, we had become old friends.

Upon arrival in Stavanger, we were met by a Phillips driver and taken directly to the Atlantic Hotel. After registering and dropping off our bags, we proceeded directly to Phillips's offices for a meeting with Phillips's Norway president, Gordon Goering. Members of Goering's staff briefed us on the situation and told us that offers of help were pouring in from all over the world. These offers ranged from the legitimate to the wildly irrational.

On-Site Damage Control

Our first task was to draft a response to such offers that would not give offense, but at the same time inform callers that the situation was under control and being well handled. Following is the response we used:

> *We appreciate your offer of assistance. Phillips, however, has employed the Red Adair Company of Houston, Texas, and given them the responsibility for bringing the well on Bravo platform back under control. Mr. Adair is recognized as the foremost authority in this type of work and we have every confidence that what can and should be done is being done.*

If callers persisted in trying to get Phillips to "do something," we followed with:

> *I'll be happy to pass your name and phone number along to our people and they can contact you if they wish further information about your suggestion (process, etc.).*

At the initial briefing we were given the facts as of that moment and the rate of flow of oil into the sea. The briefing also covered the actions already taken by the government of Norway and Phillips and Adair personnel to get the capping process underway and to deal with the environmental consequences of the spill. In short, we had enough information to put together a fairly comprehensive press briefing. However, we didn't know where the press were, how many there were, or how to contact them. Even more important, we didn't know who was in charge of media relations — Phillips or the Norwegian authorities. These were questions we pursued Sunday night.

Goering was greatly relieved to have us there. Phones were ringing constantly with calls from reporters. Operational people, needed to support capping efforts and deal with environmental problems and other essential tasks, had been pressed into service to deal with the press.

While I proceeded to sort out relationships and responsibilities, Gross gathered a considerable amount of background information from Phillips's engineering and production staff. Gross also set up and instructed Phillips operators on how to answer calls from reporters.

Initially, we responded only with a prepared statement that gave the basic who, what, where, when, and why. We also had the operators record names, affiliations, and local phone numbers of callers so we could compile a media list. Later we were able to equip operators to respond to a wide variety of questions with preapproved responses. This freed Gross and I to organize and carry out other essential tasks.

During a call late Sunday to the Norwegian Petroleum Directorate, I learned that Dr. Hans Christian Bugge, head of the Norwegian State Pollution Board (SFT), had been appointed by the Norwegian government to head a special action committee in Stavanger. Bugge, appointed by Norway's environment minister, was positioned to have authority over the handling of the oil spill, including responsibility for handling the media. While having outstanding scientific and technical credentials, Dr. Bugge had little or no experience with the media, particularly in the numbers now present in Stavanger. Not surprisingly, Dr. Bugge was pleased and relieved to have Phillips provide a public relations expert to deal with media relations.

Working late into the night, Gross and I put together plans to hold a press briefing at 9:00 A.M., Monday, April 25. The only place we could find big enough to hold a press briefing was the main lobby of the Stavanger airport. We got the word out through the Phillips operators who were taking calls from reporters, but did not know how many would show up the next day.

Among the documents we prepared were:

- A current description of the spill, its dimensions, location, and direction of drift.

- A description of the preparations underway by Phillips and the Adair Company to get the capping operation underway.

- A description of the cleanup steps being considered by Phillips and the Norwegian government, together with the commitment that Phillips was prepared to underwrite the cost.

- Fact sheets about Phillips's operations in the North Sea, including general information about the discovery and development of the Ekofisk field.

- A schedule of press briefings to be held twice each day at 9:00 A.M. and 5:00 P.M.

- A listing of Phillips and Norwegian personnel playing a role in the management of the situation, together with a brief description of their responsibilities.

We knew there would be considerable interest in the press briefing scheduled for 9:00 A.M. Monday. What we weren't prepared for was the crush of media people who began arriving at the makeshift press center at 7:00 A.M. It was a mob scene. Gross and I, assisted by some helpers, were trying to set the stage by arranging

First Press Conference

chairs at the front of the room and putting a makeshift rostrum in place on a table. There were media people everywhere. As usual, the television people were jockeying for the best camera spots. The print reporters were sniffing around trying to identify anyone who might be a possible source.

By the 9:00 A.M. start time the press crowd had become quite unruly, with some reporters showing outright hostility. In my brief introduction, I listed the handouts we had available and then introduced Dr. Bugge and Goering. Based on earlier instruction, Dr. Bugge specified that the first 30 minutes of each press briefing would be conducted in Norwegian. He would lead off with a statement in Norwegian, and answer questions posed in Norwegian before turning to English.

This practice absolutely infuriated 90 percent of the reporters in the room who were used to speaking in English. In fact, all the Norwegian reporters spoke English fluently as a second language. The English speakers regarded this as a ploy to give a time advantage to Norwegian reporters at the expense of all the others. Try as we might, we never did succeed in getting Dr. Bugge to change the order and it continued to be a source of irritation throughout the week.

Other factors irritated the media. The room itself was cramped and crowded. The public address system was inadequate and people in the back had difficulty hearing. No raised platform was available for those conducting the briefing and some of those speaking chose to remain seated. This made it nearly impossible for television reporters in the back to zero in on the speaker. Added to this, was Dr. Bugge's predilection to take questions from the front row at the expense of others in the room. As a result, a few highly vocal reporters in front were allowed to dominate the meeting.

By the time Goering got up to give his prepared statement and answer questions, many in the room were shouting questions with premises that suggested the company and the government were stonewalling and stalling. Reporters were leaving the room to phone in bits and pieces of what they learned and the entire process degenerated into an unhelpful mess.

Results from that first briefing in the form of radio and television newscasts and from wire copy convinced us that the straight story was not getting out in the form we were telling it. It was clear that resourceful reporters were listening in to company and government radiotelephone conversations, consulting "experts" in their own countries, and talking to people on the street. Anyone with oil on his or her shoes was automatically an "expert."

Reporters were taking fragments of information and weaving them together to make stories that in many instances simply didn't square with actual circumstances. Some of these stories greatly exaggerated the actual and potential impact and distorted the known facts about the blowout. If something hadn't been done to keep the situation in perspective, a tremendous amount of misinformation would have been disseminated that would have been virtually impossible to correct after the fact.

Damage Control: Battling Misinformation

Right after the briefing, I was besieged by television reporters with requests to go on camera and deliver a capsule version of what had been said at the briefing. It was a role I would play a hundred times before the week was out. In addition to giving stand-up interviews to television reporters on the ground, I was also doing voice-only actualities to radio and television stations who were calling directly to Phillips from the United States.

Of all the reports we saw following the initial briefing, the two that stood out as accurate and factual were the Associated Press and the *New York Times*. John Vinocur, Associated Press bureau chief in Paris, was covering the story in a very factual, straightforward way, without hyperbole. And, of course, Johnny Apple was performing up to standard.

The accurate, unembellished coverage by Apple and Vinocur prompted me to do something that violated one of the cardinal rules of public relations. It says: Never confer selective benefits on a few reporters because the others will eventually do you in. However, I concluded that if AP and the *Times* got it right the rest of the media would follow.

Getting together with Vinocur, I told him that I would be pleased to arrange background technical briefings with knowledgeable members of Phillips' engineering staff. Even more important, I would, in every instance possible, give him a five-minute break on any new development. I did the same with Apple. When Vinocur experienced difficulty in getting his feeds to Paris over overburdened phone lines, I "loaned" him an office and access to Phillips's telephone system.

Another problem that surfaced at the initial press briefing was a lack of depth in the information available. In some instances aspects of the blowout were described in "oil patch" language that was foreign to many of the reporters. We tried to cure some of that at the Monday evening press brief, but it still wasn't enough. Somehow, we needed to do a better job of describing technical matters in plain English.

That evening, when we discussed some of the shortcomings with Goering, he said that perhaps it would be better if he didn't participate and instead sent production engineering personnel. I told him that wasn't the answer. He absolutely needed to be there. We resolved the matter by identifying an engineer who could describe equipment and processes in lay terms and pressing him into service. I asked Gross to work with him in getting additional background information ready to hand out at Tuesday morning's briefing.

In the meantime, I was fielding calls from Bartlesville and Phillips's headquarters in London, both of which wanted to be filled in on the day's happenings. It was good that I had taken comprehensive notes during both press briefings that day because they provided the detail being sought in Bartlesville and London. It was well past midnight by the time I finished my reports and it was to be a pattern followed in successive days.

All during the day on Monday, advance preparations to cap the well continued both in Stavanger and at Ekofisk Center. Aside from preparing equipment and moving workboats into place, there really wasn't much to report to the media. We had to try to satisfy them with background information and secondhand reports about the size, dimensions, and location of the oil spill from the Norwegian authorities on the scene. In the view of both print and television reporters, the biggest problem at this point was lack of pictures.

Early Tuesday, April 26, 1977, a six-man team of experts boarded the Bravo platform. They began work at 7:00 A.M. and continued working until about 1:00 P.M. when the weather changed. The winds died and the sea calmed to the point where oil and gas were falling directly down on the platform, making it dangerous to continue to work. The crew was forced to leave until more favorable conditions returned.

Media Grows Ever More Restless

By the 9:00 A.M. start of Tuesday's media briefing, the media ranks had swollen considerably overnight. We estimated the group of 150 to 175 reporters was now crammed into a space that was cramped and crowded with 100 the previous evening. The room was overheated and uncomfortable. We sought relief by opening the doors, but airplane noise drowned out speakers' voices.

The only saving feature of the briefing was the additional material we prepared the night before, along with an excellent assessment of environmental impact prepared by Norwegian authorities. By this time we also had an expert on oil spills present to answer questions. Lt. Commander Frank Boersma of the U.S. Coast Guard was brought in to give expert advice to Phillips regarding cleanup. Boersma was quite valuable in placing the spill in perspective and in describing the degree of effectiveness of the various techniques that might be employed in containing and cleaning up the spill.

Partly due to physical conditions and partly due to lack of authoritative information, the media were still pretty hostile and unruly during the morning briefing. It
was clear that we needed to find ways to satisfy their needs in covering the story.
Following the morning briefing, I persuaded Phillips's operational people to give
us several seats on the next helicopter going to Ekofisk. I wanted to get a company contract photographer and motion picture cameraman on board to get still
and motion picture photography of the blowout.

By the time of the evening briefing we were able to distribute still photos of the
blowout. Necessary processing time for motion picture film delayed availability of
motion picture clips until the next day. While this was not completely satisfactory
to the media, it was seen as a helpful measure.

Right after the morning briefing, Apple took me aside and told me he had tried to
hire a helicopter to take him out to the platform, but had been unsuccessful. He
asked me if he might hitch a ride out on a Phillips helicopter. My initial reaction
was no. Then, on second thought, I told him I would discuss the request with
Goering. The more I thought about it the more I was taken with the idea. With
Apple reporting an eyewitness account, there was a better chance of keeping the
spill and the attempts to shut in the well in perspective.

By the time I got together with Goering, I was convinced that it was the wise thing
to do. By getting Apple out to Ekofisk Center we would be assured of fair-minded
reports driving the story. Goering accepted my rationale, but still was quite
reluctant to permit a "civilian" to, in effect, break the blockade around the platform. Gross agreed that it would be a good thing to do and together we persuaded
Goering to go along. Apple was on the next helicopter flight to Ekofisk Center,
arriving there early in the evening on Tuesday.

Apple filed his first story from Ekofisk Center, 160 miles at sea, by telephone to
New York. He stayed at the Center for the next 48 hours and filed several stories
that were bylined on the *Times*' front page. Fortunately, few in the media noticed
that they were being beat on the story until much later. Dr. Bugge raised a mild
objection when he learned of it, but decided not to make much of a fuss. Apple's
stories were excellent. He ingratiated himself with Hansen and Hatteberg as well
as the Phillips people at Ekofisk Center and they provided him with lots of color
for his stories.

Blowout Preventer

After the evening briefing, Gross and I returned to Phillips's headquarters to prepare for the following day. While walking through the engineering offices, I heard
something disturbing. If I heard correctly and understood what I heard, the

workover crew had installed the blowout preventer upside down. The implication to me was that this might have resulted in the blowout.

I went directly to Goering's office to ask what this was all about. He told me that a blowout preventer looks the same right side up or upside down and that the workover crew had mistakenly installed it in the upside down position. He quickly added that it was not significant in the capping process and was unrelated to the blowout. I told him that we would need to brief the media on this the next day. Goering and his general counsel were appalled at the suggestion. I pointed out that with the media monitoring radiotelephone traffic, the chances of keeping a lid on this were nil. If the media "discovered" the error, it would be far worse than if Phillips volunteered the facts and placed them in perspective.

Tense moments followed when I was asked to leave Goering's office while he and his counsel conferred. After a while, I was asked to return and told that in the counsel's view we should say nothing about this. At this point I suggested that the matter was of sufficient importance that it should be decided in Bartlesville rather than here. After more private discussion, Goering decided to disclose the information on Wednesday morning.

With the matter decided, Gross and I began at once to prepare for the next morning's briefing. Working with Robert Archambeault, the chief of operations for Phillips-Norway, we prepared an explanatory statement to be used the next day along with a large drawing of a well head showing a blowout preventer installed on top of the riser from the well casing. Archambeault was to give a technical explanation and then he and Goering would field questions.

The questioning was intense and probing at the briefing on Wednesday. Many in the media were looking for someone or something to blame and the upside down blowout preventer looked like a good bet. Goering and Archambeault's handling of the questions was superb. At the end of an hour's questioning, it was clear that they had convinced the media that the blowout preventer's orientation was not a factor and would not slow down or impede the efforts being made to cap the well. In fact, a most surprising occurrence happened when Archambeault finished his briefing — the assembled reporters spontaneously burst into applause.

Capping the Well: The Plan To shut in the well required several highly coordinated activities to be performed in sequence. If unsatisfactory weather conditions or technical difficulties were encountered at any stage, the entire process had to be aborted, delayed, and started from the beginning. Following are the steps that had to take place:

1. A crane barge to do the heavy lifting had to be moved into place within 50 feet of the platform and anchored.

2. The control crew of 8 to 12 men would board the platform to connect and test water and drilling mud lines.

3. Using hydraulic pressure, an attempt would then be made to close blind rams on the blowout preventer.

4. With the blind rams holding back the pressure, a spool, bonnet, and valve assembly (commonly called a Christmas tree) would be swung in place over the blowout preventer and bolted into place.

5. Drilling mud lines would then be attached to the valve on the side of the blowout preventer and the barge would pump drilling mud into the well until zero pressure was achieved and the well was "dead."

On Wednesday, crews worked to prepare to shut in the well. Shortly after noon however, work was stopped due to crew fatigue, and a decision was made to delay shut-in attempts until Thursday.

By Wednesday, a substantial amount of information was becoming available regarding the possible environmental impact of the blowout. Fortunately, most of the news was good. Much of the light crude that was spilling into the sea was evaporating due to wave action. The spill that had earlier been feared would cover a vast area was confined to a relatively small area and was fairly stable in size.

There had been a considerable amount of controversy over whether chemical dispersants should be used or whether we should rely on the use of more conventional, but more costly, pick-up methods. As it turned out, both methods were used extensively. At the height of the cleanup operation, Phillips deployed 25 vessels that used skimmers and booms to pick up hundreds of tons of oil. More than 60 tons of chemical dispersants were used to break up more than a thousand tons of spill. Evaporation and wave action eventually virtually eliminated the remainder of the spill.

While environmental data was reported, media attention was more intently focused on efforts to shut in the well. By Wednesday evening, news that the crew had not attempted to cap the well that day was greeted by disbelief and concern. The media couldn't understand why it was taking so long.

With all the coverage the event was getting in the United States, Phillips's chairman and chief executive officer, William Martin, concluded that it might help to calm the situation by sending Red Adair himself to Stavanger to personally assess

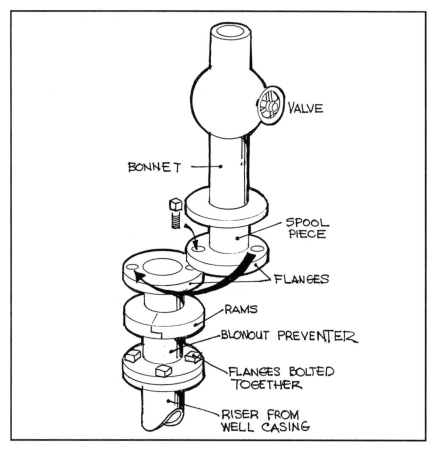

Diagram used at a press briefing to illustrate the device that would be used to bring the well under control. The illustration shows the wellhead, positioning of the blowout preventer, and the spool and bonnet assembly.

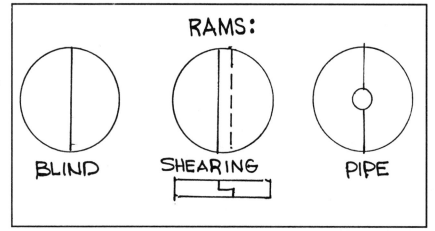

Three different types of rams that might be used to reduce or stop the flow of oil.

the situation and offer his advice and counsel. We got the word that Adair would arrive in Stavanger on April 29 and we should be prepared to handle the press when he arrived.

Three attempts were made to close the well on Thursday, April 28. The first attempt was made at 6:30 A.M., the second at 6:40 A.M. and the third at 10:40 A.M. None were successful. Descriptions of the failed attempts given to the media at the evening briefing on Thursday cast a pall over the room. Technical descriptions of why the attempts had failed didn't do much to satisfy the media and the stories filed that day reflected the disappointment at the seeming lack of progress.

The rams used in the first three attempts to shut down the well were unable to withstand pressure at the well that was estimated at more than 4,000 pounds per square inch. Specially fabricated rams made in California were being flown to Stavanger, but had not yet arrived. The new rams were designed to withstand pressures of up to 6,000 psi.

Early Friday, a fourth attempt to shut in the well failed. A description of the failed attempt at Friday's morning briefing added to the earlier sense of disappointment. Questions by the media suggested that the government's and Phillips's efforts were too little too late.

In fact the only good news we had to report was the time of arrival of Red Adair and that he would be pleased to meet with the media. Adair was due to arrive at Stavanger at 1:00 P.M. and depart shortly thereafter by helicopter to go to Ekofisk. Our plan was to make Adair available at plane-side for about 20 minutes. He would then be flown out to Ekofisk, make his personal assessment, and meet with the media for a longer period at the evening briefing.

Promptly at 1:00 P.M., Adair's plane pulled up to the gate just outside the room where our press briefings were held. All of the reporters ran outside to get a glimpse of Adair coming down the ramp. Those who might have seen *The Hellfighters*, the John Wayne movie about Adair's exploits, may have been a bit surprised when the plane's door opened and out stepped a diminutive five-foot-three-inch, slightly paunchy man.

Even so, Adair was an imposing figure. Wearing a Texas Stetson, plaid shirt, jeans, and cowboy boots, he literally swaggered down the steps, waving as he acknowledged the cameras below. As soon as the first words were out of his mouth, the tension was gone. Adair quickly had reporters disarmed and laughing.

Initial Failures to Shut In Well

A Norwegian worker finishes preparations of a valve to be used in the attempts to cap the flow of oil from Bravo 14.

Red Adair Assesses Spill

Among the points he made were these: "This is just another blowout. I've seen a lot worse. Boots is havin' a little trouble, but he does the best he can with what he's got. The blowout preventer works just as good either way. We'll just have to put a little somethin' extra on top." In answer to the question, "What if the next attempt fails?" Adair said, "If you don't have any more faith in me than that, I'll just go on home. Anything that needs to be fixed, we'll fix it. This sort of thing happens at least once in every [oil] field. I plan to stay till it's finished. You can have the best equipment and men in the world and these things still happen. One thing I can tell you, this here Phillips Company is an industry leader in safety."

When asked why Phillips brought him here when Hansen had things under control, Adair replied, "Boots is dang near blind and his face is all swole up, but he's doin' fine. I'm just here to back him up." Asked what his fee was for being there, Adair said, "I can't hear you!" This got a good laugh that accompanied Adair as he boarded the waiting helicopter and flew off to Ekofisk.

Finally, Success The blind rams from California had been expected to arrive in Stavanger Friday night. When they didn't get there, preparations were made to attempt to shut in the well using conventional rams that had been modified. At 11:00 A.M. Saturday, April 30, the rams were closed and the well shut in. Immediately the crew connected a drilling mud line and began to pump drilling mud into the well. By 3:00 P.M. enough mud had been pumped into the well to reduce well pressure to zero.

Phillips's news release issued at Bartlesville at 12:30 P.M. CDT on April 30 expressed the feelings of many people in Stavanger. In the release, Bill Martin said, "We at Phillips owe those men a great deal of thanks. They had a difficult, tedious, and dangerous job to do. The work was made even more difficult by the changing weather conditions in the North Sea. We will now concentrate our efforts on cleaning up the remaining oil film. I know that many people in Europe and around the world share our concern about the effect of the oil film on sea life. At this moment there is no indication of significant adverse effect." A *New York Times* story on May 3 noted that "The oil slick from the eight-day Ekofisk blowout had virtually disappeared." Maritime experts soon determined that the spill had no impact on the marine environment.

Aftermath Media reaction to the blowout was greater than Phillips or anyone else could have expected. An earlier blowout of a gas well in the United Kingdom sector went virtually unnoticed. With 100 reporters on site in the first 36 hours, a figure that quickly grew to 175, Phillips and the Norwegian authorities had their hands full in handling not only the blowout, but the press as well.

The Norwegian press comprised no more than 15 to 20 percent of the press corps covering the story. The event could accurately be characterized as an international interest story with reporters assigned from around the world to cover it. The ecological and environmental concerns evoked around the North Sea littoral by the early confusing stories probably served to further heighten interest and to prompt editors around the world to seek coverage.

In addition to the press corps in Stavanger, Phillips responded directly to hundreds of media inquiries from around the world by telephone. It was not uncommon to do 20 to 30 feeds a day to radio stations and to answer questions from newspapers and wire services around the world. Also involved in answering press inquiries were Phillips public relations representatives in Bartlesville and London, who were fed the latest information on a continuing basis throughout the week.

The openness, candor, and responsiveness of Phillips and the government of Norway to the legitimate needs of the media were repaid in terms of accurate, balanced, and factual reporting of events.

The voluntary disclosure by Phillips of the inverted blowout preventer did much to create a climate of trust and understanding. Although the inverted blowout preventer was not that material to the capping effort, failure to voluntarily disclose it, followed by accidental discovery by the media, could have had a disastrous effect on Phillips's credibility. After the capping of the well, I received a letter from Apple, who said, "I know as well as you do that there were moments of tension and conflict. But the important thing, and the one that impressed me, was that Phillips made a real effort to show me the situation in detail, and that made what I wrote for the *Times* much more authoritative."

Although regarded by some as a public relations ploy, the arrival on the scene of Adair did much to defuse the tense atmosphere. As an authoritative and credible expert, he was able to characterize the blowout as "no big deal." By the time the well was capped on Saturday, the press was considerably mollified and ready to do wrap-ups on the ecological aspects. However, by then, the spill was getting hard to find.

Neither Phillips, the media, nor the Norwegian authorities were prepared for an incident of this magnitude. Initially, many mistakes and missteps were made, but Phillips and the Norwegian authorities adapted quickly to the realities of the situation. Because of its willingness to deal quickly and candidly with the media, Phillips came out of the event with only minor damage to its reputation. The company got credit with many in the world's media for honesty and openness. It got credit with the countries around the North Sea for handling the emergency in a timely and competent way. It got credit with those concerned with the environment for a massive and major cleanup effort that began concurrently with the spill and continued until the job was satisfactorily concluded. And finally, Phillips got credit with the governments around the North Sea for technical competence in handling one of the ever-present risks in offshore oil development.

James A. Fyock is currently chairman and chief executive officer of James A. Fyock & Associates, Inc., a public relations firm based in Winston-Salem, North Carolina. Following a 27-year U.S. Army career that included public affairs assignments, Fyock became director of public relations for Phillips Petroleum Company in 1975. In 1977 he joined RJR Nabisco, Inc. (formerly R. J. Reynolds Industries, Inc.) as group director, public relations. Fyock took early retirement from RJR Nabisco in 1988 to establish his own firm. Fyock received a business degree from the University of Texas, El Paso, in 1963 and a master's degree in mass communications from the University of Wisconsin in 1968. He is also a graduate of the British Staff College, the U.S. Army Command and General Staff College, and the National War College.

General
Westmoreland
versus CBS

John P. Scanlon
Partner, Sawyer Miller Group

Overview

In September 1982, Gen. William C. Westmoreland, career military officer, former commandant of cadets at West Point and retired commander in chief of all forces during the Vietnam War, filed a $120 million lawsuit against CBS News, several news executives, producer George Crile, and well-known reporter Mike Wallace, charging that they had libeled him in a documentary titled *The Uncounted Enemy: A Vietnam Deception.*

The lawsuit, which eventually went to trial in the late winter of 1984, was among the most celebrated trials of the year and certainly the most famous libel trial in decades. It was also the first time that a public relations agency played a highly visible role before and during a trial. While other PR professionals may very well have counseled clients through various phases of litigation in the past, *Westmoreland v. CBS* was clearly the first time that communications specialists were so visibly present and played such a vital part in the defense strategy from the beginning.

The official documents that became available because of the trial and the depositions and affidavits that were taken in preparation for the trial provided an amazingly full and thorough record of how war is waged and decisions made during combat. To this day, scholars and military historians consider the archives of the Westmoreland case to be a treasure trove. Robert Caro, for example, a Pulitzer Prize-winning journalist-historian and biographer of Lyndon B. Johnson, said that the trial allowed him access to documents that might have taken years to obtain.

Magazine Article Leads to Congressional Inquiry

In 1975 while editor of *Harper's Magazine*, George Crile edited an article by former CIA analyst Sam Adams, titled "Vietnam Cover-Up: Playing War with Numbers." The Adams article charged that in the year leading up to the Tet offensive of January 1, 1968, a massive deception existed in which the military, with the acquiescence and support of high-ranking CIA operatives, had purposefully understated the size of the enemy troops American troops faced in Vietnam. The article further said that General Westmoreland had underreported the size of the enemy to the president, the Congress, and the Joint Chiefs of Staff. The deception intended to demonstrate that American policy was working and that the war effort should be supported since there was, in the words of Defense Secretary Robert McNamara, a "light at the end of the tunnel." A reduction in the size of the enemy would justify increasing military budgets. Time and further intelligence, of course, would later demonstrate that the enemy was far larger than officially reported. Instead of light at the end of the tunnel, a tunnel was at the end of the tunnel.

The *Harper's* article, published in May 1975, prompted Long Island Congressman Otis Pike, then chairman of the House Select Committee on Intelligence, to call for hearings to investigate the charges. The findings of the Pike Committee remain classified to this day, but the report was leaked and appeared in the *Village Voice.*

The leaked report supported the Adams charges and stated, "The numbers game not only diverted a direct confrontation with the realities of war in Vietnam, but also prevented the intelligence community, perhaps the president, and certainly the members of Congress, from judging the real changes in Vietnam over time."

Five years later, Crile, by then a producer for "CBS Reports," the documentary division of CBS News, contacted Adams and discussed the possibility of doing a special TV program on the role played by military intelligence in leaving the United States unprepared for the Tet offensive. Crile thought Adams would be the perfect person with whom to collaborate since Adams had been working on a book about the subject and had been involved in ongoing research since his retirement from the CIA. While U.S. troops pushed back Viet Cong guerrillas during the all-out Tet battle, the offensive was considered a major propaganda victory for the northern forces. Their ability to strike without notice throughout Vietnam, including the center of Saigon, was clear indication of the resiliency, power, and popular support of the Viet Cong. Even in retreat they were considered victors.

Documentary Prepared and Aired

In January 1981 Crile proposed the documentary to CBS. Bill Leonard, then president of CBS News, authorized an expenditure of $25,000 for Crile to see if he could confirm or disprove in on-camera interviews that a systematic deception had taken place. By March 1981 Crile had interviewed seven former intelligence officers, all of them career military intelligence specialists, most of whom had served in Westmoreland's own command. On film, they stated that they had served in Westmoreland's own command — and that they had been involved in a deception.

Crile was given the go-ahead for the documentary, and in the next year and a half, he and Adams compiled a massive file of evidence — military cables, enormous chronologies of enemy troop strength estimates, and 139 additional interviews. Crile's success was extraordinary. As reporter Connie Bruck said in *The American Lawyer*, "Crile had managed to persuade a group of former military intelligence and CIA officers to come on camera, not to make charges about someone else's wrongdoing, but to confess their own." As Mike Wallace pointed out in the documentary, "These men were not your average whistle blowers. They were coming forward more in sorrow than in anger and they had nothing to gain but pain." The completed documentary was entitled *The Uncounted Enemy: A Vietnam Deception* and was broadcast on January 23, 1982.

Westmoreland Makes Charges

Three days after the broadcast General Westmoreland, the commander of all troops in Vietnam during the time in question, held a press conference in Washington that was attended by an impressive group of luminaries from the Vietnam era. General Westmoreland charged that CBS had taken an honest numbers dispute between the military and the CIA and portrayed it as a purposeful suppression of critical intelligence information. He charged that CBS had wrongfully damaged his reputation and the honor of the military.

TV Guide Article Challenges CBS

Three months later, on May 25, 1982, *TV Guide* published a cover story entitled "Anatomy of a Smear," which charged that "CBS began the project already convinced that a conspiracy had been perpetrated, and turned a deaf ear toward evidence that suggested otherwise." The article charged that numerous CBS News standards had been violated in the preparation of the report. The *TV Guide* article, however, did not challenge the substance or the truth of the broadcast.

The *TV Guide* article came at a difficult time for CBS. Network and news executives were attending an affiliate conference when the story broke. They had to divert from the planned agenda and respond to very serious criticisms about the broadcast. It was Van Gordon Sauter's first affiliate conference as president of CBS News, and while he had screened the documentary prior to its broadcast, he had not been involved in its production. Sauter immediately commissioned Burton Benjamin, a highly respected senior producer at CBS, to conduct an examination of the charges made by the *TV Guide* article.

CBS Responds

On July 15, 1982, following the completion of Benjamin's report, Sauter issued a memorandum to the CBS News division. The memo stated that "CBS News stands by this broadcast," but further explained that "We now feel it would have been a better broadcast" if:

- It had not used the word conspiracy.

- It had sought out and interviewed more persons who disagreed with the broadcast premise.

- It complied strictly with CBS News standards.

Westmoreland Files Suit

Perhaps encouraged by the *TV Guide* article and the Benjamin Report, General Westmoreland filed suit against CBS for $120 million claiming that the network had libeled him. General Westmoreland was represented by the Washington-based, conservatively supported Capital Legal Foundation. Capital's president, Dan Burt, took full advantage of the suit's high visibility and in an interview by *USA Today* declared, "We are about to see the dismantling of a major news network."

Public Relations Efforts Begin

In October 1983, still feeling the sting of the negative press coverage Dan Rather received during an earlier libel trial in California, Sauter asked me to develop a strategic communications plan so that CBS could tell its story. Sauter clearly stated in the beginning of the relationship that a news organization, always demanding access on important public issues, ought to make itself fully available in a similar fashion. Sauter was also well aware that the failure to defend the Rather piece which had run on "60 Minutes," before and during trial, was a mistake. That trial had been one of the first to be broadcast on CNN, and the plaintiffs' lawyers took full advantage of the courthouse steps. Though CBS won the suit, they were severely damaged by the daily attacks of the plaintiffs' lawyers. CBS won the verdict but lost much credibility, the critical commodity of a news organization.

When we were hired by CBS in October 1983, we began a period of intense research. The agency had little sense of the facts of the case beyond what was available in the daily press. That coverage was decidedly anti-CBS, largely because CBS failed to respond to the organized and orchestrated assaults by General Westmoreland's attorneys and other supporters. Burt had clear and unchallenged control of the dialogue. CBS, a premier news organization, did not know how to respond when it was at the center of a story. Experienced news executives found it almost inconceivable that their integrity was questionable. Unlike other experienced corporate executives who frequently dealt with the press on sensitive issues, CBS personnel were stunned and paralyzed by the very fact of an inquiry. Ironically, news people invariably do not behave well when they are the focus of news stories. Their behavior gives credence to the remark allegedly made by CBS superstar Edward R. Morrow, "Newsmen are not thin skinned, they have no skin at all."

Longtime CBS lawyers Cravath, Swaine & Moore, led by lead litigator David Boies, had been gathering both deposition and affidavit testimony for almost a year prior to our involvement. In addition, thousands of pages of evidence had been acquired from various government agencies. In total, at the time the PR agency became involved, almost 100,000 pages of pertinent paper existed. This number would double before the trial started.

I was particularly blessed with my associate, Jim Noonan, who had served as a combat marine in Vietnam during the mid-1960s. His experience and specific knowledge of the events of the war were indispensable. He led me through the maze and together we read all the appropriate documents and became familiar with the sworn statements of all those on both sides who might eventually become witnesses in the case.

In total, more than 50 depositions and affidavits of both plaintiffs and defendants were taken. General Westmoreland's deposition alone was about 1,000 pages. Secretary McNamara's affidavit was 240 pages. In addition, we had numerous meetings with producer George Crile, narrator Mike Wallace, and other CBS personnel who had been involved in producing the documentary. With the assistance of CBS News personnel and Cravath lawyers, we became intensely familiar with each frame of the 90-minute documentary so that they were able to defend it in specific detail.

Problem Analysis

During the same time, the agency read and reviewed all the media coverage about the dispute and analyzed the problems that CBS was having communicating with the media. We found that CBS was essentially making no organized or strategic response to the various accusations being made regularly by Burt or his agents. Burt was defining the terms of the argument and, thus, was in control of the dialogue. While CBS News had a full public relations staff, they were generally very occupied with satisfying the daily needs of reporters who covered the television industry. Most importantly, news personnel are inexperienced at defending themselves when they are the focus of a story, and this incident was no exception.

In addition, because of numerous executive changes at CBS News during 1983–84, some uncertainty persisted about the truth of the documentary, which resulted in a reluctance to vigorously defend it. Those in charge when the Westmoreland suit was filed were not involved in the production of the documentary. Research interviews with key CBS personnel clearly showed that even at the highest levels of the corporation widespread doubt lingered about the accuracy of the documentary. Burt took full advantage of the situation and was clearly winning the battle in the press.

The agency also found that neither the Benjamin Report nor the *TV Guide* article focused its criticism of the documentary on any of the substantial charges made by the producer. Instead, Benjamin criticized the documentary for its violations of CBS News standards; for example, interviewing one witness twice, coaxing witnesses, and allowing a witness into the editing room. In addition, he found the use of the term conspiracy to be excessive. The *TV Guide* article criticized the documentary for many of the same reasons and found others in addition. Neither Benjamin nor *TV Guide* analyzed or challenged the truth of the documentary. Both focused entirely on *process* — not on truth. Clearly our task was to "spin" attention to the substance of the documentary, admit our procedural errors and oversights, and move the dialogue to a discussion about the accuracy of the charges. In most minds, criticisms of substance and process melded and CBS was perceived as not only sloppy, but unfair and inaccurate as well. In short, a widespread sense that General Westmoreland's charges were true remained because CBS had violated its own defined news standards.

At the same time, Don Kowet, one of the authors of the *TV Guide* piece, had contracted for a full-length book to be published by Macmillan & Co. which would be published just as the trial was scheduled to begin. Anticipating repetition of his *TV Guide* charges, the agency was concerned that the book would become a road map for many reporters who would be dealing with the facts in the case for the first time.

PR Execution   The agency became the sole outlet on the issues surrounding the documentary. Our designated client within CBS was the corporate legal department. This reporting protocol allowed us the potential argument that any information we received was protected by the lawyer/client privilege. All media inquiries were referred to either Scanlon or Noonan. This centralization allowed for a consistent flow of information, free of contradiction and confusion. We took full control of the dialogue. The agency was familiar with the case in detail and was prepared to give all necessary background briefings and interviews. We became the voice of CBS.

The agency then developed a list of press outlets, both electronic and print, and attempted to identify the personnel who might be assigned to cover the impending trial. By offering access to "secret" documents we, in effect, exercised some influence about who would eventually be assigned to cover the trial. Press interviews were offered and arranged with appropriate CBS staff and CBS attorneys months prior to the trial. Critical documents and evidence which would be used at the trial were made available to the working press. In effect, CBS now argued that the press had been misled by General Westmoreland's lawyers up to this point. This gave the agency the opportunity to refocus the attention on the truth issue. Slowly, the central questions changed to "Did CBS take short cuts?" "Is the documentary accurate?" and "Was there really a conspiracy?"

The agency had successfully convinced CBS of the need to go public and adopt an aggressive position. CBS was finally convinced that it could no longer allow Burt's attacks to remain unanswered.

PR Efforts Succeed

The major breakthrough came in the winter of 1983. General Westmoreland's lawyers scheduled a news conference on Tuesday, December 27, 1983, in Washington, D.C., perhaps one of the slowest news days of the year. Burt announced that he was going to release more affidavits favorable to the Westmoreland side. The agency was alerted to the pending conference on Christmas Eve. With the consent of CBS, we rented a room next to the Burt-Westmoreland press conference in a downtown Washington hotel. At the conclusion of the Burt conference, members of the press were invited next door. There, Boies and Crile met the press and responded to Burt's charges, as well as to any other questions. The results were clear and impressive. For the first time, the CBS point of view was clearly reflected. Whereas Burt had almost totally dominated the media heretofore, December 27, 1983, marked a change. It was now a contest.

While prior headlines had most often said "Westmoreland Charges," after the December 27 conference both the *Washington Post* and the *New York Times*, for example, had headlines reporting "Westmoreland-CBS Exchange Charges." CBS was finally in the game. Burt was no longer controlling the terms of the dialogue. CBS's public commitment to defend the broadcast and the aggressive response of the network became the object of new stories. The *Wall Street Journal* and

Manhattan Inc. both noted the new development and the fact that a vigorous public relations battle was underway.

More than 50,000 pages of deposition and affidavit testimony were edited, reduced, and synthesized to a 15-page "talking paper" which pointed clearly to the evidence that CBS would present at the trial. The number of sworn statements of those involved in the conspiracy who would testify on behalf of CBS was impressive. Included was the sworn testimony of career officers like Joseph MacChristian, Westmoreland's West Point classmate and chief of Army Intelligence, and Colonel Gaines Hawkins, chief of Order of Battle. It gave the first public sense of the CBS case. This talking paper was sent to almost 1,000 opinion makers and journalists throughout the country, many of whom had previously felt that CBS would lose its case.

The agency began to receive letters and other communications from people who had received the talking paper, noting that they had no idea of the strength of the CBS case heretofore. These ranged from distinguished historian Barbara Tuchman to *New Republic* editor Martin Peretz, who summed up the response of many when he said in a letter dated March 9, 1984, "Thanks for sending me the Westmoreland memo. I must say that I was on my way to believing the general's case — given what I'd read in the papers. Until, that is, I read your paper." Charles Mohr, a distinguished war correspondent who had covered the war for *Time*, and who had moved to the *New York Times*, was allowed access to all the depositions, and published two major pieces prior to the trial, which were supportive of the CBS defense. Pulitzer Prize-winning reporter Murray Kempton did the same in *Newsday*. Finally, David Halberstam, former *New York Times* Vietnam correspondent and Pulitzer Prize winner, became interested enough to read the complete depositions. In so doing, he changed an earlier position and concluded that the use of the word conspiracy was appropriate. He swore an affidavit to that effect. The tide was turning. The trial remained.

At the same time, a concerted campaign to discredit Kowet's book, *A Matter of Honor*, was initiated by the agency. Having managed to get a copy of the book prior to publication, the agency was convinced that the book might seem plausible to readers unfamiliar with the details of the case. Since the book was largely based on the testimony of only one source, Ira Klien, a CBS editorial employee, and since CBS personnel were quoted verbatim without clearance or corroboration, the book was vulnerable to serious criticism. If the book was not attacked and exposed as inaccurate and unfair it might have become a guide for reporters who would eventually be assigned to cover the trial.

One of the defendants, Wallace, who had been seriously misquoted in the book, objected by letter to Macmillan president Hillel Black. His action was followed by several other CBS personnel who objected to Kowet's verbatim repetition of unsubstantiated and uncorroborated conversations. In all, more than a dozen people quoted in the book attested in affidavits that Kowet had misrepresented or inaccurately portrayed key events. A package of these affidavits was sent to key book review editors throughout the country urging that they be forwarded to the designated reviewers.

The attack on the book became, as we had hoped, a story in itself. The first review of the book, which appeared in the *New York Times*, pointed out some of the book's obvious journalistic flaws. *A Matter of Honor* was almost universally panned by the critics. We believe that the book was tainted enough so that no journalist used it as a beginner's guide to the trial. In addition, the agency became aware of Kowet's promotional tour schedule and offered the presence of a countervailing point of view on various talk shows. Crile quite literally followed Kowet from interview to interview. This aggressive technique further discredited the book. Kowet abandoned his tour halfway through his schedule.

The Trial

The trial itself presented new challenges. Prepublicity had created a major interest in the case and even run-of-the-mill pretrial hearings were attended by large numbers of reporters from both electronic and print media. As a result, more than 100 reporters and technicians blocked the courthouse entrance as they sought a glimpse or a comment from any one of the participants on the first day of trial. In preparation for the trial, we opened an office within easy walking distance of the federal courthouse in Foley Square, in the city hall district of downtown Manhattan. The three-room suite contained sophisticated equipment which could quickly reproduce the electronic and print materials needed by reporters. Daily transcripts of the morning court sessions were available by the late afternoon. Afternoon transcripts were available by the next morning. Providing these services gave us an unusual connection to reporters covering the trial. It provided a friendly atmosphere to make our case or, in the parlance, to "spin" the story.

The courtroom itself was at first terra incognita. Federal Judge Pierre Laval, who was hearing the case, had a history of interest and publication on First Amendment issues. But no one was aware of how he would react to the real presence of PR people actually passing out evidence, during trial. CBS lawyers alerted Judge Laval to the fact that we would be doing so. He seemed to give passive consent but we were not really aware of how he would react until we distributed the first documents. His passive consent seemed to set the rule, since he registered

General Westmoreland and his lawyer outside the courthouse where his suit against CBS is being heard.

no objection as a staffer actually walked down the aisle of the courtroom and handed evidence to anxious reporters as it was introduced by CBS lawyers.

Several years later I met Judge Laval at a Manhattan dinner party and we talked about the trial. I pointedly told him of my anxiety on the first day. I also asked him how he felt about our activities. He said that he believed that the distribution of important evidence of such a complex nature would, in his mind, make for a clearer trial. In short he felt that the public would be served by full press coverage. He decided to allow us to continue for that reason. It should be understood that each judge makes his or her own rules.

In some instances we used recesses to context negative testimony by showing reporters other materials that had not yet been introduced into evidence.

The Non-Verdict   No verdict resulted from the Westmoreland-CBS trial. General Westmoreland ended his case immediately following the testimony of Gen. Joseph MacChristian and Col. Gaines Hawkins, two of General Westmoreland's trusted officers. He finally seemed to understand that he had no chance of winning in light of the MacChristian and Hawkins testimonies, which clearly and unequivocally placed him in the middle of the conspiracy.

His lawyers chose to characterize the ending of the trial as a settlement, but in fact it was a capitulation: General Westmoreland withdrew his case. CBS offered a generous statement noting the general's service to the nation and the trial was over.

Judge Laval, again acting unusually, invited the press to cross the bar and interview the assembled jury. To a person, they said that they would have found for CBS, having been convinced that the evidence clearly supported the thesis of the documentary.

Aftermath

It is a cliche, but nonetheless a truth, that one can win at trial and lose in the court of public opinion. It is also true in rarer instances that one can lose at trial and *win* in the court of public opinion.

I've been in both situations. *Westmoreland v. CBS* was a classic model of how a good relationship can work. The agency was involved from virtually the beginning. We had and kept the full confidence of our client and most importantly we had the total support of the litigators.

John Scanlon is a partner at the Sawyer Miller Group, an international strategic communications firm. Mr. Scanlon pioneered the field of litigation public relations, counseling such clients as CBS in a libel suit brought by General Westmoreland, the Boston Globe *in the John Lakian libel suit, and the tobacco industry in its product liability lawsuits. He has also advised many of America's most prominent corporations on crisis management and corporate identity, including American Express, Nissan, Citicorp, NYNEX, Ernst & Young, and Mobil. Scanlon has a particular specialty in representing media clients, having launched* New York Newsday, *the* New York Observer, *and* The National, *as well as devising ongoing programs for* Times-Mirror, The Atlantic, U.S. News and World Report, The American Lawyer, *and the* Village Voice, *among others.*

Oil Wars: Pennzoil versus Texaco

Thomas C. Powell
Vice-President, Administrative Affairs, Pennzoil Company

What is a promise worth, what is your word worth, what is a hand-shake worth, what is a contract worth? You can send a message to corporate America. —Pennzoil attorney Joe Jamail, addressing the jury, Pennzoil v. Texaco, *July 1985*

Overview

In 1985 when the Houston jury returned a $10.5 billion verdict in Pennzoil Company's favor against Texaco Inc., a naive business community was stunned. Twelve jurors had unanimously decided, after sifting evidence for four and a half months, that Texaco had deliberately enticed Getty Oil's majority shareholders to void a merger agreement with Pennzoil. By law, they concluded, Pennzoil should be compensated for its loss. But, $10.5 billion! Decided by ordinary people?

Our lead attorneys — Joe Jamail, working with John Jeffers and G. Irvin Terrell of the Houston law firm Baker & Botts — characterized this litigation as a straight-forward tortious case. To the jurors, it boiled down to judging when is a deal a deal? Yet as the jury deliberated the evidence, the issues began to range beyond the Houston court room. Seizing the opportunity, plaintiff lawyers broached inquiries into simmering moral and ethical questions involving U.S. business practices and conduct, touching nerves already raw from Wall Street merger and acquisition scandals.

Before the dust settled two years later, this straightforward dispute case had been through more appeals convolutions than a Texas sidewinder dodging 18-wheelers on the interstate outside Odessa. And the tumultuous world of corporate mergers and acquisitions wouldn't be the same.

No warning transpired that this business dispute would explode into corporate warfare, waged in diverse courtrooms around the nation. The legal arguments dissecting contract and tort law should have bored the public to sleep in 10 minutes. But undercurrents of double-dealing, greed, and dubious Wall Street morals rose to the surface of their own buoyancy. A lethargic press corps awoke to find it had been dealt an unlikely soap opera. No longer was *Pennzoil v. Texaco* a story slotted only for the business section; it was general news and editorial page fodder, growing more important as the case moved on appeal.

Cast of Characters: Extraordinary

Enter a disparate cast of characters to debate these fundamental ethical and legal questions at the bar, belabor biased positions in op-ed tracts, and pontificate law from within the halls of legislatures. This corporate tort action developed into a news story able to stand alone on the personalities of these performers. Reporters could paint this business story in human terms. But would they report the facts as well — without bias?

Among the featured and bit players: Gordon Getty, son of the world's richest man; Joe Jamail, the Texan "King of Torts"; Marty Siegel, Wall Street dealmaker, soon to be indicted; California's Getty Museum, the world's richest; the *Wall Street Journal*'s editorial board; the "Marlboro Man," Robert Norris, an advertising actor and a leading Texaco shareholder; Harold Williams, chief of the Getty Museum and former head of the Securities and Exchange Commission; the "Invisible Man," a public relations operative for Texaco; Arthur Liman, chief counsel for the Iran/Contra Hearings; 181 members of the Texas legislature; nine justices of the U.S. Supreme Court; and "the man who turned down $2 billion," J. Hugh Liedtke, chairman and architect of Pennzoil.

Embellished by this imposing cast of actors, it was not surprising diverse and strong opinions existed over *Pennzoil v. Texaco*, variously described as: "The Texas Common Law Massacre" (*Wall Street Journal*); "the most important case in the history of America" (Jamail); and "a true story of treachery and deceit" (Pennzoil backgrounder).

Abundant Media Exposure

This legal war began with a cash tender offer for Getty shares during the final week of 1983. But it wasn't until 1985, when the trial began, that it took a life of its own — and then burgeoned with an intensity that seemed capable of consuming the companies and all combatants involved. Once the depth of the story was discovered, the *Wall Street Journal* assumed something of an ownership and ran more than 100 front page stories, which may be a record. It proved irresistible for "60 Minutes" and was chronicled in three books. Law and business schools added it to case history exercises.

Pennzoil v. Texaco was the biggest business case ever, providing the largest jury award ever. The attorney count was tallied in the hundreds; included were lawyers from some of the most costly and prestigious law firms in the country, from Wall Street to Houston. Courtroom war was waged in Delaware, California, Texas, New York, and Washington, D.C. Legislative battle zones included Austin, Texas, and Washington, D.C., as well as a majority of the attorneys general offices among the states.

When the war was over and a truce negotiated in 1988, Pennzoil settled for $3 billion in cash. Texaco, the nation's eighth largest company and one of the original Seven Sisters, had been in and out of bankruptcy and restructured into a more formidable organization. The exploits of principal Pennzoil attorney Jamail had already become folklore. Participants' careers had been made and broken. And lives would never be the same for those who toiled so long on the project — especially for those handfuls of public relations practitioners fortunate to be involved.

The small public affairs shop at Pennzoil hadn't the foggiest idea what was unfolding on December 28, 1983. I was as excited as other staff members when we distributed a press release announcing Pennzoil's intent to purchase 20 percent of the troubled Getty Oil's outstanding shares. We'd waited a long time for an opportunity for Pennzoil to acquire substantially more oil and gas assets and move into a higher tier of energy companies. **Straight to the Super Bowl**

Yet within 10 days, disaster struck as Texaco preempted an agreement Pennzoil had reached with Getty's majority shareholders (and approved by Getty directors) for a Pennzoil-Getty merger. For Pennzoil's PR staff, what followed was akin to being tossed into the Super Bowl straight from college spring practice.

With little actual corporate merger/acquisition or litigation experience to draw on, those of us assigned from PR could have faced arduous odds trying to squeeze onto the project team to adequately support and counsel the legal shoot-out that was shaping up. Fortunately, we worked for a top management with a game plan. Just as fortunate, from the onset the several legal experts directing litigation gave PR a role in their project strategy. An alliance based on trust was bonded between PR and legal that remained for the duration.

When Pennzoil's tender offer for Getty stock was made in 1983, project involvement by the corporate staff was limited to a select few. Of key importance, Chairman Liedtke believed that a strong, affirmative communications strategy was an essential part of his overall effort. This support served the whole Pennzoil team well when the project flipped from a cash tender offer to a lawsuit.

Small Shop Acts Big

Being part of the team was extremely critical, because on the communications playing field, our staff was decidedly outgunned. Texaco had more than 120 PR people on staff going in, along with the largest consulting company, Hill and Knowlton, and its many offices. Pennzoil employed 20 people in its public affairs department, including government relations and employee communicators. Booke & Company, a Manhattan PR firm long associated with Pennzoil, was our only consultant. Eventually, more than 300 PR professionals and 20 public relations organizations would work for both Pennzoil and Texaco.

Much would be learned by the communicators — on both sides — often by trial and error. Hazy textbook case history memories might take shape for real at any time. It was soon clear: Be innovative or preemptive with the right tactic, or be devoured. Unshackled, the PR practitioners for both companies brought out all of the artillery when the stakes reached billions of dollars, as reflected by the op-eds and the hired-gun economists; the opinion surveys, and the counter-surveys; the skirmishes of the briefs and the truth squads; the overnight advertising campaigns and the relentless scuffles over editorial bias; the deadly sound bites; and the sometimes deadly expert witnesses.

Pennzoil's effective use of a tightly controlled, proactive communications campaign during this high-stakes crisis was crucial to the victory. As noted constitutional lawyer Larry Tribe, himself a participant, acknowledged: "... the strong Pennzoil media response ... was critical to winning."

The Case Background

A smaller oil company, Pennzoil entered the 1980s seeking a chance to expand under the right circumstances. During 1983, Pennzoil's management saw a once-in-a-lifetime opportunity to acquire a substantial ownership in Getty Oil. One of the richest domestic companies, with 2.35 billion barrels of oil and gas reserves, Getty was publicly undergoing an internal battle for control of the board of directors.

Seizing the opportunity, in late December 1983 Pennzoil tendered for 20 percent of Getty's common shares at $100 per share. Pennzoil Chairman Hugh Liedtke contacted Gordon Getty, son of founder J. Paul Getty, who controlled 40.2 percent of Getty's stock in a family trust, and who was battling with the company's other directors.

Liedtke and Getty agreed to a deal to buy up the public shares and the 11.8 percent owned by the Getty Museum and take the oil company private. If after a year the parties could not agree on a restructuring plan, the assets would be distributed: four-sevenths to the Getty Trust and three-sevenths to Pennzoil.

The deal was memorialized by a memorandum of agreement signed by Liedtke, Getty, and the Getty Museum. The Getty board approved, by a vote of 15–1, a sweetened transaction at $110 a share. A press release announcing the merger agreement was issued by Getty Oil on January 4, 1984.

However, Texaco then contacted Gordon Getty and talked him into a new deal, worth $125 a share, with Texaco agreeing to indemnify the Trust for any liability in breaching the Pennzoil contract. By January 5 the Getty board and Getty Museum had also accepted the Texaco proposal after also receiving Texaco "indemnities" against liability for breaking the Pennzoil deal.

Pennzoil eventually was able to bring suit against Texaco in Texas state court. In July 1985 a jury trial in Houston began considering the case, in which Pennzoil asked $7 billion in actual and $7 billion in punitive damages for Texaco's deliberate interference with a binding agreement under New York law. The $7 billion actual damages figure was essentially based on the value of 1 billion barrels of oil reserves which Pennzoil lost when it lost Getty.

Don't Get Mad, Go to Court

After four and a half months of trial — represented by 24,000 pages of testimony — on November 19, 1985, the jury returned a verdict against Texaco, awarding Pennzoil $10.53 billion.

Over the next two years the case was appealed through a variety of state and federal courts on different grounds, with Texaco consistently losing. Unable to legally forestall the Texas state laws requiring the posting of a bond equal to the judgment, Texaco followed up on its threat to file for bankruptcy protection.

Texaco's final appeal was denied by the Texas Supreme Court in November 1987 and the following month Pennzoil and Texaco announced a proposed $3 billion settlement, subject to shareholder and bankruptcy court approval.

Texaco paid Pennzoil $3 billion on April 7, 1988; for all of the legal appeals, the jury verdict stood to the end.

Over a period of three years, the case and related issues had been heard by 12 jurors and 23 judges in 8 courts.

The Communications Strategy

During the same time, Pennzoil's public affairs team was responsible for 40 press conferences; responded to more than 4,000 media inquiries; participated in over 100 events in and around courthouses; responded to 200 judicial decisions (verdicts, motions, rulings); placed 14 op-eds; issued 6 mail-out litigation brochure updates; made contact with 20 attorneys general; orchestrated 2 targeted national advertising campaigns; directed 2 public opinion surveys; managed 10 outside PR firms and consultants; and directed 30 state and 8 federal outside lobbyists.

The execution of Pennzoil's PR strategy — supported 100 percent by management and carried out by the internal staff — was arguably as important to the triumph as the lawyering effort. Between 1983 and 1988 staff committed not a single major Pennzoil PR blunder. With the billions of dollars at stake, this was an incredible accomplishment.

Pennzoil's overall communications strategy exploited the advantage of the company's smaller size and our strong office of the chairman, which permitted swift reaction to events. This worked particularly well because project participation was vested in only a handful of executive decision makers, who in turn ensured the PR participants entre to the war room.

We weren't caught totally unprepared. A year before the merger proposal, the PR group initiated a comprehensive study of the proxy fights for five energy companies, analyzing events from a corporate communications perspective. This was during the heyday of the merger/acquisition frenzy and Pennzoil was itself a candidate for rumors, both as a target and as a predator.

From this study we developed a repository of published information on these case studies for reference. This helped us sharpen our strategy in the Getty Oil tender offer even as we moved from a corporate merger proposal to litigation battle stations. We particularly took heed of the study's conclusions that throughout a struggle a forceful and visible CEO is essential; and corporate communications are a part of any successful plan.

Also, in retrospect we realized how important it was we had developed credibility with the media — especially the local news bureaus — before the fact. We'd earned a reputation for being responsive to reporters and for meeting their deadlines. Our group was experienced in both years and familiarity with the basic tools, and we had a solid knowledge of generally what would and would not work in a communications strategy.

Fundamental Concepts   The communications direction evolved early in the campaign with a plan based on:

- *Speed.* Make opportunities by being quick and decisive.

- *Flexibility.* Remain open to alter the game plan at any time to respond to changing developments.

- *Counterpunch.* Never take a PR hit without simultaneously delivering a meaningful reaction; yet, never interfere with the judiciary when reacting.

- *Proactive.* Remain on the offensive and promote pressure from the public, business and financial interests, and shareholders for a settlement.

Another goal, not so openly acknowledged, was to find ripe media opportunities for Chairman Liedtke, whose demeanor exudes integrity and believability. Liedtke was featured on the covers of *Business Week* and *Fortune* and his quotes remained fresh and newsworthy throughout the litigation.

Specific Strategies

Our targeting strategies were diverse and open to revision with the ebb and flow of the legal situations. Among the tactics:

- *Hub.* All outside public communications emanated from a small control group representing the chairman's office, outside counsel, and public relations.

- *One Voice.* Media and general public response was limited to the chairman's office and the principal media person — all using the same specific message points.

- *Rifle Shots.* Opportunities were sought for placements of support (especially op-eds) from an ad hoc pool of outside opinion leaders, friends, and public affairs experts around the country. These included former senators, judges, and Wall Street elder statesmen with impeccable credentials. Outside PR counselors were an important source of ideas and helped coordinate this effort.

- *Endless Flow.* The flow of information updating the project was continual to employees, shareholders, Wall Street, outside opinion leaders, and the press.

- *Intelligence.* Intelligence gathering and documentation were determined two of PR's main responsibilities. A network of "ears" and fax machines around the country proved invaluable.

> • Research. The litigation and management teams were also supplied by PR staff with information gathered as intelligence from news databases and other sources. This special service turned up old quotes and forgotten news items, as well as pertinent stories from obscure sources. Almost any newsclip from 1983 on was available in hard copy within minutes.

These tactics and staff duties were important for the communicators. They fit the resources base available and wore well with those of us assigned, as well as the new outside practitioners recruited.

Only two of Pennzoil's internal PR players — Terry Hemeyer, vice-president, and Robert G. Harper, director of media relations — participated daily with the decision makers. I was on immediate call and directly involved as required for government and press relations projects, as were Joan B. Bugbee, for external communications and opinion research, and Frank Verrastro, managing government relations from Washington, D.C. The total corporate PR personnel intimately involved during the project numbered six to eight people at most.

Problems That Never Went Away

For the Pennzoil staff, the primary issues were always understood. Chief among these were sanctity of contract; business ethics; legislative intervention in the legal process; media bias and manipulation; and legal strategies. Unfortunately, these weren't always so clear to the media — and therefore the public.

During the course of the action, several prevailing attitudes made communications more difficult. The press and Wall Street generally discounted the validity of Pennzoil's lawsuit in 1984, soon after Texaco assimilated Getty, and therefore had little interest when the trial began in July 1985 and tedium set in. The $10.5 billion verdict blew even the *Wall Street Journal* out of the water. Consequently, this was not "the media's story." Nor was it the analysts' of Wall Street, also caught with their pants down. This lack of ownership made it particularly hard for Pennzoil's press team, and easier for Texaco's communicators.

The public was led to believe — from press accounts, editorials, and Texaco's propaganda — that the verdict was absolutely wrong, the result of a runaway Texas jury that couldn't begin to fathom the complexities of a business law case. This interpretation was total nonsense. These attitudes and opinions are background for the following five accounts of battles within the PR war. They highlight the more unique examples of Pennzoil's PR effort.

To help its client, in April 1986 one of Hill and Knowlton's Texas operatives passed on to the *San Antonio Light* a tape recording and transcript of comments made by the *Pennzoil v. Texaco* judge following a speech he had given before the bar association in California. "I don't exist," the "invisible man" told the newspaper.

The judge had allegedly mentioned in an informal question-answer session after the speech that he wasn't sure of his interpretation of New York law. Attorneys attending the speech said it was apparent the judge never intended to indicate he thought the case would be overturned by a higher court, and there was nothing negative in his self-deprecating remarks.

One newspaper taking the Hill and Knowlton bait, though, was the *Houston Chronicle*, whose story, without a source, prompted a wire service follow. The *Los Angeles Times* had covered the speech and found no story, and further declined to use the wire story. The *San Antonio Light* originally chose not to do a story, but after the national story surfaced ran an exposé on the "invisible man's" visit.

After the *Chronicle* story, Pennzoil's stock plunged $4 per share, or $168 million. That's one of the reasons we reprinted the *Light's* news story in a full-page ad in several dozen newspapers, using the occasion to make arguments and question the opposition's ethics. The flap also prompted an ethics debate within the PR industry.

The day after the ad ran, Pennzoil stock rose one and one-eighth points, or $42 million, and Texaco's stock dropped one point, or $240 million, for a $282 million spread.

The editorial staff of the *Wall Street Journal* remained openly opposed to the jury verdict for the duration of the story. Six editorials lambasted the decision for Pennzoil and supported Texaco. Editorial board visits by Pennzoil executives failed to reverse the bias, which eventually spread to the news pages. In November 1987 a page one story, headlined "The Quality of Justice," critical of the Texas judicial system and of the *Pennzoil v. Texaco* verdict, was interpreted by us to be so full of distortions and misrepresentations that it required a response.

We immediately answered by creating an in-house full-page advertisement for *Journal* placement headlined "Responsible Journalism," which began: "We've paid for an ad about the Pennzoil-Texaco litigation because it's the only way Pennzoil can be certain that an accurate account of its victory in the Texas Supreme Court can be read in the *Wall Street Journal*." The *Journal* at first refused to run our ad; then wanted to change the copy; then would only run it with its own offsetting editorial response. Turning these offers down, we ran the ad in 35 other papers.

The Advertising Battle: Media Bias and Manipulation

The day after the ad, Pennzoil's stock rose three points, or $126 million; Texaco's dropped one and one-eighth, or $240 million, for a $366 million spread.

The Amicus Battles Most of us didn't know *amicus curiae* (friend of the court) from a Latin lullaby, much less how to pluralize to *amici*. But these briefs to the courts became an irritating Texaco gambit at several stages.

The first pressure came when we learned that several congressmen were circulating a letter within the Texas delegation requesting colleagues to sign a joint letter to the U.S. Court of Appeals Second Circuit to affirm a district court decision — an action in favor of Texaco.

These kinds of activities are hard to stop if they gather momentum and perhaps only an instantaneous response — telephone and Washington lobby — by all of Pennzoil's available resources saved the day. In the end, a majority of the Texas congressmen joined the two senators in refusing to sign the amicus letter; however, a number of signatures were erased after personal contact.

In another episode, Texaco mounted a blitz attack on the nation's many elected state attorneys general, who tend to be political activists, seeking their joint support for an *amicus curiae* filing to the U.S. Supreme Court arguing for the overturn of the Texas judgment bond requirements.

Only because one of our employees heard from a government friend in Kansas did Pennzoil become aware that a squadron of Texaco executives had fanned out around the country seeking amicus support from the attorneys general, some of whom were recipients of Texaco campaign contributions. Texaco was being effective. At one point, the alleged number of attorneys general signed on to the brief appeared to be heading toward a majority. Much to Pennzoil's chagrin, the American Petroleum Institute's own field personnel were helping introduce Texaco's lobbyists to the attorneys general. Both Pennzoil and Texaco belong to the trade association.

By putting Pennzoil's top attorneys and company public relations personnel onto a full-time telephone campaign, and by flying into many state capitals to lobby the attorneys general, Pennzoil was able to hold the number of signees to the eventual amicus brief to a somewhat reasonable level of 17 names.

The Opinion Research Battle The use of opinion research to support PR arguments is certainly an old and trusty tool that can be particularly effective, especially if its preemptive. That's to say, the real advantage is usually the surprise of the released favorable opinions when the other side hasn't the opportunity to adequately respond.

On the other hand, it was Pennzoil with advance knowledge that was able to negate Texaco's initial use of opinion research from an organization that specialized in political polling. That national poll of 1,200 people, taken a month after the trial, claimed to show that a majority of Americans thought the judgment against Texaco was unfair.

Our intelligence discovered the polling activity and obtained a copy of the results prior to their release. Pennzoil retained an internationally known expert in survey research from the Wharton Business School, who debunked the results. He challenged an inherent bias of the survey questions. His statement was ready for release to the press and deflated Texaco's survey results announcement.

On the proactive side, Pennzoil engaged the Opinion Research Corporation (ORC) to survey both the general U.S. population as well as 1,000 Texans for opinions on the case. While the national survey was favorable to our position, there was no need to release it. However, the Texas survey proved opportune in April 1987 when the Lone Star state's legislature was debating a bill to bail Texaco out from meeting tough judgment bonding requirements.

At a strategic juncture, prior to press release, we distributed advance copies of the ORC findings to legislators' desks in their chambers. ORC had found, among other opinions, that a majority of Texans believed the state bond laws were fair, shouldn't be altered, and certainly not changed retroactively to help Texaco.

The poll results were widely carried by the press and were believed to carry convincing weight with the legislators.

It was a journalist for a smaller Texas newspaper who tipped our PR staff that hometown legislators had secretly filed Texaco bailout legislation to set a cap on judgment bonds to $1 billion. Under law, Texaco would have had to make bond for the full judgment. With the lower cap, Texaco could forego its bankruptcy strategy. (This potential Texaco strategy had been among possibilities forecast a year earlier by Pennzoil's lobby team.)

The Austin Battle

Within an hour of the tip, it became apparent from intelligence gathering that Texaco was trying to hire every lobbyist in Austin. Only this early warning allowed the Pennzoil team and our regular contract Austin lobbyist to be able to pose a same-day counter-blitz and neutralize Texaco's sneak attack. While perhaps more of the bigger name lobbyists were swept up by Texaco, Pennzoil's

The gallery of the Texas Senate was packed with Texaco employees showing their support of a bill that would limit the bond the company must post while appealing a multibillion-dollar judgment in favor of Pennzoil.

team was equal match and soon numbered 20 to 30 people. It soon became an epic no-holds-barred lobby battle with *USA Today* reporting $2 million in lobby fees spent by both sides.

Texaco was reported to have entered the Austin Battle with mailing lists for almost 100,000 Texas stakeholders, including employees, retirees, shareholders, oil royalty owners, contractors, and other vendors. At one point, the odds were so overwhelming that I was the only Pennzoil employee in Austin, while the House and Senate galleries were packed by hundreds and hundreds of Texaco-star-baseball-cap-adorned employees bussed in by Texaco from around the state.

But PR opportunists sometimes lose control of a good thing. The Austin *American-Statesman* reported in a story, "Texaco employees wear out welcome after flooding capitol," and that "rude behavior by some of the Texaco people" reinforced legislators' decisions to oppose the bills.

We sent our star attorneys into Austin action — including constitutional lawyer Larry Tribe, from Harvard, and Joe Jamail. Other Pennzoil counsel with stature in the state, some former law school professors to many lawyers in the legislature, also worked the capitol halls and testified before committees. Texaco called on labor support, retirees, and corporate executives. In the end, it came down to a head count of votes in the Senate, where Pennzoil had the required 11 votes —

in good part secured by its lobbyists — to keep the measure from being brought up under that chamber's rules.

Pennzoil's activity during the Austin Battle extended a long-running, targeted public relations campaign to make Houston-based Pennzoil just as important a home state company as Texaco (which in reality is headquartered in New York). It included: bumper stickers for supporters ("I Trust Pennzoil"); a one-of-a-kind 9,000-name statewide thought-leader mailing list prepared from scratch by San Antonio PR counselor Jim Dublin; radio and TV ad tags ("Proud to Call Texas Home"); installation of a huge Pennzoil logo sign within the Astrodome; reprints of favorable news stories delivered to legislators; additional PBS program sponsorship in key cities; an employee letter writing campaign; personal notes from Liedtke to lawmakers; op-ed pieces in major Texas papers; truth squads, directed by George Christian, former press chief for Lyndon Johnson, flying around the state for editorial board visits; special issue brochures for thought leaders; and a retained Texas economist expert witness to deflect arguments that the action was hurting the state's economy.

The bankruptcy battle lasted from April 1987 to April 1988 and was a whole new ball game for Pennzoil. This action took the case to a New York bankruptcy court on Texaco's turf, where there had been long-held sympathy for that company.

Bankruptcy Battle

At this point, Pennzoil focused directly on its Wall Street problems. The big brokerage house analysts by and large were negative to the judgment and really did not understand the legal side of the case — especially the basis for the jury decision and the size of the judgment. For example, not many were aware that during the trial Texaco had not disputed Pennzoil's model supporting its damages claim. Many analysts were absolutely certain the damages were excessive and blamed Texas courts. An alarming side to this bias is that the press continually contacted these analysts for their "expert" opinions, which often became unchallenged quotes for news stories.

Texaco, its business prospering, remained nonetheless protected under the umbrella of the bankruptcy court — and away from Texas's bond laws — and showed little sign of wanting to negotiate a settlement with Pennzoil. It didn't help matters that Pennzoil's stock dropped $631 million in value.

To overcome this resolve, Pennzoil retained the PR firm Burson-Marsteller. Pennzoil's staff and advisors agreed they didn't have the proper calibre guns to focus on this critical assignment. Burson immediately dispensed just the right touch of counsel to our management — certainly no stranger to Wall Street —

and brought in the broad picture strategic planning experience in investor communications that counted.

Pennzoil's need was to get an accurate story across to a still somewhat disbelieving Wall Street. In turn, a more favorable message would eventually get to Texaco shareholders, creditors, and the bankruptcy judiciary. The key points: the Texas trial was over, it was fair, and appeal avenues were exhausted; the judgment was properly predicated on New York contract law; and it was time for Texaco's top management to get to the negotiating table with Pennzoil.

Counseling Pennzoil to take a more proactive posture, Burson-Marsteller, along with Booke & Company, orchestrated an event that began turning around opinions of some influential financial analysts. It amounted to a very straightforward face-to-face October 1987 session in Manhattan — billed as sort of a Wall Street town hall meeting for Pennzoil to tell its own story.

The invited analysts were offered an agenda with an enticing panel of proponents, including: Judge Simon Rifkind, the revered octogenarian, dean of New York law and former federal judge, who used his 60 years' experience to explain in detail how the Texas courts had indeed followed New York state contract law; Larry Tribe, the Harvard law professor and legal activist, who defined constitutional issues; John Jeffers, trial attorney from Baker & Botts, who explained the evidence; and Liedtke, who provided his compelling personal perspectives on the case.

The meeting concluded with a long session of thoughtful questions and answers which seemed to begin to put to rest some of the cynical observations being made by the Street. After this initiative, the "road through Wall Street" became decidedly smoother and Pennzoil bashing decidedly less frequent.

Another Gauge for Success

Pennzoil demonstrated that a small, focused PR cadre with support from carefully selected outside experts indeed can measure up to a corporate giant with all its vast resources — particularly if the stakes are mind-boggling. Was the PR campaign a success? Well, yes, if you consider that Pennzoil eventually settled out for $3 billion.

Yet another interesting gauge of success may be found in a reputable survey conducted annually for the *Wall Street Journal*, ironically a nemesis during the case. We were told that the *Journal*'s Corporate Report Cards for 1985 (during the trail) and 1986 (the year following judgement) showed these levels of readers' awareness and opinions of the top 25–30 energy companies. The numbers indicate the ranking of all companies surveyed that year with "1" representing the highest score.

	Pennzoil	Texaco
Familiarity		
1986	4	1
1985	11	2
Well-Managed		
1986	2	14
1985	12	3
Good Reputation		
1986	5	10
1985	11	3
Good Investment		
1986	2	14
1985	14	4

Well before Pennzoil received the cash settlement from Texaco, plans were underway to assure that as part of the post-trial activity the records of this epic business case would be left to scholars and others who would benefit from future study. In this way, our management involved in the five-year struggle would be assured history would not be rewritten. **Aftermath**

We donated a treasure of public relations and legal archives to Northwestern University, Stanford, and the University of Texas — to business, law, journalism, public affairs, and communications schools. Donated from the PR files were original copies of all newsclips and newscast video tapes, press releases, in-house publications, shareholder communications, and advertising.

In addition, a "living history" project was initiated by the University of Texas, with participants' taped interviews recorded to accompany written records. Where necessary, we also contributed financial support for maintenance costs along with the records donation, for those institutions requiring it.

Thomas C. Powell is vice-president, administrative affairs for Pennzoil Company. He is responsible for environmental, safety, and health (ESH) activities and the company's ESH audit program and provides support for the group vice-president/administration. Mr. Powell was a participating member of the Pennzoil communications team during the duration of Pennzoil v. Texaco, *handling media and state government relations responsibilities. He also has held media relations and general writing positions during his 12 years with the company. Prior to joining Pennzoil, mr. Powell was employed by Conoco Inc., where he was public relations special projects director, concentrating on writing, community affairs, and crisis management media projects.*

Meltdown on
Three Mile Island

Richard C. Hyde
Executive Vice-President, Corporate Counseling Division, Hill and Knowlton USA

Overview

What was once Nuclear Reactor Unit 2 at the Three Mile Island (TMI) Nuclear Power Generating Plant near Harrisburg, Pennsylvania, now stands idle. The rounded top containment building still houses the steel reactor vessel, pumps, and heat transfer piping, but the damaged fuel rods were robotically removed and are now in permanent hibernation.

The twin cooling towers adjacent to Unit 2, once the conduits for great plumes of ordinary cooling steam, now are silent symbols of nuclear power generation, and a reminder of events that were, at the time, widely perceived as the precursor of a nuclear catastrophe.

The political and economic aftershocks of the accident persist even today; the cleanup process alone has exceeded $1 billion. Though eclipsed by the deadly nuclear reactor accident in Chernobyl, Ukraine, in 1986, the accident at TMI generated enormous changes in the scientific, industrial, and communications professional disciplines.

An editorial in the "Review and Outlook" column in the March 29, 1989, *New York Times* stated:

> *The news on March 28, 1979, that an "accident" had occurred at Three Mile Island Unit 2 managed to bring together in one small place all the factions that now define and decide politics in the United States: a private company, public regulators, single-interest activist groups, print reporters, televised news, and, of course, politicians.*

Though political determinants now, these factions each played a historical role in how the accident at TMI was handled and communicated to the public. The drama they described and the way they described it has been the subject of extensive analysis. The conclusions have all been generally the same: the accident at TMI was poorly communicated by industry and governmental representatives and poorly interpreted and reported by the news media. Sensationalism on the part of the news media has consistently been blamed in large part for the near hysteria and panic exhibited by those living in the vicinity of the plant.

The accident at TMI has been exhaustively examined and, yes, technical and human error deficiencies were detected. But the fact that no one died or was injured during the evolving accident points to the successful operation of the built-in safety mechanisms.

But the damage wrecked at TMI was not isolated to the nuclear reactor. The reputation of, and public confidence in, the nuclear power utility industry was and continues to be heavily damaged. Evidence indicates that the industry will recover with great difficulty, if ever. Several state governments have not allowed fully built nuclear power plants to go into operation because of perceived inadequate emergency plans.

Approximately 108 nuclear power plants now operate in the United States. No orders for new nuclear power plants have been generated since the late 1970s and only a few plants, originally ordered in the 1970s, are scheduled to go into operation during the 1990s.

Inasmuch as the nuclear power industry was hurt by the accident, so too was media credibility. Evidence suggests that the public's confidence in the news gathering profession degenerated rapidly during the accident as conflicting reports and misinterpreted information were spread boldly across newspapers around the world, and emotionally prefaced in evening television news reports.

Public Relations Benchmark

The public relations implications during and after the accident were enormous. TMI was the seminal event for the development of a vast body of crisis communications literature and practice. It was also the single event that glaringly demonstrated the lack of crisis planning by industry; preoccupation of governmental agencies with the licensing process; lack of substantive periodic reviews to ensure information sharing between operators; and the lack of scientific understanding by news reporters who were, in many cases, unprepared to interpret the information they were provided.

The following is a synopsis of the events that took place at Three Mile Island and the subsequent repercussions. I was an observer, not an active participant, of the initial crisis. Several days after the accident my firm, Hill and Knowlton, was retained by plant operator Metropolitan Edison to provide community and employee relations counsel following the enormously damning press, radio, and television reports during and following the accident. But though an observer, I saw how the accident evolved and how it was communicated to the public by the Metropolitan Edison Company and Nuclear Regulatory Commission officials and the resulting news coverage.

Viewed as an historical event, the elements that interacted during and after the accident provide a benchmark upon which to measure what we've learned and put into practice. Those lessons, especially in communications, analyzed over the past 13 years, remain hugely valuable in our approach to every type of public and private disaster — the sort of communications disaster that grew out of the reactor accident at Three Mile Island.

To understand the impact Three Mile Island had on the nuclear power utility and the public-at-large, we should view the events at TMI from two perspectives — the technical accident that took place inside Unit 2 on the one hand, and what transpired outside the plant on the other.

The technical description of the nuclear power process and subsequent events that led to the accident have been researched from a number of sources, including *The Report of the President's Commission on the Accident at Three Mile Island* (published in October 1979) as well as other current scientific and historical publications. The description of what took place outside the plant are personal observations supplemented by research in crisis communications.

Meltdown

Though not a widely recognized term in the American lexicon prior to the early spring of 1979, "meltdown" is now synonymous with any reference to the accident at Three Mile Island. To gain some perspective of how events were played out at TMI, one must look at the general climate of public and political opinion; public support, or lack thereof, of nuclear power; and understanding of the nuclear power process by those who attempted to report the events of late March and early April 1979.

Public and media perception of the event was influenced strongly by a movie that, coincidentally, was released nationally just before the accident occurred. *The China Syndrome,* starring Jack Lemmon, Jane Fonda, and Michael Douglas, appeared to forecast many of the events and issues surrounding the accident at

TMI. Fact and fiction were skillfully blended together, making the movie appear to many as a semi-documentary. It provided audiences with a simplified way of understanding a complex process and issue. It was also the debut of terms like "meltdown," "scram," and "trip" — words that would become all too familiar, if not completely understood, to millions around the world within a few short weeks. Without question, the movie made the real life-public relations problems of TMI more difficult.

But even if *The China Syndrome* had not been released, a long heritage of entertainment films had biased many people against nuclear power, feeding the public's unreasonable fears about radiation. One need only think back to the typical horror movie of the 1950s, where the terrible monsters Godzilla, Mothra, or Rodan were spawned by radiation. The American public had been absorbing a steady diet of nuclear fears through the entertainment media for a generation since World War II.

Politically, support for nuclear power was divided, pretty much as it is today. But the energy crises of the 1970s dictated that self-sufficiency be exploited at all costs. President Carter supported the expansion of nuclear power efforts, and the electric utility industry deemed nuclear power a safe and efficient means of meeting the goal of self-sufficiency.

However, the utilities failed to adequately communicate to the public the complex process of nuclear fission and the extensive safety precautions built into the process. Further, only limited cooperation existed between the nuclear power utilities and state and local governments in planning for a possible disaster. The culprit was the widely held industry belief that the plants were so safe that emergency evacuation and communications plans were unnecessary simply because they would never be used. In hindsight, this proved to be an overtly false belief as borne out in the events at TMI.

The near total lack of journalistic knowledge about the nuclear power process was highly evident in those chosen to report the accident. Most news-gathering organizations just did not have the scientifically knowledgeable reporters well versed in nuclear power production to adequately understand, interpret, and report the sequence of events that made up the accident at Three Mile Island. Within this context, the public, politicians, industry specialists, and the press interacted during the highly volatile period.

The Accident A nuclear reactor's function in commercial power generation is basically to heat water under pressure. The hot water produces steam that drives a turbine that turns a generator to produce electricity. Heat is generated in a reactor through a process called fission — the splitting apart of an atomic nucleus. Enriched uranium is used to fuel the reactor and produce the fission process. The presence of a large number of fuel rods provides for a continuous fissioning of atoms — once the process begins, it becomes a continual chain reaction unless halted by control rods of neutron-absorbing materials. One of the products of this process is the release of energy in the form of heat.

Demineralized water is used throughout the system to cool the reactor and carry the generated heat away from the reactor chamber which, in turn, produces the steam that drives the turbines. This all takes place within a closed system of redundant safety mechanisms.

At approximately 4:00 A.M. on Wednesday, March 28, 1979, with the Unit 2 reactor operating at 97 percent power, a valve closed in the demineralizer, a system through which feedwater flows to the steam generator. This water was part of the secondary water system of "clean," unirradiated water used to generate electricity. Its closing halted the flow of water to the steam generator. Closure caused pressure to the feedwater pumps to stop. Without water, the electric turbines shut down automatically. The safety system was performing as designed.

But at this point, two more valves mysteriously failed to open auxiliary feedwater lines — the emergency backup system.

As the secondary system shut down, the primary system had no place to dispose of the generated heat, so the pressure in the primary system began to rise to over 2,200 psi. When pressure reached 2,350 psi, a relief valve automatically opened, venting water and steam from the primary system into a "quench" tank within the containment building. Pressure immediately fell. The valve was supposed to close when pressure dropped back to 2,300 psi. It did not. Engineers in the control room thought it had.

The cooling water of the primary system was escaping via the unsealed valve, allowing pressure in the reactor coolant system to fall further.

The scene in the Unit 2 control room quickly became a cacophony of incessant alarms, the control panels glowing with flashing green, red, amber, and white lights. An enormous amount of information, some of it apparently erroneous, was flooding the control room at the precise moment that radioactive water was flooding the containment building.

An operator noticed that the emergency feedwater valves of the secondary system, the initiator of the event, had not opened. He opened them manually, dumping cold water into the affected steam generator. Deprived of adequate cooling water, the pipes of the primary system had grown fiercely hot from the unchecked nuclear reactions. The shock of the sudden bath of cold water in the secondary system caused primary system pipes to rupture, permitting the remaining radioactive primary water still in the system to contaminate the formerly "clean" secondary system water used in steam generation.

Now that the steam generator was drawing heat away from the primary system again, the reactor pressure dropped further. At 1,600 psi, the emergency core coolant system kicked in as it was supposed to, forcing high pressure water into the reactor. But the water was continuing to escape through a ruptured part of the quench tank system.

Thousands of gallons of radioactive water flooded the containment building floor until an operator manually shut a valve in the pressure relief circuit. The overflow of the quench tank had already been routed automatically to a tank in an adjoining building.

General Emergency Declared

Approximately four hours into the accident, a general emergency was declared. At Three Mile Island, a general emergency was viewed as an event that had the potential to endanger the health and safety of the public-at-large.

This set into motion a notification process that involved state and federal government agencies, including the U.S. Nuclear Regulatory Commission (NRC) in Bethesda, Maryland. On the morning of March 28, Metropolitan Edison notified the Pennsylvania Emergency Management Office at 7:00 A.M., while Governor Dick Thornburgh received word of the crisis at 7:30 A.M.

The utility justified its delays in alerting state authorities by claiming that the magnitude of the accident was not sufficiently high in the earlier hours of the accident to warrant alerting state authorities. Once the emergency was declared, an immediate need arose to begin monitoring radiation levels outside the plant. Metropolitan Edison requested the assistance of the Pennsylvania State Police.

On Friday, March 30, contaminated water overflowed onto the floor in the adjoining building, where it evaporated through the ventilation system, releasing for the first, but not last, time some radioactive gases into the environment. Radiation levels of 30–35 millirem per hour were monitored at the plant gate. For comparison, an ordinary dental x-ray is approximately 25 millirem. Much higher readings were monitored within the containment building.

By the weekend of March 31–April 1, readings in the containment building were drastically down from the previous day. However, a "new twist," as it was described by Harold Denton of the Nuclear Regulatory Commission, had developed. Shortly after the emergency core coolant system (ECCS) was activated, it was manually (and inexplicably) shut off for a short time, then turned on again. The absence of ECCS water somehow formed (scientific opinions differ on exactly how) a bubble of hydrogen gas in the reactor vessel. When the ECCS was again turned on, the damage was already done — 25 percent of the nuclear fuel rods were destroyed.

The hydrogen bubble posed an unanticipated problem. Some thought it might explode, while others argued the concentration of oxygen in the vessel was too low to enable an explosion. Through a complicated mechanism — using water and pressure — technicians were able to reduce the size of the bubble. By Wednesday, April 4, one week after the accident began, the bubble was virtually eliminated. But during the course of that week, small portions of radioactive gasses were both purposefully and inadvertently released from the plant. The overt stage of the accident was over.

Media Blitz

For a brief period, the increased activity at and surrounding the plant during the initial stages of the crisis went unnoticed by the public. However, once the general emergency was declared and the notification process was fully underway, the incident was well on its way to becoming a public concern. Something was up at Three Mile Island and it wouldn't take long for the media to get wind of it. Within an hour and a half of the initial notification, the media blitz was on.

WKBO, then a Harrisburg Top 40 radio station, was the first media outlet to break the TMI story. It did so on its 8:25 A.M. (Wednesday, March 28) newscast using information gathered by a traffic reporter who, while monitoring CB transmissions, had overheard that police and firefighters were being mobilized in Middletown, Pennsylvania, for an emergency at Three Mile Island.

The reporter called TMI and asked for the public relations office, but was instead connected to the control room. No public relations representatives were assigned to the site. Once connected to the control room, the reporter was told by the man who answered that he couldn't talk now because "we've got a problem."

The reporter was referred to Metropolitan Edison's office in Reading, Pennsylvania, where he reached the manager of communications services. The gist of the conversation was that TMI had shut down due to a problem with a feedwater pump; the public was in no danger. The WKBO report was intentionally "toned down" to avoid creating alarm among the local population. But the first mistake in a long series of communications mishaps had been committed: The geographically separated public relations staff had sketchy information about the actual events that were taking place at TMI and initially were unaware of the severity of the accident.

Shortly after 9:00 A.M. that same day, The Associated Press filed its first wire story. It quoted the Pennsylvania State Police, stating that a general emergency had been declared at Three Mile Island but no radiation leak had occurred. The AP wire story, though brief (and incorrect — there had been releases of small amounts of radiation), was the first trickle that quickly became a media deluge; the accident was on its way to becoming one of the dominant news stories of the year — and the decade.

At the outset, the accident created understandable public relations problems for Metropolitan Edison. Small amounts of radiation were escaping into the environment. The problems quickly became a nightmare when a burst of radiation Friday morning, March 30, was widely reported as "uncontrolled." This prompted Governor Thornburgh to advise individuals within a ten-mile radius of the plant to stay indoors. He also asked for the evacuation of pregnant women and preschool children residing within five miles of the disabled plant.

Governor Thornburgh originally minimized the accident in his public statements. A few days later he said publicly, "You are being subjected to a conflicting array of information from a variety of sources. So am I."

It was immediately apparent that Metropolitan Edison was faced with a unique communications problem that imposed burdens on a small staff geared to dealing with a public utility's traditional publics: employees, customers, state regulatory bodies, media in the service area, and, periodically, the financial community. These traditional publics were augmented — instantaneously — by all residents within a 20-mile radius of the nuclear plant, by state and county civil defense authorities, by local elected officials, by the governor of the state, by the Nuclear Regulatory Commission, by the Pennsylvania legislature and Pennsylvania's Congressional delegation, by the White House, by business and industry in the region of the plant, and by regiments of media representatives from the United States and a number of foreign countries.

Within hours of the first wire story, the media descended on the plant. But Metropolitan Edison's technical people, those competent to describe accurately what had happened and what was happening at any given moment, were totally occupied with bringing the reactor under control.

A large number of employees in the Reading headquarters, about 60 miles from the crippled plant, were pressed into service manning telephones. Demands for information from the media were unceasing. For a brief time, the badly strained

Reporters and spectators stand in front of the main gate of the Three Mile Island Nuclear Generating Station in Middletown, Pa., on Sunday, April 1, 1979.

telephone system threatened to collapse. Eventually, Metropolitan Edison had three divergent information centers operating: one at the Reading headquarters, one in Hershey, Pennsylvania, and finally, one at the accident site.

Besides the public statements being issued by the three Metropolitan Edison information centers, other sources (including local, state, and federal officials) were issuing reports. Some were based on theoretical possibilities, some on probabilities, and some on observations made from locations away from the site. Widespread public fear and uncertainty grew. The mood was aggravated by media pronouncements that focused on the possibilities for catastrophe.

Hydrogen Bubble to Burst?

Media interest was accompanied by an equally avid political interest. Members of the Pennsylvania congressional delegation, state officials, and the president of the United States were on the scene within days.

The absence of a single qualified spokesperson at the site during the initial stages of the accident, armed with a comprehensive crisis communications plan, severely hindered any attempt to get consistently valid information to the public. The communications staff at Metropolitan Edison was overwhelmed, with the possibilities for gaining control of such a massive media event growing more remote with each passing hour.

At the request of President Jimmy Carter, the NRC descended on the area via helicopters on Friday, March 30. The director of Nuclear Reactor Regulation at the NRC, Harold Denton, was among those to arrive.

On Saturday, March 31, concern grew at the NRC about the potential of a hydrogen explosion in the crippled reactor. During the early afternoon, NRC chairman Joseph Hendrie met with the press in Bethesda, Maryland. He explained that an evacuation of 10 to 20 miles surrounding the TMI plant might be invoked if engineers at the plant decided to force the hydrogen bubble out of the reactor. The NRC concluded that if this course of action was taken, it might ignite an explosion of the bubble.

Hendrie's statements about the hydrogen bubble were misinterpreted by the media, leading to reports of a possibly imminent "meltdown" of the reactor core and possibility of widespread radioactive contamination. In Pennsylvania, Denton disagreed with Hendrie's assessment and said so during a late evening press conference in Harrisburg. In sum, a variety of sources in different locations variously interpreted a story that changed from minute to minute.

Efforts by Metropolitan Edison to keep the story in perspective were widely misunderstood. This gave rise to prevailing and lingering doubts regarding the company's credibility. The notorious hydrogen bubble is a good example: it has since been firmly established that the bubble was never the danger it was portrayed to be at the time.

More Panic and Confusion Contributing to the confusion was the absence of a definable emergency evacuation plan. Site evacuation plans were being kept under wraps because (1) nobody was sure what was happening, (2) the evacuation plans were poorly drawn up, and (3) the plans shifted daily as the wind shifted. In the three counties within a five-mile radius of the plant lived 630,000 people. An evacuation alert was announced by the weekend, even though shelters for those people were neither selected nor prepared.

The continuing nature of the accident was also a major contributor to the vast communications problems. Friday brought the release of radiation and talk of a core meltdown. Saturday and Sunday brought the hydrogen bubble. Confusion by technicians and scientists reigned and was reflected by the media. The public naturally responded with fear and panic.

Adding to the confusion and fear, John Herbein, vice-president of Metropolitan Edison and its chief technical spokesperson, disagreed with NRC staff on the seriousness of the accident, the size of the hydrogen bubble, and the extent of the damage. Early Saturday, March 31, Metropolitan Edison announced it would hold no more news conferences but would allow the NRC to speak on its behalf. Denton became the NRC's chief spokesperson. At this point, Metropolitan Edison relinquished control as the primary source of information.

The NRC's stepping in may have represented the public relations axiom of speaking with one voice. However, it did not necessarily improve cooperation in the technical management of the problem. Metropolitan Edison people were not well coordinated with NRC staff.

In general, three reports of the accident attracted attention for supposed sensationalism. They were the United Press International story on the third day of the event, March 30, reporting on the chances for a meltdown; the CBS News broadcast, March 30, when newscaster Walter Cronkite began, "The world has never known a day quite like today"; and an AP story on the fourth day of the event, March 31, that reported the hydrogen bubble might explode.

Sensationalism versus Perspective

It is impossible to arrive at a definitive answer as to whether these reports sensationalized the event, since such a judgment is highly subjective and means different things to different people. One person may think a story is sensational if it appears on the front page rather than on page B6. Or the photograph accompanying the story may play on the emotions. The twin cooling towers became the foreboding symbol of TMI, and many people wrongly thought that the radioactive contamination that was inadvertently and, in some cases purposefully, released from the plant was released through those cooling towers.

When considering TMI, it is difficult to understand how any discussion of a possible meltdown during an accident could be anything but sensational. NRC people announced that a meltdown was possible. Metropolitan Edison countered that "reports of a meltdown are unfounded." They, of course, were reluctant to discuss a meltdown.

The issues for public relations, industry, and the media are really risk communications and communication of uncertainty. Few reporters covering TMI were experienced in these kinds of issues. The solution lies in preparation, in developing more sophisticated approaches to discussing the inevitably raised "worst case scenarios," and putting risks in perspective.

Public relations must anticipate "what if" questions and provide background prior to an accident. Communications should not just provide stark facts but should place the facts in perspective. Risks, such as nuclear power in general, should never be discussed without references to alternative activities that also have risk. If the risks of nuclear power is the subject, it must be discussed along with the risks of alternative power generation methods.

Nuclear Fear and Loathing

Disagreement among scientists over the seriousness of low doses of radioactivity fueled public fear and confusion, as did widespread ignorance of radioactivity. One school of scientific thought among scientists described a linear relationship between radiation dose and negative health effects, concluding that no safe radiation threshold exists. Another school argued against a linear dosage-effects relationship, stating that only higher doses would cause ill effects. Still others argued that somehow lower doses were worse than high doses since cells damaged at lower doses could continue to reproduce and pass on their damaged characteristics. Cells killed outright by radiation would die and not reproduce the ill effects.

Scientific controversy and uncertainty were reflected by TMI media coverage, leading to increased public fear. Both the public and the media were virtually ignorant of radiation issues and related nuclear science and had to learn day by day during the accident — a difficult set of conditions for public relations people. Reporters assigned to cover this event were, for the most part, unprepared. And the most knowledgeable had trouble getting the story out in the clear, calm manner the public might understand.

Positions among university professors were divided because of such controversies over radiation. Anti-nuclear academics, such as those in the Union of Concerned Scientists, gained support for their views; pro-nuclear professors such as Norman Rasmussen of MIT and Alvin Weinberg of Oak Ridge National Labs proclaimed that the nuclear safety systems worked.

President Carter, a nuclear engineer himself, took a personal interest in TMI and quickly dispatched the NRC to the scene. He visited shortly after the accident was under control in order to demonstrate his administration's vigilance and concern.

Planning for the Next "Accident"

On Wednesday, April 4, 1979, a week after the accident occurred, Hill and Knowlton was retained by Metropolitan Edison to develop an immediate program for employee communications and community and governmental relations. In the weeks that followed a comprehensive written document was prepared to address communications when a mishap, accident, or crisis occurs.

Dealing with a crisis imposes a new kind of communications discipline, which must be formalized so that when and if a crisis occurs it can be managed. Certain guiding principles help facilitate crisis management. They include speaking with one voice, providing regular updates, covering all the bases and all the subjects that are important. And they include, of course, the cardinal rules of "tell it all," "tell it fast," and "tell it accurately." These are normal informational imperatives associated with crisis management. However, the accident at Three Mile Island was not a "normal" crisis.

There is no analogous situation for the several days of crisis and uncertainty at Three Mile Island. It was a continuing accident whose potential for causing widespread damage and radiation injury was constantly and carefully examined by the media.

The accident in itself was unique. Unique, too, were its ramifications. National, indeed worldwide, indignation was directed against Metropolitan Edison. This was reflected in news and opinion columns. As an example, a Harrisburg newspaper editorialized that whether or not the utility went bankrupt was not a matter of public concern. Regulations, including the Pennsylvania Public Utility Commission, were following rules that hadn't been written for such a situation.

Hard Lessons

But given the unique situation, certain hard lessons in crisis communications were learned:

- In an atmosphere of confusion and rapid change, a voracious media needs to be fed.

- A fluid and continuing crisis needs special attention for the public and media to be satisfied, and for the crisis to be adequately controlled by public relations.

- If the public is closely involved, unknowns about the crisis at hand have to be communicated by the industry, in cooperation with the press, in order to serve the public responsibly.

- To a certain degree, the industry, press, and public relations have to cooperate to assist and reinforce the civil authorities who are the agents responsible for the public's safety.

To handle a public crisis like that at TMI, communications must have top priority. A single platform for issuing official statements and answering media queries is essential. This became very apparent during and after the TMI accident, and is just as valid today. When public anxiety is elevated to the level of general panic, a persuasive argument must be advanced; public health and safety requires a unified voice. But is a single spokesperson the right approach? Perhaps a team approach is best, with the provision that team members only appear together. A plant management person, a state emergency authority, and a regulatory scientist might make an appropriate team.

But no team will be effective if the public and media are not continually educated prior to a crisis, through seminars, plant tours, and short courses. And no crisis will be managed effectively unless a comprehensive plan is in place long before the crisis hits.

Out of the same consideration for public health and safety, public announcements must be limited to official statements, and firm discipline must be imposed on all communications personnel who have contact with the media. This becomes even more important when non-communications personnel are pressed into service by the scale of media inquiries. Ad lib comments are eagerly seized upon by reporters, all of whom are eager for fresh angles to the running story.

Constant contact must be maintained with the proper authorities, and when evacuation becomes even a remote possibility, the state executive and civil defense officials have decisive roles that require their access to immediate and reliable information.

Aftermath In April 1979, shortly after the accident was under control, President Carter named John G. Kemeny, then president of Dartmouth College, to head a special commission to investigate TMI. On May 12, 1979, the Kemeny Commission made its preliminary report.

The report faulted both the operators and the design of the plant, as did the NRC report. It also criticized the NRC for not ordering its priorities properly, getting bogged down in day-to-day licensing requirements without taking a broad view on whether licensing was addressing safety capacity.

After TMI, there was an immediate congressional outcry calling for more effective licensing and oversight by the NRC. Senator Gary Hart, for example, then chairman of the Senate Nuclear Regulatory Subcommittee, offered legislation to establish continued federal monitoring of all reactors in the U.S. He asked for federal experts to be ready to move into all reactor areas in the wake of an accident in order to take full control. Democratic majority leader Senator Robert C. Byrd called for greater reliance on coal-fired electric power.

In the aftermath of TMI, a common theme emerged. The media criticized the utility for lying, obfuscating, and attempting to sooth with public relations finesse. The utility criticized the media for irresponsible sensationalizing. It now will fall to history to determine the truth.

The thesis has been raised that the image of nuclear power has suffered because of media treatments of accidents such as TMI or, for that matter, Chernobyl. An article in the *New York Times* published on April 3, 1980, reported that mental stress among the population around TMI was "greatly exacerbated" by news media coverage of the accident. Then Congressman Mike McCormack particularly took CBS News to task as well as a New York City newspaper.

As mentioned earlier, one result of TMI has been the complete halt of nuclear power growth in this country and stricter regulation of existing plants. Since 1979, not a single new plant has been announced. A number of generating stations well along in their construction were converted to use other fuel sources such as coal or natural gas.

The industry's position in TMI-type accidents points up a quandary: If industry admits error it invites lawsuits. Metropolitan Edison was sensitive to this possibility. They, and any other utility that experiences an accident, have the unenviable public relations position of handling the costs of the accident and the adverse impact on stock value.

As a result of the Three Mile Island accident, there will be no such thing as an insignificant nuclear accident. The terrible accident at Chernobyl reinforces this thesis. Crisis preparation remains the key to effectively communicating the event and creating an orderly flow of information.

Dick Hyde started his professional career in public relations with Hill and Knowlton in 1962. Initially, he was assigned to New York where he worked on H&K's largest corporate and association accounts. Over the years, his work has covered corporate, energy, and trade association public relations; employee communication; financial relations; and public affairs. He now heads up the Corporate Counseling Division at Hill and Knowlton USA headquarters. In addition, he specializes in crisis communications and issues management planning and training.

Anatomy
of a Crisis

Ron Rogers
President, Rogers & Associates

Ron Rogers
President, Rogers & Associates

Throughout this book, we learn that no two crises are alike and that they tend to arrive unannounced, exploding on a company and then evolving in fast-moving, unpredictable directions as many conflicting factors come into play. Advance planning for these eventualities is essential, because once underway, a crisis takes on a life of its own and is constantly changing course as various constituent audiences are affected — and react. Their response to events often triggers reaction by other interest groups, some of them new to the fray, and these audiences must now be dealt with as part of an ongoing communications campaign.

Overview

We will explore the anatomy of a crisis — the key, potentially explosive forces that should be taken into account by a company's crisis management team from the very outset of trouble. Ideally, whether the company is faced with a major product recall, a strike, an executive scandal, a lawsuit, or a major natural disaster, these guidelines will help the team formulate strategy decisions across all areas of concern as the crisis unfolds. While every crisis acquires its own scope and personality, management should follow three hard-and-fast rules from the beginning to help ensure the most effective containment and resolution of any crisis.

First, the crisis team must be ready to act and make decisions quickly and decisively. Crisis managers get just one shot to frame their strategy and must get it right the first time, because they rarely get a second chance to keep the crisis from spinning off in undesired directions. In fact, the company's ability to ride out the storm is largely determined by these initial actions, as it makes decisions in response to the various forces that have already come into play. Numerous other factors need to be anticipated and assessed, from establishing credibility with the media to communicating with key constituent audiences. These early hours are critical as the company adapts strategy that becomes the basis for all future actions.

Second, companies that deal successfully with a crisis always try to anticipate next moves and take control of a given situation. Companies that are reactive, or try to minimize damage through inactivity, inevitably prolong the crisis. Therefore, when the crisis team first meets to decide how the company is going to respond, members must be ready to analyze all these different scenarios and anticipate what might happen, depending upon the particular strategy selected. Initial questions include: How are people going to react if we take this approach? How big could this problem become? But the team's thinking must obviously go further than that, with members anticipating, If this particular audience reacts one way, how might that affect the crisis? And if this other audience reacts in another way, how could that trigger reaction by this interest group, and, in turn, affect our strategy? This initial flexible thinking is critical in the effort to take control of the situation with a confident, overall strategy based upon a comprehensive understanding of the issues and audiences involved. However, it is equally important to remain vigilant of the reactions by audiences and be flexible to respond to them.

Third, as they head into a crisis-mode operation, crisis team members should resolve to keep a sense of perspective and objectivity. Otherwise, the realization that every decision the team makes could have a long-term impact on the company can become overwhelming.

Following are many of the critical factors that will likely come into play during a crisis and influence not only the initial strategy decisions but those that will continue to be made for days, weeks, even months to come.

Preparation: A Key to Success Whatever the size, corporations today all operate in a "crisis environment," and having a crisis response program in place should be viewed as a fundamental business requirement. While a crisis plan will rarely cover every contingency, all the groundwork preparations — crafted, ideally, when cool heads are at work in "normal" circumstances — will ultimately pay off when the pressure is on and fast but well-reasoned decisions are demanded. This advance planning by a company can ultimately help minimize the damaging impact of a crisis, since key executives will have already anticipated key issues and can thus more effectively deal with the crisis at hand. How much or how little the company prepares — and the perceptiveness of these plans — will shape the company's response and response time.

Here are several important planning steps to take into account so that systems are in place and a company can respond immediately.

An in-house staff or outside crisis firm should research the company and identify the potential crises that could arise — and assess how management dealt with any of these emergencies in the past. Taking this a step further, Rogers & Associates help clients identify a range of worst-case scenarios and devise plans for dealing with them. This involves sitting down and having "creative crisis" sessions with staffers, in which they raise every imagined eventuality that could strike the company — and types of responses to each scenario. We also determine the important audiences that will be affected by each of these potential developments and how the company plans to communicate with them during a crisis, including employees, dealers, distributors, customers, consumer interest groups, stockholders, the media, industry experts, competitors, and government officials and regulators.

Appoint a crisis team, which normally includes top management, legal counsel, public relations professionals, and technical experts. A final decision maker, usually the president of the company, should be determined in advance, since each team member will have his or her own agenda and points of view.

Select a corporate spokesperson who will be solely responsible for speaking with the media in the event of a crisis. In these times when presidents and CEOs are starring in their companies' television commercials, the public expects to see top brass representing the company. However, if the president is an excellent manager but an ineffective spokesperson, the crisis team should carefully select someone else to personify the company.

Whoever is chosen, this spokesperson should be trained to work with the media and should participate in mock interviews and press conferences on a regular basis, to ensure he or she will be prepared to handle media inquiries when the time comes. This means putting spokespeople through all the possible scenarios ahead of time, asking them the toughest, rudest questions imaginable, so that when they're on camera or leading a press conference, nothing shakes them.

In one instance, we were unable to convince a client's CEO about the importance of being prepared for an unsuspected media ambush. We felt media training was critical, so we arranged for a camera crew and one of our own people acting as a reporter to show up at his house early one morning and ask him some very embarrassing questions. They posed as an investigative news team from the local network station and he went off to work, chastised and frightened at what might air that night. As soon as the CEO arrived at work he called the agency and said,

"We need to have a meeting — immediately." We knew we were either going to be fired or would now be able to help his company. Fortunately he had a sense of humor when we revealed our scheme, and we went on to help him develop effective media skills.

Develop actual plans of action for responding to the potential crises situations. These plans should be reviewed on a regular basis so that as a company's business and/or the business environment changes, the anticipated crisis management strategy remains comprehensive and viable.

Aggressive Damage Control: the Suzuki Samurai

Early on, the crisis team must establish the basic strategic groundwork by deciding if the company is going to adopt an overall aggressive strategy or take more of a reactive approach. Either way, this decision sets the tone for most other decisions. There are times to be aggressive and times when it's more appropriate to try to avoid or minimize any further controversy as best as possible. Whatever approach is taken, fact-based candor seems most appropriate in today's society and gains a better response from the public than calculated evasiveness.

Various factors tend to collide during a crisis, influencing one another and dictating certain courses of action and ensuing responses. The Suzuki Samurai case in 1988 illustrates how these dynamics can force an aggressive communications campaign by a company under siege and how this chosen strategy subsequently affects many other decisions that have to be made.

On June 3, 1988, *Consumer Reports* magazine held a press conference in New York to announce that for the first time in ten years it had determined that a vehicle was "not acceptable" and should be recalled. Specifically, the magazine was talking about our client's vehicle, and the ominous headline read: "The Suzuki Samurai Rolls Over Too Easily." The Samurai was a four-wheel drive sport utility vehicle that had been introduced in the U.S. with great success just three years earlier. It was also Suzuki's only automotive product in the U.S. market, up against fierce competition, and a public controversy of this nature — spearheaded by the country's most respected consumer advice magazine — obviously threatened the company's American-based operation.

At 6:00 A.M. in Los Angeles, prior to the press conference, Suzuki's crisis communications team assembled at a local television studio. We agreed from the beginning that Suzuki should adopt an aggressive campaign. Fighting back was the appropriate action to take with its key audiences because the vehicle was safe and the allegations unfounded. The Samurai had been extensively tested before its introduction and Suzuki's data indicated the vehicle had an excellent safety

A 1988 Suzuki Samurai on the Consumer Reports *test track.*

record — it had nothing to hide. We also knew that a public battle would invite more media coverage, but Suzuki didn't have any choice. It could not simply stop selling the only vehicle it was distributing because of inaccurate allegations, and the company had to convince dealers that Suzuki was here for the long run. Moreover, if we harbored any hopes of successfully challenging *Consumer Report*'s allegations and credibility with a highly public campaign, Suzuki certainly couldn't appear to be passive.

What followed the magazine's announcement was a case of damage control. Within three hours (shortly after watching a video of the press conference, shot by our own people and transmitted to us by satellite), we transmitted by satellite a one-take-only videotaped response by American Suzuki's general manager, refuting the magazine's charges and defending the safety of the Samurai.

Simultaneous to our videotaped response, we distributed releases over the wires, in time to make the evening news and the next morning's newspapers, so that consumers would hear both sides of the story. We also distributed mailgrams to dealers, field personnel, and employees, alerting them to the situation and Suzuki's response. Suzuki requested that all media inquiries be referred to Rogers & Associates, and we prepared a statement for Suzuki's customer relations department. Working virtually nonstop, we took phone calls from more than 1,200 reporters in 48 hours, while providing press kits, news releases, statistical data, and background information.

A week later, Suzuki held its own formal news conference in Los Angeles, with live two-way satellite communications to locations in Detroit and New York. We felt it was imperative that the automotive press in Detroit and the national press in New York be given the opportunity to see Suzuki's presentation firsthand and to ask questions. We supplied the media with Samurai safety facts that refuted the unscientific findings of *Consumer Reports*. We brought in an independent engineer who explained and demonstrated the safety testing that had been done on the Samurai. We showed videotaped footage of other vehicles turning over to demonstrate that almost any car or truck (with expert steering-wheel manipulation) can be made to turn over. And we provided an independent analysis of government data showing that the Samurai was safer than many vehicles in its class.

We had warned Suzuki in advance that media coverage of our counterattack would certainly include video and photographs of the Samurai rolling over, and this indeed happened on virtually every news telecast. But Suzuki had to take this gamble, knowing it was imperative that the company be seen by its customers and dealers as aggressively denying the unfounded charges while defending its reputation and its only product. Ultimately this strategy worked. We got the message out. While media coverage was, understandably, extensive and aggressive, Suzuki's side of the story was given substantial coverage.

Yet still — despite our best efforts — June sales plummeted by 70 percent to 2,200 vehicles. Our counsel was to keep fighting, rather than retreat. We worked with Suzuki's sales director to devise a generous dealer incentive program ($2,000 for each vehicle sold) and we cooperated with automotive editors on editorials about Samurai safety. Most of the automotive editor experts indicated that *Consumer Reports* should concentrate on testing toasters and leave the automotive reviews to the experts.

These strategies began to work. July sales returned to normal levels, and August sales soared to 12,208 — by far Suzuki's best month since entering the U.S. market. And then on September 1 came the company's ultimate vindication. The National Highway Traffic Safety Administration, a federal agency, determined not enough evidence existed to even open an investigation on the Samurai. And it refused two separate petitions by the Center for Auto Safety — a so-called consumer organization — to force a recall of the vehicle. In uncharacteristically strong language, the government said what we knew was true all along, that the *Consumer Reports* testing was biased, unscientific, not properly calibrated, and not representative of real-world driving. Suzuki's aggressive response to the allegations had paid off, demonstrating the company's faith in its vehicle and concern for its customers.

Anticipation Fuels
Proactive Campaign

When a company is alerted to a potential crisis ahead of time, all contingencies should be evaluated and crafted into a proactive campaign. For example, our firm had been quietly working on behalf of a major non-profit organization in Los Angeles for several years when, in the spring of 1992, a series of events threatened to put the CEO in an uncomfortable and unaccustomed spotlight. In the midst of a continuing recession, a growing public disenchantment with highly publicized executive salaries, and a financial scandal involving the CEO at United Way, we learned that a leading financial magazine was coming out with a major story about CEO compensation at nonprofit, charitable organizations — and that our client would be highly visible in the story. We were able to read the article before it appeared on the newsstands, and our client came off well, but we worried that daily newspapers and local TV newscasts would pick up on the overall theme of the story, do their own sensationalized reports, and create further setbacks for organizations that had already been tainted by the United Way scandal.

So rather than promote or facilitate media interviews at that point, we recommended that our client take a responsive approach. We prepared a media campaign designed to put the CEO's salary and the financial outlays by his organization in the context of his industry to demonstrate that his compensation was well within the acceptable parameters of companies of similar size and revenue. We anticipated six contingencies, but then had to wait and let events dictate our actual strategy. We were ready for an onslaught of media coverage, but nothing happened when the article came out. Not only had intense interest in the subject begun to fade, but the Los Angeles riots broke out within two weeks, completely overshadowing and minimizing the issue. The anticipated "crisis" never occurred and we never had to implement our program.

Setting the Agenda

Once the nature and extent of the crisis has been determined, if it's apparent that a strategic advantage to media exposure or to going public remains, the crisis team should try to gain control of the flow of information by issuing a preliminary statement as early as possible. If the team allows the controversy to simply unfold, then its campaign becomes automatically reactive and is much more vulnerable to getting swept along by events or having the other side dictate the course of action.

Instead of letting this happen, the crisis team must remember: The first player frames the debate that follows. The company should use only confirmed facts in this initial statement, but provide as much background information as possible to reduce speculation by the media and other sources. The public relations member should assure reporters that additional information will be made available on a timely and consistent basis — and then make sure he or she follows through and delivers. In this day and age, stonewalling the press rarely works and invariably creates new problems that are not easily overcome. Also, failure to keep the media informed and updated will force many reporters to speculate or to rely on secondary news sources that are at least one step removed from the primary news source.

Worst-Case Preparation   Our work with the Jeffries Securities firm in Los Angeles illustrates how even with the "luxury" of knowing in advance that a potential crisis is headed its way, a company must still prepare for several worst-case eventualities.

When the management team at Jeffries learned that president and founder Boyd Jeffries was under government investigation for securities violations in 1989, they retained Rogers & Associates to develop and execute a damage control plan that would separate the company from its president in the minds of employees, clients, shareholders, and media in the event he was indicted (as he indeed was, six months later). After studying the company, we felt strongly that Jeffries management could successfully handle the crisis in a convincing manner and that the majority of their employees, customers, and stockholders would stick with the company, insuring its survival. Yet despite these convictions, we knew we had to twist our prognosis around and ask ourselves, Okay, what happens if we're wrong? What happens if the brokers bail out and take their clients to other brokerage houses? If new customers are scared away? If the stock plunges — and stays there?

This meant we had to design separate marketing campaigns for three different scenarios, to the point where we had advertising programs approved by Jeffries management and locked away, ready to implement at a moment's notice, as well as a new marketing brochure touting the aggressive management team Jeffries had in place. We also had three different versions of letters to employees, customers, and stockholders all finished and ready to mail, depending upon the indictment and its relative harshness.

Fortunately, after the indictment was made public, the company successfully retained its client base and its employees and, in fact, continued to do business virtually uninterrupted.

Responding to Emotion   When a crisis arises, the company's communications team must instantly size up the human emotions involved and anticipate how this will influence the various affected audiences — and, in turn, the company's strategy as it strives to cope with conflicting amounts of fear, anger, frustration, and resistance. In fact, crises are rarely diffused by facts, they are dissipated by people's feelings about a company, or a product, or a chief executive as the controversy unfolds in the public eye. Many "publics" are out there, so an effective crisis team will stay sensitive to the emotional needs of these various constituencies. Too often, companies that are in the process of defending themselves forget to acknowledge how various audiences feel about the crisis, and spend too much time defending the quality of their products, financial status, or management — at the risk of alienating these other important audiences. This can ultimately undermine a company's efforts to resolve the crisis on favorable terms.

Employee loyalty and fears about job security are two examples of personal factors that often come into play during a company crisis. At Jeffries Securities, for instance, emotions ran high among top management because intense loyalty to the company's namesake was mixed with their obvious personal fears: Will we stay in business? Should I start to look for a job now? Where am I going to be working next year? These executives also had nightmares about the best employees taking their clients and Rolodexes to competing firms, further threatening the company's prospects for survival.

In contrast to this, at American Suzuki during the Samurai crisis, personal job security and the threat of people leaving the company were never really an issue. The major concern was to make sure that employees were confident about the safety of the product they were selling and promoting. By communicating with them and waging a high-profile defense, we reinforced the Samurai's safety record so that when customers and friends asked questions such as, How could you work for this company? they had positive responses.

This same philosophy applied when we represented a medical products company that came under picketing by an animal rights group. Maintaining employee morale was a key factor in our strategy here. This was a company with considerable pride of ownership among the employees (most of whom owned stock in the corporation) and we needed to make sure they had the background knowledge and reassurance to think, I work in a facility where animal tests are required to produce the artificial human ligaments and arteries we manufacture. I know that our company pays particular attention to the care of the animals being used.

Dealing with the Facts

Depending upon the nature of the crisis, a company's ability to marshall and disseminate as many facts as possible will obviously impact how it conducts its campaign. The facts enable a crisis team to deal from strength and stake its strategy around honestly held positions and to more easily take the high road, which is ultimately the best approach. But remember an important caveat: Never assume that "facts" will necessarily win out. One of the fundamental mistakes companies make in dealing with the media is assuming that the media is interested in printing the facts, rather than "the story." Most reporters strive to be objective, but with few exceptions, the media does not have a vested interest in either the success or failure of a particular company. The media's primary concern is to be first with a breaking story, even if key facts are unconfirmed or only cursorily reported. When a confrontational type of crisis erupts, the first side to the media usually frames the story, often contributing to a further undermining of sound journalistic judgement.

Still, while the facts may not always prevail, they help level the playing field (for better or worse). In the eyes of the press and the public, the facts are the facts and can be used as an enormous weapon, so that if a company is "David" in a battle with "Goliath," this can work to its advantage. That's why tiny consumer groups can take on Proctor and Gamble, or why just one outraged citizen can suddenly gain a significant voice, because the facts carry the same weight, no matter who's saying them. The press doesn't buy its news according to the size of the news source but according to the credibility of the specific facts. That's why a crisis team has to be so careful when dealing with the press, particularly a big company under attack by a consumer group, a feisty little competitor, or someone who has a patent right.

In our campaign on behalf of Tengen (a division of Atari Games) versus Nintendo, we took advantage of an enormous disparity between the size of the companies. Tengen, a $30 million company, sued Nintendo, a $3 billion giant, for allegedly creating a monopoly of the U.S. video game market and locking out competitors through the use of proprietary technology. Yet, when Tengen announced its $100 million antitrust lawsuit, the press gave the company's side considerable attention. As large as Nintendo was, Tengen carried the same weight and Nintendo, through its reactions to the lawsuit, turned Tengen into a formidable opponent.

Rumor Management   Every crisis is rife with rumors and speculation, which calls for constant monitoring of media coverage, consumer activities, and the "buzz" within constituent audiences. From the beginning, the crisis team must make sure these audiences (employees, shareholders, government officials) are informed about the situation and the company's response, to minimize and help contain the rumor mill. The team should also remember that internal communications are crucial; a vacuum is filled with speculation.

Overall, rumors tend to spawn when a company fails to provide a high-level, accessible, and knowledgeable spokesperson who is close to the situation. This quickly frustrates the media and encourages them to seek out secondary and tertiary news sources who often don't have a stake in the company and are simply speculating.

When our firm went to work for Jeffries Securities, which already existed in a rumor-hungry industry, the scuttlebutt was rampant as word leaked out about the impending indictment. Would Jeffries himself be the only person indicted? If not, who was next? How many other people were involved? Were the top brokers going to jump ship? Were major corporate/pension accounts going to disappear when they saw the bad press? Would a business even be left?

We couldn't do much about all this speculation. But we could help fortify the company by preparing a professional marketing communications program to implement when the indictment actually came down.

Credibility

A company's ability to deal with a crisis successfully is dependent upon the ability of senior management to be honest with itself and its constituents, as well as the media. One important reason for our firm's success in this field is the fact that while we're advocates for our clients, we urge them to take the high road during a crisis campaign by remaining factual and realistic. Our counsel is to avoid mud-slinging tactics — despite the emotional temptation to do otherwise against certain foes — because we never want to undercut our client's ongoing credibility.

This philosophy is reflected by our experience that if the news is bad, it won't improve with age, so company management should face up to it, acknowledge the downside realities, and then get on with damage-control efforts. Surely that attitude would have helped Exxon minimize the negative publicity generated by the *Valdez* oil spill in Alaska. Moreover, one would assume that a corporation the size of Exxon that transports environmentally sensitive materials would have had a crisis plan in place. And yet, a combination of slow response to the media, insensitive answers to questions, and an apparent lack of concern for the citizens of Alaska resulted in extremely negative media coverage and, enraged consumer and environmental groups. Thousands of consumers were motivated to return their Exxon credit cards. Most importantly, the positive steps that Exxon later took to pay for and manage the cleanup process were largely obscured by media coverage which started out and continues to be highly critical. Examination of how Exxon mismanaged that incident and the lack of clarity that characterized its PR campaign reveals that management would have fared much better by announcing from the beginning: "We are taking responsibility for this tragedy.

We're very sorry it happened, but now we're going to get down to the facts, find out why it occurred, and then fix the damage the best we can."

Who's the Adversary? When a specific adversary has created the crisis or looms as a company's dominant opponent, learning all about this opponent will make a big difference in how the crisis team designs its strategy and anticipates developments.

"Keeping your enemy close" is an important part of crisis intelligence, and means that the more a company knows about the opponent, the better it can manage a communications campaign. This includes understanding public perceptions of the company and the foe, since this will shape how the issue at hand is discussed. For example, animal rights activists who picket and harass medical science facilities are often regarded as unsympathetic opponents in the public's eye because they tend to do things that undermine their credibility and make people uncomfortable, such as vandalizing facilities, throwing paint on innocent bystanders, or simply acting like fanatics. Conversely, when the adversary has the stature of a *Consumer Reports*, as in the Samurai skirmish, a carefully researched, fact-based defense tends to win over skeptical consumers.

Knowing the "enemy" involves having a grasp of the industry, knowing the financial climate surrounding this particular company, sensing how the political climate might affect the situation, and understanding how both sides relate with the media. When our firm began working for Atari Games, just days before it filed its lawsuit against Nintendo, we gathered all the news clips about Nintendo from the previous six months. When they arrived in huge boxes, we knew we were going to be dealing with a media-savvy opponent. Since then we've tried to learn everything possible about Nintendo — reading the company's financial statements, attending speaking engagements by its executives, interviewing its licensees — so that we know the company's business as well as we know our own. This helped us anticipate Nintendo's moves and fine-tune our strategy on behalf of Tengen and Atari Games.

Government Involvement The government's actual or potential involvement in a particular crisis (either at the federal, state, or local level) can certainly play an influential role in how the crisis evolves. If, for example, a company is involved in a consumer product-related controversy, the crisis team can be sure that some arm of the government will eventually investigate, very often drawn simply by media attention.

Fortunately, this interest is not always detrimental to the company's cause. When Tengen and Atari Games filed a major lawsuit against Nintendo, we took an aggressive media relations approach on its behalf. The deluge of media attention helped motivate the government to launch an investigation into Nintendo's practices, which in turn helped our client's own campaign.

Alas, government investigations can also serve to keep a crisis churning at a time when public relations efforts have finally managed to resolve or quiet the key issues. For example, after *Consumer Reports* came out with its attack on the Samurai, seven state attorneys general announced they were going to conduct their own investigations into Suzuki's marketing of the vehicle. Subsequently, nothing substansive resulted from these investigations, but the attendant news coverage of the requisite press conferences certainly didn't help the Samurai's cause. This also reiterates our emphasis on the fact that as a crisis evolves, problems can deepen as different audiences are affected and get involved. In this case, the press responded to the *Consumer Reports* allegations, and this reaction surely helped trigger interest by the attorneys general.

Staying keenly attuned and sensitive to the public mood about various issues not only makes good business sense, it becomes critical during a crisis when a company is seeking support or trying to avoid the spotlight.

Understand the Public Mood

A good example is the *Exxon Valdez* disaster, which occurred at a time when U.S. consumers were becoming increasingly sensitive to environmental abuses, not only in their neighborhoods but faraway locales. Exxon officials seemingly failed to take that into account, reacting as though the oil slick was "no big deal" — what's a few fish and birds? This attitude only made the situation worse. If these executives had really understood the public mood, they certainly could have shaped a much more sensitive and constructive PR campaign, instead of one that came across as self-serving and callous to what American consumers were feeling at the time.

Here's another perspective on the problem. In 1991 and early 1992, when many Americans were in a Japan-bashing mood, our firm's work with existing Japanese clients was significantly affected as we tried to shape their marketing and media campaigns. That was a time of crisis for Japanese businesses in this country. Some of our Japanese clients had a large number of American employees, their products featured a high percentage of local content, and the companies themselves had a great deal of involvement in their local communities. Their American-based Japanese executives really wanted to speak out on the issue and we encouraged them to do so. However, we also had Japanese clients with a small number of American employees, whose companies imported all their materials, and who paid scant attention to community affairs and concerns. We urged these clients to stay quiet and avoid proactive media coverage, knowing they were not in a position to promote a positive image of Japanese business in the U.S.

Advertising   What to do about advertising is, of course, a critical decision to make during a crisis. Should it continue or be discontinued until the storm clears? In normal circumstances, Rogers & Associates plays a supporting role in advertising decisions, but in a crisis mode, the crisis team — and specifically the PR executive member — should take charge.

In the case of Suzuki's Samurai, we responded to the *Consumer Reports* allegations by recommending that the company's advertising them be changed and that the new commercials air the night of the *Consumer Reports* press conference. We felt that it would be inappropriate to run the old commercials, which emphasized free-spirited fun, when the Samurai was under such serious assault. But we knew that to stop advertising would be ill-advised for several reasons, a major one being the need to reassure Suzuki dealers, owners, and potential buyers that the company stood behind its product. Therefore the new commercials, in network news timeslots, featured quotes from automotive media experts praising the Samurai.

Assessing the Media   The type and quality of the journalists who are reporting the crisis plays an influential role in how a company wages its communications campaign. When the crisis team is dealing with business or consumer reporters who know the industry and are familiar with the topic, it can take a much different approach than when working with a general interest reporter who has been thrown into an unfamiliar, technical situation.

For example, we didn't have to spend much time with the journalists who came from the automotive industry and covered the Samurai developments; we simply gave them the facts and they had the background to understand and interpret the important factors involved. General interest reporters, who invariably knew little about automotive technology and the auto business, posed a much greater challenge, particularly those from television who had a short amount of air time but the potential to deliver a devastating report.

Another important dynamic here has to do with database reporting. While databases can help reporters get quickly up to speed on a story, the process can greatly impact the course of a crisis. The potential problem, of course, is the fact that the first major article reporting the crisis lays the groundwork and sets the tone for other reporters covering the story, and is virtually impossible to change. In effect, it becomes the primary news source. If this story is filled with errors and replete with inflamatory quotes detrimental to a company, the crisis team will fight an uphill battle trying to set the record straight with the media. Even then, this initial story, whether or not it is fair or accurate, will be perpetuated and enlarged by future reporters using the database.

Given these realities, it's crucial that the company spend time with each new reporter covering the crisis to make sure he or she is working with accurate information. This also means communicating with the same kind of clarity and enthusiasm as exhibited the day the story broke — no matter how many hundreds of times the story has been told by an individual spokesperson.

Location

A company's geographic location can have a major influence on how a crisis is approached, especially when dealing with the media. In a major metropolitian area, companies under siege must cope with the sometimes voracious demands of television, radio, newspapers, and magazines — and the greater likelihood of unwanted national exposure. Yet working to a company's advantage is the fact that many other stories are competing for attention or can suddenly surface and deemphasize coverage of the crisis.

In a smaller market, with only a few media outlets, it's easier to contain the crisis to a limited geographic area. However, the downside is that everybody reads the same daily publication and watches the same local news show, so everybody knows about a company's alleged problem.

For example, Rogers & Associates represents a medical products corporation which is a large employer in a small Arizona city. When they were picketed by animal rights activists, everybody in town knew about it, because word of mouth travels quickly and the city's only newspaper put it on the front page. But this local knowledge wasn't of great concern to the company. Management told us they were confident they knew enough of the influential "stakeholders" in the area that even if picketing continued and was covered by the local media night and day, they could repair the damage and maintain their business. Their concern was that the controversy would spread beyond their geographic border and that as soon as it started leaking outside their area of influence, that's when problems might arise, such as unannounced visits by "60 Minutes" reporters. So we were brought in to help keep the news contained to local press.

Legal versus Marketing

Clearly, the long-term legal concerns of the company impact how you react and proceed in a crisis, starting with the classic in-house confrontation between lawyers and marketeers. As a general rule, legal counsel will want to protect the company from any lawsuits and reduce its long-term liabilities. Conversely, marketing and public relations personnel tend to focus on corporate image, sales, and the immediate impact of the crisis. This is why the crisis team must take responsibility for weighing short-term and long-term objectives and balancing the public's perceptions with the potential lawsuits.

When a company is in a crisis involving litigation, the lawyers will prefer that the crisis team resort to "no comment" — and that it come up with statements that are basically unacceptable for the press, addressing the issue by saying as little as possible in the most confusing style, when what is needed in crisis communications is clarity. In the Suzuki Samurai campaign, we couldn't say anything in our news releases that wouldn't hold up in court, because we knew that these releases could ultimately be used in court cases where media coverage of the Samurai controversy was deemed a major issue.

Meanwhile, the marketing people are understandably worried about how they are going to sell their product in the midst of a public crisis. They want to remain visible at this time because they know they're going to lose customers if the company basically clams up. So what we have here are opposing forces, with the legal side pushing for containment — keep the issue in a box until it can be decided in court — while marketing argues for high visibility in order to keep selling its products.

What the crisis team must do in this situation is have everybody in the room talk about both issues, knowing that a compromise must be effected, with one person ultimately making a final decision. Drafted statements must be concise and clear but legally acceptable, while at the same time move the company's business forward. This can't be an either/or type of campaign, because purely legal communications can kill the company if the marketing department can't sell the product.

A good illustration of this potential problem occurred in June 1992, when California's Consumer Affairs Department accused Sears Automotive of systematically overcharging for car repairs, making unnecessary repairs, and charging for work that was never done at many of its 72 auto centers in the state. Initially, Sears used lawyers as its primary spokespersons. The lawyers denied any fraud and called the accusations politically motivated. However, this stance proved untenable in the face of growing consumer outrage and the admission by Sears employees of some truth to the allegations. Subsequently, as the crisis spread to other states, including New York, New Jersey, and Florida, Sears shifted to a response tied to customer concerns. This change in tactics came too late to control the immediate damage and help repair the company's credibility. According to an article in the *New York Times*, crisis management experts judged the initial Sears strategy as "absolutely atrocious," and that by using lawyers to frame the defense, Sears alienated their automotive repair customers and turned public opinion against the company.

Sales and Distribution

Get right down to it and the most effective PR advocates for a company embroiled in a crisis are the sales and distribution people who interface directly with the consumers. They are the crucial mouthpieces (along with media coverage), for their attitudes get reflected directly to the customer and that, of course, impacts sales for the company in the midst of turmoil. We found with Atari Games that as long as their retailers held tight against intense pressures from Nintendo, video game sales held up, but once these retailers grew increasingly nervous about the company's future and continued to be pressured by Nintendo, major problems arose and sales erosion set in. Direct communications between management and sales/distribution is the key to success.

Aftermath

Ultimately, win, lose or draw, the actual crisis comes to an end — or at least subsides to a point where crisis team members can return to their regular lives, putting an end to 18-hour (or more) working days, fast-food diets, and the grinding, draining pressure to stay atop the situation at all times. And then a curious thing happens — a total letdown, emotionally, when members try to return to business-as-usual. The crisis work has been so intense and all-consuming, moving so fast in so many directions with rarely an opportunity to take a break for days and weeks on end, that once members have weathered the storm, the emotional letdown can be severe. One of our executives has admitted that when he returns to the normal tasks of publicizing his client and talking about the client's next marketing campaign, the work seems not nearly as demanding, and it's difficult to recapture the intensity he feels when he's caught up in the unique throes of crisis management. Yet he rests assured, knowing another crisis is headed his way, destined to challenge one client or another.

Ron Rogers formed Rogers & Associates in 1979. It is one of the largest independent public relations agencies headquartered on the West Coast. Rogers began his career in 1964 with the promotion of television programs, feature films and other entertainment events. He served as partner and executive vice-president at Rogers & Cowan, the world's largest public relations entertainment company. Top public relations magazines rank Rogers & Associates as one of the nation's leading crisis communications firms. In recent years, the company has developed and implemented risk management and communication plans for a wide variety of clients, including American Suzuki, Atari Games, Sir James Goldsmith, Jeffries Securities, medical institutions, fast-food chains, large retail stores, and package goods companies. The firm has also handled crises for companies involved in investigations, bankruptcies, toxic issues, threatened product recalls, management changes, and labor relations and negotiations.

CONSUMER TROUBLES

Condom

Crises

Alfred Geduldig
President, Geduldig Communications Management, Inc.

By law, every condom is entitled to have one hole. But, in 1988, a batch of **Overview** Lifestyles brand condoms were found to have two — one at either end. Unfortunately, this was only one of three major crises the manufacturer, Ansell-Americas, faced in the course of nine months. The other two crises involved a government sponsored study caught between science and politics, and a *Consumer Reports* piece caught between integrity and publicity.

In May 1988, Louis Capozzi, then the newly named president of N.W. Ayer **The Environment** Public Relations, got a call from Ross Campbell at Campbell Public Relations, Ayer's affiliate in Australia. Campbell represented Ansell International, a division of Pacific Dunlop Ltd., a publicly traded Australian company. They needed someone to help their U.S. affiliate, Ansell-Americas, to prepare for an impending crisis.

Ansell-Americas used a PR firm for product publicity, and Pacific Dunlop retained an investor relations firm in the U.S., but preferred a separate crisis management firm. All firms would, of course, have to be kept in the loop at all times. In fact, Campbell had to be apprised of plans in advance, in case clearances were required in Australia.

Capozzi, who had considerable crisis management experience as vice-president of corporate affairs at Aetna, was eager to take on the job. And while Ayer had its share of good marketing PR people, Capozzi knew he would need backup if the situation heated up. He called me in as an independent crisis consultant.

Even today, it is no easy matter to represent a condom maker. That simple latex sleeve provokes extraordinary controversy and ire. Powerful groups, including Catholics and Orthodox Jews, marshall their forces against it. However, the advent of AIDS and the courageous stance of former surgeon general C. Everett Koop to promote widespread use of condoms have since opened the subject to discussion. But, fearing reprisal, many influential publications and television networks continue to resist condom advertising.

While Lifestyles held only a small portion of the over-the-counter market (Trojans dominated the market with about 60 percent of sales), Ansell's modern manufacturing facilities in Dothan, Alabama, enabled it to produce vast quantities of unbranded product needed for hospitals and clinics throughout the country and, most important, to meet the requirements of a huge annual contract with the U.S. Agency for International Development (AID). The AID contract specified that the condoms had to be manufactured in the U.S. and were required to meet Food and Drug Administration (FDA) standards. Because the AID distributed product abroad, foreign competitors, notably the Japanese, were eager to carve off a piece of the AID contract, and had long been angling to modify the contract specifications regarding test standards and country of origin.

Latex condoms are amazingly strong: just ask any kid who has tried to blow one up to the bursting point or fill it with water until it is the size of a bed pillow. But in another sense, condoms are fragile: sensitive to heat, humidity, aridity, oxidation, sunlight, petroleum-based oils, animal fats, and contact with certain metals.

The manufacture of condoms is an exacting process. The product is considered a medical device, and its quality is therefore regulated by the FDA. U.S. condoms are formulated to meet stringent FDA standards. Testing is rigorous. Every condom made undergoes an electronic test for the presence of pinholes. Large batches of condoms are taken off line and subjected to water-filling and other tests. In fact, condom makers spend more money testing their product than manufacturing it.

For safety's sake, condoms are required to have an expiration date, after which they must not be sold or should not be used.

Ansell was very proud of its manufacturing facility and its quality control. In fact, Ansell was the only major condom manufacturer that had never — in more than 50 years — had a product recall.

In the early 1980s, the combined advertising expenditures for all U.S. condom manufacturers were estimated at $250,000. It was a classic push business: The manufacturers sold their products in large numbers to a relatively small group of distributors and dealers who, in turn, got it into the hands of retailers. But as the decade progressed, condom makers felt a need for greater visibility with the ultimate consumer. Thanks principally to increasing awareness of the efficacy of condoms in preventing AIDS and the growing volume of purchases by women, industrywide condom sales increased over 40 percent between 1986 and 1987. By 1987 advertising expenditures had risen to about $10 million.

Some of this growth could be attributed to former surgeon general Koop's highly publicized statement that, next to abstinence and mutually monogamous relationships, the use of condoms is the best means of preventing the sexual transmission of AIDS. In fact, in August 1988, Koop took the unprecedented action of mailing an AIDS-awareness booklet to every home in America.

The industry saw boom times ahead. In fact, one manufacturer was admonished in the press for saying what was on everyone's mind: "AIDS is a condom marketer's dream."

AIDS was, in fact, on everyone's mind. Condom makers were aggressively seeking promotional opportunities to boost sales even higher, but resistance to advertising and publicity remained high and somewhat puritanical. Even the liberal *New York Times* said, in 1988, "We accept condom advertising, provided the emphasis is on the prevention of disease." And many media would not take condom advertising under any circumstances. Koop, who had a $40 million advertising budget, was turned down by the networks when he tried to buy prime commercial time to promote condom use.

It wasn't until November 1988 that the three major networks agreed to air an Advertising Council public service campaign promoting the use of condoms in preventing sexual transmission of AIDS.

Having a modicum of brand awareness in the Lifestyles name, yet far behind Trojans, Sheiks, Ramses, and the other brands, Ansell felt that a strong advertising and promotional push would help it gain market share. Around January 1987, Lifestyles unveiled its "I'd do a lot for love but I'm not ready to die for it" print campaign, which won critical acclaim in the advertising community but couldn't get enough consumer exposure to build measurable awareness or sales.

In 1988 the company asked ad pro George Lois to develop a high-visibility television campaign. Lois forsook fear in favor of light comedy: "It's a matter of condom sense." The commercials were parodies: A male in a formal black cape, black slouch hat, and a half mask is taking his date to the opera ("But you didn't have to wear that mask to ask for them," says the saleswoman), and Azania, draped in a scanty leopard skin, swings into a drugstore on a vine to buy some mousse and some Lifestyles condoms ("Good thinking, Azania," says the salesman, "'cause it's a jungle out there.").

An example of Lifestyles advertising.

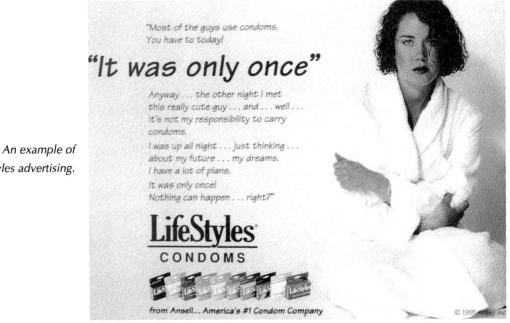

"Most of the guys use condoms. You have to today!

"It was only once"

Anyway . . . the other night I met this really cute guy . . . and . . . well . . . It's not my responsibility to carry condoms.

I was up all night . . . just thinking . . . about my future . . . my dreams. I have a lot of plans.

It was only once! Nothing can happen . . . right?"

LifeStyles
CONDOMS

from Ansell... America's #1 Condom Company

© 1991 Ansell Inc

A few cable stations accepted the commercials for broadcast, but the commercials probably got more exposure in news stories than they did as an actual campaign.

Despite the communications barriers, things seemed bright for Ansell and the industry in 1987–88. Demand was strong among homosexuals and heterosexuals alike. Then, unaccountably, sales flattened. Heterosexuals were concerned about AIDS, to be sure, but their panic was subsiding.

The Secret Government Study While condom sales were cooling down, some members of the media were heating up — in particular, a *Los Angeles Times* reporter named Allan Parachini. Parachini had at least one source who was feeding him the results of secret condom tests the FDA's National Institute of Health (NIH) had quietly commissioned from UCLA in the spring of 1987. In October, the industry learned a study was underway, but it was not privy to many of the details. Nor, it seemed, was the sponsor, the NIH.

The study, which UCLA farmed out to an organization called the Mariposa Foundation, was aimed at determining the effectiveness of latex condoms as a barrier against the spread of the HIV virus. The objectives of the study were certainly reasonable, but the way it was conceived, conducted, and communicated was not.

U.S. condom manufacturers knew that Japanese condom companies were trying to get a foothold on the West Coast and that they had close ties to Mariposa. In fact, one saline test Mariposa used was a Japanese procedure not required or approved by the FDA. It was said that Mariposa used one of the Japanese companies to test all companies' condoms in its American plant, which had recently been shut down by the FDA for manufacturing violations. Had Ansell known the nature of the study, it could have warned that substance used in the manufacture of Lifestyles — sal soda — caused false-positive results in this test.

Another nonstandard test in the UCLA study involved inflating condoms with air until they burst. In view of how condoms are used, this test, while dramatic, had long been questioned by the FDA and U.S. condom makers as a valid measure of condom strength. In short, the UCLA study was to use tests that were 1) of questionable validity, and 2) that U.S. condoms were never designed to pass.

Working through the Condom Task Force of the Health Industry Manufacturers Association (HIMA), the U.S. manufacturers lodged a protest with the NIH. Parachini got wind of their action and wrote an unflattering article whose focus was that U.S. condom makers were resisting the UCLA study.

In early June 1988 the industry heard that the study had been completed and that Trojans and Lifestyles had fared badly. In fact, the brands that scored best were from Japanese companies thought to have close relationships with Mariposa and whose products were formulated to pass Japanese tests.

The American companies were understandably upset. Ansell knew that a year or so earlier, scientifically valid tests conducted at the University of Colorado and the University of Massachusetts had confirmed that Lifestyles condoms were impermeable to the AIDS virus, and these findings had been presented at the Third Annual AIDS Conference in Washington in 1987. Now, the industry learned, results of the UCLA study were scheduled to be presented at the Fourth Annual AIDS Conference, in Stockholm, June 12–17, only one week hence.

Capozzi and I immediately found ourselves in an emergency meeting of the Condom Task Force called to address the UCLA issue. The other manufacturers and their PR counsel were represented. A lot of work would have to be done in a very short time. Under great pressure, each company developed its best arguments, gathered its materials, and made its strongest case.

At the Condom Task Force meeting, it was decided that HIMA would put together a briefing document for the FDA, NIH, and the surgeon general indicating that test protocols were flawed, that tests were conducted by competitors, and that, if results were made public, the resultant coverage would be enormously damaging to the government's AIDS-prevention program. Moreover, HIMA reminded the agency that the study was intended to study the resistance of latex condoms to the passage of HIV virus, not to rank brands.

It is difficult to be critical of, or even to take a strong stand against, a government agency that regulates your business. Companies fear retaliation: obstinacy, obstacles, and opposition. And for good reason. While political appointees come and go, an offended civil servant is entrenched, and can have a very long memory. But despite possible long-term repercussions, a confrontational approach may be needed when short-term stakes are high.

The strategy worked. The NIH advised UCLA that, while the Stockholm presentation could proceed (although results had presumably never been seen by the NIH nor undergone peer review), no brands were to be identified. Moreover, UCLA researchers were to present their findings to the FDA immediately upon their return from the conference. They were warned that under no circumstances were they to release their unsubstantiated findings publicly.

But release they did: they leaked the study to Parachini. On June 29, 1988, the *Los Angeles Times* ran a lengthy article by Parachini, complete with brand names and rankings. Capozzi and I urged HIMA to recommend that the FDA disavow the findings if queried by the media, which they may have done because, while the story saw some extension in Times-Mirror papers, notably the *Hartford Courant*, it received surprisingly little attention elsewhere.

Ansell and the manufacturer of Trojans breathed a sigh of relief. Presenting a solid front had served the industry well, and the condom makers continued to profess their solidarity. But Ansell, whose record of quality manufacturing had been unblemished for 50 years, was officially incensed. And so, it seemed, were the FDA, NIH, the surgeon general, and other government health officials who had very nearly been embarrassed publicly by UCLA.

But Ansell's indignation did little to avert damage in the marketplace. Copies of the Parachini article were everywhere, and, at the sales level, competitors were advising wholesalers and other distributors to avoid potential problems of handling inferior condoms. Of course, the Lifestyles brand was more vulnerable than the formidable Trojans.

Working closely with Ansell executives, Capozzi and I developed letters to dealers and distributors, and memos and notices to employees. We armed the company's salespeople with Q&A's covering the political, social, scientific, and technological issues. We couched arguments for them in sound bites. And all the while, we were advising the other agencies in New York and Australia of our progress.

Meanwhile, of course, the company was doing a full-court press on AID to ensure that the contract was in no jeopardy and that Ansell would be a welcome bidder in the next contract round. During July, in the midst of the furor, Capozzi and I worked toward strengthening the product's reputation and building a solid base of credibility for the future. We planned to submit a PR program to the client when the furor abated.

Based on the Parachini article, activist college students, principally on the West Coast, began to protest the sale of Lifestyles condoms in bookstores and vending machines, claiming they were inferior protection against AIDS. There were some graffiti scrawls but also a hint of conspiracy when anti-Lifestyles stickers began to appear on vending machines.

On August 9 the NIH cut off funding to UCLA. The action was welcomed by the U.S. condom makers, but the reason NIH gave was vexing. The NIH said the potential failure rate of all brands of condoms was much higher for anal sex than vaginal sex, so the study could mislead the gay community into thinking they were better-protected than they actually were. The NIH did not admit it had commissioned a flawed study, nor did it offend UCLA by challenging the integrity or validity of its research methods and procedures.

But the worst was over ... at least for a few weeks.

Capozzi and I continued to develop the communications plan, sending it back and forth to Australia for review. During this period, Campbell began work on a global crisis plan for the parent company, and we were closely involved in the drafting and review procedures.

The Recall

In late September 1988 a gentleman in Hawaii purchased a pack of Lifestyles brand Extra Strength condoms with Nonoxynol-9, Ansell's flagship product. Later (presumably), removing the condom from its foil wrapper, he found the product unusable, with holes where no holes were intended.

Perhaps the circumstances under which he discovered the flaw added to his annoyance, but he reported his findings immediately to the Hawaii Department of Health. That agency sought additional packages of the product, and soon confirmed that the problem was not an isolated incident. They contacted Ansell: it was the first the company had heard of the defect.

The Department of Health told Ansell they would recall the product from the market, but we suggested a voluntary withdrawal by the company. The agency agreed. Ansell coordinated with the FDA and followed its guidelines on recalls.

Within 24 hours, on October 5, Capozzi and I had prepared a recall notice, identifying two lots by number. We developed an extensive media list, hired a media distribution firm, prepared employee notices, reviewed customer letters, cleared the release with the firm's outside counsel, discussed the strategy with Australia, and released the story to the media.

The recall notice was distributed to the Associated Press, United Press International, and PR Newswire, as well as to local media where the company had plants and offices. We also targeted 40 major trade publications that would have even remotely been interested in the story.

The affected condoms had been distributed throughout the country, and Ansell did its best to call them in. Ansell people sent hundreds of letters to dealers and distributors, made scores of phone calls, and encouraged consumers who purchased the affected condoms to return them to the company for replacement or refund.

A product recall is not, in and of itself, a crisis. And certainly not in the condom business, which has issued recalls covering up to one percent of its annual output. The reason for this high figure, of course, is that when one condom is found defective, tens of thousands may be recalled.

Ansell was now somewhat agitated about its dealings with AID. An aborted university study that did not apply standard FDA procedures was one thing, but a major recall — and so soon after the UCLA hubbub — was quite another. Ansell was sensitive to the coverage the recall would generate.

To determine the impact of the communications effort, we contracted a clipping service to do a comprehensive sweep of daily papers over the next few days. No clippings were found. Not one.

Meanwhile, Ansell was conducting a exhaustive study into the cause of the product failure. The problem could have been a trace of copper in the Nonoxynol-9 spermicidal cream, or possibly the use of a petroleum-based lubricant in the machinery by an unenlightened employee. To ensure that all affected product was covered, the company bracketed the condom lots produced within a wide time frame as well as those lots that used a particular shipment of Nonoxynol-9. That double-bracketing led to a second recall notice, on October 11, of four additional lots. In all, 9,713 gross were affected. Once again, Capozzi and I made a thorough distribution of the recall notice, and once again a clippings search produced no clips.

It can be argued that all crises are media crises, meaning that without involvement of the media, there is no crisis. But that does not necessarily mean the media must have widespread circulation. Environmental, health, and other newsletters can reach targeted audiences and have a powerful impact on a crisis. Trade publications can reach selected groups, raising their awareness and sensitivity. And it only takes one article and one copying machine to get the news into the hands of the right people: regulators, distributors, activists, and others. Moreover, the mere fact of issuing a news release and sending copies to the FDA, NIH, and AID was tantamount to media involvement.

The battle soon broke out on another front. While the general public's fear of sexually transmitted AIDS was diminishing, the fear of contamination from other sources was not. So every health worker was expected to wear surgical gloves when in contact with patients. Like many other condom manufacturers, Ansell made latex surgical gloves as well. Manufacturers were having difficulty keeping up with demand. But if Ansell's condoms were "unsafe," insinuated the competitors, could their gloves be trusted?

It was clear that the UCLA study and the recall were being used by salespeople in the industry to beat Ansell in the marketplace. But the glove matter indicated that the broader reputation of the company was being undermined. Capozzi and I believed Ansell was a good company, and Lifestyles condoms were as good as anything on the market. The company was just having a series of bad breaks. The extensive public relations program we had prepared would help Ansell regain its footing. It would strengthen the company's reputation in the marketplace and with the regulatory agencies, and boost the morale of company employees.

In it, we proposed, among other things, 1) media tours of the company's manufacturing facilities; 2) a media seminar on AIDS that would travel to four major media centers; and 3) a long-range non-publicity public relations campaign. This campaign would be aimed at priming the media environment for accepting product publicity produced by Ayer and others. It would encourage media inquiries by positioning the company as expert in the field of condoms and AIDS, as well as other STDs; build the company's image in various markets, among key customers and public policy decision makers; and help the company assume a position of leadership within the industry so that its views and position would have an impact commensurate with its size, energy, and integrity.

The elements of the program included op-ed ads; op-ed articles; a speakers bureau for use by Ansell people before dealer and distributor groups, local business and community leaders, and health groups; a videotape useful both as a sales tool and as a visual aid in interviews; speeches and classroom presentations; and the development of a program to handle future crises.

We completed a working draft of the program in late July, right about the time we learned that *Consumer Reports* was planning a major article on condoms for its March 1989 issue. The industry had known about it for several months.

Consumer Reports Prepares Condom Issue

Nearly a decade earlier, in November 1979, the venerable *Consumer Reports* had run its first condom ratings. At that time, a private company called Akwell protested the low rating of its product on technical grounds, and, in March 1980, won what has been characterized as the first-ever retraction from the magazine. Akwell and its Lifestyles brand were subsequently purchased by Ansell to become Ansell-Americas.

Now, in March 1988, Ansell and the other condom makers learned that *CR* was planning to run its second condom rating a year hence. But subsequent events — in particular, the UCLA study and the recall — had diverted Ansell's attention from the matter.

Not that there's much that can be done about *Consumer Reports*. *CR* tests product it buys on the open market. Often it uses questionnaires to survey its readership (an Ansell memo noted that *CR*'s readership averages over 30 years in age, and is an economically upscale group, which is hardly a valid demographic cross section of condom users).

Reporter Bill Appel, who was preparing the *Consumer Reports* article, had called HIMA and the various companies with technical questions regarding condoms. The companies, including Ansell, had showered Appel with information, including articles, papers, research, and anything else they could find that would educate him about the value of condoms. They paid particular attention to disease prevention, which was the direction in which Appel seemed to be taking the story.

By midsummer 1988 the industry learned that CR was using outside contractors for some of its work, including a laboratory funded by one of the Japanese companies. It appeared that the magazine was planning to conduct air-inflation tests as well as the same saline test that had given false indications of pinholes in Lifestyles condoms back in 1979. In addition, the readership questionnaire was being administered by none other than the Mariposa Foundation.

The matter was turned over to HIMA, which wrote a letter to *Consumer Reports*, advising the magazine of the necessity of using standardized FDA tests and challenging the kind of procedures it was planning to use.

By the time Ansell emerged from the turmoil of the UCLA study and the product recall, the opportunity may already have passed to affect the *Consumer Reports* story (if any opportunity ever existed). The industry was deeply concerned. Once again, members of HIMA agreed to put up a united front while each company planned its own strategy.

With the companies' help, HIMA developed a fact book that might have been carried around in a wheelbarrow. It contained all the usual materials, plus an extensive list of audiences, with different messages tailored for each audience, depending on the outcome of the article. Back at Ayer's offices, Capozzi and I did the same for Ansell, gathering materials from the company and our own files, and enlisting the help of the Ayer's media people. Our own fact book was no less extensive than the industry's. We were ready for anything, we thought.

By late fall, a rumor began to spread that Lifestyles had not done well in *CR*'s tests. Ansell used every means at its disposal to confirm the validity of these stories but was unable to penetrate the CR wall. There was nothing tangible to go on, and Ansell was understandably paranoic at this stage. The company began to speculate about possible reasons why it had possibly rated badly in whatever tests *CR* may or may not have conducted. Sal soda? Japanese standards? Air inflation? And then an unnerving thought dawned on the company: What if *Consumer Reports* had picked up some of the company's recalled product for testing? Ansell placed a hurried call to Appel, and after several days of consideration, the magazine provided the serial numbers of the five Lifestyles lots it had tested. Three of the five were from Ansell's recalled batches.

These events transpired during October and November, and *CR*'s condom article was scheduled to appear in the March issue. Even allowing for the fact that the publication would be mailed in the middle of February, there were still at least two, and possibly three, months in which an unfortunate error could be corrected. The company appealed, implored, and applied every form of pressure it could, but to no avail. The magazine stonewalled, saying it was too late to make any changes. But Appel was still interviewing in early December, so the story could not have been entirely wrapped up. And still we were uncertain of Appel's tack, the specific methodology used, or how Lifestyles condoms ranked.

Without that knowledge, Ansell was whistling in the dark. Capozzi and I prepared as many strategies as there were possible permutations: our statements were, variously, shocked and dismayed, pleased, outraged, and gratified, and ranged all the way from a bellow to silence. All the while, we pressed Ansell to undertake the overall communications campaign we had developed to build credibility and strengthen the company's position regardless of the outcome of the *Consumer Reports* article.

On January 27, 1989, predicated on the belief that the *Consumer Reports* article would generate negative fallout even if the coverage was predominantly positive, the HIMA public relations committee met to plot its strategy. Assignments given out to employees of the member companies included:

- Coalition-building and third-party endorsements.

- Developing a policy statement on testing.

- Developing a policy statement on quality.

- Preparing Q&A's.

- Writing a counter news release, based on most likely negatives.

- Conducting a spokesperson training refresher.

- Conducting advance meetings with science and medical writers.

- Compiling a condom briefing book.

- Collecting footage of manufacturing and testing operations.

CR Gives Lifestyles Bad Rating

By early February word began to trickle out, principally through regulatory sources, that the story was strongly positive about condoms. And, HIMA learned, "the only thing adverse in the story is about Lifestyles." So much for HIMA solidarity. Support at HIMA evaporated overnight. Ansell's competitors could hardly be blamed for leaving the company to twist in the wind. If the information were true, the efficacy of condoms had been confirmed, and the fact that one brand scored low was simply a cruel reality.

Consumer Reports scheduled a news conference for Wednesday, February 15, to announce the results of the study. By the prior Friday, Capozzi and I had contacted the assistant director of Consumers Union (*CR*'s parent organization) responsible for communications to get an advance copy of the story. We were allowed to pick one up on Tuesday, but no earlier. But we already knew the story. The prior week, the entire story had been read to HIMA by a source at one of the regulatory agencies.

The results were in, and Ansell's worst fears were realized. Ansell's leading product was called "grossly defective," although the identical product, without Nonoxynol-9, was ranked in the superior group.

As usual, "Good Morning America" consumer editor John Stossel (whose wife held a senior position at *Consumer Reports*) had the story a day earlier than the rest of the media.

There is an old saying in the public relations business that it is not wise to argue with someone who buys ink by the barrel. But this time, Capozzi and I believed, the client had to take up arms. We were girded for a fight. We had answers to every question *CR* raised and many they hadn't. And we felt we had them on a couple of serious breaches of ethics, not counting the leak to Stossel.

First, if a magazine is dealing with a material matter that concerns a publicly traded company, is it acting honorably by releasing the information selectively and providing certain individuals with advance information on the subject? Stossel aside, several people in government had sufficient advance warning to act on that information, as did members of HIMA and Ansell's own competitors.

The second breach requires some backgrounding: When we asked the assistant director of Consumers Union to justify inclusion of a recalled product in its tests, and thereby risk damaging the product's reputation and the company's business, he said that *Consumer Reports* had a duty to its readers and the general public to reveal potential health hazards, especially in light of the AIDS epidemic. Our questions to him were: If public health were *CR*'s concern, and lives were involved, why did *Consumer Reports* wait several months to hold a press conference to report its findings? Or, in fact, did the magazine simply need a dramatic case to hype its March issue? We received no answer.

Despite our knowledge of the story, Capozzi and I were hobbled by not knowing how *Consumer Reports* was going to handle the Lifestyles ranking at its news conference. We were prepared for the worst, and we got it.

Simultaneous with *Consumer Reports*'s press conference and news release, Ansell released its own story challenging the magazine's findings on several counts discussed earlier. From a scientific point of view, the most damaging may have been that *CR* extrapolated results from an insufficient statistical sampling. In the scientific community, this fact, which was confirmed by the FDA, would have been enough to invalidate *CR*'s research.

Despite *CR*'s protestations that its story was a positive one, the media did what the media does: highlight the negative. The Associated Press referred to the Lifestyles rating high up in the story, as did *USA Today* and many other newspapers and magazines. Capozzi's heated jab to the media, "*Consumer Reports* does not understand condoms," got some play of its own.

Other communications had been prepared and were ready for the *CR* release. Memos to its employees and letters to 2,500 customers were sent that day, telling Ansell's side of the story and blasting *Consumer Reports*. Personal calls were made that day to contacts at the FDA, NIH, AID, and others, following up on earlier contacts that had forewarned them of the result of the *CR* study. Capozzi and I pressed for a letter to the head of Consumers Union detailing our position and the specific flaws in the article and in the treatment of Ansell throughout the process.

In a rare moment in communications history, Capozzi and I (the public relations and crisis management people) suggested the possibility of a lawsuit to embarrass *Consumer Reports* and to provide a platform for public statements excoriating the magazine for its loss of credibility and integrity. But true to form, lawyers disagreed with communicators. The company's outside legal counsel thought more could be gained by negotiating with *CR*'s outside counsel. Communications people were not welcome at these meetings, of course.

Capozzi and I remain convinced that the aggressive strategy was the right one, and were frustrated at the company's acquiescence to the advice of legal counsel. The matter had come down to "our lawyers against theirs," with both sides arguing legalities. But we knew Consumer Reports had won virtually every legal battle it had ever fought, and this cordial negotiation wouldn't even leave it winded. We believed the proper strategy was not based on legal arguments but on a challenge to the magazine's integrity and prestige, where we felt it was highly vulnerable. In the end, Consumers Union did not concede a single point to Ansell's attorneys, and the matter was quietly dropped.

Aftermath   The hardest lesson for client and practitioner alike is that some crises are so big, so ugly, so fast-changing, and so expensive to fight, the most feasible goal is not solution, but survival.

The people at Ansell were smart, strategic, aggressive, tough marketers. When, ultimately, they concluded they might win the battle but lose the war, they chose survival. Looking back, our approach to handling these crises evolved as events unfolded, but they were built on three core strategies:

> • *Solidarity.* Because there were broad issues involved — and our client was not a dominant force in the industry — we championed a strong industry front in dealings with media and regulatory agencies. This was not an easy sell in a group of independent, entrepreneurial types, but an unusually assertive and proficient association staff helped this strategy work.

- *Self-Protection.* Because the reputation of the company and its products was being assailed, we took positions that were "assertively protective." Despite our desire to educate journalists, customers, and employees in advance of attacks, we often had to wait for bad news to get a platform for our statements. And the adversaries kept changing. So whenever "they" took a shot at us, we fired a salvo. We called it counterpunching.

- *Direct Contact.* Because the company had little media clout but a lot of business credibility, and because it dealt with a relatively small universe of customers and employees, we advocated an affirmative program of direct contact. This included face-to-face meetings, phone calls, direct mail (and memos), and other means to encourage dialogue and provide the opportunity to answer questions.

Certain background elements of these condom crises remain an enigma. Someone, somewhere may understand all the convolutions, complexities, and even conspiracies, but the consultants who handled communications during these crises — Lou Capozzi and me — had to operate with the information available to us.

In the client's view, we had done an excellent job. The head of marketing, who was our key contact with Ansell, said we had turned a potential disaster into a position from which the company could regroup and recover. "Without you," he said, "it could have been an overwhelming debacle."

There was some marketing erosion, of course, and competitors continued their sharp practices in the marketplace. But the majority of customers remained loyal, and the AID contract was, at least for the moment, preserved.

Alfred Geduldig established the consulting firm of Geduldig Communications Management, Inc. in 1988 after three years as president of Chester Burger Co. For more than two decades as a senior executive in corporate communications, public affairs, and management consulting, he has helped management define and achieve internal and external communications objectives in media, marketing, crisis management, environmental matters, investor relations, image and reputation, corporate identity, agency selection, organization, and publications. Recent clients served include Aetna, American Express, Apple, Carrier, First Nationwide, BF Goodrich, GTE, Levi Strauss, Lufthansa, Manville, Miles, MONY, MCI, Ocean Spray, Union Carbide, Waste Management, and the AARP. His career has included positions at Mobil, where he was an architect of its public relations program, including "Masterpiece Theatre" and op-ed advertising. He helped guide Mobil's communications through such public relations crises as the Arab-Israeli Wars and gasoline shortages. As vice-president, public affairs, at GAF, he helped negotiate the sale of its asbestos mine.

A Red Herring in

the Chicken Coop

Jane E. Redicker
Vice-President, Fleishman-Hillard, Inc.

On March 29, 1987, CBS's "60 Minutes" featured a segment that would become a defining moment for poultry producers throughout the United States. This 20-minute broadcast marked the first serious public threat to a product that had become increasingly popular with American consumers.

Overview

Titled simply "One Out of Three," the segment reported that 30 percent of chicken sold in the U.S. was "contaminated with harmful salmonella bacteria." It focused on allegations made by a disgruntled former U.S. Department of Agriculture poultry grader, a handful of government inspectors, and a former employee at a processing plant in the Midwest. They charged that the USDA's inspection system had become "increasingly lax," allowing poultry companies to "routinely violate health standards" and "ship products tainted with harmful bacteria." They further pointed to chicken as the culprit in a "dramatic increase" in reported cases of food-borne illness.

Following the broadcast, the industry faced an onslaught of negative publicity repeating the charges and questioning the safety of eating chicken. The industry was caught by surprise and astounded by the misinformation, half-truths, and false conclusions contained in the charges. The immediate priority for the National Broiler Council, the industry's trade association, and PR agency Fleishman-Hillard was finding a way to help protect sales. Yet as these efforts evolved, it soon became obvious that the "60 Minutes" crisis had merely been the first salvo of what would become an ongoing attack on both the government's meat and poultry inspection program and the poultry industry — an attack that those inside and close to the industry believe is nothing more than a red herring dragged in by elements of organized labor who were looking to expand their ranks.

Working on behalf of the National Broiler Council, Fleishman-Hillard undertook a year-long public relations effort that succeeded in helping the industry achieve its initial goal of maintaining chicken's popularity with consumers and its strength in the marketplace. What has evolved is an ongoing crisis and issues management communications program that continues today.

Fowl Fiend or Fried Chicken? By the mid-1980s, the U.S. poultry industry had become one of the beneficiaries of an increasing interest in health and nutrition. In 1986 the average American consumed 55.4 pounds of chicken. Industry sales topped $12 billion at wholesale. Low-fat, nutritious, economical, and versatile, chicken was well on its way to becoming America's favorite meat. The industry had become a marketing success. But it was ill-prepared to face the kind of threat to its product's image posed by the allegations in the "60 Minutes" piece.

Because the impact of negative media coverage was felt throughout the entire industry, not just the company singled out by "60 Minutes," the job of leading an effort to counter the problem fell to the National Broiler Council. Yet the association had even less experience than the member companies in dealing with this kind of media crisis. The situation was even more challenging because it was clear early on that the real target of the attack was the USDA, which is charged with inspecting all meat and poultry marketed in the United States. Yet the Department was not aggressively stepping forward to defend its inspection system.

At the same time, surrounding the "60 Minutes" broadcast were other events that seemed timed to fuel media interest in the inspection system and the industry. The previous Friday, March 27, a whistleblower advocacy group, Government Accountability Project (GAP), issued a news release embargoed for publication until Monday morning. The release included the same charges made on "60 Minutes." Written on behalf of a handful of poultry inspectors, it placed the blame for the alleged shortcomings on the USDA's initiatives to improve and streamline the meat and poultry inspection system — initiatives that would, in effect, move away from the current labor-intensive system to one based on scientific testing and risk analysis. That same day, Senator Patrick Leahy of Vermont offered a floor statement citing affidavits from the same USDA poultry inspectors who alleged that the USDA was "gutting the inspection system."

A week later, representatives of GAP and the American Federation of Government Employees (AFGE), the union that represents USDA inspectors, generated more negative publicity when they testified before the House Agriculture Subcommittee on Livestock, Dairy, and Poultry. Resulting media coverage included further allegations of a deteriorating inspection system and "filthy" conditions in chicken processing plants.

By early May, the National Broiler Council had commissioned a consumer survey to assess the extent of the damage to the reputation of both the industry and its products. The results were as expected. The "60 Minutes" broadcast and ensuing negative publicity had heightened consumers' awareness of salmonella on chicken and negatively affected both consumption of chicken and confidence in the existing inspection system. Within one month, the National Broiler Council retained Fleishman-Hillard and I joined the firm shortly thereafter. It was no surprise that what most of Council's member companies really wanted us to do was make the bad publicity go away. That would be easier said than done. For the moment, we needed to start damage control and lay the groundwork for efforts to restore public confidence in chicken.

Media Roast

We realized that our first priority was to begin steps to correct and stop the flow of misinformation in the media. We had to get out the facts quickly, with the ultimate goal of reassuring consumers that they could continue to enjoy chicken. We also knew this would be an uphill battle. This was not a one-time media crisis. Instead, it appeared to be a carefully orchestrated campaign that was working. The industry's critics had already seized control of the debate and they had a story that the media couldn't resist. Articles seemed to appear everywhere. Coverage was mostly negative and singled out chicken as the primary culprit for food-borne illness from salmonella. These quotes represent some of the more benign examples of what we faced:

> *Americans concerned about their diet are eating less red meat and more chicken these days, but the evidence is now clear that what's eaten in the interest of health can also make you sick. The problem lies mainly in how chickens are processed and later prepared.* —Los Angeles Times, May 19, 1987

> *Flaws in the federal inspection process allow millions of chickens tainted with ... disease-inducing germs to reach American consumers each year, a top Agriculture Department official acknowledged yesterday.* —Washington Post, June 3, 1987

The latter quote appeared subsequent to a June 2 House Agriculture Subcommittee on Livestock, Dairy, and Poultry hearing on modernizing the USDA meat and poultry inspection system. Among those on the witness list were representatives of AFGE and the first two consumer groups to join labor concerns in criticizing the USDA and the industry — the Community Nutrition Institute and Public Voice for Food and Health Policy.

If we were to be successful, our communications strategy had to combine reactive, responsive tactics with aggressive media and consumer education efforts. After "60 Minutes," the industry had virtually shut down to the media. Who could blame member companies? They marketed their products under brand names and didn't want to be connected with yet another "dirty chicken" story. Reporters who did try to contact companies for comment got one of three responses. Their calls were not returned. They heard "no comment." Or they were referred to the National Broiler Council. The first two created what every public relations professional dreads — an atmosphere of stonewalling that leads the media to believe you really do have something to hide. The third caused a deluge of media inquiries for which neither we nor the National Broiler Council were yet prepared.

Our job was to get out the truth and correct misinformation. Part of the problem was that most of the critic's charges often contained a grain of truth. However, they also omitted a lot. It was true, for example, that the Centers for Disease Control (CDC) statistics showed an increase in reported food-borne illness in the U.S. It was also true that chicken consumption was at an all-time high. But there was no evidence of a meaningful connection between these two facts. Even some CDC experts admitted that their data may not reflect an increase in food-borne illness, but instead, a vastly improved system of identifying and collecting data on food-borne illness in the U.S.

Also, poultry industry critics' success was enhanced, in part, by the unavoidable fact that any effort to describe the details of how animals are killed and processed for human consumption is unattractive, to say the least. Recognizing this, poultry companies have never talked about the details of how and why current processing methods developed. As a result, when images of chicken processing were shown on TV or in articles, it was easy for reporters and consumers to be persuaded that something was wrong with all this.

Allaying Consumer Fears Our challenge was to develop a strategy that would communicate truth about chicken, salmonella, and food-borne illness and, at the same time, effectively allay consumers' fears about eating chicken. The first priority was to find out what kinds of messages would accomplish this objective. Later, we would address some of the specific misinformation being perpetuated.

One of our first actions was to arrange a series of consumer focus groups to reassess the impact of negative media attention and to test our messages. We found that most people responded positively to one reassuring message: Making sure your food is safe is really simple. Just cook it. And, don't let raw meat come into contact with any foods you don't plan to cook. That became the basis for our consumer education efforts.

Our challenge was to convince consumers that they need not worry about salmonella and chicken, but to do so in a way that would not bring more attention to questions about the safety issue. Therefore, we decided our consumer education program would focus on three areas:

- Educating consumers that salmonella is a common bacteria found on all fresh animal products and that normal cooking destroys the bacteria and eliminates the need for concern about food-borne illness.

- Reminding consumers of simple food handling and preparation techniques.

- Balancing information about food safety with health and nutrition messages to reinforce the industry's position of strength.

Safe Chicken Strategy

The centerpiece of our consumer education campaign was a national media tour featuring two well-known experts in food handling and preparation. From a list of chefs and cooks who featured chicken in many of their recipes, we selected Kathleen Perry, author of a cookbook entitled *the everyday gourmet,* and Merle Ellis, who appears as "The Butcher" in his syndicated food column.

Perry would demonstrate how to prepare simple, quick, and delicious chicken dishes from her cookbook, making sure she wove into her instructions our basic safe food handling messages. Ellis was the showman. He could cut up a chicken in 30 seconds and debone a whole chicken in two minutes — all the while talking about food safety in the kitchen.

Their messages were simple and reinforced the overall program strategies:

- If you cook your chicken, you'll never have to worry about salmonella.

- Don't cut up foods like lettuce for the salad with the same knife or cutting board you used for the chicken.

- Take the same easy precautions with beef, pork, fish, and other meat, because they too can have salmonella on their surfaces.

Before we took our show on the road, we conducted a day-long media training session with Perry and Ellis to work on messages, give them an understanding of the USDA inspection system, and prepare them to handle questions about some of the charges made by industry critics. The next day, we traveled to North Carolina to tour a chicken processing operation. We wanted Perry and Ellis to have a full understanding of how chickens are produced and processed so they could speak confidently from firsthand experience about the "sanitary conditions" in a chicken plant.

Our first placement was an August 26, 1987, appearance by Perry on "CBS This Morning." The positive reception she received from the show's hosts would set the stage for the rest of a 21-city tour over the next eight months. We traveled to large- and medium-sized markets, booking at least one television appearance (noon news, morning talk, cooking show, or cable programming) plus a series of print and radio interviews on each stop.

Early in the tour, the impact of negative publicity on the poultry industry was quite clear. Despite the fact that in pitching appearances, we never mentioned the word "salmonella" — in keeping with the industry's desire that we not raise the specter of the issue — every reporter or producer with whom we spoke asked whether Perry and Ellis could address how to avoid bacteria and food-borne illness.

The good news was, we often found reporters or particularly talk show hosts who helped carry the message for us. In a September 30 appearance on "AM Los Angeles" host Steve Edwards asked Ellis, "So, what about salmonella?" Before Ellis could respond, co-host Cristina Ferrare piped up, "Just cook your chicken! What's the big deal?" That comment set the tone of the segment and opened the door for Ellis to point out that, not just chicken, but all fresh meat, fish or pork — indeed virtually everything — can have salmonella on it. He explained that all the chef has to do is cook it and make sure to use different utensils and cutting boards to prepare raw foods like salads.

Cookbook author Kathleen Perry (right) with WAGA-TV's Sharon Summers on "Eyewitness News at Noon" in Atlanta, Ga.

The next day, across the country in Atlanta, we faced one of every PR person's nightmares — having your client bumped by breaking news. We'd spent hours selling this soft story of quick, economical ways busy consumers can prepare healthy chicken dishes and had succeeded in landing an October 1 appearance on the only noon news show in Atlanta. Perry, all set up with her cutting board, utensils, cooking and serving dishes, and just-out-of-the-oven sample for the host to taste, was scheduled to appear just after the news update. About halfway through local run-down, the wires started ticking with news of an earthquake in Los Angeles. Within moments, we were politely told that our appearance had just been cancelled.

Maybe it was because the crew liked Perry's chicken roll-ups so much. Maybe they realized that since Georgia is one of the top-producing poultry states, this was an important story. Whatever the reason, the station rescheduled our appearance the next day. In addition to this high-profile media tour, we took a number of additional steps to place reassuring messages in front of consumers. To reach beyond the major markets to food, consumer, and nutrition writers with whom we could not arrange interviews in our target cities, we wrote and distributed a kit of information that included:

- A "Consumer Guide to the Care and Cooking of Chicken" that provided simple, reassuring food preparation tips for all raw foods.

- A fact sheet on salmonella.

- Nutritional information on chicken.

- Answers to the most commonly asked questions about chicken, salmonella, and food safety, including information about the industry's efforts to assure product quality and safety.

Repackaging the information from the media kit, we also developed a mailing targeted to reach rural America. As a former 4-H club member, I knew every county in the country has a team of "county agents," or cooperative extension specialists in agriculture and home economics, who provide information and assistance to rural communities. I also remembered that Marge Klink, our home economics agent back in Jackson County, Indiana, had a weekly radio broadcast and a column in the local newspapers. Food safety would be a perfect topic for Klink — and hundreds of other home economists just like her.

Working with the USDA Cooperative Extension Service, we arranged to make our information kit available to all poultry and home economics cooperative extension specialists. This was among our most successful outreach activities, resulting in impressive coverage in local newspaper columns across the country.

Speaking for the Industry

At the same time we were working to reassure consumers through the media tour and other positive outreach efforts, we had to deal with a steady drumbeat of media events in which the industry's critics — almost always labor-related — repeated their charges. One of the agency's first tasks was establishing a news bureau to assist the National Broiler Council in effectively managing the day-to-day media coverage of the issues. At least one story was in the works each week during the beginning of the crisis. Armed with a series of statements on steps the industry takes to assure product quality and safety, facts about salmonella and other meats, descriptions of how food-borne illness data is collected, and a host of other topics, we attempted to get the industry's perspective included in every story possible. We also arranged telephone interviews or one-on-ones with the Broiler Council's food science expert whenever we found a willing reporter.

Our goal was to begin encouraging more balance in the coverage. Sometimes we were successful. Sometimes not. Often stories ran without any evident attempt to present industry comment. We spent a lot of time writing letters to the editor or to individual reporters during those early months. Not that we really expected many to be published, but we hoped, at least, to set the facts straight with the reporter, in anticipation that he or she would do another story. Each letter closed with an invitation to call the National Broiler Council any time the reporter wanted to write about the chicken industry.

Speaking on behalf of an industry trade association presented an interesting communications challenge — one I'm not sure we were ever able to overcome. Unlike speaking for an individual company where the spokesperson can refute specific charges with facts, we had to respond in very general terms while speaking for the national organization representing some 95 percent of the industry. While accurate, our answers and our overall messages were never as strong as I would have liked. Quite simply, it was hard to sound credible, and not sound like you were just mouthing the company line.

The Neverending Challenge Fueling the continued negative media coverage of the industry were a series of events, each of which created a forum from which the industry's critics could repeat their charges.

The week of July 2, four months after the "60 Minutes" broadcast, we learned that a coalition of labor and consumer groups, including AFGE and GAP, had scheduled a news conference for July 7 to demand that the USDA require warning labels on all fresh poultry. The news conference never materialized. It would have occurred during the week that Oliver North's testimony at the Iran-Contra hearings dominated the media.

What did occur right before the Fourth of July — historically the day of the year more chicken is consumed than any other — was a news conference in which the Community Nutrition Institute, who had joined labor critics at a hearing the previous month, called for a consumer boycott of poultry "until the poultry industry and the Department of Agriculture take steps to eliminate bacterial contamination of poultry and poultry products." We covered the news conference and issued a statement assuring consumers about the safety of eating chicken and questioning the timing of the announcement. Coverage was inappreciable and the boycott never materialized.

Later that month, on July 21, a coalition of consumer, labor, and whistleblower protection groups announced their proposals for strengthening the USDA's food inspection system. The stated purpose of the news conference, held at AFGE's office, was "to make the public aware of the crisis faced in meat and poultry inspection process in the country."

Kenneth Blaylock, national AFGE president, Tom Devine, legal affairs director for GAP, and Delmar Jones, president of the National Joint Council of Meat and Poultry Inspection Locals, were joined by representatives of CNI and the National Consumers League.

They contrasted the dramatic increases in chicken production and consumption with a decrease in the number of inspectors. They criticized the USDA's move toward a more science-based inspection system, which they said would rely less on visual inspections and more on microbiological testing and risk analysis. In short, they misrepresented what the Department was attempting to do. The bottom line of their proposals was to keep the inspectors on the line and in the plant.

Part of our success in responding to other news conferences and events had been the ability to monitor the proceedings and review media materials, then quickly develop an industry statement on the issues. This event presented a somewhat different obstacle, since it was held at AFGE headquarters and closed to all but credentialed media. We finally found a way to get someone in who recorded the presentation, obtained copies of the handouts, and identified reporters who were there. Back at the office, we quickly developed a statement from the industry and distributed it to media who attended the news conference and to selected Washington-based agricultural media.

Initially, I think we all hoped that the "60 Minutes" broadcast and ensuing barrage of negative coverage would be a short-lived crisis event. We hoped that through our consumer education effort and an aggressive media response system we would be effective in laying the issue to rest. Yet when the attacks on the industry and the inspection system didn't stop, when the same players continued to repeat their charges in forum after forum, and when their momentum increased as consumer groups joined the original labor critics, we had to take another look at the situation. What was really going on here?

Anatomy of a Red Herring

If the critics' allegations were true, why weren't chicken companies being overwhelmed with complaints from people who claimed they got sick from eating chicken? There wasn't evidence that consumers were complaining, to either their retailers or brand name companies — even the increased publicity wasn't matched by an increased number of customer complaints.

Logic told us something else was at play here. Since we could find no evidence of an increase in human illness directly attributable to chicken, we began to suspect that the focus on food safety was merely a red herring — this time, an effort to divert attention toward an issue that would further the motives of those responsible for the diversion. Because the initial criticisms came from labor activists within the ranks of USDA inspectors, we decided to take a closer look at what was going on within the USDA.

We learned that during the late 1970s and early 1980s the Department had been exploring improvements in meat and poultry inspection to incorporate scientific advances made in the years since the current system was adopted in 1957. (That system requires that every chicken be inspected after slaughter and that an inspector be present in every facility where chicken in processed. This is in addition to the bird-by-bird inspectors.) As a committee on the National Academy of Sciences (NAS) pointed out in a report on federal poultry inspection, "the current visual inspection system was not designed to detect microorganisms." NAS recommended a move toward a risk-assessment model for poultry inspection, incorporating hazard analysis and critical control point monitoring — a system more like that by which the FDA inspects and monitors the safety of all other food produced in the U.S.

In 1986, Congress gave the USDA the authority to vary the type of inspection in meat processing plants, depending on the product, the compliance history of the plant, and the commitment of plant management to control its operations. Although the agency already had this authority for poultry plants, it did not want to use it in the absence of similar authority for red meat plants. With this legislation, the USDA would have been able to make the kinds of changes modern science supported — changes that could threaten jobs of meat and poultry inspectors. However, the act was never implemented.

Buffeted through the 1980's by budgetary anxieties and threats of temporary shutdowns, job security had become an increasing concern within the ranks of USDA inspectors. Continuing maintenance of the USDA's labor-intensive inspection program reflected considerable public investment, particularly compared with other food safety programs. (The budget for the Food Safety Inspection Service of the USDA, which oversees only meat and poultry inspection, was roughly seven times that of FDA, which has responsibility for all other food inspection.)

The 1986 legislation, current and former USDA officials told us, fueled already strong opposition from leaders within the ranks of the poultry inspectors' union. What we were facing, they believed, was a steady, rear-guard effort to undermine the successful implementation of a streamlined inspection system. Labor's objective was to shift the focus to food safety and position the inspector as the lonely figure in assuring that giant corporations don't get away with short-changing the consumer.

Understanding this backdrop didn't cause us to alter our basic strategy. But it did help the industry realize that whatever we did, we would not be able to quickly make all the bad publicity go away. We were reminded of that shortly before Labor Day.

In late August, while we were on the way to our tour of a chicken processing operation with Perry and Ellis, we learned that "60 Minutes" scheduled a rebroadcast of "One Out of Three" on Sunday, September 5, the day before Labor Day, the second most popular day of the year for chicken consumption. From a phone booth in the Charlotte, North Carolina, airport, we began attempts to dissuade CBS producers from rerunning the show. When it appeared that our efforts were to no avail, we burned the midnight oil in our hotel room, developing a letter that highlighted the errors and misrepresentations in the original segment. With the client's approval the next morning, we dictated the letter back to the office and sent it off to CBS, urging that they provide some balance to the story by including our rebuttal in the rebroadcast. When they refused, we responded with yet another letter, this time addressed to the show's Mailbag section.

"60 Minutes" Revisited

Fortunately for the industry, the rebroadcast had little if any impact on consumers. And it did not immediately generate a second wave of negative media interest. Was our program, still in its relative infancy, working? Were people getting fed up with food scare stories? Were we lucky? We weren't sure, but at this point, we'd take every break we could get.

Shortly after the "60 Minutes" rebroadcast, we got a call from reporter David Beeder, of the *Omaha World Herald*. He'd heard about the show, but hadn't seen it. Did we have a tape? he wanted to know. And, would we watch it with him and talk to him about our reaction? A bit uncomfortable with the prospect, but committed to cooperate with the media in an effort to get out the facts, we agreed.

Negative Coverage Continues

"USDA Calls Chicken Safe Despite Publicity," read the headline of his October 4 story. Quoting the late Dr. Donald Houston, then head of the USDA's Food Safety and Inspection Service, Beeder's lead began, "Despite televised reports about problems with federal inspection of poultry, Americans have no reason to worry about eating chicken that is well cooked." He went on to report that a "long-running USDA dispute with a government labor group may have helped stir publicity about the presence of salmonella in some poultry." Still quoting Houston, he wrote, "...members of the American Federation of Government Employees have used the salmonella problem to publicize their disagreement with changes the USDA has made in the inspection system in the last 10 years." Unfortunately, that story was a rare exception to the approach most of the media took. Continued labor activities guaranteed a steady drumbeat of negative coverage.

The continuing negative coverage in 1987 also attracted a number of less-than-ethical opportunists, attempting to take advantage of the industry's unfortunate position. One of the most blatant was a fledgling microbiology firm that began marketing an instant salmonella test for consumers. "Chik Chek," according to the company's release, was a "breakthrough in the battle against food poisoning." The company generated a flurry of publicity through its release and a considerable number of consumer inquiries when ads for the product began appearing. But it was gone from the horizon a couple of months later after the USDA announced that tests on the product showed it to be "ineffective and unreliable." The kit registered a positive finding from plain tap water.

In mid-December, we faced what appeared to be another coordinated effort by labor elements to generate unfavorable coverage of the USDA and the industry. On December 14, GAP, on behalf of seven other organizations, made public a letter petitioning the USDA to "commission a study by NAS of the relation between federal poultry inspection methods and microbial contamination." The request was made despite the fact that NAS had already conducted a study and issued a report earlier that year calling for a more scientific, risk-assessment model for meat and poultry inspection.

GAP also chose the occasion to lead off its fundraising letter by calling chicken "a lethal substance in your refrigerator," and seeking contributions to support "some courageous people who work in (chicken) plants and who have personally witnessed the shameful wrongdoings in them." The next day, we learned that GAP, AFGE, the Food and Allied Services Trade Department of the AFL-CIO, UFCW, and a few consumer groups had distributed a mailgram to House and Senate conferees calling for a tightening of poultry inspection regulations.

None of these efforts generated much publicity, but we were troubled by something we found in the mailgram. For the first time, the American Association of Retired Persons (AARP) appeared on the list of consumer supporters.

We immediately arranged a meeting between Broiler Council officials and AARP policy staff to discuss their concerns and reassure them of the industry's commitment to producing the safest, most wholesome chicken products in the world. The dialogue continued and, at their request, we arranged a tour of a chicken processing operation for the staff. We didn't know — until we got to the plant, that is — that one of our AARP guests was a vegetarian. Our presentation must have been effective, though, because that was the last time AARP was among the industry's labor and consumer critics.

Year-end brought another small victory. Just before New Year's Eve, we got a call from CNN. The reporter was planning a piece on a National Consumers League's 1987 Report Card that gave the broiler industry and the government a poor grade for "allowing contaminated poultry to be sold to consumers." After talking with us, the CNN reporter proceeded to prepare the broadcast, and agreed to quote Council information. However, he indicated, "In light of what you've told me, this piece will probably be put on the back burner." To our knowledge, it was never broadcast.

By the time the new year arrived, things were relatively quiet. We were moving forward with our nationwide media tours and had begun arranging a series of background briefings with Washington-based reporters. We had arrived at a point when the fear of generating a negative story lessened somewhat. We were able to begin laying some groundwork that had not been possible in the previous months.

One Year Later — A Successful Turnaround

An analysis of media coverage one year later revealed significantly more balanced and positive coverage than that which followed the original "60 Minutes" broadcast. When our efforts began in June 1987, almost 90 percent of the clips we found singled out chicken as the primary source of salmonella, and most of those placed the blame on the industry. Few mentioned other meat, fish, or egg and diary products in connection with food-borne illness. After the first year, that trend virtually reversed. More than 95 percent of the articles on food safety and food-borne illness pointed out that the bacteria may be found on all meat, fish, and poultry. These quotes represent some examples of our success:

> *Most food-poisoning outbreaks in the United States come from meat, milk, or eggs, but it is difficult to determine whether the contamination occurs on the farm, in the processing plant or during preparation.* —Atlanta Journal, April 8, 1988

> *Most salmonella outbreaks are traced to contaminated meat, poultry, eggs, or milk. But even vegetables can carry the bacteria.... Salmonella bacteria are killed when the food is properly cooked.* —USA Today, April 8, 1988

Any food of raw animal origin can carry salmonella. Meat, poultry, raw milk, fish, and shellfish are common culprits. The most common food handling mistakes are improper cooking, undercooking, and infected person handling cooked food, inadequate reheating of cooked chilled foods, improper storage of cooked food ... and eating raw meat or poultry. Fortunately, all these mistakes can easily be corrected. —Auburn (CA) Journal, March 23, 1988

In short, our efforts on behalf of the National Broiler Council achieved our ultimate objective of maintaining the industry's position of strength in the marketplace. Perhaps the best indicator of success is industry sales. By the end of 1988, chicken consumption was up to 58.7 pounds per person (from 55.4 pounds in 1986) and wholesale sales had risen to $13 billion (up $1 billion from 1986).

Aftermath Five years later, we still see evidence of labor and consumer efforts to cast aspersions on industry and USDA practices and policies. For the most part, the chicken and food safety story continues to be reported fairly. Food reporters and publications, on whom research shows most consumers rely for food safety information, provide the most responsible coverage. Even reporters whose primary focus is criticizing the industry include safe food handling information, reassuring consumers that all they have to do is cook their chicken, and make sure they handle all raw meat with care. And most stories acknowledge that bacteria is found on all foods. There are the occasional sensational exceptions, but by and large, coverage of the industry on the food safety side is dramatically more balanced than it was five years ago.

The real turnaround has also been the industry's response to this success. In the past, the companies' reactive posture made PR specialists' jobs difficult. But in recent years, they have realized that stonewalling doesn't work. It's still difficult for some companies and industry officials to be open about their businesses or to say anything that may raise consumer concerns about their products — despite the fact that there is bacteria on everything.

The red herring dragged in back in the 1980s can still pull the occasional reporter away from the real facts, particularly since labor groups have expanded their focus far beyond food safety. But dealing with that reporter, attempting to influence a more balanced industry story, is more likely to be successful today because most companies have realized that unless you are involved in the story, you cede all control to your critics. What's more, many companies have realized that there are benefits to laying some groundwork by educating the media before you find yourself in the midst of a crisis.

As such, several have initiated media outreach programs that include briefings with top executives, inviting the media into processing operations, and talking about their efforts to assure product quality. In 1991, the industry, through its trade association, undertook an initiative to test the effect of various improvements in processing systems on the microbiological quality of their products. Though research efforts had been undertaken in the past, the industry had not sought public and media attention for its activities. This time was different. We assisted the Broiler Council in announcing the test and subsequent results. Coverage was some of the most positive we had ever experienced.

At the same time, the true test for these companies is the bottom line. Here, too, we can report success. In 1992, for the first time ever, chicken topped beef as America's most popular meat.

Jane E. Redicker is a vice-president in the Washington, D.C., office of Fleishman-Hillard, Inc., the largest independent public relations firm in the U.S. She was brought into the firm in 1987 to handle the salmonella crisis for the National Broiler Council. Other corporate and association clients have included Anheuser-Busch, INTELSAT, Beverly Enterprises, G.D. Searle, AARP, the "Baby Bells," the USO, the United Network for Organ Sharing, and the Vision Council of America. She has also held communications management positions in a number of associations and businesses.

Villains and Victims of Product Tampering

L. James Lovejoy
Former Director of Corporate Communications, Gerber Products Company

On Valentine's Day 1986, a New York woman complained of finding glass in a jar of Gerber baby food. The local territory sales rep picked up the jar of peaches alleged to contain glass and air expressed it and samples from the identical code to the Gerber laboratory in Fremont, Michigan. New York State health officials also picked up samples of the same product produced in the same batch at the same time for analysis. Before the tests could be completed, a local television station pressured two chain store grocery stores to remove Gerber baby food from the shelves. They accomplished this by stopping young women in the grocery parking lots to ask, "Did you know this store is selling baby food containing glass?"

The wire services picked up the story and by the time the New York health authorities gave Gerber a clean bill of health, copycat complaints were cropping up from as far away as Florida. This despite the Food and Drug Administration (FDA) being unable to substantiate any claims of broken glass in baby food jars.

Overview

Regardless of what you may have read or heard, the 1986 baby food glass scare was *not* the 1986 Tylenol capsule poisoning revisited. The only *real* connection between capsules and baby food was in the timing.

Three days after a New York woman died from poisoned Tylenol, another New York woman called local television stations and reported she had found glass in Gerber baby food. This timing and a superficial understanding of the Tylenol recall response was sufficient to foster preconceived perceptions in the minds of some reporters and others that precluded objectivity.

Not Like Tylenol: The Critical Differences

First, people died from poisoned capsules. The most serious of the unsubstantiated claims against glass in baby food was a cut lip and mental anguish to the parents.

Second, capsule poisonings were localized: five in Chicago in 1982, one in New York in 1986. Thus, media calling from anywhere in the country could be satisfied with identical facts. Baby food complaints, on the other hand, occurred in 40 states and countries as far away as Australia. In more than half the cases, complainants called the media before notifying local authorities, the FDA, or Gerber. Media myopia ignored the overall picture and reporters were interested only in the local angle of specific claims on which they often had more information — albeit one sided — than anyone at the company or a government agency.

Third, Tylenol is a market leader, but represents only one of the many brands marketed by its parent. Prior to the poisonings, consumers had little occasion to know or care that the parent company was Johnson & Johnson. Gerber is also a market leader. But 168 food products and the parent corporation share the same name and symbol. The Gerber "baby head" logo enjoys a 95.6 consumer brand recognition among its target market audience of parents and grandparents.

With no documented proof of the cause or a credible corrective action, emulating Tylenol's effective public relations response of demonstrating concern by recalling one or more products would only confuse parents and would betray the employees who were totally committed to maintaining Gerber's heritage of excellent quality control. If strained peaches were recalled because of alleged glass, for example, how could parents be expected to trust Gerber pears, plums, peas, or 164 other food products packaged and manufactured identically with the peaches?

Fourth, the capsule poisonings were clearly the result of tampering. No tampering ever was indicated for baby food. The FDA checked 50,000 unopened jars without substantiating any of the glass claims based on consumer-opened jars of baby foods produced at the same time, in the same plants, and where possible, removed from shelves in the same retail stores.

Fifth, the entire general public — except children — was the target market for the capsules. The baby food market, on the other hand, is restricted to only about 4.6 percent of the population. That market segment of American parents with children aged three and younger arguably is the most careful, knowledgeable consumer group of all. For nearly 60 years, Gerber had built its success on earning and deserving the trust of those parents.

No magic formula or "right way" to handle a crisis exists. When a company is faced with a real or alleged product tampering situation, its response is not dictated by a textbook solution. The variables of the corporate culture, the market, the product involved, the source of the complaint, the company's previous complaint history, and many other factors will give each situation a personality and a priority of its own.

Emergency Reaction

All crisis response programs are divided into three distinct phases:

- Identify the problem.

- Develop the solution.

- Communicate the action.

**The Phases of
Crisis Response**

Gerber was unable to move beyond the first step of its crisis plan — to identify the problem. No pattern to the complaints emerged, either by type of product, location, or type of retail outlet, warehouse site, shipping point, production facility, or date of processing.

Identify the Problem

Gerber and FDA analyses showed no glass in jars that had not been opened previously by a complainant. According to the evidence, no problem existed. Yet, the copycat complaints continued to mount and the media and public relations "experts" clamored for Gerber to recall its baby foods as a demonstration of its concern for its tiny consumers.

Gerber earlier had tried the recall route in 1984. At that time, baby juice alleged to contain glass was recalled, although regulatory agencies found no manufacturing or packaging problem. Instead of crediting Gerber with concern, the media and consumers interpreted the recall as proof that a problem existed and copycat glass complaints on a broad range of baby foods spread across the country, finally dying out in California months after the initial report.

In 1986 Gerber adopted a no-recall strategy unless such an action was justified by the facts.

Based on consumer research that showed the FDA enjoyed higher credibility than any commercial enterprise, Gerber decided its consumer communications effort should rely heavily on the FDA's data and spokespeople to present the truth on baby food safety.

**Develop the
Solution**

While continuing to respond to local press calls that totalled up to 80 per day, including weekends, Gerber corporate communications kicked off a proactive communications effort aimed at specific target audiences: the media, consumers, trade customers, investors, employees, government agencies, and health care providers.

Communicate the Action

Gerber's first priority was to reach *the media* to curtail every unconfirmed local complaint becoming a national front page story. Toward this objective, we invited the *New York Times*, Associated Press, and the *Wall Street Journal* to tour Gerber plants, interview CEO William McKinley, and talk to whomever they wished to get the facts. The philosophy behind our strategy was that in-depth, balanced stories by these three influential media outlets would have more impact on fellow journalists than a press conference with the Gerber CEO responding to localized questions on the latest complaints.

While these stories were being developed, we continued to issue news releases citing FDA and state health authority findings, backed up by our own analyses.

For the broadcast media, we decided the unbiased views of the FDA commissioner were the most effective statements to meet "Good Morning America" demands for interviews. For the "Today" show, we provided the facts to the network's expert

Glass in baby food jars was widely reported, but never substantiated.

pediatrician, who reviewed the glass scare and went on the air to assure parents absolutely no documentation of any problem in baby foods had surfaced.

CNN, which featured glass in food stories around the clock — and around the world — for days, was given an interview with Gerber's director of research and quality control.

Wire services were targeted for special attention since they were the conduits by which local complaints were being fanned into national coverage.

Special updates and instant access to Gerber spokespeople for the wire services soon convinced them the company had nothing to hide. They also began to realize that the volume of new complaints correlated closely with media coverage. The result was a dramatic drop in national wire stories about glass in food products. I was even invited to present Gerber's side of the story to newspaper editors attending the Associated Press annual meeting in Michigan.

While this media effort was underway, Gerber launched an aggressive *consumer* communications effort to stop the erosion that market research indicated was occurring among our users. Since the story wasn't getting across in the media, we decided to direct mail our message to the 2.6 million U.S. households that included infants. "Ask Gerber" mailings included a letter from our president, tips on serving baby food, and a return card inviting consumers to submit questions or request free coupons.

Within weeks, more than 250,000 replies were received. Seventy-five percent of the responses were favorable. Many parents urged us to stand our ground. Others recommended we "sue the people who are filing false complaints." Twenty-four percent did express serious concern over the reports of glass in baby food. The remainder posed questions such as, "When should I start my baby on solid food?" and "Is it true that Humphrey Bogart was the model for the Gerber baby?" (The answer is no.)

With the aid of a laser printer and 150 letter formats, we responded to con-sumers' individual concerns and specific questions with 75,000 personal letters from the president of Gerber. This personal touch was reinforced by a media tour that booked broadcast and print interviews in markets most severely impacted by glass in baby food publicity. Four Gerber spokespeople conducted 112 interviews in the first 60 days.

One of the first avenues of consumer communications to be investigated was tele-vision advertising. Ironically, at the same time the nightly news was tearing up Gerber with undocumented claims, our proposed ads featuring our president inviting viewers to call or write him with their questions were held up by network lawyers until they could review our answers! The Gerber Baby roared at this point and network management overruled their lawyers.

Trade Customers represented another critical audience. Our commitment was to keep Gerber customers as up-to-date as possible in what was a very fluid situation. All news releases were faxed or mailed overnight to retail and wholesale customers. Many grocers were under heavy pressure from local television stations to pull all Gerber products and provide their Minicams with footage, despite continuing FDA and state health authorities assurances that no risk to public health was indicated, much less proven.

Through the 700-person Gerber sales force, we kept tabs on local media by calling news directors and convincing them no recall or health hazard was present. Gerber's president, Leo Goulet, appeared in a half-hour interview on "Supermarket Insights," a newsmagazine show distributed to all major retailers. Most food and grocery trade media supported Gerber after they were filled in on the facts.

Communication with *investors* is critical during any crisis. During the baby food glass scare, it proved particularly beneficial as Gerber stock never dipped, even at the height of the burgeoning claims and negative publicity. Security analysts and major investors were kept up to date with regular phone calls and meetings, such as the Food Securities Analysts' Conference.

The company got a lot of credit from the investment community when McKinley spoke to the New York Society of Security Analysts on March 14 — less than a month after the "scare" began. We got extra mileage out of the New York Society meeting by mailing a reprint of McKinley's remarks to every Gerber shareholder. Shareholders also were kept informed with a special letter from the CEO and updates in the annual and first quarter reports.

Employees were a particularly critical audience in this crisis communications effort. Located across the country in food, apparel, and youth furniture plants, 102 Gerber child care centers, and several service subsidiaries, our employees deserved to know the facts. They were ideally situated to present the company's side of the story, if they were kept informed. In addition to distributing news releases and positive media clips to all Gerber facilities, we previewed the president's television commercials in employee cafeterias and published a special issue of the *Gerber News*, Gerber's six-issue-per-year employee newsletter.

In a gesture of appreciation for employees' extra efforts during the glass scare, the Gerber board of directors passed a special resolution that was reprinted and distributed in payroll envelopes.

Two other crisis communications audiences were special to Gerber: *federal, state, and local authorities* and *health care providers.*

In addition to telephone and personal contact at many levels with FDA and U.S. Department of Agriculture officials, we personally talked with or distributed information to health and police authorities in all 50 states. An insert in *Pediatric News*, Gerber's quarterly publication to 45,000 pediatricians, supplemented briefings in doctors' offices and hospitals by company medical services representatives.

Despite the strength of this crisis response program, villains remain in the product tampering scares that add to the consumer's everyday stresses. In many cases, these villains are motivated more by personal bias or greed than by any concern for the public.

Villains

The key group of villains were the *terrorists* — those arrested for alleging baby food or other products had been tampered with:

> *An unmarried mother in Illinois admitted to filing a false report to regain her family's attention after her married sister brought her new baby home from the hospital.*

> *A North Carolina woman was charged with felonious child abuse for deliberately feeding her baby bits of window screen wire — using baby food as the vehicle.*

> *Two 12-year-old baby-sitters in Minnesota admitted putting glass in baby food as a joke ... after the Minicams had made them ministars on the nightly news.*

These complainants are guilty of trying to manipulate the media to gain their own objectives.

Some *self-style consumerists* are also active seekers of media coverage. These "modern Chicken Littles" see disaster everywhere and don't pass up the opportunity to regulate or control every aspect of American lives. They also can be a source of some totally irresponsible demands.

Responding to consumer pressures, the city council in a New York community passed an edict banning all food products packaged in glass. The statute was quietly rescinded when others pointed out the impact of such a limitation on voters' eating enjoyment.

Crisis consultants thrive in today's environment and some are doing their best to turn "crisis management" into a growth industry.

Mostly they are easy to ignore. But one author did get under my skin as he toured television talk shows across the country promoting his book and castigating Gerber for not following Tylenol's example by recalling every jar of baby food.

Let us not forget the *ambulance chasers*. Not to be confused with legitimate personal injury attorneys, these modern-day alchemists hope to change threatening letters into fat fees. This excerpt from a letter sent to Gerber provides some idea of their professional qualifications:

> *My client gave me the jar of the baby food when she first saw me. I saw the hair in it. I emptied the baby food from the jar into the plastic bag and I washed the jar and put both items in the box you sent. I put the address label on the box and had the intention of stuffing the box with appropriate packaging material. However, the box has disappeared from the office and I'm unable to send it. I hope this does not hurt our claim. I can state that the hair was in the baby food and the hair was long blonde or brown hair. My clients do not have hair similar to this hair.*
>
> *We ask for settlement in this case in the amount of $9,000. I look forward to a quick resolution of this matter.*

Political opportunists practice another brand of alchemy — seeking to turn frightened consumers into votes.

In his press release that announced banning a Gerber baby food product (over the recommendation of state and federal health agencies), Maryland governor Harry Hughes pointed with pride that his state was the "first to recall and ban a Gerber baby food product." After 30 days, during which time Gerber successfully pointed out that 49 other governors had not seen fit to follow his lead, the governor rescinded his ban. Then, Gerber dropped its $150 million lawsuit against the governor to compensate for lost sales attributable to his unwarranted action.

Newsmongers dedicated to keeping the traditions of sensational journalism alive can be found in both print and broadcast media — happily not in large numbers.

For example, a Georgia newspaper reporter called and said he would serve as a witness if Gerber sued the local television station that continued to erroneously broadcast that a baby was in intensive care after eating contaminated baby food. When I called the station to point out that the baby had been released two days earlier from the emergency room without any treatment being required, the news director said, "I don't have time to check out every story that is called in by a viewer!"

The harm done by these "guardians of consumers" is unmeasurable in terms of unnecessary human fear and anguish, as well as in dollars. Some of their victims include: **Victims**

Consumers, who in addition to being needlessly frightened and forced to pay higher prices for "tamperproof" packaging and other "safety" programs, are deprived of their favorite products — forever, as in the case of Tylenol capsules, or until products can be restocked, as with Gerber, Heinz, Beech-Nut, Kellogg, Kraft, Jell-O and other brand leaders victimized by tampering claims during and subsequent to the 1986 tampering scare.

Taxpayers, another name for consumers, also pay a heavy price in skyrocketing costs for federal, state, and local health authorities to process real and alleged tamperings. The FDA alone estimated that investigations relating to unsubstantiated "glass in baby foods" reports cost $1.3 million in the first 38 days.

The *media* can be victimized by manipulators seeking notoriety or other benefits under the guise of reporting health hazards that seemingly warrant coverage.

Regulatory agencies, police, and other *government organizations* suffer increased workloads and expense not related to their primary objective of protecting the public welfare.

Shareholders can be penalized heavily as unexpected recalls, legal expenses, and increased advertising and promotion to regain lost market share siphon off profits and reduce stock prices.

Finally, *consumer goods producers* suffer lost sales, higher quality control expenses, and unnecessary packaging changes that raise costs without enhancing user benefits.

What was the outcome for Gerber's crisis management response? By January 1987 Gerber baby food brand share was back to 66.3 percent, versus 66 percent before the glass scare and a low of 52.5 percent in March 1986. **Aftermath**

The most rewarding sign was that the number of consumers surveyed who indicated concern over glass in baby food dropped from 81.1 percent in March 1986, to 27.9 percent in January 1987. That documents that parents — that careful, knowledgeable consumer group cited earlier — recognized Gerber as a victim rather than a villain.

L. James Lovejoy had been director of corporate communications of Gerber Products Company for less than six months when the baby food glass scare followed on the heels of the 1986 Tylenol tamperings. The recipient of many peer awards, Jim's public relations career spans 30 years. Since October 1991, he has been vice-president of corporate communications for Wolverine World Wide, Inc. An accredited public relations practitioner, he is past president of the Chicago chapter of the Public Relations Society of America (PRSA), and former board member of the Publicity Club of Chicago and the West Michigan chapter of the PRSA.

The *Exxon Valdez*
Paradox

James E. Lukaszewski, APR
Chairman, The Lukaszewski Group, Inc.

Joy A. Gmeiner
Editorial Researcher

Exxon and *Valdez* have become the *sine qua non* for the mishandling of both an environmental disaster response and the corporate communications surrounding it. The events of the first few hours of Friday, March 24, 1989, in the pristine, icy waters of Alaska have dramatically changed how many companies plan for emergencies and disasters. *Exxon Valdez* crystallized world environmental sensitivity on a scale and with a depth of emotion never before seen.

Overview

Nightmare is the perfect metaphor, except, of course, that the spilling of 10 million gallons of oil really did happen. Like a nightmare, it recurs, is recollected, and is relived in similar but slightly different ways. Yet, Exxon can never wake up to find this problem has disappeared with the night.

> [Exxon Valdez] *has been categorized as this country's worst environmental disaster. When asked about preparedness and response to this incident, Secretary of Transportation Samuel Skinner said that on a scale of 1 to 10, response was zero. No doubt* Exxon Valdez *is a world-class catastrophe. On a list of the largest spills worldwide, however, it ranks number 30. In 1978 [the* Amoco Cadiz], *one of the largest tankers in the world, six times larger than the* Exxon Valdez, *spilled 70 million gallons of oil off the coast of France. In fact, there have been 21 larger tanker accidents, nothing to be proud of. The difference is that none of those spills occurred in U.S. waters. The* Exxon Valdez *spill is the nation's largest spill by four times.* —Joel D. Sipes, rear admiral, U.S. Coast Guard[1]

We thought the first task should be to assist our operating people to get the incident under control. We were more concerned with that than with external perception. —Lee R. Raymond, president, Exxon[2]

Exxon is a very, very proud company that has done a lot to protect the environment.... The public's reaction is totally irrational ... how much good is this really doing? We're not willing to make [the commitment] to go anywhere and do anything anybody says. — Frank Iarossi, president, Exxon Shipping Company[3]

What are the cleanups and the lawsuits going to cost Exxon? Are we talking billions of dollars? "We're not talking billions, but I don't know what we're talking." —Lawrence G. Rawl, chairman and chief executive officer, Exxon[4]

The reputational effects of *Valdez* are expected to last for many years, or at least until another disaster of greater consequence to public interest occurs. Some effects may indeed be permanent. The incident galvanized public attention and opened wallets to increase funding for dozens of environmental groups. The major environmental funds — World Wildlife, Natural Resources Defense Council, Isaak Walton League, Audubon Society — were principal beneficiaries of enormous new public concern and sense of the need for action. In the years since *Valdez*, hundreds of other environmental efforts, publications, and organizations have also benefitted.

The magnitude of *Valdez* managed to eclipse this century's other giant, nonwar, nonnaturally caused environmental disaster, Union Carbide's deadly explosion in Bhopal, India, where more than 2,000 people died. Public reaction to the *Valdez*'s massive environmental damage and destruction of wildlife clearly overshadowed the fact that no human deaths resulted from either the tanker's spill, the effects of the spill, or the cleanup operations that lasted nearly two years. Analysis of what actually happened as compared with public perception of what was done shows that many permanent negative myths now exist about Exxon's performance. What caused this?

On the other hand....

Exxon's ability to weather the *Valdez* spill has created an important set of powerful questions used by senior executives to challenge extensive efforts to prepare for emergency management beyond operational imperatives. These questions, in a sense, aren't new to those interested in crisis prevention and mitigation, but they have new force and power based on the Exxon experience.

- How much effort really needs to go into a crisis disaster response/business recovery development process? Once government and health and safety regulations have been met, why gear up beyond that level of preparation? After all, most emergencies and disasters last only a very brief period of time. There's always time to respond, repair, and remediate, if necessary. What's really at stake?

- Does an organization really pay a permanent price if it doesn't prepare and, therefore, responds "poorly" — either from the public's or some other interested audience's point of view? The fact is, most companies, both those in America and elsewhere around the world, don't prepare in advance for crises and emergencies beyond those actions required by law or government regulations. Yet, they survive. What companies, products, or processes have been terminated by disasters other than bankruptcy or takeover? Does the "small" price a company is likely to pay in public perception, government reaction, or public abhorrence justify potentially enormous expenditures of both monetary resources and executive time for crisis management preparation and practice?

- If Exxon can survive ... with the visibility and size of the *Valdez* spill ... just how does an organization gauge how much preparation is necessary? How much money should be invested in getting ready? How much executive time should be diverted from day-to-day operations to plan for effective communication with communities, employees, the public, government, and others when something bad happens? What is the justification from an operating standpoint for significant organizational commitment to crisis preparation?

The Paradox

The impact of a *Valdez*-like incident on an organization's image has fostered increased interest in planning and selective preparation for serious problems at lower management levels. Yet the incident has not caused crisis preparation to become a permanent part of the thinking process among American top management.

No environmental disaster in the 20th century has captivated the world's attention to the extent of the *Exxon Valdez* oil spill in March 1989. It certainly captivated the attention of public relations practitioners and corporate communicators, triggering exhaustive new crisis planning and crisis preparation efforts in many organizations. Yet, top business management often use the Exxon spill as a key platform for raising questions about the need for crisis planning beyond that necessary to operationally manage a problem. In discussing Johnson

& Johnson's handling of the Tylenol matter during an interview for this chapter, the senior corporate executive being interviewed seriously questioned whether it was worth it. He argued that J&J would have been better off financially if it had just hunkered down — low visibility — and let it pass. I sensed a lot of approval from other executives in the room.

It's true, the public relations crisis management industry created by the tanker's spill is quite robust and likely to remain so. But now nearly four years later, management may be at odds with public relations practitioners over the lessons to be learned from the incident. It's a paradox well worth exploring.

In fact, analysis of the *Exxon Valdez* situation raises a series of contradictions. It seems appropriate to begin discussion with this series of dichotomies. Beginning in this way allows us to take a much more managerially oriented approach — looking specifically at the facts of the situation and then examining the questions and impact *Exxon Valdez* could have on an organization's ability to be prepared.

Bottom Line Health
One of the first and more interesting paradoxes is that Exxon has continued to be a profitable company, with the spill having very little apparent impact on its business. Within a few days of the incident, the average price of a gallon of gasoline in the United States seemed to jump as much as $.10 a gallon in some areas. The perception was that the increase was due to the impact of the *Valdez* spill and the potential tie-up of the port of Valdez. Exxon Company, U.S.A. senior vice-president J.T. McMillan denied this accusation in testimony before the Senate Energy Regulation and Conservation Subcommittee on April 17, 1989. "The idea that Exxon raised prices to profit from the spill is completely unfounded."

Even though shipments of oil from Valdez resumed their normal level rather quickly, no obvious drop in gasoline prices occurred to countermand the earlier increase. The industry maintains that the price of oil fluctuates daily, subject to world market conditions, and that it's almost impossible to isolate a specific incident as the causal factor for price increases and decreases. Review of average U.S. price per gallon at the pump (self-service unleaded gasoline) statistics during the period demonstrates a gradual reduction in the average price per gallon beginning in early April and continuing through the end of July 1989. Nevertheless, *the perception at the time* was that this single incident triggered a new level in oil prices, benefitting all oil companies at a time when the public wanted to see some punishment delivered to the industry in general and Exxon in particular.

Chairman Stays Home
The chairman's paradox is another interesting aspect of analyzing the *Exxon Valdez* spill. Exxon chairman Lawrence G. Rawl made his first visit to the port of Valdez on

April 14, 1989, 22 days after the incident occurred. His decision to delay going to Valdez for this lengthy period of time created the nearly permanent impression that he never did go. At 22 days into the incident, Chairman Rawl was already under serious challenge, as were his handlers, for not having gone to the site immediately.

Exxon held its annual meeting in New Jersey on May 18, 1989. Among the resolutions brought before the shareholders was one demanding Rawl's resignation. Although it failed by a substantial margin, the action was driven by his apparent unwillingness to apologize, his vigorous defense of the company's response, and his attacks on those criticizing the company.

The paradox? Rawl remained the robust chairman of Exxon — combative, aggressive, and vigorously defending Exxon's actions against criticism until his scheduled retirement in 1993. He provided a kind of pugnacious, corporate punctuation to the ongoing debate about just how badly his company handled the perception of this problem. Rawl's longevity is a lesson not lost on the chairpeople of other major U.S. corporations.

Public Boycott Dissipates

Another paradox. At the very early stages of the oil spill recovery operation a number of environmental groups, disc jockeys, and talk-show hosts around the country began a campaign urging Exxon customers to cut up their credit cards and return them to Exxon. Two things occurred. First, U.S. independent gasoline dealers responded quickly, pointing out that they were independent business owners who were just as ashamed and aghast at what happened as anyone else, but they were caught in the middle as sellers of Exxon products. Second, despite the valiant efforts of the disc jockeys and activists, the public never seriously boycotted the company. The net result was that 40,000 credit cards were returned to Exxon out of a card-carrying customer base of more than seven million. The effort failed substantially.

Despite the enormous political and public pressure placed on the oil industry as a whole, the industry has proven to be extraordinarily resilient (some say unbelievably arrogant) throughout the entire process. The industry did suffer the enactment of the Oil Pollution Act of 1990 — imposing vast new restrictions and liability on transportation and associated activities which endanger the environment.

What Actually Happened

If you doubt that bad press can wound a company, consider what happened to Exxon. Since the Exxon Valdez *dumped 260,000 barrels of crude oil into Alaska's Prince William Sound, TV and print reporters have portrayed the world's third largest industrial com-*

pany as an uncaring, incompetent, penny-pinching despoiler. Almost everything Exxon says and does — from criticizing the Coast Guard to running stiffly worded apologies in the press — seems to make matters worse. Shareholders, including some heavy hitting institutional ones, have attacked the company and even demanded CEO Lawrence Rawl's resignation. Rawl's conclusion, "Our public image was a disaster once that ship went on the rocks." [5]

We will observe closely the first 48 hours of the disaster. I refer to this time frame as the "crisis cocoon." If a company gets trapped inside the walls of confusion, fear of the media, lack of preparation, and unwillingness to talk, the public's expectations won't be met. And worse, because the cocoon effect causes decisions to be made in isolation, events are likely to get out of control operationally and perceptually. Crisis management perception planning is geared primarily toward managing the first minutes, hours, and day or two of an emergency … and staying out of the crisis cocoon.

Little Switzerland The picture painted of Prince William Sound in late March 1989 is one of beautiful, deep snow; tumbling waterfalls; rolling, thundering surf; the inevitable spring migration of gray whales from Mexico; salmon headed toward their spawning streams; sea birds coming in from across the Pacific; swans, geese, cranes, and hosts of shore birds flying the coastal winds. [6]

"The little Switzerland of Alaska" is the way Valdez is known. It became a place on the map in a very big way once Alyeska, the consortium of six oil companies that own the Trans-Alaska Pipeline, chose it as its base of operations for shipping crude from the North Slope. Valdez is now an industrial complex consisting of dozens of enormous storage tanks, huge floating tanker berths, a ballast receiving facility, and a group of giant incinerators, plus a maze of feeder lines and valves. [7]

Hazelwood Unwinds Here's how author Art Davidson describes the events surrounding the disaster in his book, *In the Wake of the* Exxon Valdez, *the Devastating Impact of the Alaskan Oil Spill:*

On Thursday, March 23, 1989, at the port of Valdez under gray evening skies, the crew of the Exxon Valdez *readied the ship for the five-day run to Long Beach, California. The three-year-old, 987-foot tanker was the newest, best-equipped ship in Exxon's fleet. Its captain, 42-year-old Joseph Hazelwood, had sailed for*

Exxon Shipping for 19 years and had made the Valdez-Long Beach run many times. By 6:00 P.M. that Thursday, the Exxon Valdez *was loaded with 1,264,164 barrels of North Slope crude, and Captain Hazelwood was anticipating a routine passage through Prince William Sound and down along the West Coast.*[8]

At 5:00 P.M., Hazelwood and his chief engineer, Jerzy Glowacki, stopped in at the Pipeline Club, a popular bar and dining room. With a seaman's cap set over his prominent forehead and his dark beard laced with silver, Hazelwood's appearance reflected his experience. After graduating from maritime college in 1968, he had advanced quickly through the Exxon ranks. He had earned his master's license at age 32, 10 years earlier than most Exxon captains. Captain Hazelwood had a vodka.[9]

On the way back to the tanker, Hazelwood and Glowacki stopped at the Club Valdez for pizza to go. The captain ordered another drink. At 8:10 P.M., they called a cab to run them back to the terminal. A guard cleared them through the security entrance.[10]

Davidson carefully chronicled the next several hours.[11]

Disaster Unfolds

9:00 P.M. AST[12] The *Exxon Valdez* was ready to depart.

Thursday, March 23, 1989

9:12 P.M. AST … the tanker's last mooring line was detached from the pier and two tugs nudged the *Exxon Valdez* from its berth. On the bridge were harbor pilot Ed Murphy and Captain Hazelwood.

9:21 P.M. AST … Murphy, directing the vessel's speed and course settings, began to steer the *Exxon Valdez* out of the harbor toward Valdez Narrows, seven miles from port.

The *Exxon Valdez* steamed through the Narrows in relatively calm weather: a 10-mph breeze from the north, with a four-mile visibility through low clouds and some snow and fog. With Murphy at the helm of the vessel, Hazelwood left the bridge.

11:20 P.M. AST … Captain Hazelwood returned to the bridge and took control of the *Exxon Valdez*.

As the *Exxon Valdez* approached the edge of radar coverage, Hazelwood radioed the Coast Guard that he was "heading outbound and increasing speed."

11:24 P.M. AST ... harbor pilot Murphy, who had already turned over command to Hazelwood, left the tanker and boarded a pilot boat that would speed him back to the port of Valdez. Hazelwood radioed Traffic Valdez, the Coast Guard's radio monitoring station.

Shortly after Hazelwood notified the Coast Guard that he was going to divert from the Traffic Separation Scheme (designated one-way inbound and outbound tanker lanes), he radioed that he was going to angle left and reduce speed in order to work through some floating ice.

11:40 P.M. AST ... the night shift took over at the Coast Guard station back in Valdez. Radar man Taylor had seen the *Exxon Valdez* "blinking on and off the screen" but had lost the vessel by this time.

Meanwhile, back on the *Exxon Valdez*, third mate Gregory Cousins had joined Hazelwood on the bridge to make a navigational fix on the vessel's position in the sound. The night was too dark for the seaman on watch to see any bergs, but ice was silhouetted on the radar screen. It was an extensive floe — thousands of chunks massed together by the current. Cousins and Hazelwood discussed skirting the ice. Some of the ice, broken into pieces the size of a car and smaller, were of little consequence to a tanker.

A well-timed right turn would be necessary to avoid Bligh Reef, which lay six miles ahead in the darkness. There would be little room for error. The vessel needed at least six-tenths of a mile to make the turn, and the gap between the ice and Bligh Reef was only nine-tenths of a mile wide. The tanker itself was nearly two-tenths of a mile long.

11:46 P.M. AST ... [Seaman] Maureen Jones left her cabin to go on duty. Captain Hazelwood relayed an order to her to stand on the bridge wing instead of standing her watch from the bow.

11:53 P.M. AST Hazelwood left the bridge "to send a few messages from [my] cabin." Cousins was now the only officer on the bridge. The chief mate and second mate were off duty, resting.

11:55 P.M. AST ... Cousins called Hazelwood to say, "I think there's a chance that we may get into the edge of this ice."

... Cousins assured the captain that he could handle things and then told the helmsman to make a 10-degree right turn.

11:59 P.M. AST ... Jones, now on watch, noticed that the red light on the Bligh Reef buoy was to the ship's right. Red navigational lights are placed to the right of ships returning to port, and almost every sailor knows the adage, "red, right, returning." Since the *Exxon Valdez* was leaving port, the light should have been on the left side, to port.

12:02 A.M. AST Jones called Cousins a second time. She had a more accurate count on the red light; it was flashing every five seconds. It was still on the wrong side of the ship.

Cousins ordered a hard right and called Hazelwood, saying, "I think we are in serious trouble."

Good Friday, March 24, 1989

12:04 A.M. AST ... the *Exxon Valdez* shuddered. Hazelwood raced to the bridge. After first impact, the tanker advanced 600 feet before it ground to a halt on Bligh Reef.

12:27 A.M. AST ... twenty-three minutes after grounding, Hazelwood finally
3:27 A.M. CST[13] radioed the Coast Guard traffic control in Valdez. "It's *Valdez*
(Spill + :23) back. We should be on your radar there. We've fetched up, run aground north of Goose Island, around Bligh Reef. And evidently we're leaking some oil. And we're going to be here awhile. And if you want to say you've been notified. Over."

12:30 A.M. AST ... the Coast Guard officer on duty woke Commander Steve McCall, asleep at home. "This is the big one. We have the *Exxon Valdez* aground at Bligh Reef."

... the Coast Guard called Alyeska and alerted night-shift superintendent Dave Barnum that the *Exxon Valdez* had run aground and was leaking oil. Barnum notified a crew that was loading a tanker.

12:35 A.M. AST ... Alyeska terminal superintendent Chuck O'Donnell was awakened by the phone. Told that a tanker had "possibly gone aground," O'Donnell called Alyeska marine supervisor Larry Shier and sent him over to the Coast Guard office.

1:23 A.M. AST
4:23 A.M. CST
(Spill + 1:19)

... Darryl Warner, president of Exxon Pipeline Company in Houston, was notified of the spill. He immediately called Frank Iarossi, president of Exxon Shipping (also in Houston), who at his bedside phone, initiated Exxon's response. Meanwhile, in Valdez, Alyeska's Shier assured the Coast Guard and Dan Lawn, of Alaska's Department of Environmental Conservation (DEC), that Alyeska was implementing its contingency plan.

1:30 A.M. AST
4:30 A.M. CST

... Iarossi was in his bedroom on the phone with Ulysses LeGrange, senior vice-president of Exxon U.S.A. "I told him we had a problem and I didn't know the magnitude of it yet." LeGrange gave Iarossi full authority to do whatever had to be done, "no limits, no bounds, total open authority."

During the next two hours, Iarossi made phone calls from his bedside, waking executives and oil spill specialists.

1:59 A.M. AST
4:59 A.M. CST

... Coast Guard Commander McCall radioed the *Exxon Valdez* for a status report. He was told that no one knew how many of the tanker's 16 oil-storage compartments had ruptured or how much oil had been lost.

3:00 A.M. AST
6:00 A.M. CST

... Coast Guard Lieutenant Thomas Falkenstein and Lawn had reached the *Exxon Valdez* aboard the *Silver Bullet*.

Lawn ascended the pilot's ladder and saw a turbulent pool of oil rising two feet higher than the surrounding water. He would later describe it as "a boiling cauldron. The oil was rolling up, boiling up, like it was cooking."

3:19 A.M. AST
6:19 A.M. CST

Falkenstein radioed Valdez. He informed McCall that at least 138,000 barrels of oil had already been lost and that 20,000 barrels were escaping every hour. As the oil rushed out, the tanker balanced precariously over Bligh Reef.

3:30 A.M. AST
6:30 A.M. CST

... George Nelson [Alyeska president] called Iarossi to say the vessel had lost an estimated 138,000 barrels. Iarossi didn't feel panic, just a tremendous sense of urgency.

4:00 A.M. AST
7:00 A.M. CST

... Iarossi arrived at his office to meet with his top managers. Calls were made to mobilize skimmers and boom in San Francisco and Southhampton, England. Half an hour into that meeting, Harvey Borgen, Exxon Shipping's West Coast fleet manager, called Commander McCall to ask if dispersants could be used.

4:00 A.M. AST 7:00 A.M. CST	... DEC's Dan Lawn called Alyeska from the tanker's satellite phone and then stared into the darkness, awaiting the light of Alyeska's response boat.
	Alyeska's contingency plan stated that a vessel with containment boom and skimmers would arrive at the scene of a spill in no more than five and one-half hours, and that period was now nearly over.
5:00 A.M. AST 8:00 A.M. CST	... thirty-nine workers had arrived at the Alyeska terminal expecting to be handed equipment and assignments. However, the boom required to contain the oil and skimmer attachments needed to suck it up were not on the response barge — and the barge itself was in dry dock.
6:00 A.M. AST 9:00 A.M. CST	... Mayor John Devens was awakened by a call from the local radio station. "You'd better put on your mayoral hat. We've got an oil spill."
	Before rushing to his office, Devens tried to call Alyeska and Exxon but couldn't reach anyone.
6:05 A.M. AST 9:05 A.M. CST (Spill + 6:01)	... as dawn crept over Prince William Sound, Alyeska officials flew over the spill for the first time. They saw a slick three miles long and two miles wide drifting south from the tanker.
6:23 A.M. AST	First official word from the Exxon and Alyeska Anchorage Center that the tanker *Exxon Valdez* had run aground on Bligh Reef.
6:30 A.M. AST 9:30 A.M. CST	... Lawn on the *Exxon Valdez* called Shier again at Alyeska. "You need to get that equipment to Bligh Reef. The oil is moving away from the ship and has to be contained immediately."
8:36 A.M. AST 11:36 A.M. CST (Spill + 8:32)	... Iarossi and Exxon oil spill response coordinator Craig Rassinier leave Houston for Valdez in an Exxon jet. They were accompanied by Gordon Lindblom, a scientist who had helped pioneer the use of chemical dispersants on oil spills, as well as a lawyer, a claims adjuster, and one of Exxon's senior mariners.
9:30 A.M. AST 12:30 P.M. CST	... Hazelwood was given a sobriety test aboard the *Exxon Valdez.* Hazelwood told a state trooper who witnessed the test that he had drunk only one beer in town before reboarding the ship but had drunk a low-percentage alcoholic beverage after the incident.

10:00 A.M. AST ... the *Exxon Baton Rouge*, en route to load oil in Valdez, was
1:00 P.M. CST diverted to Bligh Reef to take on oil from the *Exxon Valdez*.

*On March 26, the
Exxon Baton Rouge
attempts to offload
crude oil from the
larger* Valdez.

11:00 A.M. AST The Alyeska barge, loaded with 50,000 pounds of boom and
2:00 P.M. CST skimmers, sets out from Valdez.
(Spill + 11:04)

1:48 P.M. AST Exxon's corporate jet refueled in Seattle. On that stop,
4:48 P.M. CST Rassinier called Alyeska to discuss the possibility of *in situ*
burning — ignition of a floating pool of oil cordoned off with
fireproof boom. Other calls, to the Houston command center,
confirmed that planes were *en route*: a DC-8 picking up dispersant equipment in Phoenix.

2:30 P.M. AST [The Alyeska barge] arrived at Bligh Reef.
5:30 P.M. CST
(Spill + 14:24)

4:00 P.M. AST 7:00 P.M. CST	… Governor Cowper arrived in Valdez from Fairbanks, Alaska, and Dennis Kelso, the commissioner of Alaska's Department of Environmental Conservation, flew in from Juneau, Alaska.

Commissioner Kelso told the governor that "Alyeska's contingency plan is very specific about what kind of equipment they would have here within five and a half hours. It's quite clear that what was promised has not been delivered."

5:30 P.M. AST 8:30 P.M. CST	… an estimated 240,000 barrels of oil had escaped the *Exxon Valdez* into Prince William Sound. Since first light, the slick had spread from 6 to more than 18 square miles.

5:37 P.M. AST 8:37 P.M. CST (Spill + 17:33)	… Exxon's corporate jet landed in Valdez, and Iarossi immediately opened the company's command post at the Westmark Hotel. On his way to a press conference, Iarossi ran into Coast Guard Commander McCall. "He said we needed to test dispersant. That was the first time we heard that we were required to do tests," Iarossi said.

That afternoon, Alyeska had made the first dispersant trial from a helicopter, and as Gordon Lindblom had predicted, the test failed … the helicopter test, "clearly demonstrated that because of the calm conditions and thickness of the oil, dispersants were not effective."

6:30 P.M. AST 9:00 P.M. CST (Spill + 18:36)	At the press conference, Iarossi announced that Exxon accepted responsibility for the spill. He then drove to the Valdez tanker terminal and assumed responsibility from Alyeska for the lightering (fuel unloading) operation, dispersants, and public relations.

Commissioner Kelso was puzzled by Exxon's assumption of responsibility for the spill response…. Together, these confusions would add up to the most profound unanswered question surrounding the cleanup: Who, in fact, was in charge?

… according to a prior agreement with Alyeska, [Exxon] was mobilizing. However, when Exxon started to assume command, the state was surprised. Iarossi expressed surprise in turn. "I am very puzzled by Kelso's comments about never being informed of our taking over a large spill."

10:00 P.M. AST ... Captain William Deppe, Exxon's marine expert, boarded the
1:00 A.M. CST *Exxon Valdez* to take charge of the precarious process of sal-
(Spill + 21:56) vaging the tanker without losing any more oil. Hazelwood was
being relieved of command and, after questioning by authorities in Valdez, would be free to return to his home and family in
Huntington, New York.

Communications
Countdown

Davidson concludes his chronicle of the first 24 hours in this way:

> As the first day of the oil spill came to a close, deeply troubling
> questions were beginning to appear. Was Alyeska shirking its
> responsibility and letting Exxon shoulder both the burden of and
> accountability for spill response? Or, had the state been unaware of
> an established chain of responsibility in the event of a large spill?
> Should the state have been reviewing oil spill plans of the shipping
> companies, such as Exxon, as well as that of the consortium? Why
> had the Coast Guard failed to observe that there wasn't an adequate
> oil spill response system in place? While these questions might be
> answered in court years hence, the most pressing concern now was
> whether Exxon's people, flying into Alaska from thousands of miles
> away and marshalling equipment from around the world, could
> actually contain the disaster unfolding at Bligh Reef. [14]

Media Lockout

As the spill spread, so did the communications problems. On March 25 and 26,
Exxon issued several news releases, including an announcement stating that
Exxon had begun its informal investigation of the *Exxon Valdez* accident. Media
advisories were issued announcing that the transfer of oil from the *Exxon Valdez*
had restarted and that the workforce on-site was growing, with the number managing, advising, or supervising response activities approaching 100 people.

On March 27, Exxon Shipping Company issued a media advisory about the
National Transportation Safety Board (NTSB) beginning its investigation. "All our
efforts and comments will be focused on these priorities [the cleanup].
Reconstructing the events of the accident has lower priority, and we will have
further information available only when the investigation has been completed."[15]
On that day, twice daily briefings and press conferences at the Westmark Hotel
started being canceled.

According to Keith Schneider, a *New York Times* national correspondent attached
to the Washington bureau, "Suddenly you couldn't get near the place. There were

armed guards all over the place. It was like a fortress."[16] The press also began complaining about their inability to get outgoing telephone lines. Exxon decided that company policy questions were to be handled and answered only by Houston and New York, and not in Alaska.

On March 28, William Stevens, president of Exxon U.S.A., was sent to Alaska to be chief spokesperson. The next day, Exxon Shipping Company announced that the oil off-loading on the *Valdez* was going well. The local fleet had mobilized and was in full operation. Samuel Skinner, secretary of transportation; William Reilly, EPA administrator; and Paul Yost, U.S. Coast Guard commandant, reported to President Bush that the cleanup was going well enough that there was no need for the federal government to take over despite increasing public concern.

Rawl Comments, Hazelwood Out

On March 30, Exxon Chairman Rawl made his first comment, but refused to visit the scene. That day, Exxon announced the termination of Captain Hazelwood.

> *Iarossi said that the decision to terminate the employee was made because he violated company policy concerning alcohol. "We are all extremely disappointed and outraged that an officer in such a critical position would have jeopardized his ship, crew, and the environment through such actions. Our policies in this area are very clear."*

On March 31, Exxon issued a news release, "Exxon USA President Meets with Alaska Governor, Legislators." The following day, Exxon advised the media on general mobilization issues including tons of equipment, command issues, and communications. Eighty vessels and 14 aircraft were under contract to Exxon. The company also issued a news release stating that, "Exxon Ready for Full-Scale Dispersant Application March 25." Iarossi explained that Exxon did not get unconditional authority to use dispersants in the most important zone until 6:45 P.M., Sunday, March 26. On that same April 1, Exxon Shipping Company issued a news release describing how the company was funding the Alaska Bird Rescue Center.

On April 3, Exxon's full-page "apology" ad ran in 166 U.S. newspapers. On April 4, Exxon Shipping Company issued a media advisory announcing that the oil off-loading was completed and that the focus was now on refloating the vessel. On April 5, Exxon issued a release stating that the *Exxon Valdez* salvage had succeeded. On April 6, almost two weeks after the initial disaster, Exxon issued a news release headlined: "Exxon Mounts Massive Effort to Contain and Clean Up Oil Spill."

For several days thereafter, Exxon went into high funding mode, announcing a $250,000 advance to the Cordova District Fishermen United, an offer to fund seafood and tourism marketing efforts, and an advance of $1 million to the Aquaculture Corporation. It also announced the construction of an expanded sea mammal rescue center and the funding of a grant to the Alaska Public Radio Network. On April 13, Exxon issued a news release announcing that, "Exxon Shipping Company will support a combined federal-state natural resource damage assessment of Alaska's Prince William Sound."

Rawl Makes First Visit

The following day, Chairman Rawl made his first trip to Valdez to inspect the site and cleanup progress. On April 15, Exxon issued a news release describing its expanded oil recovery operations.

By mid-May, Exxon estimated it had received 18,000 credit card cancellations due to the national radio talk show "Cut Up Your Exxon Credit Card" campaign. On May 18, Exxon held its annual meeting. Rawl handily survived the movement for his resignation.

By the end of May, the Valdez economy was booming from the requirements of the cleanup process. "... as summer approaches, Valdez booms again. Its population has been doubled by the cleanup crews, and rent for a house with room for four spill workers can run as much as $11,000 a month. The 4,000 cleanup jobs offered by Exxon will increase petroleum employment statewide by 44 percent, and some estimate that $1 billion will be expended in the next five years. The cleanup itself will soon rank with fishing, tourism, logging and mining as a major employer of Alaskans."[17]

Damaging Memo Leaked

On June 10 Exxon hired Griffin Bell, a nationally known attorney, to conduct an "independent" investigation of the entire matter. The following month, Otto Harrison, Exxon's Valdez general manager, distributed an internal memo stating that: 1) Exxon will demobilize when it chooses; 2) For safety reasons, no operations will be continued during the winter months; 3) No commitment will be made for future action other than a survey of the shore in the spring of 1990.

That memo was leaked to the news media. A firestorm of criticism followed. By October, approximately 40,000 cut-up credit cards had been returned to Exxon.

Hazelwood Trial

As of April 1990, 170 lawsuits had been filed. Exxon estimated its expenditures to be at the $2 billion mark.

During June, Captain Hazelwood was acquitted in state trial of one felony and two misdemeanor counts. He was convicted of one misdemeanor — pollution. The Coast Guard promptly suspended Hazelwood's mariner's license for nine months.

(On July 10, 1992, an Alaskan appeals court threw out the criminal conviction of Captain Hazelwood on grounds that a federal statute gave immunity from prosecution to those who report oil spills. The decision would not affect several civil law suits against Exxon and Captain Hazelwood.)

In August of 1990, the NTSB ruled that contributing factors to the spill included:

Contributing Factors

- Drinking by the captain.

- An overworked crew.

- Inadequate traffic control by the Coast Guard.

On August 18, 1990, the Oil Pollution Recovery Act of 1990 was signed into law. The legislation addresses oil pollution liability and compensation, licensing and license revocation issues, as well as maritime training programs. It sets new tank vessel construction standards, addresses directly issues in Prince William Sound, and establishes an oil pollution research and development program.

Legal Ramifications

During a hearing held in U.S. District Court in Alaska in October 1991, Judge H. Russell Holland approved a settlement, acknowledging that Exxon had moved immediately to get the cleanup underway. He pointed out that Exxon had stepped forward and started paying private claims, many of them unsupported by documentation, to the amount of $300 million.[18]

In the summer of 1992, Rear Admiral D.E. Ciancaglini, federal on scene coordinator for the U.S. Coast Guard, notified the Alaska Department of Natural Resources that the cleanup was officially at an end.[19] He also notified Otto Harrison of Exxon Company, U.S.A. that the *Exxon Valdez* oil spill cleanup operation should be concluded.[20]

According to scientists gathered at Anchorage for the 1993 *Exxon Valdez* Oil Spill Symposium, the cleanup process has netted just 14 percent of the 11 million gallons of crude oil spilled. Some 20 percent of the oil evaporated from the water's surface, mostly in the first month after grounding. Another 12 percent sank to the bottom of the sea. As of late 1992, the remaining 50 percent had broken down, much of it into components and chemicals remaining on beaches and in the water. The spill eventually contaminated 1,567 miles of shoreline; scientists estimate that 300,000 to 645,000 birds and 1,000 to 5,000 sea otters were killed.

Environmental Ramifications

The disaster may have caused irreversible damage to entire species of animals and fish in Alaska's Prince William Sound. Scientists at the symposium also suggested that cleanup techniques may have damaged the environment. High-pressured blasts of hot water used to clean oil-fouled coastlines may actually have harmed those areas. "I'm beginning to wonder if the effects we're seeing now are the effects of the spill, the effects of the cleanup, or the effects of both," said federal government researcher Alan Mearns.

Work crew cleaning oil-slicked rocks.

Crucial Criticisms of Exxon's Response

During open-ended discussions I conducted with dozens of operating and staff executives throughout corporate America since April 1989 about the *Exxon Valdez* incident, the audiences consistently identified specific action or behavior mistakes. Examination of these actions and behaviors provides a unique and powerful checklist against which any crisis response plan could and should be tested.

Exxon's Mistakes

1. *Was Slow to React*: This perception is described both in terms of the Exxon's response to managing the spill itself as well as communicating about the spill publicly. The most common observations are that Exxon apparently was not ready to deal with a spill of this magnitude and that Exxon was reluctant to talk about what it was doing and how it was going to go about resolving the problem.

2. *Shifted Blame:* Here public comment relates mostly to focusing attention on (1) the condition of Captain Hazelwood, allegedly under the
influence of alcohol at a critical time when piloting the ship required
his skills to be at their highest level, and (2) his specific behavior at the
time.[21] The public perception was more that it was the company's
responsibility and problem, and not just the sea captain's.

Later, when there was a delay in using chemical dispersants, the company blamed the government and environmentalists for delaying the
use of these chemicals beyond a point when they could be helpful and
weather conditions would permit.

> *... It was the state and the Coast Guard that really wouldn't
> give us the go-ahead.... The basic problem we ran into was that
> we had environmentalists advising the Alaskan Department of
> Environmental Conservation that the dispersant could be toxic.
> In fact, the dispersant has been approved for use in California,
> which is a difficult place to get these kinds of things approved,
> and it was approved by the EPA.* —Lawrence G. Rawl, chair-
> man, Exxon.[22]

3. *Ducked Responsibility:* The perception almost from the beginning was
that Exxon was trying to limit its exposure, resist the efforts of others
to help, and refuse to publicly take the responsibility the public seemed
to demand. At one point Alaskan officials suggested that the chairman,
and perhaps other key Exxon officials, publicly accept responsibility
and, following the Japanese model, resign their positions.

> *In hearings held by the Senate Commerce, Science and
> Transportation Committee, Exxon Chairman Rawl faced a mer-
> ciless grilling. Rawl said once again that the company has taken
> full responsibility for the spill and will pay cleanup costs, but
> the senators were not satisfied. Slade Gorton, a Republican
> from Washington, pointed out to Rawl that when Japanese com-
> panies cause serious accidents, their executives often resigned
> in remorse. "I'd suggest that the disaster your company caused
> calls for that sort of response," said Gorton. Replied Rawl: "A
> lot of Japanese killed themselves also, I refuse to do that."* [23]

Despite the facts that during the very first public statement by an
Exxon officer (Iarossi, on March 24, the day of the accident), Exxon
expressed regret and stated clearly that it assumed responsibility for

the cleanup, and that at subsequent press conferences and congressional hearings, Rawl and Raymond repeatedly apologized for the accident and took responsibility for the cleanup, the perception persists through today that the company did not meet the public expectations for taking responsibility for the accident.

4. *Wasn't Prepared:* The incredibility of a company being able to operate a ship this large but being unable to manage what to most seems a pretty obvious scenario — the spilling of a large amount of oil — was one of the great frustrations felt by the public. It seemed unbelievable that no plan existed, no immediate process for containing the spill was in place. The notion that spills could occur is not nearly as damaging as the reality that spills beyond a certain size might not be containable simply because appropriate precautions are not taken.

5. *Showed Arrogance/Lack of Concern:* Throughout the process, top management's position was that Exxon "could handle it," didn't need any help from outsiders, and, in fact, resented the growing public concern about damage to Valdez. From the various accounts available and the millions of words written about the spill, it's clear that Exxon employees and their managers were quite concerned and sorry as the disaster progressed, seemingly out of control. From the public's point of view this concern and caring simply never came through.

We would have liked to recall the oil off Prince William Sound. We called, but it didn't hear us. Now, let's talk about that word arrogance. Last year customers boycotted us and cut up 40,000 credit cards. But, on average, those cards weren't being used much, while many other customers had ordered more than 160,000 cards in that same time period. So the media asked, "Has this hurt you? Do you think your company will survive?" Well, certainly we will survive. Ralph Nader says, "Boycott!" And when we're asked, we say we haven't noticed it. Is that arrogance? Maybe I should have said that I'm wringing my hands or something. I guess I'm supposed somehow to be generating sympathy, but's it's very hard to do if you ask me a straight question and I want to give you a straight answer. — Lawrence G. Rawl, chairman, Exxon.[24]

6. *Resisted Solutions:* It's surprising how many remember Exxon's initial attempt to take over and manage the entire affair, keeping — even

demanding — that everyone else become supportive to their efforts and, at a minimum, stay out of Exxon's way. Even as Exxon lost the initial battle to control the spill, it seemed apparent that its goal was to keep everyone else out of a position to help. Ultimately, the president ordered the U.S. Coast Guard to manage the problem.

7. *Took an Unrealistic Approach:* Even three years after the spill, the public remembers what appeared to be Exxon's inadequate ability to respond. The perception is that the company based its response on a completely unrealistic appreciation of the extent of the disaster. The news media repeatedly depicted Exxon's efforts as minuscule and more focused on cost than solving the problem.

8. *Presented Unprepared (Unwilling?) Spokespeople:* While the perception relates to spokespeople's lack of preparation, when probed the real issue relates to the visibility and availability of Exxon spokespeople. Most importantly, where was the company's chief spokesperson in this disaster, namely the chairman of the board? This question is raised repeatedly among audiences analyzing the Exxon Valdez incident.

   When the media asked for a comment at Exxon's headquarters in Houston several hours after the disaster in Alaska, it was coolly stated that this was a question for the Exxon Shipping Company, the manufacturer responsible for oil tanker transportation. They could not, and did not want to, make any further comment. To the question regarding whether Rawl could possibly be interviewed on the TV news program, a statement was issued to the effect that the chairman of the board of directors of Exxon had no time for that kind of thing.[25]

9. *Profited from the Disaster:* When the price of gasoline rose within several days of the spill, many felt that Exxon should have foregone the price increase both as a sign that it cared about the spill and its cleanup, and that money was no object when it came to fixing this environmental disaster.

10. *Minimized the Impact:* Constant attempts to allay public concern, fear, and public suspicion made analogies of one kind or another to minimize the effect of the spill. Perhaps the most interesting was a comment attributed to a petroleum industry spokesperson urging the public not to worry about the spill because it represented only one thirty-eight thou-

In its July 1989 issue, O'Dwyer's PR Services Report "edited" an Exxon ad that appeared in 166 U.S. newspapers on April 3, 1989.

sandth of the oil that passed through Valdez in a typical year. One late-night TV comedian commenting on this characterization agreed that a failure rate of one in 38,000 is probably not all that bad ... unless, of course, you're either in the oil business or manufacture condoms.

There were 30 million birds that went through the sound last summer, and only 30,000 carcasses have been recovered. Just look at how many ducks are killed in the Mississippi Delta in one hunting day in December! People have come up to me and said, "This is worse than Bhopal." I say, "Hell, Bhopal killed more than 3,000 people and injured 200,000 others!" Then they say, "Well, if you leave the people out, it was worse than Bhopal." —Lawrence G. Rawl, chairman, Exxon [26]

11. *Lacked Top Management Involvement:* The refusal of Rawl to proceed immediately to the site, or to visit the site at all in the early days of the disaster raised for all of corporate America the very serious question of when to involve the chief executive in a problem or disastrous situation.

12. *Missed Window of Opportunity with the News Media:* Many have suggested that a more aggressive media exposure policy early on would have exposed the efforts and attitude of the company in a much better light. But the perception among most observers who commented to me, as well as that of journalists who covered the disaster, was that there were far more attempts to hinder the media's activity than to help. Lack of enough knowledgeable spokespeople was frequently cited.

But the most important issue raised related to the media's willingness early on to learn and to help explain. The media's initial disbelief of Exxon's unreadiness and the unmanageability of the situation quickly turned to incredulity and negative news coverage as reporters began to feel hampered, excluded, and disliked. They finally felt it necessary to get even.

13. *Missed Window of Opportunity with Government:* One of the major lessons from a public policy perspective — and now embodied in the Oil Pollution Act of 1990 — is that those who create large disasters, especially in this industry, must not have the option of inviting government into the process. Government by definition will manage the ultimate problem. In 1989, without the benefit of this public strategy, Exxon appeared to fight off attempts by the U.S. government to step in and help. Exxon even fought off offers from the governments of several

foreign countries including Norway, the Netherlands, and the Soviet Union to send equipment and experts to assist in cleanup. Ultimately, the Coast Guard was ordered in by the president of the United States.

14. *Missed Window of Opportunity with the Public:* Many have suggested that Exxon should have found ways to involve the public in the cleanup. When I was asked for suggestions in April 1989, I recommended that Exxon charter aircraft to carry volunteers from several major U.S. cities to and from Valdez. Other counselors recommended the recruiting of college students. These volunteers would help wipe rocks for two or three days and then return to their homes. This gesture would have allowed several thousand Americans and even citizens of other countries to have a personal stake in the cleanup. At the time of the suggestion, the cost seemed outrageous. But in the context of what Exxon has ultimately paid — more than $3 billion at this writing — the cost of a few chartered aircraft for three or four months seems like very small change indeed.

15. *Missed Window of Opportunity with Environmentalists:* Initially, Exxon again appeared to do its best to distrust, deny, and delay the active intervention of environmental organizations. While the company appeared to be blocking the voluntary efforts of these huge organizations to rescue endangered wildlife, Americans saw devastating scenes around the clock of wildlife injury and death. Since 1989 Exxon has invested millions in a host of wildlife reclamation activities, studies, and remediation strategies. Yet, no amount of investment will recoup the damage created by the perception in those first few hours and days.

Powerful lessons ensue from even this qualitative analysis. Public perception will be determined by official pronouncements, or the lack thereof, together with the organization's public behaviors. We've learned that major, high-profile, publicly sensitive events like the *Valdez* spill can have enormous impact at the grass roots level and become standards against which similar events in other localities will be measured, and that significant events will be interpreted over a long period of time by government, the media, activists, and other outsiders in ways that can be accurately forecast.

Aftermath

The effect of the *Valdez* spill was to shift public and world opinion quickly and powerfully into unified horror at the nature of the disaster. Very quickly vast numbers of people became crucially interested in hearing and seeing whether Exxon would perform effectively. Exxon simply didn't understand where public

Three months after running aground, the Exxon Valdez *is towed from Prince William Sound to a San Diego shipyard.*

attitudes were, or the growing level negative public emotion which coalesced into expectations nearly impossible to accommodate.

The paradoxes caused by the *Exxon Valdez* spill remain, but so do many of its important lessons:

- Public perception of how a company handles a problem ultimately matters more than the facts.

- A rapid apology-fact-action plan will put many people on a company's side quickly.

- Mistakes and arrogance can overshadow the most positive actions.

- Focusing on a few critical, positive messages early on will help a company counteract the mistakes the media always make in reporting these situations and the company's mistakes in responding.

Review of literally dozens of articles, my own early research on the communications surrounding the spill, and materials provided by Exxon reveal a rather startling final paradox. While it is clear that many voices spoke for Exxon constantly from very early on the morning of March 24, 1989, those in charge of communications at Exxon and the executive offices couldn't seem to speak with a single set of messages. A colorful, combative chairman; operating executives who, I believe, while sincerely trying to be responsive, sympathetic, and helpful were simply overwhelmed by the emotional magnitude of the event; and a senior executive corps caught up in its own emotional involvement and embarrassment — all moved forward without a very specific and useful plan of action.

Analyzing the visibility implications of the *Exxon Valdez* oil spill provides an extraordinary number of operating and staff level management lessons. Experience from using a variety of approaches with operations managers and communications professionals has yielded even more paradoxes and fundamental realities. Here are some of the most important:

- The more complex the planning process, the less management seems genuinely interested or willing to pay attention to visibility and reputational issues —"We'll deal with it when it happens."

- Crisis management plans that do not include those individuals the boss trusts are doomed never to be executed, no matter how thorough or interesting the training, installation, or simulation happens to be —"All you communications people want to do is to tell everything to everybody."

- Effective management participation in the crisis disaster planning process can be successfully achieved only when the level at which managers are asked to participate is consistent with the level of their perceived need for preparation. (Translation: Keep it simple, positive, useful, and managerially oriented — "If the boss only understood, we'd all be better off.")

- Once bad things occur, those who plan for bad news in an organization often feel tagged with the blame — "Why can't your friends in the media ever get it right?"

The key issue facing Exxon was reacquiring public trust. As we compare how Exxon managed its visibility efforts to those themes which constantly surface in media interpretation, public expectations, government comment, and the criticisms of activists and other outside organizations, we see a pattern of actions which can initiate public forgiveness. This pattern, if executed quickly, clearly responds to the kinds of questions repeatedly asked and explored by the news media. Using this model can mean increased control over the media and the clear potential for diminishing its continued interest in exploring and reporting negative situations. When I discuss this with clients about to be in trouble, I refer to it as the "penitential model." It involves seven specific steps to obtain public forgiveness:[27]

- Voluntarily admit that mistakes have been made.

- Explain why the mistakes occurred (no matter how stupidly).

- Show/say/demonstrate contrition and sincere concern.

- Agree to take the steps necessary to fix the problem.

- Ask for help from the victims/accept counsel from the community.

- Promise (or publicly commit to) never to let it happen again.

- Find a way to pay (do penance)/alleviate/remediate.

Responding effectively to an emergency by fulfilling public expectations seems far easier than having to explain why things weren't done, were delayed or denied, or simply not thought of. The public now has little tolerance for companies that behave below these standards. In fact, when it comes to environmental infractions, the public clearly is demanding increased government response, tougher and tougher regulations, and criminal penalties for those who violate the stringent new rules.

Why Worry?   The toughest question management asks is, Why plan for situations that are extremely unlikely to occur? I've had clients tell me that extensive planning could cause those very problems to occur. My view is that if an organization is worthy of its reputation and interested in maintaining its credibility, then emergency preparations are an absolute necessity. When bad news happens, critical audiences, including employees, have expectations of a company's behavior and its ability to manage problems.

The community expects a company to know in advance what its vulnerabilities are and to be prepared for them. The community also expects to be warned, if at all possible, to minimize the damage and pain, and that the company will handle the problem in a competent fashion.

Employees may have the greatest expectations in emergencies. They expect a company to be caring, concerned, sensitive, understanding and, most of all, communicative about what is going on and when it will end. If management isn't, they will be, even if uninformed or misinformed.

Government agencies expect good organizations and companies to be able to respond and manage emergencies in a credible fashion. If a company can't, won't, or don't, government may step in and do it instead.

The victims of an organization's mistakes also expect it to be able to manage and handle these situations with the appearance of, if not the actual practice of skill, ability, caring, and sensitivity.

Most important of all, a company should expect competent and expeditious management from itself because if it isn't ready to handle a crisis situation, and as a result makes things worse, its reputation will be diminished.

The fact is that every organization and business is vulnerable to mistakes, mishaps, unanticipated events, and human error. We are all vulnerable. The prudent organization studies its vulnerabilities, identifies those most dangerous to the organization, and prepares to manage them.[28]

> *I've been with Exxon for 38 years, and the thing that has bothered me most is not the castigation, the difficulties or the long hours; it's been the embarrassment. I hate to be embarrassed, and I am.*
> —Lawrence G. Rawl, chairman, Exxon[29]

Notes

1. "The Alaskan Oil Spill: Lessons in Crisis Management," *Management Review*, April 1990: 20.

2. Allanna Sullivan and Amanda Bennett, "Critics Fault Chief Executive of Exxon On Handling of Recent Alaskan Oil Spill," *Wall Street Journal*, March 31, 1989.

3. Jerry Adler, "Alaska After," *Newsweek*, September 18, 1989: 54.

4. Peter Nulty, "In Ten Years You'll See 'Nothing'," *Fortune*, May 8, 1989: 54.

5. P. Sherman Stratford, "Smart Ways to Handle the Press," *Fortune*, June 19, 1989: 69.

6. Art Davidson, *In the Wake of the* Exxon Valdez, *The Devastating Impact of The Alaskan Oil Spill*, (San Francisco, CA: Sierra Club Books, 1990): 3.

7. Davidson: 3.

8. Davidson: 5.

9. Davidson: 9.

10. Davidson: 10.

11. Davidson: 9-36.

12. Alaska Standard Time.

13. Central Standard Time.

14. Davidson: 36.

15. Exxon Shipping Company, Media Update — *Exxon Valdez* Spill, "Accident Investigation," Valdez, Alaska, Monday, March 27, 1989, p.1.

16. "That Sinking Feeling with Keith Schneider of the *New York Times*," *Relate*, April 24, 1989, p. 25.

17. John Greely, "Alaska Over the Barrels, The Spills and Spoils of Big Oil," *The Nation*, May 29, 1989, p. 740.

18. Alfredo N. Vela, III, Manager, Public Affairs Operations, Exxon Corporation, Letter to the Author, October 19, 1992: 3.

19. D. E. Ciancaglini letter to Commissioner Glenn A. Olds, Alaska Department of Natural Resources, June 10, 1992.

20. D. E. Ciancaglini letter to Otto Harrison, Exxon Company, U.S.A., June 11, 1992.

21. Mr. Hazelwood is now an instructor at the Maritime College in New York.

22. Nulty: 51.

23. Michael D. Lemonick, "The Two Alaskas," *Time*, April 17, 1989: 57.

24. Richard Behar, "Exxon Strikes Back," *Time*, March 26, 1990: 62.

25. Behar: 62.

26. Behar: 63.

27. Dr. Peter M. Sandman, Director of Environmental Communications Research Programs at Rutgers University, uses a similar concept in "Risk = Hazard + Outrage: A Formula for Effective Risk Communication," a video program distributed by the American Industrial Hygiene Association.

28. James E. Lukaszewski, *Executive Action Crisis Management Workbook, Step By Step Process to Develop Your Crisis Plan*, (White Plains, NY: The Lukaszewski Group Inc., 1992): 1–2.

29. Behar: 63.

James E. Lukaszewski is a corporate problem solver who advises, coaches, and counsels the men and women who run America's largest corporations. He believes that the communications difficulties they face can be solved through superior personal leadership skills combined with positive, strategic communications. He is a nationally known expert in troubleshooting tough, touchy, sensitive corporate communications problems. He works primarily with Fortune 500 companies facing serious internal and external crises involving the environment, labor organization and negotiations, and public policy issues. He is frequently retained by senior management to directly intervene and manage bad news situations. He is a specialist in contingency planning and its components, business resumption, disaster recovery, and crisis communications.

An author of several books and more than 130 articles, lecturer, trainer, counselor, and public speaker, Lukaszewski is an assistant adjunct professor of communications at New York University's Management Institute and is civilian advisor to the International Disaster Advisory Committee, U.S. Department of State, and the U.S. Marine Corps. He is a nationally recognized speaker in crisis management, ethics, media relations, and public affairs topics.

Trial by Media

Christopher P.A. Komisarjevsky
Executive Vice-President, Hill and Knowlton, Inc.

Overview

Today, the thought of product liability sends chills up and down the spines of corporate leaders. Nearly 20,000 product liability lawsuits were filed during the 12 months that ended June 30, 1990, according to the Administrative Office of the U.S. District Courts. This was well more than double the number filed ten years earlier in 1980. These suits cover a range of different products, with the single largest number coming from a rapid growth in the number of asbestos-related product liability suits.

The effects of these lawsuits can reach far beyond the immediate legal and financial outcomes. Media coverage of a drawn-out battle can test the underpinnings of a company's values. Regardless of whether or not a lawsuit is successful, the product may die, the company's reputation may suffer, employee morale may plummet, and shareholder and management confidence may be shaken.

The media — from the stark black and white of newspapers to the full-color drama and tragedy of television — play a critical role in the perception of the facts surrounding a product liability trial. Human interest, emotion, alleged disclosures, and so on are potent forces that the media thrive upon and that cannot be ignored by corporate attorneys or public relations staffs. Now, before the first lawsuit is announced, is the time to examine your corporate public posture and develop a realistic communications strategy. During a product liability trial, there is no substitute for a practical plan that is based on a thorough understanding and realistic assessment of the media.

**Product Liability
and the Media**

The prescription drug Bendectin was the subject of a trial in U.S. District Court in Orlando, Florida. After 23 years of worldwide use in millions of pregnancies, Bendectin, for the first time, was accused of causing birth defects. The Orlando jury found in behalf of the plaintiff, but awarded no compensatory or punitive damages. When the presiding judge ordered a retrial, the new jury reversed the earlier decision, finding in behalf of the defendant. In spite of this vindicating verdict, in spite of scientific evidence, and in spite of favorable findings by an FDA Drugs Advisory Committee hearing, more than two years later the Associated Press reported:

> *Merrell Dow Pharmaceuticals has doubled the price of Bendectin, a widely used morning sickness drug, to help pay legal costs of a prolonged defense against charges Bendectin causes birth defects.*
>
> *Merrell Dow has won the only suit against the anti-nausea drug that has come to trial but faces more than 100 similar suits seeking millions of dollars in damages.*
>
> *Worldwide sales of the pill, which has been used for an estimated 33 million pregnancies since 1957, reportedly dropped sharply over the last few years as a result of pending litigation.*

Within a few years the product was taken off the market by Merrell Dow for reasons that had nothing to do with safety or efficacy.

All of this was in the face of scientific evidence — including reviews by health authorities throughout the world and published epidemiological studies — which had shown no data to link Bendectin with an increased risk of birth defects. The medical community consistently supported the use of the drug. But the media persisted in their public trial of Bendectin.

The media coverage had repercussions throughout the world: in legislative circles, in regulatory corners, among scientists, and in the marketplace. It pitted scientific experts against one another, lawyers against the FDA, the plaintiff against her attorneys, and physicians against their patients. Sometimes unwittingly, other times in the interest of sensationalism, the media often ignored the scientific evidence and played on emotion.

Arousing "sympathy" and "outrage" appears to be the key to plaintiffs' winning product liability judgments.

This 1973 Ford Pinto exploded and burst into flames when struck from behind on U.S. 33 south of Elkhart, Ind. The Ford Motor Co. was indicted for responsibility in its design of the auto.

In what was perhaps one of the more publicized product liability cases — the Pinto case — Ford Motor Company's design, construction, internal correspondence, management, and post-marketing policies were examined by the press. Three girls had died after a rear-end collision during which the fuel tank in their Pinto burst into flames. Ford was charged criminally with reckless homicide. The trial took place in the small town of Winamac, Indiana, while crusading magazines and investigative reporters took out after Ford. The case was tried not only in Indiana, but in front of television sets throughout the nation. At the end of a 10-week trial, the media had provided columns, wire service stories, cartoons, photographs, magazine features, and broadcast coverage. In the end, the jury found Ford not guilty, but for months, Pinto owners, Ford customers, employees, and salespeople couldn't help but be affected by the reporting.

Effective Communications Strategy

From a communications perspective, a product liability lawsuit, no matter what its outcome, can be devastating. And the smarter trial lawyers know it. Increasingly large judgments are the goals, with contingency fees as the prize and large corporations as the targets.

No one who has been involved in a substantial product liability case would deny that a product liability lawsuit puts great strains on the company, on management, on staff, on all levels of employees, on legal counsel, and on public relations staffs. It is virtually impossible to quantify the effects, but it takes only one lawsuit to start the boat rocking. However, the underlying public relations posture of the company can help to keep this controlled.

Here are some important points to keep in mind in laying the foundation for a sound and effective public relations strategy before, during, and after a trial:

Regarding Corporate Communications

- Credibility and honesty are critical and should have the highest priority. There is no substitute for a posture that is honest and will stand the test of time.

- Communications with all audiences should be consistent and timely.

- There must be a spokesperson available and authorized to be interviewed. That person should be trained in how to deal with the press, be armed with facts, and field questions in a way that is credible and will be respected.

- Whenever there is a development which is important to the company, it should be followed by an immediate announcement of the company's response or position so that the press knows and can report on the company's stance. The company's interpretation of the development can also influence press coverage.

- Timing is critical. The company will have a better chance of affecting news coverage if it acts swiftly.

- Third-party support — such as independent physicians and scientists — of the company's position is essential in dealing with the media.

- On health issues, a medical spokesperson is extremely valuable, at times even essential.

- Both consumer and professional audiences are important to the perception of the company and the product.

- All communications should be viewed regarding their effects on employees, the financial community, shareholders, existing and potential customers, the local plant and office communities, and regulators and legislators.

- Every effort should be made to communicate openly and regularly with the corporation's overseas offices so that they are informed about developments that affect their businesses.

Regarding the Media

- Briefing the press prior to a major event is essential. Without that step, balanced publicity is doubtful.

- In a sensational or highly charged situation, the best press you can hope for is balanced press.

- On medical and health issues, patients are influenced by the general media and today appear to be less likely to accept without question the advice of their physicians. Over the past years, the controversy surrounding unnecessary drugs, operations, and other medical care has heightened a patient's skepticism. In addition, the proliferation of articles and sections in the general media dealing with medical/health topics has encouraged a more discriminating approach toward medical care.

- As efficient as the wire services may be, they cannot be relied on solely to get the story told. Even dissemination of a favorable press release from a government regulatory agency must be leveraged by company action in order to generate the kind of coverage wanted. If the company does not take steps on its own to publicize favorable comments, those comments may be misinterpreted in the interest of a sensational headline or may not reach some of the audiences important to the company.

- One can never be assured that reporters, researchers, or editors will get in touch with the company before doing an article or broadcast.

- Even the most irresponsible reporting can gain a life of its own and may be used by responsible reporters.

Working with the Legal Staff

There should be a close-working, mutually respectful, and trusting relationship between public relations counsel and legal staff. This may be difficult at first — and for some it may seem next to impossible — since the legal staff is apprehensive about what public relations might do with sensitive information and public relations tends to feel that legal hasn't told them enough.

Nevertheless, both public relations and legal counsel have important jobs to do. At the top of the list is winning the case in court. That task takes priority over all others and is the ultimate goal of all efforts during the trial time. No public relations work should take place if, after serious discussion, the company concludes that it might actually jeopardize the legal battle.

Public relations, too, has its own battle. The media will tend to focus on the sensational and the human interest aspects of the case and will be prone to side with the plaintiff's case. In this David versus Goliath struggle, a number of important steps can be taken to help balance publicity and make sure that the media have the company's side of the story in hand. In order for public relations to be effective, though, it must have facts and deal with the media in a straightforward, objective, and credible way. This requires a close working relationship with the legal staff, which has to begin long before the case comes to trial and extends beyond the announcement of a jury verdict.

The best relationship is one in which public relations and legal work hand in hand, both aware of the facts and of the strengths and the weaknesses of the lawsuit.

Legal will have its perspective and public relations will have its own. Regular discussions, increasing in frequency as the trial approaches, are indispensable. If at all possible during the trial, there should be daily meetings between legal and public relations staffs to deal with the following:

- An assessment of that day's courtroom activities.

- A review of that day's trial publicity in the town, the country, and other worldwide markets.

- Any media coverage known to be still in the works.

- A briefing on courtroom activities and on likely "disclosures" and testimony anticipated for the next day.

- Preliminary drafting of any company statements to be issued.

- A discussion of whether possible spokespeople, and a decision about whether a member of the legal team, would be available for interviews or background briefings with the press.

- A discussion of sensitive issues in the case and establishment of guidelines for dealing with the press the next day. For example: Will a statement be issued? Will on-camera questions from television stations be avoided? Will photographs be permitted?

It is the responsibility of public relations to assess the media each day and provide a daily report. In past experience, such reports — covering local as well as worldwide media — have been valuable in assisting the legal team members to review their various options. If the public relations staff is experienced and professional, it will become an integral part of the day's strategy session and welcomed in the lawyers' "war room."

It is very difficult to generalize about a public relations strategy for a product lia- **Strategy During**
bility trial. Each case is different, each company is different, and so, too, are the **the Trial**
public relations considerations.

At the root of the issue is the concept that a strong legal defense should be
accompanied by a strong communications posture. Defense of the product in
court deserves a similar defense of the product out of the courtroom. The rules
that bind testimony and depositions do not bind the media. And, even though the
presiding judge may not want the media to cover the trial, they will cover it. Each
night, the local television stations will broadcast their reports, the wire services
will distribute their copy and, if the issue or corporation is of national interest,
the networks may decide to do their own piece. Evening and morning news broadcasts and weekly television "magazines" have viewers which number in the millions. With the growth of cable television, the likelihood of in-depth, hour-long
feature coverage increases.

Before developing a strategy, a number of facts should be examined:

- Research prior to the marketing of the product.

- Latest available research findings.

- Legal strengths and weaknesses of the lawsuit.

- Any similar lawsuit settlements.

- Total number and dollar value of lawsuits filed.

- Assessment of public attitudes — nationally, regionally, and in the town
  where the case will be tried.

Publicity is likely to surface before the opening date of the first trial, escalate
during the opening arguments and plaintiff's arguments, drop off toward and during the defendant's arguments, and peak again at the time of a jury verdict. If the
case involves a death, serious injury, or a permanently disabling accident, the
publicity is likely to be even more extensive.

Publicity may be generated not only by the media, but also by plaintiffs, potential
plaintiffs, aggressive attorneys, researchers, activists, and politicians. Hardly a
sensational or potentially lucrative product liability trial goes by without activist
attorneys talking to the media to tell their sides of the story. They also may be present in the courtroom to watch the corporation's defense and prepare strategy for

their own future cases. In some situations, lawyers have appeared on television talk shows, been interviewed by newspapers in various parts of the world, openly courted reporters at the close of testimony each day, and placed advertisements seeking information and potential class-action litigants. More and more people involved in product liability are becoming increasingly sophisticated in various kinds of public relations techniques and in generating media coverage.

An effective public relations strategy can only be built on thorough knowledge, credibility, and confidence in the company's testing and marketing of the product. Any nagging areas of doubt need to be discussed thoroughly. Whatever comments the company makes publicly must be able to stand the scrutiny of further product safety testing, courtroom depositions and testimony, and investigations by experienced reporters. It is impossible to foresee all potential problems, but as many as possible must be considered.

Reaching Corporate Audiences

In developing a public relations strategy, three objectives should be kept in mind: (1) increasing the likelihood of balanced media coverage, (2) establishing the company as an objective, accessible source of reliable information about the product and its testing and about the company itself, and (3) determining in advance what media coverage is being planned so that the company will have a better opportunity to provide information or a spokesperson to balance adverse statements being made.

Any kind of publicity — negative, as well as positive — has bearing on communications with many corporate audiences, including customers, shareholders, the financial community, and employees. A public relations strategy needs to consider all those audiences.

It also needs to consider that corporate management must be kept informed on a regular basis. With the legal team tied up in the details of courtroom activities, it is the responsibility of public relations to develop a system for communicating with management and with the company's offices throughout the United States and in worldwide markets. A trial in a small United States town can become an international issue, and its repercussions can shake a corporation's product markets.

Witnesses from abroad may travel to the United States and generate news coverage in both countries. Reporters often are calling in to news desks thousands of miles away, the wire services use correspondents to file stories for the state, regional, and national wires, and networks may send film crews to cover a trial. In some cases, a trial's publicity may be more intense abroad than it is in the U.S. and overseas managers may be deluged with media calls; hence, they too need to know about events concerning the suit and what they can say publicly.

Accurate and timely information — which can be in the form of approved company statements telexed worldwide each night — do wonders to demonstrate a strong defense and to reduce internal problems. These statements can be issued to the press and, moreover, can be distributed to employees, local communities, and members of corporate management.

Regular corporate statements, when leveraged by effective public relations techniques, can also reach customers, shareholders, and the financial community. Since product liability lawsuits can surface issues of "materiality," communication with these audiences is important.

At the core of a public relations strategy are five principles:

1. The development of factual, scientifically based background material.

2. An initial briefing of carefully selected members of the press — not to generate press coverage but rather to position the company as a source of objective, factual data.

3. The identification and training of a spokesperson or spokespeople for the company who would be available at all stages of litigation.

4. A daily monitoring and assessment of media interest and coverage, reporting regularly to corporate management and legal staff.

5. A plan of action, including various options for announcing a jury verdict — win, loss, hung jury, or other — and a plan for responding to inquiries after the trial.

Responding to the Call

In dealing with the media, a central question must be asked: What do you do when that publication or broadcast station comes knocking on your corporate door? There are no hard-and-fast rules, but in general, it is a good idea to speak with all reporters no matter what the publication, station, or network, including those from overseas. To ignore them is to lose the opportunity to provide balanced information, even though that information may not actually appear in the article. If a corporation later decides to sue the publication or station, it can then do so with the knowledge that it had done all it could to provide the facts.

Moreover, refusing to talk may signal the reporter that he or she's on the track of something big. But where would a company draw the line? When a company suspects that a story is in the works, there are a few guidelines to follow:

- Be sure the reporter is from the publication or station he or she claims to be from. Don't talk to a reporter without checking first. Record the name and the affiliation.

- Send background material to the reporter by registered mail; the reporter cannot later deny that he or she received the material. Follow up with a call.

- Inform the reporter that you are going to record all interviews, and then do so. If the reporter objects, you then have an indication that a negative story is being prepared and, in any case, you have a record of the interviews.

- Prepare yourself thoroughly before proceeding with each interview. Know your main points and state them in a clear, concise manner.

- Be very conscious of the media's need for simple, straightforward answers that can be retold in one or two sentences or 30 seconds.

- Limit the amount of time you spend with the reporter. Your time is valuable. If you continue to let a reporter dig, he or she will make something out of his or her efforts.

National Enquirer Exposé

In most situations, companies do not want to deal with the press on such sensitive matters as legal defense. In particular, they don't want to deal with the more sensational and, perhaps, scandalous publications. A supermarket tabloid, for example, conjures up an image of bold headlines, flashy pictures, bright colors, sensational allegations, untold stories, and suspect reporting. These images appear regularly, staring out at countless shoppers as they pass through supermarket checkout aisles.

Disdain is probably the most common response felt by corporations when they face an exposé in the pages of such a tabloid. Often they would like to ignore it, claiming that it was just an irritant and would be only short lived. However, articles in such publications can have a ripple effect, and the story can go on to live a life of its own long after the last issue leaves the newsstand. Moreover, material in those magazines may become a source of information or ideas for stories in other publications, including business and financial journals.

An appropriate example is the *National Enquirer.* In the *Consumer Magazines* edition of *Standard Rate and Data Service (SRDS)*, a directory for advertising and marketing professionals that provides basic information on periodicals, the magazine provides an editorial profile of itself: "*National Enquirer* is a nonfiction, general interest publication. It covers contemporary topics from around the world. Articles cover news events, original investigative reporting, celebrity and political personalities.... Special emphasis is placed on human success...."

While differences of opinion exist over its description, there is no denying this publication's visibility. "What's Happening America" reported that almost one out of every ten literate Americans glances at the *National Enquirer*'s headlines each week. The most significant numbers concern readership of the magazine. While its base circulation is over five million, the magazine itself looks at a total readership of 23 million people, based on an average of four members per family.

It was the *National Enquirer* which — more than three months before the trial began — broke its story on the prescription drug Bendectin with a front cover headline that claimed: "New Thalidomide-Type Scandal — Experts Reveal ... Common Drug Causing Deformed Babies." The effects of this cover story can never be fully measured. But based on the letters that poured into many magazines and medical columns, and based on the articles that in subsequent months referred to the article, it appears that the story had far-reaching effects and lived a life of its own.

National Enquirer readers were not the only ones who sat up and took notice of the Bendectin cover story. The article did not single-handedly set things off, but it did help to escalate a controversy that involved parents, lawyers, doctors, legislators, the FDA, and the media. Women who were taking Bendectin during pregnancy feared that their unborn children would have deformities. Some had given birth to babies with abnormalities and associated their children's defects with Bendectin. At least one lawsuit appears to have been brought on by the story.

Later on, lawyers placed advertisements searching for Bendectin cases, and disputes among doctors and scientists occurred over conflicting evidence on the drug. Media attention was a constant. Soon afterwards, the German popular magazine *Der Stern* (The Star) also took out after Bendectin, rocking the European market. Complete with pictures of deformed children, the magazine accused the company of hiding evidence. Within weeks, that article appeared to lead to a call by a member of parliament for removal of Bendectin from the market. It then became an issue for the German health authorities.

The point here is not to indict any particular publication but to demonstrate potential effects. The impact of a supermarket tabloid cannot be underestimated or ignored. It is valuable to make some observations about the potentially sensational story and about the drama of supermarket tabloids:

- Supermarket tabloids have large readerships and high visibility; it should be assumed that their stories will be widely disseminated.

- Subjects will be treated in a sensational manner in order to appeal to the widest audience.

- Controversial subjects that affect women are likely targets since the majority of supermarket tabloid readers are women.

- The views of these publications may find their way into more reputable publications, fueling further public debate.

To Sue or Not? An intriguing question regarding media treatment of product liability trials is whether a corporation should sue a publication if it believes it has been damaged by the publication's irresponsible reporting. Obviously, this is primarily a question for legal counsel. Nevertheless, there are some public relations considerations.

From a public relations perspective, it is possible that if a corporation were to sue in response to a damaging article, the following could happen:

- Segments of the public that were previously unaware of the issue would learn of it or would go back to read the damaging article.

- Media support would galvanize behind the publication, as the press is more likely to defend its First Amendment rights when attacked by a large nonpersonal entity such as a government agency or large corporation.

- The initial rush of stories following the filing of a suit would further stoke the fires. Subsequent rehashing of the issue would damage the corporation's reputation, while its day in court against the publication would not come for several years.

- Negative attention could spread to other company products, increasing the chances of a public boycott.

These observations should not be interpreted as counsel against suing a publication. Each case needs to be discussed after the article has been reviewed line-by-line for possible inaccuracies and false reporting.

Significance of the Spokesperson Few tasks are more difficult than those of the spokesperson during a product liability trial. Before the trial, any efforts to brief the press must be done in a manner that says, "This is a potentially dramatic situation. The opportunities for sensationalism are great. I am not there to dissuade you from doing a story, nor am I here to encourage you in writing a story. I would like to provide you with some factual background information which explains our point of view and gives you the scientific data surrounding the testing of our product. If you need any further information, please let me know."

Before and during the trial, that spokesperson must be cool under the hot lights of television, respond in a factual way, and be familiar with all the techniques of media confrontation. When a jury verdict is announced, the spokesperson must be able to show sensitivity and compassion. Especially in the case of a favorable jury decision, the spokesperson must be able to balance victory with the tragedy of someone who had been hurt or harmed.

In light of the fact that a spokesperson plays such an important role in public relations, especially during a trial, a corporation should take great care in selecting and training that person.

Furthermore....

Obviously, the primary goal of any public relations effort surrounding a product liability trial should be to support the corporation and its efforts to be successful in court; public relations should not take any actions which might jeopardize the legal defense and its chances for a victory. Furthermore, what happens in the lawsuit can have a profound effect outside of the courtroom. Communications systems for anticipating press reactions and dealing with them effectively are fundamental. Likewise, a communications system for keeping members of the corporate management team informed is very valuable.

The media can be powerful, especially when dealing with emotionally charged issues. However, sound planning — based on a careful, objective assessment of the media and the facts surrounding the case — can help create a strong public relations effort that will serve the company well.

Christopher Komisarjevsky is executive vice-president of Hill and Knowlton, Inc., the international public relations and public affairs counseling firm. He is general manager of the Hill and Knowlton New York office and the eastern region. He is responsible for client counseling covering a broad range of industries and companies, both in the United States and internationally. In 1988, Mr. Komisarjevsky was named president and chief executive officer of Carl Byoir & Associates, relaunching the firm to provide high-level corporate communications counseling with an international perspective. Prior to that, Mr. Komisarjevsky was president and chief executive officer of Hill and Knowlton International S.A., the headquarters for Hill and Knowlton operations in Europe, the Middle East, and Africa, with responsibility for the network of 11 offices in 10 countries. Since joining Hill and Knowlton in 1974, Mr. Komisarjevsky has served major corporate and trade association clients engaged in such fields as financial services, building materials, entertainment, pharmaceutical, health care, communications, real estate, management consulting, and consumer products.

Repealing
Gibson's Law

Peter S. McCue
Senior Vice-President, Fleishman-Hillard, Inc.

Whom can we trust?

Overview

After having been bombarded for decades with prophesies of doom about the foods they eat, the air they breathe and the products they use, American consumers are still without a satisfactory answer to this question. Whether the controversy has concerned the threat of poisoned grapes or automobiles that accelerate suddenly and seemingly without warning, the buying public has been left with the daunting task of defining for themselves where the truth lies.

In a real sense, consumers have become victims, and what they have to say about their situation indicates the emergence of a bemused sense of resignation. The view of consumer Brandon Margoulis is typical. He told a reporter from the *Boston Globe* a couple of years ago that "Going to the grocery store these days is like taking a walk on the wild side. It seems like every day there's somebody telling me what I shouldn't eat. I try to heed the warnings, but it's getting so I may have to go on a water diet — and even that isn't as safe as it used to be."

Like Mr. Margoulis, millions of other consumers are showing signs of a civilian form of battle fatigue. Since it would be impossible for them to escape all or even most of the alleged dangers in their environment, they have had to cope with them. Their response has ranged from detachment to studying product labels and fixatina on health foods.

All too often during public health and safety scares, the basis for sensible decision making has remained buried beneath a hysteria-triggered avalanche of scientific data. Each crisis has tended to follow a familiar pattern:

The Anatomy of a Consumer Crisis

- A public interest group sounds the alarm or bullies a federal agency into sounding it for them.

- The media create widespread awareness of the charge, whether it is legitimate or not.

- Industry responds with studies of its own and proclaims its products safe. Few consumers even hear this defense, much less believe it.

- In the face of shrill charges and sketchy, often irrelevant advice, the public becomes agitated and fearful. It avoids the product in question until more reliable answers are made available.

- Sales suffer and continue to decline as the regulators equivocate and issue confusing and conflicting guidelines.

- Relying upon exaggerated emotional appeals, the activists step up the attack.

- The press faithfully covers their every move, thus magnifying consumers' concerns.

- Industry reacts strenuously and occasionally resorts to exaggerations of its own in an effort to restore calm and boost sales.

- For weeks or months, everyone loses perspective on the issue.

- Eventually, a more accurate and balanced assessment emerges.

- Industry digs out and braces itself for another day.

- Those who make their living from consumerism find somewhere else to promote gloom and doom in order to maintain the vital flow of tax-free contributions.

- The media move on to the next crisis after giving short shrift to clarifications of the original inflated charge.

- And, the government goes back to studying the issue so that it can write new regulations that make little sense.

Granted, this is an oversimplified picture of what actually happens. Nonetheless, this view is held by an ever-increasing number of consumers.

Opinion polls show that the public largely blames economic stagnation on a lack of leadership throughout society. The White House has been faulted consistently for turning a blind eye to domestic issues, preferring instead to concentrate on international affairs. Congress is thought to be mired in perennial scandal and incapable of passing any meaningful legislation.

Public Remains Skeptical

Business suffers from the perception that its leaders have become complacent and soft. Moreover, they are seen as greedy, unconcerned about the long-term welfare of their companies or employees, and, in many instances, inept. Government regulators are considered to be the handmaidens of industry, the agents of bureaucratic paralysis, or both. The press is widely believed to distort and sensationalize the news as the means to establishing its own agenda for the country. Consumer activists, once thought of primarily as advocates for constructive change, are more and more frequently and harshly being criticized for exaggerating the dangers confronting the public.

To one degree or another, the perceived impotence or manipulations of all these authorities has been amply evident in their response to the glut of food, product safety, and environmental scares that have occurred over the past three decades. With varying degrees of success, all these protagonists have attempted to portray themselves as agents of public good. However, in their zealous pursuit of consumer affection or trust, few of them ever pause long enough to evaluate how their attacks and counterattacks actually sound to real consumers.

Judging from their predictable stances each time a crisis erupts, it is apparent that they have failed to recognize the growing discount factor that consumers apply to everything they say and do. In the words of the most current populist outcry, "They just don't get it." They appear incapable of seeing themselves the way the public does.

To consumers, these self-styled leaders have come to represent caricatures of themselves. When confronted with controversy, they act like robots, as if they were programmed to fly on automatic pilot. Their roles have been predetermined and they play them as scripted, mimicking stereotypes from the past. Their positions have become inflexible and hardened, allowing little or no room for sensible compromise.

Today's information pollution can trace its roots back to The Great Cranberry Scare of 1959, which marked the end of an age of innocence for consumers. The announcement came just three weeks before Thanksgiving. The federal government had discovered samples of cranberries laced with a weed killer known to be

The End of Innocence

carcinogenic in rats. Consumers were urged to avoid all cranberries except those which had been tested and approved by the government.

Until then, the American people believed that food items available at the supermarket were automatically safe to eat. As a result of chemical contamination, the public now had reason to fear the safety of their food supply.

The cranberry scare was followed, in the late 1960s, with the ban of cyclamates, an artificial sweetener. Since then, Americans have been almost routinely subjected to food crises, with consumers dealing with more than one crisis per year. For more than 25 years, consumers have been unable to find refuge from dire warnings about the foods they eat. The list of these public scares is virtually endless, but here are a few of the more memorable ones: DES in meat; botulism in canned mushrooms; the banning of violet dye number one; the banning of red dye numbers two and four as well as carbon black; Kepone contamination of fish in Virginia; Saccharin; PCBs in fish in New York and in animal feed in Montana; sodium nitrite used in cured meats such as bacon, hot dogs, and ham; residues of the pesticide ethylene dibromide (EDB) in breads and breakfast cereals; salmonella in chicken and later in cantaloupes; and the specter of entire boatloads of Chilean grapes riddled with cyanide.

Whether issued by governmental agencies or by public interest groups, the announcements about alleged dangers in the public food supply have resulted in headlines that have sent consumers scurrying to their kitchen cabinets in search of the carcinogen of the moment. Interspersed among these frightening episodes have been countless horror stories about such public safety issues as faulty nuclear power facilities, unlawful dumping of hazardous wastes, highway safety, and terrorism at the pharmacy counter. A few of the most notorious incidents were Three Mile Island, Love Canal, Times Beach, toxic-shock syndrome associated with Rely tampons, silicone breast implants, the Tylenol tampering, and cases of sudden acceleration in the Audi 5000.

To current shoppers, frequent consumer anxiety has become a way of life. Having been exposed to a seemingly uninterrupted series of false and premature alarms since the late 1960s, they feel isolated, vulnerable, powerless, and angry. From the preservative-laden juice they drink in the morning to the flame-retardant pajamas they slip on their children at night, they remain hostages to the incessant public debate over their safety.

It seems that everywhere the American consumer has turned during the past 25 years, he or she has bumped into a perceived health or safety calamity of one kind or another. This is not to suggest that the bulk of them have been false alarms. Many, in fact, such as the Tylenol case, have ultimately saved lives and led to long overdue reforms in industry practices.

On balance, however, I think it's safe to say that most of the food and safety scares Americans have endured since the late 1960s have been exaggerated out of all proportion to their actual threat. Some even have turned out to be dead wrong. For instance, after nearly 25 years in marketplace exile, cyclamates seem poised for a comeback on the heels of regulatory admissions that the substance is safe after all. In 1989 Robert Scheuplein of the Federal Drug Administration's (FDA) Center for Food Safety and Applied Nutrition said, "I have no reluctance in saying that with cyclamate we made a mistake." He cited the results of a long-term study on a group of monkeys at the National Cancer Institute. Since 1972 each of them had been fed enough cyclamate five days a week to sweeten 30 cans of diet soda each day. The Institute's first progress report, issued 17 years later, showed that the monkeys had experienced none of the adverse effects which some rats had suffered 20 years before when cyclamate pellets had been implanted in their bladders and tumors later developed.

Crying Wolf?

And while dioxin has long been considered to be one of the most toxic substances known to humans, the Environmental Protection Agency (EPA) has come to recognize, grudgingly, that its effects are not as lethal in humans as officials had once concluded. Some 10 years after the crisis at Times Beach, the government is tempering its grim view of this chemical compound. News of the reassessment appeared on the front page of the *New York Times* on August 15, 1991. "We are seeing new information on dioxin that suggests a lower risk assessment for dioxin should be applied," announced William Reilly, EPA's administrator. "I know the stakes and that I'm unraveling something here ... but we need to be prepared to adjust, to raise or lower standards, as new science become available."

The reaction of former Times Beach mayor Marilyn Leistner was one of bewilderment: "You just don't know what to think. If dioxin is less dangerous, that should be good news. The truth is, it's not. People have been hurt, their lives ruined by what happened in this area. One minute it's bad, the next, it's good. It's a roller coaster that just won't stop." Mayor Leistner was one of 2,240 residents of Times Beach, Missouri, whom the federal government evacuated from the town in 1982 after finding high levels of dioxin contamination in soil samples.

While food and product safety scares have caused nowhere near as much devastation and dislocation as have Times Beach and Love Canal, they have produced considerable consumer distress and, often, needless economic loss. Only after weeks of panic at fruit counters across America and the near destruction of

Chile's grape producers was the source and true magnitude of the problem finally revealed. The contamination of just two single grapes had caused all this ruckus.

Following the startling charges about sudden acceleration in mid-1980s Audi 5000s, it took many months and several investigations to clear the company's name. The culprit indeed had been driver error all along. Nonetheless, some six years later Audi still is struggling to recover in the marketplace.

Measuring Individual Risk

In 1985, more than a year after consumers had been warned about cancer-causing pesticide EDB residues in their breads and cereals, the EPA issued itself an unusual public rebuke concerning the manner in which it had handled the emergency. The report agreed with critics who claimed that the entire affair had been overblown. It attributed much of the blame to the agency's inability to communicate properly and clearly with the public. "EPA's decisions were based on a statistical analysis of the aggregate threat from EDB, and this was the focus of much of what EPA said about the issue," the document said, "but the individual newspaper reader and television viewer was asking the very personal question: Can I eat the bread?"

People who heard the EPA's warning, the report determined, didn't know what to make of it. "The public has little patience for a risk evaluation that concludes with EDB is 1,000 times less risky than aflotoxin, or than smoking a pack of cigarettes," it found. At no time during the crisis did the agency try to lend perspective to the issues it had raised by addressing the fundamental questions on consumers' minds: Am I at risk? If so, What do you suggest I do to minimize that risk?

The report went on to find that overreaction by the press compounded the level of public fear. It cited one network's egregious reliance on theatrics to convey the story. Whenever a studio reporter offered the latest news about EDB, a skull and crossbones was featured behind him or her.

In general, the EPA said, the press tended to oversimplify matters. While the agency generated "macro-risk" data relating to the population as a whole, the media translated those findings in terms of an individual's risk. This magnified the actual hazard "a thousand times," according to the report. "Macro-risk becomes a science-fiction monster, and what was intended by the EPA to be the soothing voice of assurance is conveyed or heard by the public as the crack of doom."

And the resulting consumer response can be as unanticipated as it is extreme. Three Mile Island, for example, left in its wake at least one unexpected and bewildered casualty. Months after the fabled event, The Book-of-the-Month Club (BOMC) was still reeling. The warehouse and distribution site for its Quality

Paperback Book Club (QPBC) subsidiary was located in Camp Hill, Pennsylvania, only a few miles away from ground zero. This fact was not lost on many customers. Fearing radiation poisoning from the books they planned to order, they chose instead to purchase them elsewhere. QPBC's sales plummeted and remained flat until the mushroom cloud of hysteria dispersed.

Today consumers find it virtually impossible to determine the real facts. In matters of public health and safety, emotionalism understandably clouds the debate. Warnings about cancer-causing food additives, botulism, airborne lead contamination, highway fatalities caused by defective automobiles, and retail terrorism are anything but academic concerns. They are deeply troublesome and personal subjects to consumers.

Ball of Confusion

Further obstructing the consumer's pursuit of truth are the tactics that have been employed by activists. They have come to recognize that the best way to secure a headline is to create a sense of alarm. Merely suggesting to people that there is something in general for them to be concerned about in their food supply packs nowhere near the news punch of a charge that apples, for example, are unsafe to eat.

Rarely, in all of this alarmism masquerading as public service, can consumers find so much as a molehill's worth of sensible guidance concerning what to do under the circumstances. The danger usually is defined in parts per million and billion and theoretical equivalencies rather than in actionable terms. Should I keep feeding my child apple juice or switch to cranberry juice? Concerned parents want to know.

An example of such forces at work is the Alar scare of 1989. That year, following an announcement by the Natural Resources Defense Council (NRDC) that a growth regulator (daminozide, known popularly as Alar) used in apple production was a potent carcinogen, apples and apple products were removed from supermarket shelves and school lunchrooms across America. Six months after the initial uproar, the Washington apple growers alone, who produce nearly 60 percent of the country's apple crop, were said to have lost approximately $125 million. And one of the leading producers of apple juice admitted publicly that its sales were down 25 percent. When asked by the growers why apples had been singled out when countless other fruits and vegetables also had been treated with Alar, the NRDC's Janet Hathaway said that she, too, was surprised, claiming that her group's study has spotlighted 23 chemicals used on 17 commodities.

Anatomy of a Consumer Crisis: Alar and Apples

The simple fact is that scientific conclusions and legal assertions suggest certainty in a world where none exists. Consumers must make choices based on the process of continually weighing relative risks against relative benefits. There are no hard and fast answers.

During the Alar controversy, in fact, consumers received no useful answers at all from the NRDC, the originators of the panic and perhaps the only ones who credibly could have restored perspective at the time. The EPA had become discredited as little more than an agent of the apple growers and processors. And the industry itself, of course, was perceived as being self-interested and therefore an unreliable source of information. It was up to the individuals who had sounded the alarm to show consumers how to respond to it.

But instead of telling consumers that no immediate cause for concern existed (as subsequent headlines proved), the NRDC needlessly fanned the flames by launching a series of public service spots featuring actress Meryl Streep. The actress also appeared on the talk-show circuit to spread the gospel. Her basic message, beyond inveighing against the greed of corporate America, was for parents to wash all their fruits and vegetables before serving them to their children. Generally speaking, that probably is sound advice. It is a simple and effective way to remove pesticide residues from the fruit.

Meryl Streep speaks on behalf of the Natural Resources Defense Council, warning of potential health hazards from Alar, a pesticide used on apples and other produce.

The trouble is, her helpful hint failed utterly to address the issue that she and the NRDC had raised. Substances such as Alar are used to regulate growth and promote uniformity of color. They work inside of the apples and other crops rather than on their surfaces. No amount of soap and water or hard scrubbing can remove Alar from apples.

So instead of providing customers with some reasonable way of responding to its warning, the NRDC treated them to the sorry spectacle of Ms. Streep addressing a separate issue. This added to the confusion and convinced many consumers to avoid apple products altogether until the controversy had passed. The resulting erosion of sales, in turn, caused a secondary panic among growers and producers and reinforced the impression that the public threat was more serious than it actually was.

Gibson's Law in Action: Enter the Experts

Once consumers read past the headline of a crisis story, they often are left with columns of warnings, reassurances, and useless tips from the so-called experts, all with axes of one sort of another to grind. Instead of working together to provide the public with a balanced assessment of the situation, these experts seem inclined to engage in statistical combat. Confusion reigns as scientific gladiators struggle for their places in the limelight.

Fletch Waller, a General Mills spokesperson during the FTC's 1979 hearings in San Francisco about children's advertising, might well have been speaking for all beleaguered consumers during his locally televised debate with a representative of the Consumers' Union. In the initial few minutes of the show, Waller was barraged with the results of numerous scientific studies "documenting" the nutritional inadequacy of his company's breakfast cereals.

So savage was the attack that a few of Waller's advisors standing behind the studio cameras became very nervous. Why is Fletch allowing this nonsense to go on? they wondered. Apparently, the show's host was thinking along the same lines. In the interest of fairness, the host said, he felt compelled to interrupt the activist's oration in order to give Waller a chance to defend himself.

Fletch leaned forward and said, "Whenever someone hurls stacks and stacks of scientific research at me, I am reminded of Gibson's Law." Then he paused, giving his advisors further reason for concern. "What's that?" asked the host. "Simply this," responded Waller. "For every Ph.D. there's an equal and opposite Ph.D. You see, I could refute every one of those charges with more reliable data from the studies we cite. If we had more time, perhaps I would. This isn't the first time people have been needlessly frightened by an alarmist. No, I'm not going to trot out all the scientists we know and trust. That would only bore and confuse your viewers now. Instead, let's examine the real issues here, shall we?"

The relief he had brought to his advisors was nothing compared to the beating he administered to his opponent for the remainder of the show. In the cab ride back to the hotel, one curious companion wondered where Waller had ever come up with this law. He allowed as how he was familiar with the laws of Parkinson, Murphy, and others but had never heard of Gibson's. Waller shot back, "Oh, that's Larry Gibson, the research guy who works just down the hall from me."

Consumers and Gibson

Squeezed for so long between the various hardliners who insist upon nothing short of "zero tolerance" when it comes to additives and pesticides that might cause cancer and the "acceptable risk" crowd, which believes that everything in life including safety is relative, the public is worn out. It has begun to retreat from all who curry its favor since none of them has proven reliable or trustworthy over time.

Gibson's Law goes to the heart of the dilemma consumers are facing. No matter where they turn for answers during each crisis, consumers are confronted with dueling Ph.D.s, who leave in their wake piles of statistical chaff. Joe and Joan Q. Public are left to rummage through it all in search of a few kernels of guidance.

It is next to impossible for consumers to make an informed assessment on the merits of what they are told. So they have learned to do the next best thing. They make their determinations by conducting credibility contests. The optimists among them ask themselves which authority they trust the most. The pessimists make their decision on the basis of which one they distrust the least.

Activists Flex Political Might

Today, many disgusted members of the general public, when asking Whom can we trust? might answer — nobody. Increasingly, consumers are coming to the conclusion that each of the groups vying for public support has its own axe to grind. Hidden behind the sanctimonious words of their leaders lurks the real agenda, which is less the protection of public interests than the acquisition of greater political power.

For all their high-minded rhetoric about public safety and the need for environmental purity, the activist groups seem to be spending the bulk of their contribution money on the propaganda war rather than on the propagation of health, safety, and environmental enhancements. In 1989, according to Dallas oil pro L. Frank Pitts, as featured in the March 1992 issue of *World Oil*, "The top 12 (environmental) groups had operating budgets totalling over $336 million a year, from a donor base of just under 13 million contributors. That's over 10 million more people and $250 million more in money than the entire combined Democratic and Republican parties have available to them." He claims that "a full 90 percent of those funds go, not to environmental improvement, but to political purposes."

Applying the same discount factor that consumers use, let's assume that Mr. Pitts is exaggerating a bit just to sharpen his own political axe. After all, some would argue, if only the public interest groups would leave him alone, he could harvest a considerably fatter profit. So let's say the amount the environmentalists spend on politics amounts to just 70 percent of the funds they generate each year. That still adds up to more than $235 million per year that is being set aside for lobbying and proselytizing purposes.

And what precisely is all this newfound political muscle achieving for these groups and the millions of consumers whose interests they profess to defend? To illustrate, Pitts cites the case of the spotted owl. The Sierra Club, he says, "openly admits (that its) suit to protect the ... spotted owl was really to stop tree cutting." He points out, however, that there is 23 percent more timber around today than 70 years ago and that the planting of new trees is triple the level it was then and expanding each year. "The spotted owl ruling," he concludes, "has put 30,000 families out of work and set aside 12 million acres for the use of owls at a cost of $660,000 per owl."

The overemphasis activists have been placing on gloom-and-doom scenarios throughout the years appears at last to have boomeranged on them. A spate of recent news articles in major national publications has been skewering the environmental movement for its overblown rhetoric. Headlines such as "The End Is Not at Hand" and "A House of Cards" tell the story. It seems that the media finally have decided to send the activists a message of their own: Enough is enough.

Scientists Debate

Even many of the scientists who have been drawn into the protracted public debates on health and safety issues are no longer safe from the withering glare of public scorn. Despite having compiled enough data over the years to fill every warehouse in America, they remain unable to provide consumers with the definitive answers they seek during most crisis situations. By proving Gibson's Law correct, they have unwittingly helped to reduce their own stature in the eyes of consumers.

The evidence to support most food and safety scares is usually inconclusive. It frequently comes down to one scientist's word against another's. Pure science, it turns out, is anything but pure truth with a meaning obvious to all. At what point can substances that cause tumors in mice, when administered in high dosages, be considered dangerous to humans? How is it possible to determine safe human thresholds at all when it can take 30 years or more for certain forms of cancer to develop? And once they appear, how certain can we be that they were caused by consumption of a single substance? Just how protected are we by the Delaney Clause and the Ames Test? Even when the government tells us our food products are acceptable to eat because they contain only a few parts per million or billion of a suspicious substance, can we really be sure they are safe?

For all the data we have been able to amass in our laboratories, we simply do not know the definitive answers to these questions. How then can consumers be expected to understand them? The sheer complexity of the data alone is enough to befuddle most of them. Add to this the attempts by various groups, vying for public acceptance during a crisis, to bend the news their way and everyone becomes confused.

Government Stumbles, Business Fumbles

Government regulators are known more for their indecision than for their ability to protect the public. The activists, when they are not prodding one of these agencies into issuing dense and ill-conceived rulings, often dismiss them as being industry dupes. And whenever industry is displeased about what it sees as over-regulation, somebody in a pin-striped suit invariably seems to scurry out of the executive suite to condemn the bureaucrats for toadying to the public interest groups.

Industry voices, in fact, are the easiest of all for consumers to ignore. The public expects business people to rush to the defense of their products. Even when their own companies are not being attacked, they are known as fervent boosters of free enterprise, prone to exaggeration to maintain the status quo.

PR Reaction   Whatever the crisis concerns, the corporate public relations reaction generally follows a prescribed, if proven, set of rules. While management doesn't always accept the advice it is given, the recommendations it receives fall into roughly these categories.

Create an ad hoc committee with responsibility for handling all aspects of the crisis. In addition to someone from senior management, all pertinent functional areas should be represented on this committee — sales and marketing, legal, government relations, human resources, research, public relations, and other departments deemed important to resolving the crisis. Individuals selected should hold positions of authority so that decisions can be made quickly.

Conduct an inventory of internal and external resources that can be relied upon as needed.

Prepare a position paper that summarizes the situation, conveys the company's key message points, includes evidence of third-party support, presents the company's own scientific case, and so forth. This document is intended to be the company's primary resource document for the duration of the crisis. It will ensure consistency in the company's position and facilitate public actions.

Conduct baseline research to gauge public opinion and establish what impact the crisis in having upon sales. Repeat at regular intervals and use the findings to guide decision making.

Develop a scenario-based crisis plan keyed to the various courses that events could take.

Identify critical audiences, within and outside of the company, and rank them in order of importance.

Establish a news bureau to handle all media requests and to prepare and distribute news releases and other materials, such as Q&A's for management's use. This body will arrange press briefings, editorial board meetings, and other affirmative activities considered useful.

Ensure that all communications with designated regulatory bodies are maintained. Enhance contact if necessary to minimize surprises.

See what assistance the company might obtain from trade associations to which it belongs.

Identify a cadre of spokespeople to convey the company's side of the story. Then provide them with media training so that they can get the messages across under any circumstances. The news bureau will schedule their appearances.

Identify third parties, particularly scientists, whose credentials are unassailable and whose views support the company's position in this case. Enlist them to speak out in the company's behalf.

Develop a trade support program for dealers, supermarkets, retailers — whichever avenue the company's products take en route to consumers — to help them respond most effectively to customer inquiries and demands.

Continuum of Fear

In the abstract, these are all logical and appropriate steps to take. The trouble is that, in recent years, they have become less and less effective in terms of extricating companies from crises. One reason for this is the sheer amount of time it takes to find, motivate, and mobilize all of the resources, primarily the most credible ones located outside the company. The controversy is often on the wane by the time they get into the act.

This alone, however, does not account for the growing problem facing crisis communicators. Its roots are in the profound changes that have been occurring elsewhere, among consumers and within the information environment. Until practitioners first note and then act upon these differences, they will remain frustrated in their attempts to get their messages across to the public.

It is simply no longer safe for crisis communicators to assume that each crisis they face is unique, with characteristics all its own and with little or no connection to others that have preceded it. The curvature of the lens through which consumers examine each controversy has been altered permanently, misshapened by the relentless battering of all the product and environmental scares over the past three decades. Science has become synonymous with danger. As a result, consumers now see each health or safety scare as part of a continuum of fear. It has become difficult for them to separate one crisis from another. The issues tend to overlap and the same activists and regulators dominate the headlines. Their information environment has become polluted.

The Erosion of Trust

Another factor contributes to the emergence of an entirely different type of consumer: public trust has evaporated. Suspicions abound. All messages, regardless of their source, are being filtered through layers of consumer doubt, mistrust, and cynicism. True, the public cannot be frightened as easily as it once was. But it also has become wary of any positive news. Punching a company's messages through this cloud of misgiving has become a formidable task.

The results of recent national opinion polls would seem to indicate that the task of reaching the general public in the years ahead will be a daunting one. As late as 1967, the majority of polls showed that Americans had great confidence in most institutions. Even Congress had a 40 percent approval rating. But by the mid-1970s, after Vietnam and Watergate, Congress's rating had fallen to below 15 percent. The White House was down from 41 percent to 13 percent and major companies had dropped from 55 percent to 20 percent. Under the circumstances, the press was doing fairly well with its 26 percent approval rating.

Attitudes have deteriorated further since then, however. A March 1992 Harris Poll placed public confidence in major companies at a mere 11 percent, the worst score for big business in 26 years. The press limped in with a shameful 13 percent approval rating, also an all-time low. Only 16 percent of the public has confidence in the White House today and just 10 percent think that Congress is doing a good job. The entire executive branch, including the regulators who watch over the products we consume, managed just a 13 percent confidence rating, a drop of nearly 30 percentage points from 26 years ago.

Establishing a New Perspective

Like an army of shell-shocked veterans, consumers are numb and wish only to be left alone. In growing numbers, they are resigned to the sad fact that they have nowhere to turn for answers in times of public controversy. And, like Diogenes, holding out a lantern in perpetual search of one honest man, they are looking for someone, anyone, to give them reason to put down their lamps. For too many of them, regrettably, their arms have grown weary before succeeding in their quest. It has become pointless even for them to conduct their own private credibility contests. How can there be any winners in an atmosphere where credibility no longer exists?

Long ago, crisis communicators should have noticed this for the threat it represents to their profession and to the businesses they serve. They should have detected its symptoms in their diminishing effectiveness. They should have paused now and then to ask themselves why, after so diligently doing what they had been taught to do, were they having so much trouble getting their messages across.

Given the nature of crisis communications work, it is only natural for its practitioners to lose sight of the larger context in which they ply their craft. The issues frequently involve matters of economic life or death to their corporations. The pace can be as exhilarating as it is exhausting. And the degree of involvement with top management it affords crisis communicators exceeds that of virtually every other facet of corporate communications.

Nevertheless, the present overwhelming danger facing all practitioners requires them to jettison their blinders. They can ill afford to believe any longer that their livelihoods depend solely on their ability to extinguish a single company's fires.

Until credibility has been resurrected, every corporate message will evaporate along with all the others into the heavily polluted information environment. No matter how professionally crisis communicators execute their plans, they will not succeed so long as consumers refuse to hear the message. And blaming failure on factors beyond a company's control will only lead to complacency and perpetuate the problems.

Misinformation, hyperbole, and other distortions, as well as the sheer information overload, must be seen for the toxins they are. They have contaminated the atmosphere of robust debate Americans once enjoyed. Imperceptibly, yet inexorably, they have eroded the public's ability to seek constructive change. Plenty of noise remains, but there is little progress to show for it.

For meaningful change to occur, a new sense of perspective must be established for consumers. The arteries of communication, which have been abused for decades by all the deadlocked factions of the health and safety debate, must be unclogged. If at all possible, they must be restored to their condition prior to the 1950s.

Toward this end, crisis communicators, in fact, are in an enviable position. If they can only be persuaded to come out of isolation and work together on this problem, they can make an appreciable contribution to the cleansing of America's fragile information environment. And they will be one of its eventual beneficiaries.

Toward Repealing Gibson's Law

The first step, then, is to help everyone — business people, governmental officials, scientists, the media, even environmentalists — redefine the enemy. No single one of these constituents is the villain here. While each of them has contributed to this dismal circumstance, none can be credited with having sired it. To fault only one group for such damage would be like blaming a lone pocket of warm air somewhere out in the mid-Atlantic Ocean for all the devastation that Hurricane Andrew brought ashore to southern Florida and coastal Louisiana. Even if it could be faulted, this would do nothing to start the rebuilding process.

The single largest barrier to progress on health and safety issues since the late 1960s has been information pollution. This has been the insidious enemy common to all of the adversaries. The problem hasn't been the Environmental Defense Fund, the Sierra Club, or Jeremy Rifkin. Nor has it been the FDA, Dow Chemical, or the *New York Times*. Alone, the excesses and oversights of each would have been negligible. Their harmful effects would have been neither serious nor lasting. An atmosphere of reason could have been restored through healthy debate.

Together, however, all these forces have combined to create an environment in which it is virtually impossible to assess, objectively and dispassionately, which information regarding health and safety concerns is truthful and which is tainted by hyperbole and politicking.

SCARED Straight   In order to clear the air of unsubstantiated claims and invective, a truly impartial body needs to be created. Ideally, such a group would be composed of leading research scientists and physicians from a variety of scientific and medical disciplines — including chemistry, environmental studies, nutrition, pediatrics, oncology, physics, public health, and others — drawn from across the nation.

To facilitate public trust and identity, the organization would adopt an easily recognizable name. One that would apply is SCARED, an acronym for Scientists Concerned about Research Exaggeration and Distortion.

This new group would be independent. Its aim would not be to target any particular point of view as incorrect or disreputable. Rather, SCARED would seek to preserve the integrity of scientific and medical research as a source of accurate information upon which the general public can rely. In that light, SCARED would provide the public and the media with an independent, objective source of evaluation on scientifically or quasi-scientifically based controversies.

The group would take to task publicly any individual, company, organization, or association that engages in unsubstantiated claims designed to mislead the public on health and safety issues. This willingness to identify and expose the introduction or perpetuation of misinformation by any source — be it government, the media, public interest groups, corporations, activists, celebrity spokespeople, universities, or whomever —would all help rebalance the public health equation in a vitally necessary and productive manner.

An important cornerstone of SCARED's independence would be its sources of funding. Perhaps the best way to ensure that the group would be beholden to no specific constituency is to establish a blind trust fund to finance the operations of the organization. Any person or group would be welcome to contribute to this fund — including the NRDC, DuPont, the Rockefeller Foundation, or concerned members of the public. Contributors' identities would be kept strictly confidential, thus helping to insulate the group from attacks that it is biased toward any special interest.

SCARED could issue a challenge to the nation in general, and to regular players in health and safety dramas in particular, to put their money where their mouths are. If these groups are truly concerned about the health and safety of the American people, they should likewise be willing to support an initiative, as epitomized by SCARED, to reintroduce sanity and the dissemination of accurate information to the public safety debate.

To get started, at least several respected and well-known scientists would have to stand up and issue a rallying cry for support from the scientific and medical communities. These should be scientists with the stature of former surgeon general C. Everett Koop or Nobel laureate Joshua Lederberg. At long last, a bewildered public and a beleaguered press corps would have someplace to turn for reliable guidance whenever these scares arise. Needless and costly panics could be averted in the true interest of the public good.

The success of the group would ultimately depend on four factors: its commitment to ideological and financial independence; its devotion to preserving the ideals and standards of scientific research; its avoidance of single-issue campaigns; and its ability to emerge as a single, authoritative voice that is equal to any scaremongers who may emerge down the road.

To perpetuate the effectiveness, independence and visibility of SCARED, the group could engage in several ongoing projects designed to educate important audiences about the need for information relating to science to be accurate if it is to be effective.

For example, SCARED might arrange a series of seminars for the media across the country in which it describes, say, 10 signs of distortion often used by participants in public safety debates and offering suggestions on how to guard against them. Likewise, SCARED members could write a series of op-eds for newspapers around the nation offering consumers similar warning signs regarding distortion. Town meetings could be held to better educate consumers about practical ways in which they can sift through all they hear about safety issues so that they can make informed choices. Eventually each state could form its own chapter of SCARED drawing on responsible scientists from within its borders to deal with local and statewide health and safety misinformation. These ongoing activities would help establish SCARED as an impartial voice of reason and perspective in the noisy and swirling area of public debate.

Eventually, the success of SCARED could spawn a similar organization with a grass roots focus. Such an organization could be composed of consumers, who are fed up with riding the roller coaster of fear that accompanies each new health scare. Health and safety issues often are portrayed as threats to the welfare of the American family. Consequently, both sides regularly attempt to skew debate by influencing the nation's mothers who, correctly or incorrectly, are viewed as the custodians of America's family structure.

In order to reintroduce perspective in this emotionally charged arena, a group would be formed to provide sensible, responsible information on which consumers can base family food buying decisions. To discourage further attempts at family manipulation by all parties, the group could be called MOM, or Mothers Opposed to Misinformation.

MOM, or any similar organization, is not intended to replace the use of credible scientific or industry authorities and supporters. Rather it would provide a base of consumer support that could balance public debate and demonstrate that concern for healthy American families does not preclude advocacy for the responsible use of scientific data in public debate and against the needless fulmination of public hysteria about safety threats that may or may not exist.

Back to Apples   To invoke the Alar example again, it would be interesting to speculate how the daminozide "crisis" might have run a different course had groups such as SCARED and MOM existed in 1989.

Two events prompted the national attention that was focused on Alar. The first was a study issued by the Natural Resources Defense Council entitled "Intolerable Risk: Pesticides in Our Children's Food." The second was a report by the CBS News magazine "60 Minutes" on the NRDC findings, which generally accepted the study's apocalyptic assertions at face value and introduced the public to the first wave of hysteria.

What "60 Minutes" failed to do was carefully examine the NRDC claims and point out a host of glaring inconsistencies and factual errors in the report. Instead the CBS program chose to gloss over these factual lapses and cater to the public appetite for yet another safety crisis. (A move reminiscent of its treatment of the Audi 5000 acceleration issue several years earlier.)

Among the inconsistencies in the NRDC report that never made it to the CBS broadcast were: claims by NRDC that its study, at the time, represented a present danger to American consumers. It was only after carefully examining the report and its appendix dealing with methodology that a careful reader discovered NRDC claims were based on 1986 data. No effort was made to determine if the situation in 1989 was the same as it was in 1986.

The 1986 data showed that the detectable levels of daminozide in apple products were between 9 and 400 times less than the level of acceptable tolerance established by the EPA.

The NRDC study implied that testing of then-present levels of Alar in apples and apple products was done by NRDC itself. In fact, NRDC did no studies on the presence of Alar in apples or apple products in 1989 or in 1986. All NRDC's data was derived from a 1986 study by EPA — a fact a reader does not encounter until footnote 26 on page 217 of the appendix to the NRDC report.

What NRDC presented to the public as facts were, actually, estimates. The infamous appendix to the report reveals that estimates of exposure to Alar were derived "by multiplying the consumption data for individual foods by a calculation of the amount of residues found in these foods." No testing of current residues was done in 1989.

None of the primary authors of the report were chemists, toxicologists, or cancer specialists. The two principal authors held master's degrees in public health. One contributing author had a master's degree in science and the other was a lawyer. The project coordinator was also a lawyer. Of the 14 other people who helped in the preparation of the report, 2 were lawyers, 11 had no academic credential listed, and only 1 had a doctorate in a relevant field. He performed statistical assessments of carcinogenic risks.

NRDC portrayed its study as statistically valid, drawing on a 1985–86 food consumption survey by the U.S. Department of Agriculture's Human Nutrition Information Service on women ages 19 to 50 and their children ages 1 to 5. Yet only 333 children completed three days or more in what was supposed to be a nonconsecutive six-day study. The EPA said that this small sample was not large enough to be valid.

NRDC flatly charged that Alar was a carcinogen and its presence in apples posed a threat to consumers. Yet, many highly regarded scientists — including Dr. John H. Weisburger, former National Cancer Institute official, Dr. Bruce Ames, professor of biochemistry at the University of California at Berkeley and inventor of the widely used Ames Mutagenicity Assay, and Dr. James Witt, professor of agricultural chemistry and a specialist in chemical toxicology at Oregon State University — shed doubt on the risk presented by minute amounts of residual Alar in apples.

Had a group such as SCARED existed in 1989, CBS might not have accepted NRDC's assertions so readily. After the NRDC report was issued SCARED could have thoroughly examined the study and presented a full critique of the methodology used in the report.

The role of SCARED would not have been to refute NRDC's claims by presenting countervailing arguments. Rather its job would have been to assess the scientific foundation on which NRDC's claims were based and determine if they indeed were based on good science or slipshod generalizations, estimates, and inconsistencies.

The presence of such an organization would have forced the media to examine more closely the claims made by all sides in the Alar controversy, thus, one hopes, introducing perspective rather than hysteria into the national discourse.

Of course groups like SCARED and MOM are only a beginning. It is important to recognize that they are not panaceas for all the problems surrounding health and safety issues. Additionally, they, like any group, are susceptible to politicization. The best way for such groups to guard against this type of danger is to keep firmly focused on their charters — namely, to remain dedicated to cleansing the information environment and keeping watch on all sides that cross the line separating responsible and valid scientific reporting from fantastic fear-inducing pseudo-science.

A group like SCARED is a good start because it begins to rechart and redefine the murky waters in which the current debate on health and safety issues is submerged.

SCARED can't provide all the answers to all questions of science and it can't replace the choices consumers of food, finished goods, and information must make for themselves. What it can do, however, is present a better way to evaluate what people hear and, in turn, provide a more factual foundation for the decisions that ultimately will be left to the consumer.

SCARED gets the ball rolling and begins to change the behavior of those who would now have to answer to an unbiased authority with impeccable credentials and a growing track record of neutrality, fairness, honesty, and impartiality. This alone would make SCARED worthwhile.

Many experts, including those in the White House, have pegged the economic future of the United States to industries such as biotechnology in which health and safety issues currently operate in ambiguity. This nebulous atmosphere of charge and countercharge leaves open a wide door for endless fears of killer tomatoes and crippling litigation. This environment eloquently argues in behalf of an organization like SCARED which can help clean up the pollution of information so decision makers, the media, and consumers can make well-informed choices about what to accept and what to dismiss. In this case, no less than the economic well-being of the nation's future may depend on it.

What society needs to do is to repeal Gibson's Law, where differing views are forever locked in opposition and the loser is the nation. SCARED can begin to break this deadlock by reintroducing clarity and perspective to the information process. This will allow our nation to act responsibly and decisively for the health and safety of today's consumers and for the economic and scientific achievements of tomorrow.

Peter McCue is senior vice-president and director of Fleishman-Hillard's Corporate Relations Group in New York. He and his staff specialize in strategic communications counsel, crisis communications, litigation support, issues-response management, labor communications, and promotion of foreign investment and tourism. Clients include corporations, trade associations, and foreign countries. Prior to joining Fleishman-Hillard in 1987, McCue had been senior vice-president and managing director, corporate relations, for Hill and Knowlton, New York. For more than 10 years there, he was responsible for developing and implementing scores of strategic communications and crisis plans for Fortune 500 corporations. A communications strategist for Texaco during its fabled court battles with Pennzoil concerning the Getty Oil acquisition, he has also counseled hundreds of other companies, including Monsanto, Campbell Soup, RJR Nabisco, Texaco, Northrop, GTE, Cargill, Caterpillar, General Mills, and Anheuser-Busch.

HUMAN TRAGEDIES

Disaster at

Lockerbie

Raymond J. O'Rourke
Director of Crisis Communications, Burson-Marsteller

Overview

The long, pioneering history of Pan American World Airways, which began in the warm, sunny skies of the Caribbean in 1927, ended 61 years later on the night of December 21, 1988, on the cold, wind-swept hills around the tiny village of Lockerbie, Scotland. That night 270 people — 259 aboard Pan Am Flight 103 bound from Frankfurt via London to New York and Detroit, and 11 on the ground in Lockerbie — died, victims of the most vicious terrorist attack in aviation history.

Though Pan Am would struggle on for another two and a half years before bankruptcy forced the end of all operations, few would doubt its final chapter began that night at 6:25 P.M. (GMT) when Flight 103 departed Heathrow Airport, 25 minutes behind schedule. Half an hour later, a powerful bomb tore through *Clipper — Maid of the Seas* as it approached 31,000 feet, 175 miles north of London. A nightmare storm of debris — shredded aircraft, flaming jet fuel, luggage, cargo, brightly wrapped presents, and horribly mangled bodies — rained down over several hundred square miles of the Scottish countryside. The largest pieces, including one of the massive Pratt & Whitney jet engines, fell directly on the center of Lockerbie, igniting a fire storm of incredible proportions.

Initial Response

Word of the tragedy crossed international news wires within minutes of the radar controllers in Scotland losing contact with Flight 103. Both NBC and ITN, the British television network, were credited with the initial reports. At Pan American headquarters in New York, where it was midafternoon, a well-rehearsed disaster plan went into action. Guards restricted access to the company's executive offices on the 46th floor of the landmark Pan Am Building. A

Damage from the wreckage of Pan Am Flight 103 was spread over a wide area of Lockerbie, Scotland.

dedicated 800 telephone line for relatives and friends of passengers was activated. At the Pan Am WorldPort at Kennedy International Airport, arriving-flight status boards flashed "SEE AGT" ("See Agent") next to Flight 103. Specially trained teams of passenger service agents prepared for the grim task of meeting and assisting relatives and friends.

In response to the first wire service queries, Pan Am spokesperson Pamela Hanlon was able to confirm only that radar controllers had lost contact with Flight 103. Moments later Pan Am confirmed that a crash had, indeed, occurred, that there were no indications of survivors, and that there were casualties on the ground. Inevitable confusion developed over the number of passengers on board. Reuters wire service initially quoted a Federal Aviation Administration (FAA) spokesperson who reported that there were 244 people on board and that the crash had occurred 10 minutes after takeoff.

Both misstatements were quickly corrected. Pan Am's initial count was 255 on board, subsequently increased to 259. By the time Pan Am's chief spokesperson, Jeff Kriendler, senior vice-president of communications, addressed assembled reporters at the company's headquarters at 7:00 P.M., he was able to confirm the actual passenger count. Following standard procedure, he declined to release passenger lists, pending notification of next of kin. He also declined numerous requests to speculate on the cause of the accident.

As Pan Am spokespeople answered questions at headquarters, the scene at the WorldPort was growing increasingly frantic. Still, initial stories on the families were well disposed to Pan Am. The first accounts tell of escorts providing help and support for the families.

At the WorldPort

In fact, wire service reports noted the grief and attendant rage directed at television news cameras and photographers. Associated Press reported that one grieving relative knocked a camera from a photographer's hand and added, approvingly, that a Pan Am security guard intervened asking for understanding from the assembled photographers and escorted the person from their prying lenses.

Unaware of the real cause of the disaster, reporters initially speculated about a mechanical or a structural failure. They recalled an accident earlier that year in which an Aloha Airlines Boeing 737 came apart in midflight, a result of stress fractures in its frame and skin. The crippled aircraft landed safely thanks to the heroic efforts of pilot and crew.

Mechanical Failure?

Both Pan Am and the FAA quickly produced and answered questions from the *Maid of the Seas'* maintenance logs. The aircraft was delivered to Pan Am in 1970, the 15th 747 built by Boeing. There was nothing out of the ordinary in its log.

In fact, two years earlier the aircraft had been completely rebuilt as part of the U.S. government's Civilian Reserve Air Fleet (CRAF) program. CRAF was intended to ensure that there would be sufficient high quality airlift capacity available in the event of a national emergency. Said Kriendler at the press conference, "It was virtually a brand new plane."

Officials in the U.K. and the FAA and the FBI knew that 747s simply did not disintegrate in midair. The sturdy plane had one of the best safety records of all commercial aircraft. They quickly dismissed the possibility of mechanical or structural failure. They knew there could be only one explanation for what happened. And within an hour of the first reports, they were organizing what would become the largest manhunt in the history of international terrorism.

It is often said that how an organization is perceived to be managing a crisis is determined by its actions in the first 12 to 24 hours. While an expert response will not necessarily resolve the crisis, the contrary proposition should be self-evident: A bungled response will worsen the problem and prolong the recovery.

Pan Am Responds

Pan Am executives did as much as they could that night and the next day to organize an effective response. Once questions about aircraft integrity were disposed of, media reports acknowledged the company's concern for those with family and friends on Flight 103 and firmly positioned the company among the victims of the tragedy.

However, the destruction of Flight 103 had profound long-term implications for Pan Am and no amount of short-term damage control would change that. In fact, Pan Am's experience after Lockerbie illustrates the point that there is no objective standard of success in crisis management. Each situation is unique. Judging a company's performance requires a thorough understanding of the underlying conditions that predated the crisis and some reasonable definition of what constitutes success, given those preexisting conditions.

Pan Am ultimately succumbed after Lockerbie, but also after years of financial distress, contentious labor relations, and operating in a fiercely competitive, deregulated market. Against that backdrop, and through the Lockerbie crisis, the management team quickly recovered a large share of their customer base, minimized the sense of despair among shocked and beleaguered employees, and preserved a large measure of the company's historical reputation for safe, professional operations.

How they managed the issues that emerged in the weeks and months following Lockerbie is instructive for anyone interested in the complexities of crisis management.

Why Pan Am? If a terrorist group had wanted to strike out at a symbol of American prestige and leadership around the world, they could hardly have chosen a better target.

Pan Am had pioneered international aviation, starting in Latin America. The airline expanded service throughout the Pacific and, finally, across the Atlantic. Few companies were so identified with the U.S. around the world. Even the name *Clipper — Maid of the Seas* evoked the rich heritage of the Pan Am flying boats, and the ideals of ingenuity, adventure, and pioneering spirit.

In 1988, despite years of financial difficulties, a shrinking international route system, and a problematic service image at home, Pan Am's blue and white logo still scored high in international brand recognition studies. In fact, the logo was as well known overseas as it was in the United States.

As a practical matter, in 1988 Pan Am was still the largest American carrier to Europe, serving more cities with more flights and carrying more people than any other U.S. airline. On either score — visibility or opportunity — Pan Am was a likely target. These facts did not escape the attention of the families of the victims of Flight 103. They asked, "If Pan Am was such an obvious target, why wasn't security better?"

If international visibility was the terrorists' objective, they accomplished more than they could have hoped. And more, it seems, than they had planned. Investigators quickly surmised that the bomber intended that his device explode as Flight 103 proceeded out over the North Atlantic, taking with it all clues to his handiwork. However, as noted, Flight 103 departed 25 minutes late. The delay at Heathrow, and a northerly routing, resulted in an explosion over land, enabling investigators to gather enough evidence to identify a likely suspect and the route his bomb followed to Lockerbie.

Police officers carry the body of one of the passengers past the cockpit of the Maid of the Seas.

More important, from a communications perspective it also enabled television crews to record the gruesome results. The *Maid of the Seas'* cockpit lying in a Scottish meadow became the visual symbol of the horror of Flight 103. The power of the visual images helped this act stand out among other terrorist attacks.

One day before the crash at Lockerbie, Pan Am Chief Executive Officer Thomas Plaskett, who had been at the helm less than a year, told Dow Jones News Service he was optimistic about the airline's prospects for the coming year.

The Death of Hope

He predicted year-end results for 1988 would be substantially better than the $265 million loss recorded in 1987. He even raised the prospect of a modest operating profit for the year. Overall, Pan Am's prospects at the time were better than they had been in recent memory. In 1988, a significant rebuilding of transatlantic traffic ensued from depressed terror-conscious lows of 1986 and 1987.

Pan Am, given its dominant position in the market, had capitalized on the surge. Its share of the transatlantic market rose to 16.7 percent compared with 13.5 percent in 1986. Though still cash strapped, Plaskett and his team were confident the improved performance could make lining up additional cash — or an outright buyer — considerably easier. Pan Am employees, if not quite optimistic, were justifiably proud of their tenacity. They had earned a grudging respect from competitors and analysts for their ability to keep the airline going.

In one sense, that pride and dogged determination was another victim of the crash at Lockerbie. With the crash, many Pan Am employees resigned themselves to the idea that the airline would not, in fact, survive and that the end was coming sooner rather than later. It was against those prevailing currents that Plaskett and his team set their course in the days immediately following the disaster at Lockerbie.

News from Moscow   On Day Two reporters began asking about a new story from Moscow. Early in December, FAA officials issued a warning to other government agencies about an anonymous threat received by the U.S. Embassy in Helsinki from a caller who said a Pan Am flight bound from Frankfurt to New York would be bombed and that the bomb would be carried on board by a woman.

Officials at the U.S. Embassy in Moscow posted the warning on an embassy bulletin board advising staffers that despite the warning they were not relieved from their obligation to fly on U.S. carriers. Word that government employees had the benefit of a warning that was denied to the American public was reported the next day. And though Pan Am had no control over the government posting, the issue became one of the organizing points for families of the victims of Flight 103.

Ironically, law enforcement and intelligence organizations knew of the Helsinki threat and had dismissed it as meaningless long before it was posted in Moscow. Finnish intelligence sources knew the caller and said that he was a disturbed man who had made similar threats before. Word that the threat was in all likelihood empty was communicated to U.S. officials and to Pan Am. Still, the idea that Pan Am negligently failed to warn its passengers of a threat fueled the growing anger of the families.

In the days following the crash — after notifications of next of kin were completed and it had been firmly established that Flight 103 was the victim of a terrorist bombing — Plaskett and his team turned to the question of how to appropriately express the genuine grief and sorrow that was so palpable throughout the organization.

A national day of mourning was scheduled in the United Kingdom for January 4, 1989, with a special memorial service in Lockerbie. It quickly became the focus of international attention. Members of the Royal family, the prime minister, and numerous foreign dignitaries attended. Plaskett, as CEO, represented Pan Am. He was accompanied by employees representing every Pan Am location around the world. The gesture was widely noted in the U.K. and served the important purpose of unifying a disheartened work force.

In a prepared statement that Plaskett brought with him to Lockerbie, Pan Am expressed its gratitude "to the many heroic men and women who have emerged in the face of this tragedy, (who) have worked virtually without rest for 15 days to bring order to chaos, aid to the injured, and comfort to the bereaved."

In addition, a simple "in memoria" advertisement was prepared and ran in newspapers in the United Kingdom. It stated simply: "We extend our deepest sympathies and condolences to all who lost relatives, friends, and co-workers in the tragedy of Flight 103."

If the efforts helped to restore Pan Am's reputation in the United Kingdom or better position the company among the victims of the tragedy, that was never their stated purpose. Therefore, no assessment was ever undertaken to measure "effectiveness." The delegation, the statement, and the advertisement were Pan Am's best efforts to express the organization's grief over a uniquely horrifying event.

Reaching the Public and the Work Force

In the weeks following the Lockerbie disaster, normally slow winter Pan Am traffic across the Atlantic dropped dramatically. In an effort to understand the decline, Pan Am surveyed air travelers, specifically those who intended to fly in the next six months. The results were disturbing. Although 81 percent of those who responded said they had no plans to change their travel itineraries, 36 percent said they were able to identify particular carriers about which they were concerned. Of those, 45 percent said they were concerned about flying Pan Am, compared with only 13 percent who said they were concerned about flying Delta or TWA and 9 percent who expressed concern about American.

More than three times as many travelers expressed concern about Pan Am than about their nearest competitor. Pan Am officials were also aware of recent sur-

Travel Declines

vey results that indicated the traveling public at large expected airlines and airport operators — not government officials — to bear the primary responsibility for the safe, reliable operation of the air transportation system. The surveys were particularly troubling because they contrasted sharply with similar research that had been done in the summer of 1986 after a series of terrorist incidents in Europe, including the hijacking of a TWA aircraft in Beirut, caused a dramatic fall-off in traffic to Europe. In that case, travelers identified Europe — the destination — as the source of their concern. In the current research, travelers cited a particular carrier — Pan Am — as the source of their concern.

Anecdotal evidence tended to support the data. Pan Am sales executives reported that travel agents were having difficulty convincing travelers that Pan Am was a secure choice. In response, Pan Am produced an eight-page brochure on safety and security that was eagerly accepted by travel agents around the U.S. Distributed by travel agents and Pan Am ticket offices in response to any expressions of fear or concern, either about the airline or about safety generally, the brochure attempted to familiarize passengers with the level of security already in place at airports and aboard aircraft.

Plainly identified as a Pan Am brochure, it instructed the traveler on what to expect at the airport and in flight. It also noted that some of the most critical aspects of air travel security were consciously kept out of public view. It noted Pan Am's cooperation with law enforcement and government intelligence organizations, "to ensure that the most up-to-date intelligence is always available." The advice applied to all international flights. And while the focus was definitely on the actions and responsibilities of the airline and airport operators, the traveler was reminded several times about the need to guard against letting one's luggage out of one's control and against accepting any packages to check in or carry on.

Letter to CEOs While the brochure was being prepared, Pan Am's commercial sales staff — those calling on corporate customers — learned of plans by some major customers to book all their transatlantic flights on foreign carriers. They feared that U.S. airlines were to be the target of a new wave of terrorism. In a letter to the chief executives of 1,000 of the largest service and manufacturing companies in the United States, Plaskett called such actions "unprecedented, unwarranted and unlikely to increase the safety" of American business travelers.

He noted that U.S. carriers, particularly Pan Am, were operating at maximum security levels and that since supplemental security measures ordered by the FAA in January 1989 for flights inbound to the United States applied only to U.S. carriers, flying on foreign flight carriers provided, at best, a false sense of security.

"Unfortunately," the letter stated, "all airlines operate in the shadow of terrorist threats. In fact, there appears to be no meaningful distinction in the level of threats faced by the major Western nations. Terrorists seek targets of opportunity, and in recent years foreign flag carriers have been the targets of more incidents than all U.S. airlines combined."

Plaskett offered to have his chief of security meet with travel managers and security directors at any concerned company. The response was overwhelmingly favorable. Chief executives and travel managers who responded expressed their sympathies over the disaster and their continued support for Pan Am. Volume levels among this critically important segment showed no drop traceable to a "corporate boycott."

Pan Am executives recognized that their immediate response to Lockerbie did not address the underlying vulnerability of the international air transport system to terrorist attack. The reality was — and remains — that a determined terrorist, with access to the best available technology, could repeat the attack on Flight 103.

Longer Term Strategy

Plaskett mounted an aggressive effort to raise awareness among key government and industry officials about alternatives to the current structure of the aviation security system. In government testimony, and in speeches before the International Conference on Airline Operators and the American Society of Industrial Security, Government/Industry Conference on Terrorism, Plaskett laid out a six-point plan that called on governments, air carriers, and airport operators of all nations to:

1. Recognize that all *airlines* are subject to the threat of terrorism, and agree that strong actions are required to safeguard passengers and crew members of all nations.

2. Agree to establish and implement a uniform international standard of practices and procedures for airport and airline security, worldwide.

3. Recognize that governments of all nations must take direct responsibility for airline security as distinguished from a solely passive, rule-making, or regulatory role, by providing whatever resources are necessary for improving the security of international air travel.

4. Concur on the means to fund the necessary resources, including law enforcement personnel and equipment to screen passengers, cabins, checked baggage, mail, and freight.

5. Accelerate development of advanced technology, equipment, and qualified operating personnel.

6. Establish a timetable for implementing these new standards, focusing initial efforts on airports deemed to be most in need of improvement in view of their threat profile.

Aftermath Perhaps a measure of how far the threat of air terrorism has receded from the current agenda is to note that the needs Plaskett described are rarely discussed in public policy forums.

Pan Am and Lockerbie are forever related; part of each other's story. Pan Am has now entered the annals of aviation history, to be listed among the great pioneering accomplishments of the 20th century. Lockerbie remains very much with us today, part of the darker reality of this era. It neither will — nor should — be forgotten.

Ray O'Rourke is an executive vice-president and the director of the corporate crisis counseling practice at Burson-Marsteller, New York, and a leading authority on crisis preparedness. A veteran of some of the most widely publicized crises in recent corporate history, Mr. O'Rourke has led teams for Pan Am after the disaster at Lockerbie and for Perrier through its worldwide product recall. Mr. O'Rourke also helps clients anticipate and prepare for potential crises. He created the disciplined process by which Burson-Marsteller assists clients in developing formal crisis plans for their operations. A frequent author and lecturer on crisis management, O'Rourke resides in New York City.

The Calnev Pipeline Fire

George S. Lowman
Director of Communications, GATX Corporation

Overview

On May 12, 1989, a runaway Southern Pacific freight train rolled down from the mountains through San Bernardino, California, at 90 miles per hour. Sixty-nine rail cars and six engines derailed into a slumbering neighborhood on the city's west side. Four people were killed, including two Southern Pacific employees, and six homes were destroyed.

Thirteen days later, tragedy struck again in the same neighborhood. Almost 13,000 gallons of gasoline leaked from a rupture in an underground pipeline buried in the railway right-of-way where the train derailed. Two residents of the neighborhood died and 31 others were injured after the leaking gasoline ignited. Ten more homes were destroyed in the fire and five were damaged.

Calnev Pipeline Company, which owns the ruptured line, and GATX Terminals Corporation, Calnev's parent company, were plunged into a crisis. Both companies worked quickly to provide relief and recovery efforts, preserve Calnev's reputation, and resume operations following the first fatal pipeline accident in Calnev's history. The incident challenged our management and communications skills and showed once again why companies must be ready to move quickly when the unexpected occurs.

Tragedy Strikes

The 248-mile Calnev pipeline, built in 1970, supplies 90 percent of the unleaded gasoline used in the Las Vegas area. It supplies the city's McCarren International Airport with all of its jet fuel, transporting more than 2.7 million gallons a day. The pipeline also plays a key role in national security as it provides jet fuel to Edwards, George, and Nellis Air Force bases.

Calnev was purchased in late 1988 by GATX Terminals Corporation, a subsidiary of Chicago-based GATX Corporation. Besides its pipeline business, GATX operations include railcar leasing; real estate leasing and financial services; bulk liquid terminal storage, warehousing, and logistical services; and Great Lakes shipping.

Calnev was a relatively low-profile part of GATX until a chain of disastrous events began to unfold beginning on the day of the Southern Pacific freight train derailment. When the train derailed, Calnev officials acted immediately to depressurize the pipeline to 50 percent (800 psi) of its normal operating pressure. As clean up of the derailment progressed, it was determined that one of the train engines had come to rest, inverted, directly over the pipeline.

Under the watchful eye of local officials, the state fire marshall, and representatives from the Office of Pipeline Safety (OPS), Calnev engineers began safety inspections that included:

> *Exposing the pipeline for 15 feet on either side of the locomotive to determine depth of cover and possible damage. The pipeline was found to be eight feet below grade and no debris or damage was detected.*

> *Removal of the train engine and re-excavation of the same area; no debris or damage was found.*

> *Lifting all railroad cars up and over the pipeline, rather than dragging the cars across, which is typical of other train cleanup activities.*

> *Numerous excavations of approximately 20 to 50 feet along the length of the affected area. The depth of the pipeline, its condition, and the absence of debris were all inspected at each excavation site.*

> *Soft-digs ranging from eight to 14 inches directly over the pipeline were made at 50-foot intervals and stakes were placed to mark the location and depth of the pipeline.*

After the safety tests were completed, Calnev and local, state, and federal officials determined that the line was safe. Operations were resumed at noon, May 16, four days after the train derailment.

While the pipeline was closed, investigators from the National Transportation Safety Board (NTSB) combed through the mangled wreckage of the train. Southern Pacific brought in heavy equipment to remove the train cars and its cargo of potash from the area. As the bulldozers cleared away the destroyed houses and train cars, residents returned to the neighborhood.

Fire erupts from burst pipeline with flames engulfing this San Bernadino neighborhood, recently stunned by a runaway Southern Pacific freight train.

Pipeline Rupture and Fire

On May 25 at 8:11 A.M., disaster struck again without warning. A 300-foot pillar of flame erupted from what had been the backyard of one of the homes destroyed in the train crash. Thick black smoke billowed thousands of feet in the air. A pipeline operator's worst nightmare — a pipeline rupture and fire — became Calnev's reality.

The flow of fuel through the pipeline was quickly shut off when an automatic control at the Colton station registered a lack of pressure, indicating a rupture somewhere in the line. It took firefighters several hours to bring the blaze under control and the flames were not extinguished until after 4:00 P.M. Approximately 1,000 people, representing 200 families, were evacuated from the Duffy Street neighborhood.

Crisis Strategy As the parent company of Calnev, we at GATX were thrown into the midst of a full-blown crisis. We had to work quickly to communicate what had happened to the community, to our customers, to our employees, and to other affected publics, and to share with them our plans for providing relief from the disaster. We also had to respond to a sudden firestorm of media interest without precedent in the history of our company.

I received the first call shortly after the explosion and immediately pulled together a team of operations, communications, and legal experts for a meeting to begin mapping out our strategy.

Our crisis team assembled in two locations. At GATX headquarters in Chicago, I was supported by members of my staff and public relations professionals from public relations company Berkhemer Kline Golin/Harris Communications. GATX Terminals President Bob Claypoole and Vice-President Anthony Andrukaitis immediately flew to the scene of the disaster in San Bernardino, joining Calnev officials, crisis management experts from Berkhemer Kline Golin/Harris in Los Angeles, and attorneys from the law firm of O'Melveny & Myers. Together, we moved quickly to learn the facts and take action.

Many tough decisions had to be made during the first days of the crisis — through Memorial Day weekend into June — calling for 18-hour days, seven days a week, for every member of the crisis team. In many ways, the situation grew even more difficult to manage after the immediate danger passed.

Key Areas of Concern We realized immediately the magnitude of the situation, the devastating impact on the community, and the implications for the continued operation of Calnev and the pipeline.

Our overall strategy for managing the crisis included:

- Maintaining openness and responsiveness to concerns and inquiries.

- Focusing on cooperative plans, together with Southern Pacific Railroad, for community relief and recovery.

- Cooperating with local, state, and federal safety authorities investigating the cause of the accident.

- Containing the crisis and controversy within local confines as quickly as possible.

- Reaching and communicating decisions on critical issues as soon as possible, including reopening the pipeline and reaching settlements with the city and with community residents.

> • Preparing to deal with the issue of gasoline pipeline safety at the state and national levels.

The crisis team had to quickly develop its own methodology for dealing with the crisis. We identified each audience and determined what actions had been taken to date, what next steps were needed, which member of the team would be responsible, and assigned deadlines. Each team member worked on his or her assigned elements to keep all audiences informed and progress moving forward.

We also applied a lesson learned painfully by other companies faced with crisis situations: the importance of moving quickly to fill the information void. Responsive, honest communication is essential if a company's credibility and reputation are to be preserved through a crisis.

With these principles in mind, we hit the ground running. Much needed to be done, with our customers suddenly cut off from their sole source of fuel, a devastated neighborhood, an angry community, and a sudden onslaught of calls from the news media.

As Claypoole made his first statement expressing concern for the residents, he clearly conveyed that the company was cooperating fully with the investigation mounted by the NTSB, which is responsible for interstate pipelines such as Calnev. He also made it clear that the company, focused as it was on relief and recovery efforts, would not seek to place blame for the incident elsewhere or speculate on the cause of the rupture.

Aiding the Victims

Within hours of the disaster, we distributed a news release to the media and the local community offering aid to the residents of the evacuated area. More than 200 families were evacuated from their homes and immediately housed and fed in nearby hotels at the expense of Calnev and Southern Pacific.

Calnev, Southern Pacific, and the local unit of the American Red Cross set up a communications center at the San Bernardino Hilton to assist residents. Calnev and Southern Pacific representatives quickly began making personal visits to residents at the hotels to distribute checks for food and living expenses and investigate their other recovery needs.

At the site of the rupture and fire, Calnev secured the pipeline area to ensure that there was no possibility of further fire or damage to the neighborhood. The key

GATX decision makers — Claypoole and Andrukaitis — were on-site taking the pulse of the situation and making the important decisions.

Following the pipeline rupture, residents in the area demanded an opportunity to voice their feelings directly to community leaders and other involved parties. Claypoole, with the support of the crisis team, offered to meet with community residents at a time and place of their choosing.

Five days after the tragedy, a crowded public meeting took place at a hotel where many of the residents were staying. Claypoole expressed his personal sorrow and concern and then listened as residents vented their frustrations and fears. The meeting was covered extensively by the news media, with angry neighbors featured on every major Los Angeles-area radio and television station that night and the next day.

"More than 100 angry Duffy Street residents packed into a tiny meeting room Tuesday night and begged for answers to the disaster that hit their neighborhood last week," wrote Mike Gordon of the *San Bernardino Sun*, the local daily newspaper.

Immediately following the community meeting, Claypoole met privately with a smaller group of Duffy Street residents to establish direct dialogue. This meeting proved to have a valuable and important effect on future plans for settlement with the community. At that closed meeting, our crisis team began the long, slow process of establishing trust with the residents, a process that continues to this day.

Our crisis team quickly recommended several community outreach initiatives to show the residents that we cared about their needs and well-being. For example, we initiated a matching funds gift program with the *San Bernardino Sun*. Calnev agreed to match funds donated to the newspaper's "Lend-a-Hand" program for community relief, up to a maximum of $15,000. As of July 1989, when the program closed, $13,230 had been donated by the community and matched by Calnev. Media coverage of the matching funds program contributed to Calnev's public credibility as a caring company.

Media Response
One of the most pressing problems in the hours immediately after the tragedy was coping with the sudden avalanche of news media interest. National, regional, and local television and radio news crews were on the scene within minutes, including network affiliates and reporters from the Associated Press and United Press International. Phones began ringing in Calnev offices in Las Vegas and San Bernardino as reporters quickly began preparing and filing stories on the tragedy.

Immediately following the rupture, David Andries, manager of Calnev operations, answered media questions and gave interviews at the site. Within the first few hours, Berkhemer Kline Golin/Harris Vice-President Fred Cook joined him on-site to begin managing the media response. After being briefed by Andries when he arrived in San Bernardino, Claypoole assumed the role of primary spokesperson, charged with communicating Calnev's position on the tragedy and its relief efforts and directing emergency measures at the pipeline.

We monitored and analyzed all media coverage from the beginning of the crisis to determine key concerns. On May 25 alone, there were 24 video news segments that aired on local and national television. In addition to television coverage, local and regional newspapers in southern California and Nevada devoted extensive coverage to the rupture.

Each day during the crisis, we reviewed the coverage to determine key message points for Calnev and how to present them. Monitoring the daily media reports also allowed us to evaluate and respond to positions being taken by local authorities and residents as each day passed.

Rapid media training for the Calnev spokespersons was another critical task coordinated by the crisis management team. On-site preparation for all media events and public comments included training sessions with the crisis team and attorneys from the GATX corporate staff and O'Melveney & Myers, asking every imaginable question. Question and answer sheets also were created by the team and used to train both Claypoole and Andrukaitis on key message points.

Positioning was extremely important, as in any crisis. The following points were established early during the crisis and used consistently throughout:

- The pipeline will only be reopened after its safety and integrity are established by Calnev and the U.S. Office of Pipeline Safety.

- The pipeline represents a vital part of the regional economic infrastructure, serving as the sole source of unleaded gasoline and jet fuel for southern Nevada, and also plays an important national security role.

- Pipelining is the safest form of transporting petroleum products (i.e., versus tanker truck).

- Calnev is confident the future safety of the pipeline is not compromised by its present location; it would be difficult if not impossible to move the pipeline to the other side of the railroad tracks into the flood control channel, as demanded by some in the community.

Proactive Communications

In addition to gaining control of our response to the news media, we also recognized the need for proactive communications. In fact, one of our first steps was to release a statement on the tragedy, which said that Calnev employees "are grieved at this accident and share in the sorrow of the people in San Bernardino who are victims of this fire."

We also placed an ad in the *San Bernardino Sun* on the Sunday following the fire, headlined "Our Deepest Sympathy to the People of San Bernardino." The ad described the fire as "a tragic accident" and expressed condolences to the families of those killed, injured, or displaced. The ad noted Calnev's history of safety and promised a thorough investigation to ensure a similar tragedy never happens again.

Relationships were established quickly with the key media covering the fire and its aftermath. All reporters received prompt responses and periodic update calls. Claypoole and Andrukaitis responded to every press inquiry daily and willingly made themselves available for every television interview to answer questions and express the company's position.

Internal Communications

Effective communication with internal audiences is vital during crisis situations, yet these important constituents are often overlooked. Customers and employees, for example, not only have as much interest in a crisis as the general public, but also have a genuine need to know. A company's shareholders also have concerns that must be addressed.

In the hours immediately following the tragedy, we focused our efforts primarily on the news media and the community. The following day, letters from Claypoole were sent to Calnev customers and employees to update these audiences on the crisis.

The letters stressed cooperation with investigators and emphasized concern for the victims of the accident and their families. Calnev also pledged to resume operation of the pipeline only after the line's safety, and that of Calnev's employees and local residents, could be assured. Similar letters went out to the parent company's employees.

We also distributed a letter to GATX shareholders the following week which emphasized many of the same key points and provided necessary reassurance that the tragedy would have little or no impact on the company's financial results. Calls were made to securities analysts, key institutional investors, and ratings agencies. As a result, the days following the tragedy saw no adverse impact on the company's stock price.

Recognizing that the support of government officials would be necessary to resume pipeline operations once the investigation was complete and the damage repaired, we moved to establish relations with key legislators in southern California and Nevada within days of the tragedy. Research was conducted with local and state legislators whom we felt could be either beneficial or detrimental to the company's position. Letters were distributed stressing cooperation with all investigations and assuring legislators that the pipeline would only resume operation with concurrence from the OPS, the state fire marshall, and other involved agencies. Telephone contact with key officials important to the company also was carefully maintained.

We worked closely with San Bernardino city officials from the time the crisis began to negotiate settlements with residents and with city agencies that provided vital relief and recovery services, including the police and psychological and medical services, in the aftermath of the disaster. In order to help resolve these challenges, we established a dialogue with area Congressman George Brown and newly elected San Bernardino Mayor Bob Holcomb, who took office on June 5, 11 days after the tragedy.

Working closely with Brown and Holcomb, and at the request of Calnev and GATX executives, city officials reached a settlement agreement for residents with Calnev. Two hours after his inauguration, the mayor announced the settlement and plans to reopen the pipeline at a city hall news conference. The announcement was covered by all major media and provided Calnev with its first public ally.

The following day, a local radio station conducted a call-in poll to determine public acceptance or rejection of Calnev's settlement plan. The poll showed 72 percent of the callers were in favor while only 28 percent opposed the plan. Another public battle had been won by Calnev.

Governmental Communications

NTSB, as the primary investigating agency, was on the scene within hours of the accident. Other offices with jurisdiction in the investigation were the OPS and the city of San Bernardino. Numerous court proceedings had determined the pipeline was under federal jurisdiction.

Investigators were quickly on the scene taking measurements and photos, conducting metallurgical tests, and surveying the site. The section of ruptured pipeline was removed and shipped to NTSB labs in Washington, D.C., for further examination. Throughout this process, our engineers cooperated fully with NTSB investigators. Interviews were conducted and depositions were taken from Calnev employees, Southern Pacific employees, cleanup crews, and residents.

The Investigation

The NTSB investigator held a news conference to convey the facts before returning to Washington, approximately 10 days after the incident, but did not speculate or attribute blame to anyone. Federal investigations of this type take approximately three to six months. We cooperated fully with the NTSB and, as requested, did not speculate on causes of the incident.

Resuming Pipeline Operations

Safely resuming operation of the pipeline was our primary business goal after the tragedy. We anticipated that this community, which was charged with anger and grief, would oppose the continued operation of the pipeline. Public officials, reflecting the concerns of their constituents, quickly raised questions about steps Southern Pacific and Calnev had taken to ensure the safety of the pipeline after the train crash.

We had to do everything possible to assure the community that the Calnev pipeline was safe. But, as we expected, there were some community members who were not easily convinced. Commenting on assurances that the pipeline was safe, the San Bernardino city attorney said, "Obviously, in this case the experts were wrong. Calnev has a lot of explaining to do."

The city attorney, with other city officials, fought plans to reopen the pipeline in its current location. After visiting the scene several days after the tragedy, he demanded the line be rerouted outside city limits. Evelyn Wilcox, mayor at the time of the tragedy, said "We were told the pipeline had been inspected and was safe. At this time, they can move the pipeline to anyplace but inside San Bernardino."

Our response to the city attorney's request to move the pipeline was established after extensive discussions with Congressman Brown and city officials. We wholeheartedly supported a federal study of the pipeline's route, and pledged to cooperate in any way, including moving the pipeline, if the study arrived at that conclusion. Several times the city attorney sought injunctions seeking to halt the repair and reopening of the pipeline, all of which were rejected by the courts. Each time legal action was taken, the crisis team prepared our legal counsel and made them available to respond to the media.

Personal injury attorneys sought to use the media as a forum to solicit clients. We responded aggressively to the media and in court each time the attorneys took legal action, with consistent messages of caring and concern.

While the first priorities were aiding the victims of the tragedy and cooperating with investigators, we were anxious to reopen the pipeline. Customers in the Las

Vegas area, as well as key air force bases, were cut off from their primary source of gasoline and jet fuel, jeopardizing commerce and compromising important military operations.

The shutdown also raised concerns about the safety of alternative transport methods, such as tanker trucks. While the pipeline was closed, a tanker carrying 8,700 gallons of gasoline exploded and burned on an interstate highway in the desert between southern California and Las Vegas. No one was hurt, but the incident, well covered by the media, underscored the fact that underground pipelines are the safest way to ship petroleum products. More than 200 tanker trucks a day would be needed to carry the same amount of fuel as the pipeline.

Prior to opening the pipeline, we took extensive steps to review its safe operation. These included replacing 600 feet of pipeline in the area of the train derailment with thicker pipe; burying the new line 16 feet deep (twice as deep as required by OPS regulations); and encasing the entire 600-foot length of pipe in a concrete slurry for added protection. The new pipe also faced extensive hydrostatic testing before reopening.

As expected, the city attorney filed suit in an attempt to prevent Calnev from making repairs and resuming operations. But a California Superior Court judge refused to halt the repairs, noting that petroleum pipelines are governed by federal regulations beyond city or state jurisdiction.

Test results and safety efforts were announced to the press immediately. A news conference was called on June 9 at the site of the rupture to officially reopen the pipeline. At the news conference, the mayor's office distributed a statement endorsing the safety of the line. Standing on the very spot of the rupture, before dozens of reporters, Mayor Holcomb and Andrukaitis, via cellular phone, called Calnev's Colton terminal with instructions to reopen the line. The symbolism and confidence created by the mayor announcing the reopening did not pass unnoticed.

Even with the pipeline open, the crisis team's work was far from over. In the following weeks and months, preparations for legislative, congressional, and NTSB hearings would be made. Written and verbal testimonies were given at legislative hearings by Claypoole and Andrukaitis. Question and answer documents were prepared by the crisis team and used in prehearing meetings.

As the crisis began to subside, there was time to reflect on the experience and knowledge gained by all affected, which provides a valuable lesson in crisis communications and management for the pipeline industry.

Aftermath   Through effective crisis management and communications efforts, Calnev achieved its primary objectives of preserving the company's reputation in the community and restoring customer confidence. Within two weeks the results were evident. The company:

- Established effective communications within the community to ensure fast response to its needs.

- Reopened the pipeline in 15 days.

- Retained 100 percent of its customer base.

- Did not cause its parent company's stock price to suffer.

- Avoided a federal or state order to reroute the pipeline.

- Reached a fair and reasonable settlement with the city and residents.

- Contained media interest to the regional level within one week.

- Did not adversely impact GATX Terminals Corporation's long-term business plans.

Since the pipeline explosion, Calnev and GATX have developed formal crisis communications plans to assist in effectively communicating with all key audiences in the event of another disaster. Corporations have a duty to their shareholders, customers, employees, and the communities in which they operate to be prepared to communicate effectively when the unexpected happens. Calnev and GATX fared well considering the circumstances surrounding the fire. Had we failed to be both responsive and accessible during this crisis, both companies would have had a much more difficult time recovering — not only financially, but also socially, in regaining community, customer, and shareholder confidence.

George S. Lowman has served as director of communications for GATX Corporation in Chicago since 1983 and is responsible for investor relations, advertising, public relations, and strategic planning. Prior to joining GATX, Mr. Lowman was a corporate planning analyst at USG Corporation and a chemist for United Technologies. He also served as a research associate at Yale University. Lowman serves as chairman of the Public Relations Committee for the Railroad Progress Institute and is a member of the Public Relations Committee for the National Institute of Investor Relations.

The Wall Street
Murder

Richard H. Truitt
Partner, Public Affairs, Arnold Consultants

Early in 1987, several months before Wall Street was stunned by Black Monday, the prestigious stock brokerage firm of Josephthal & Company was rocked by a one-day catastrophe all its own.

Overview

A Florida man walked into the firm's office in New York's Financial District, shot his older brother three times with a small derringer, then slumped on a couch and told the horrified receptionist that she'd better call the police. As might be expected on a slow news day, the murder played big on television that evening and in the next day's newspapers.

But two very important things happened. The company's name didn't get much exposure — the event quickly became the "Wall Street Murder," with the Josephthal name appearing only marginally in news reports. And several minor mysteries that developed in the early hours following the event never made it into the media.

Within hours, other happenings took over the news reports. Crisis management based on the principle of one-day containment had moved the situation into the news properly and out of the news quickly.

It doesn't always work that way. Most often, to the distress of many managers, crises tend to happen in a methodical way. Which means they hang around far too long. Emerging with a subtle warning that's not unlike the first faraway glow of the morning sun, these kinds of crises travel a predictable course — giving early hints of the heat to come and growing quickly to midpoint high intensity before they cool and fade. Here are ways in which business crises and their effects can be tempered and perhaps speeded up a bit.

This event shows that the standard rules of handling a crisis apply also to any short-term emergency that strikes unexpectedly, but apply differently because unanticipated crises can develop with lightning speed.

It shows that, given fast and skillful response, an organization's exposure in the media often can be contained within one news day.

And it shows that it's almost always impossible to anticipate the specifics of the next crisis, proving the value of crisis communications training in dealing with the unexpected.

Murder at the Firm Here's the scene as it unfolded. Early on a blustery Wednesday morning, February 24, 1987, just after the glass front doors of Josephthal & Co. had been unlocked on the 22nd floor of one of Wall Street's most prominent buildings, Sol Koch, who was 56, walked into the firm's small, paneled reception area.

He didn't give his own name, but instead asked to see his "friend," Harvey Koch, who was actually Sol's older brother. When Harvey appeared, the younger brother fired two shots into Harvey's chest. Bystanders dived behind desks and ran down an adjacent hall as the victim, who remained standing, yelled, "This is my brother, call the police!" Sol Koch managed to reload the gun and fire one more shot at his brother. Then he placed the pistol on Harvey's fallen body and sat down to wait for the police.

Police officers on the scene shortly after Sol Koch murdered his brother, Harvey.

Within minutes, the day's agenda had changed for many people. Curious workers from nearby offices began to congregate outside the glass doors. The firm's own employees rushed to the reception area. Only two people actually had seen what had happened, but within minutes information was flowing freely.

"Why would a guy just come in and shoot his brother?" asked one of the bystanders. "He blamed him for taking poor care of their father," another announced.

A third bystander said he had heard the accused killer shout, "You murdered our father," as he fired the first shots. In this scenario, a story that picked up steam quickly, the killed had become a killer, too. In fact, the father of the two men, Nathan Koch, had died of natural causes in a Jersey City nursing home three years earlier.

Talk about a motive for the bizarre killing flashed through the crowd and reporters were taking notes. Revenge was mentioned frequently by the onlookers. One person said, authoritatively, that the New York brother was killed because the Florida brother felt the nursing home decision, which he opposed, destroyed his father's will to live. She wouldn't provide her source to a reporter who asked.

Addressing Public Relations Needs

At this confused and out-of-control moment, public relations help clearly was needed to provide straight information to reporters who had begun to crowd the corridor.

The situation prompted a number of questions that could develop into a long-term disaster for Josephthal: Where did the man get the gun? Why wasn't there better security? Why did the crime take place in this crowded office building? Was there a link to the company's security business? In the worst of situations, the Josephthal name could be attached to all of these questions.

As the struggle for accurate information was developing, the directors of Doremus and Company, a prominent financial advertising agency, were assembling for a board meeting in the same building, 13 floors below. Doremus also developed crisis communications plans for corporations, but it had not (yet) done any public relations work for Josephthal. The directors were scheduled to hear a review of public relations at Doremus, a report that ultimately was not presented that day.

Grasping quickly for the best communications help they could put their hands on, officers of the Josephthal firm and two police officers rushed to the ninth floor and literally invaded the Doremus board meeting.

Establishing Control

Within minutes, as the head of Doremus's public relations department, I had rushed upstairs and directed reporters to a corner of the hallway with the promise of "a press conference here in 20 minutes." It was a gutsy move; I had no idea what I would say.

But Rule Number One of crisis communications had just been followed. It says, essentially: Tell the media who the source of information will be, establish credibility for that source, establish when and where the information will be delivered, and deliver the news accurately and when promised.

Some crisis communications managers feel that if Rule Number One is followed carefully, there is no real need for a Rule Number Two.

Once inside the closed doors of Josephthal, I found a jumble of conflicting records and confused information about the case. In my efforts to put together some concrete information about the main participants, I battled two big problems: lack of information and lack of time.

As the newly named crisis manager, I knew little about the company and nothing about the names or positions of any of the dozen people who crowded the small planning room. So getting credible information seemed to be difficult. Where could information be obtained? Who could be trusted? How much would the company reveal? Would the company's law firm be an obstacle to communication?

There were conflicting reports about where Sol Koch actually lived. Reporters, police, and one person within the brokerage firm had provided conflicting information. Also, a reporter for one of the city's major papers had information about where the victim lived that differed from the company's own records. These conflicts could have become part of the story. In fact they almost did when the newspaper reporter suggested the victim actually lived at two permanent addresses, one in Long Island and one in Manhattan.

Fortunately the cooperative nature of the firm's management and its lawyers saved the day. Once it was established to the company and its attorneys that the crisis communications manager was responsible for the information flow, a team spirit developed that helped the process importantly. Sources identified themselves patiently and office workers jumped to provide materials and information needed for the press conference.

Identifying Needed Information

The second problem, lack of time, was self-inflicted. It is true that as the crisis manager I had established the tight time limit myself. But a longer time limit would have frustrated the media and fueled the rumors. Something had to be said quickly.

Not much information could be drummed up in the 10 to 12 minutes that were left after the process had begun to work. But, as the crisis manager and a former news reporter, I knew these pieces of information must be delivered accurately:

1. The name of, and other information about, the victim, including a picture, if possible.

2. The name of, and information about, the alleged attacker.

3. Information about the event that the company was able and willing to disclose.

4. Information about what was due to happen next (police custody, notifications, etc.).

5. A statement about the nature of the event, probably from the company's attorney.

6. A statement assuring reporters that they knew everything the company did.

Relaying Information Quickly

I decided the company, as such, should not be the source of information because the murder was not a corporate event. The company's officers, after all, knew only what they were told by witnesses.

The media conference took about 20 minutes. It involved a brief statement from the crisis manager and one of the police officers who had been on the scene early. The statement was followed by distribution of a biography of the victim plus a copied photograph from the victim's personnel file. Between the police officer and myself, half a dozen questions were answered.

Two or three of the questions required follow-up. A Doremus secretary took notes and the reporters got answers to these questions within half an hour after the end of the conference.

From that point forward, the communications work was assumed by the police. Calls that came into Josephthal were referred either to the police, if they were about the case, or to me if they concerned Josephthal.

Lessons Learned This short-lived case provides examples for anyone who might anticipate a fast-developing crisis situation. They include following four fundamentals that could, if properly applied, limit the organization's negative exposure to one news day.

> • The organization must maintain tight control over the communications function.
>
> • The spokesperson is key to clear commnication and should be picked and trained carefully.
>
> • The organization must have a plan, even a modest one, to deal with emergencies.
>
> • A well-done crisis audit can solve problems in advance.

The organization must maintain tight control over the communications function. If two or more people are doing bits and pieces of the job, there's a good chance it will be botched.

In the Josephthal case, it would have been easy for the company's lawyers to begin talking with the press or even for the receptionist, who witnessed the murder, to speak out. But even in this unplanned situation, these people waited for me, as the trained crisis manager, to take over and run things. This paid off in terms of clear, accurate, and timely communication.

The person in charge must have either a very good plan or lots of experience. The heart of a crisis is not a good point at which the manager should act on book knowledge alone. The manager must enjoy the confidence of both the organization for whom he or she is working and the media, and this normally comes with experience.

And he or she must understand how to manage the release of information. In most cases, the way an organization handles the flow of information determines whether the crisis is successfully managed.

Finally, it's critical that the crisis manager be a trained newsperson — or at least a person with substantial experience working with the media. The determining factor in a crisis —particularly a short-lived one — is the media and the way they handle the situation.

A skilled newsperson knows, for example, that an obscure television station can put together a three-part series that can cause you more harm than the cover of a news magazine, depending on how the rest of the media react and pick up information for their own reports.

Once a crisis story breaks, the organization should take the initiative by releasing information promptly rather than remaining in a reactive mode.

If it has it, the company should go to the public with bad news before being asked, or it will lose the initiative. The danger in withholding negative news sometimes is described as "sausage slicing" in crisis control practice. In "sausage slicing," the crisis manager (or political candidate) releases small pieces of the problem at a time, hoping with each slice that the problem will go away. But what normally happens is that the story builds with each revelation and the communicator's credibility suffers much more than if he or she had simply released the entire "sausage" at the outset.

When the organization in crisis takes the initiative by releasing positive information rather than remaining in a reactive mode, certain advantages come into play. One of these is that the organization, not the rumor process, becomes the source of information.

The spokesperson is key to clear communications and should be picked and trained carefully. Perhaps no one is more important, as a crisis develops, than the person who is speaking (and answering questions) for the organization.

It really doesn't matter whether this is a senior officer of the company or a support person. He or she can be an insider or an outsider as long as the company gives that person total authority to speak from the top.

All information must flow from that one person. This will work well as long as the media understand he or she knows the subject, has access to all of it, and is forthcoming.

The organization's spokespersons should be designated in advance, if possible. They should be trained to be informative, responsive, and assured. They must understand the needs and motives of the media.

Many people will have the opportunity to speak during the crisis, of course. The remarks or observations of a disgruntled customer or an afraid employee can carry as much weight with the media in a crisis as the measured statements of the company. In fact, the views of such people often are kept alive as the local media launch "in-depth" series on the subject. Anecdotal reporting can muddy the waters dramatically and this should be tracked and addressed in follow-up interviews by the spokesperson.

Also, the spokesperson can be effective in protecting investor relations objectives as well as the company's general reputation by keeping the company's own name out of the news if it is not directly involved with the issue.

The media tend to identify a crisis with a brand or corporate name, as with the "Tylenol crisis" or the "Hyatt Hotel disaster." Protecting the company or organization sometimes can be accomplished by using a location name in reports.

Sometimes the company's attorneys can help with this job, although working closely with the company's lawyers doesn't always sit well with public relations experts. Some lawyers may be overly cautious at a time when open communication with many groups clearly is essential.

But a lawyer's job is not to plan the communications program — it is to protect the organization against the kinds of future threats that a crisis manager might not immediately envision.

As an example, attorneys know that people exposed to internal information about the planning for a crisis can later be called into court to give deposition, sometimes against their own organization. They also know the communicator's natural attempts to console victims and assuage the public could put the organization at risk.

It's a good plan to work out communications rules and systems ahead of time with legal counsel and to include that person on the crisis management team.

Crisis Planning — a Necessity
The organization must have a plan, even a modest one, to deal with emergencies. Structured organizations, including businesses, thrive on planning. They abhor crises which, by definition, can't be planned. Crises are momentous, urgent, threatening, and unplanned.

But they can be anticipated, and the organization's response can be planned in enough scope and detail to control the damage.

Crisis plans normally are designed to handle situations such as product recalls, computer breakdowns, labor disputes, and business setbacks — the horrors that senior executives spend a lot of time thinking about anyway.

If the crisis plans are thorough, they will be well stocked with "if-then" scenarios such as: "If the local papers get the story, then we do this; if the regulators get involved, then we do that; if '20/20' comes calling, then we go to Plan C."

The best organizational planning for those crises that can be reasonably anticipated includes elements such as these:

- Be scrupulously honest in each statement.

- Keep the record straight with quick responses.

- Don't permit anyone to speculate.

- Grab and maintain the news initiative.

- Provide all news from a central, credible source.

Research conducted among the 1,500 largest U.S. companies shows that only about six out of 10 of these firms have a crisis communications plan. Of that number, 70 percent said they had a plan in place before problems developed and the remainder had developed one following a crisis.

Yet demands on the time of managers of modern business and the diligence of the news media in reporting on irregularities require that companies create, in advance, some kind of system for dealing with time-robbing crises.

"It is axiomatic that whenever a major problem arises in a large institution, and is not solved quickly and informally, the institution eventually finds it necessary to confront the problem in a formal manner," says David McClintik in *Indecent Exposure*, his authoritative book about an internal crisis at Columbia Pictures.

"If the institution has a problem-solving apparatus appropriate to the task, it is activated. If it doesn't, one is created. In either case, a large measure of control over the problem-solving process inevitably passes out of the hands of those who discovered the problem and into the hands of the apparatus."

While the CEO never wants to relinquish total control of a crisis situation to a plan — even one approved in advance — clear, truthful, and consistent communication is mandatory in a crisis. The ability to communicate effectively at such a time, and to hold the crisis to a one-day affair, increases significantly with a road map and good preparation.

This varies from company to company. Some, for example, are comfortable with thick manuals offering step-by-step instructions on what to do when adversity strikes. For firms of this culture, dozens of pages of contact lists and detailed instructions make sense. But other companies operate in a more freewheeling manner. For these, a brief list of responsible executives to be contacts in an emergency is sufficient, and anything more is a burden.

The crisis plan must have a set of objectives, and these should be written into the plan and should form the basis for the rest of the plan. For example, one objective might be to shorten the life of the crisis — to make it a one-day affair, if possible. To accomplish this objective, supporting strategies would deal with establishing an early-warning system to prevent surprise and developing fast and accurate information for the media to assure accurate and complete coverage.

Finally, the crisis plan should provide for a crisis team that would take charge of the situation and report to the CEO. The team's leader probably should be the organization's senior communications officer and it also should include people in charge of operations, personnel, legal affairs, and possibly community relations.

A well-done crisis audit can solve problems in advance. The degree to which a crisis plan works effectively depends on the amount of intelligence and sensitivity that went into structuring the apparatus.

When an organizational problem is institutionalized — taken from the hands of one or two persons and put into the system — flexibility and freedom of movement are likely to suffer, outside issues are likely to intrude, and delays are inevitable.

Hence the crisis audit. Properly performed, it identifies a procedure for handling crisis communication that does almost exactly what the CEO would do if the CEO were to drop everything, become fully informed, and handle each detail personally.

The crisis audit rapidly is becoming mandatory for companies that anticipate the possibility of crisis. And what responsible company does not?

One of the useful functions of a crisis audit is convincing management that something catastrophic actually could happen to the organization — today.

Even when convinced, many officers tend to think only in terms of the most obvious cases — an explosion, a product failure, a major layoff, or employee crime. But the best crisis audits include consideration of a variety of potential crises, resulting in a brief plan for each. These include such chilling situations as "officer caught" or the unexpected situation at Josephthal — "murder in the reception room."

When the audit is followed by an "ambush," the crisis auditors get a chance to see how well the plan is put into action. Sometimes things go smoothly, depending on how well the company has implemented its plan.

Most good audits focus on how information actually flows within the organization in any given situation.

With that knowledge in hand, and knowing where information is likely to be modified or delayed, the crisis auditors can eventually write a crisis plan that opens communications channels when and where they are needed most.

Richard H. Truitt is a partner ot Arnold Consultants, in charge of the firm's public affairs practice. Previously, he was president of Doremus Public Relations, one of the world's largest corporate/financial firms, for six years. Truitt served for 26 years at Carl Byoir & Associates, where he became executive vice-president in charge of the research, public issues, and corporate divisions and supervised the firm's regional office in Washington, D.C.

Death of the

Asbestos

Industry

Matthew M. Swetonic
Former Director of Environmental Affairs, Johns-Manville Corporation

Overview

It's almost impossible to comprehend, but little more than a quarter-century ago, asbestos was still referred to as the "magic mineral." The dozen or so major corporations that were major asbestos miners and/or producers of asbestos-containing building materials, such as Johns-Manville, Cetrain-Teed, GAF, National Gypsum, and Raybestos-Manhattan, were rich, sassy, and riding high. Asbestos was used everywhere: in floor tile, in pipe, in brake linings, in a dozen different types of insulation, in acoustical tile, in house siding. It was in our homes, our schools, the places we worked, our cars and trucks, our planes, our ships ... everywhere. If there was a dark cloud on the horizon, it might be that housing starts were down or commercial construction was slowing. A handful of scientists in the U.S., Great Britain, and South Africa were starting to uncover some disturbing things about the consequences of inhaling too much asbestos fiber, but few were listening to their concerns.

Today that industry is dead. The major asbestos corporations have either been driven into bankruptcy by billions upon billions of dollars in liability claims or have long since moved into other ventures, abandoning the use of asbestos altogether in most products. Once flourishing asbestos mines in Canada, the United States, and southern Africa lie abandoned or are operating at a fraction of their previous output. Where it was once treasured, it is now dreaded. A multibillion-dollar industry has arisen for the sole purpose of removing it from wherever it is found. The Environmental Protection Agency (EPA) has even proposed banning its use in any product anywhere in the United States, but was rebuffed by the courts on a technicality.

What happened? What drove that once mighty industry into the dust? It's simple. During a relatively short period of time from the mid-1960s through the early 1970s, the "magic mineral" was exposed for what it really was — probably the most hazardous industrial material ever unleashed on an unsuspecting world. I know. I was there.

The Right Place at the Right Time

In June 1965 I took a job as an assistant editor in the public relations department of the Johns-Manville Corporation in New York City. The man who hired me, William P. "Bill" Raines, the head of public relations, had recently joined J-M from the Koppers Company in Pittsburgh. Like myself, he had done his under-graduate work at the University of Pittsburgh and had worked on the school newspaper.

My job was not very demanding. I was the number two man on the company's monthly employee magazine. Mostly I traveled around the country from J-M plant to J-M plant, taking pictures and interviewing plant personnel for stories on a new product line or new plant addition. If nothing else, I got to know the company pretty well: where asbestos was used, how it was handled, what products it was in and why, although it never occurred to me at the time how valuable that knowl-edge was to become in later years. In 1967 my boss was promoted to head of all J-M publications and I was given the editor's job on the employee magazine. Life was fine and uncomplicated. And then it happened.

In the late summer of 1968 I was called into the office of Jack Solon, who was Raines's boss and vice-president for advertising and public relations. Raines's was there, too. Solon said he knew I had specialized in science journalism and he wondered if I would be interested in leaving the magazine and joining him and Raines to work on a new problem that had recently arisen in the company. He asked me whether I had ever read anything in the press about recent allegations regarding the safety of asbestos. I said I thought I recalled seeing an article or two but since Manville's name was not mentioned, I didn't pay much attention to them. He assured me it was time to pay attention. I left Solon's office with a new but ambiguous title, coordinator of special projects. My first take on my new assignment was to learn all I could about the asbestos-health issue. I discovered a long and interesting story.

History of the "Magic Mineral"

To begin with, asbestos is not synthetic; it is a mineral mined from the earth, gen-erally from open-pit mines. There are three commercially valuable types of asbestos: chrysotile, which comes primarily from mines in Canada and a few, now closed, in the United States; and the two so-called amphibole varieties, cro-cidolite and amosite, which are mostly found in the southern part of Africa.

China and the former Soviet Union also contain sizable deposits of asbestos, but they play little part in our tale. Some chrysotile asbestos will be found wherever there are outcroppings of a form of rock called serpentine, but these are not com-mercially useable. These outcroppings can be found in almost every state in the U.S. Practically the entire northern half of California rests on a bed of what is referred to as "crud grade" asbestos ore. While totally unusable, it is the main reason why California cities such as San Francisco and Sacramento have the highest levels of asbestos in their drinking water of essentially anyplace in the world. Rain put it there by washing it out of the ground and into the drinking water. Wind and erosion also release small but detectable quantities of asbestos into the air. It has even been found in ice samples dating back thousands of years. It is everywhere.

What made asbestos so valuable was its ability to be separated into long silky fibers that could be woven or wound into a wide variety of products; and it is practically fireproof. The word asbestos, in fact, comes from the ancient Greek and means "unquenchable," not because it wouldn't burn but because when used as wicks for oil lamps, it wouldn't go out or burn down. To this day I keep a chuck of asbestos ore on my desk. To illustrate its attributes I pull a few fibers and hold them over a cigarette lighter. Far thinner than a human hair, the fibers will glow bright red in the flame, but not burn or be consumed. It is the fineness and near indestructibility of the fibers that made asbestos so valuable, and, as it turned out, so lethal.

Health Problems?

The first indications that there might be something amiss with the "magic min-eral" arose in the years prior to the First World War in Great Britain. In the late 1940s, reports, once again from England, began appearing in the medical litera-ture linking asbestos exposure to an elevated risk of lung cancer among heavily exposed workers, primarily in the British asbestos textile industry, where condi-tions were recognized to be particularly dusty. While efforts were undertaken to reduce exposures, it was not known how much asbestos was "too much."

In the United States and Canada, the industry was sufficiently alarmed by the reports crossing the Atlantic from England that it commissioned a study of lung cancer among the Quebec asbestos miners. It was assumed — incorrectly, as it later turned out — that asbestos miners would have the highest exposure of any group of asbestos workers, including the textile workers, and that if a problem were to be found, it would be found in the Quebec mines. The study, which was completed in 1955, found only a handful of cases and concluded that whatever was going on in England it wasn't happening here.

Complacency was finally shattered in the early 1960s when reports started surfacing in many countries of an exceedingly rare cancer of the lining of the chest or the abdominal cavity. It was called mesothelioma. Not only was it being found among asbestos workers, but it was also showing up in communities adjacent to asbestos mines and factories, and among the families of asbestos workers — people whose only exposure to asbestos was the dust on the clothes worn home from work. Most of the cases being reported were in Great Britain and South Africa, but, unlike lung cancer, because there were no known causes of mesothelioma other than asbestos exposure, it was difficult to ignore.

Too Little Too Late? In the United States, additional dust control equipment of varying degrees of sophistication began to be installed in plants from coast to coast. But was it enough, and was it too late? The problem was, no one knew for sure how much dust was too much, nor, in the United States at least, were there standards that were enforceable in all plants and mines nationally even if someone did come up with a safe exposure level that everyone could agree upon. The basic law governing exposure to occupational hazards in the U.S. was at that time the Walsh-Healey Public Contracts Act, which had been passed in the 1930s but applied only to those companies doing business with the U.S. government. Because there were no inspections nor record-keeping procedures enforceable under the law, compliance was for all intents and purposes voluntary. The standards themselves were developed by an independent group called the American Conference of Governmental Industrial Hygienists (ACGIH), which set and revised standards for a whole range of occupational hazards, including asbestos.

For many years, asbestos exposures had been measured in particles per cubic foot of air, which was more a reflection of the crude nature of the measurement equipment then available than it was of the conviction of the scientific community that the volume of asbestos inhaled by a worker was an appropriate gauge of its level of hazard. By the 1960s, in fact, most scientists had come to the conclusion that volume meant little; it was the number and size of the individual asbestos fibers that a worker inhaled that was the true test of its danger. If a fiber was too long or too thick, it was incapable of penetrating into the deep recesses of the lung where it could cause disease. In the same regard, if the fiber was too small, it would be either cleared by normal lung cleansing mechanisms or else would be totally encapsulated by certain types of lung cells to form a non-hazard phenomena called an "asbestos body."

General agreement existed as to the size of asbestos fiber that caused the problem; no agreement existed on was the number of fibers per cubic centimeter that should be the limit in factory air in order to prevent disease. Some said 12; some said 5; some said 2. It was this argument that roared through the late 1960s and early 1970s — and which to some extent persists to this day — but I am getting ahead of my story.

While awareness was growing in American government and industry in the early 1960s that something needed to be done about the asbestos threat — and many things were being done in terms of improving factory conditions — it was not an issue known to any except a handful of scientists, government officials and enlightened industry leaders. Those in industry who were either unaware of the hazard or who chose to discount it, could ignore it with impunity because of the weaknesses of the Walsh-Healey Act. Something or someone needed to come along to stir up the country. It was a someone. His name was Irving Selikoff.

Dr. Irving Selikoff was a chest physician who throughout the more public part of his career was head of the Division of Environmental Medicine at the Mount Sinai School of Medicine in New York and director of its Environmental Sciences Laboratory. In 1962 he began a decades-long study of the mortality of union workers in the asbestos insulation industry in the New York City area. These were not workers who manufactured asbestos-containing insulations; instead they were the people who installed asbestos insulation in New York area skyscrapers and schools and, when the insulation deteriorated and needed to be replaced, ripped it out.

The First Large-Scale Study

The health experience of the asbestos insulation workers, as Dr. Selikoff discovered, was disastrous. Their rates of asbestosis, lung cancer, and mesothelioma were higher than any other asbestos researcher had found among any other asbestos-exposed population anyplace in the world. Equally as important, it was the first large-scale study of an asbestos industry group in the United States that produced results similar to studies done in Great Britain and South Africa. It was no longer possible to say, It can't happen here. Dr. Selikoff published his study of the insulation workers in the *Journal of the American Medical Association* in the spring of 1964. The asbestos problem was starting to enter the limelight.

The next four years witnessed increasing efforts from Dr. Selikoff and his associates at Mount Sinai to focus American public attention on the plight of the insulation workers, and by implication on workers throughout the asbestos industry, both here and abroad. While his studies produced no data that could help in the development of an appropriate numerical fiber standard — all he knew was the diseases the union members died from and how long they had been working in the industry — he nonetheless argued passionately to anyone who would listen that the existing standards were woefully inadequate. It was impossible to know whether he was right or not since the existing standards — whether measured in particles or fibers — had never been monitored except in the most rudimentary fashion, and for his own insulation workers had never been measured at all.

It was not that an environmental engineer could not enter an asbestos mine or construction site and take a precise asbestos fiber count — many were doing it — but there was no way to compare these exposures with those that existed decades ago when workers experienced the exposures that had led to the fatal diseases of the 1960s. Over dozens of years, gradual improvements in conditions in mines and plants, plus numerous changes in the composition of finished asbestos products and in work practices for handling those products at the job site, had made it essentially impossible to reconstruct the exposures of the past. In short, the only thing Dr. Selikoff had to offer the American public in the 1960s was the woeful health experience of the insulation workers and a plea that something be done about it.

Proactive Health Efforts

By the time I became involved in the asbestos controversy in the late 1960s, Johns-Manville had undergone a major transformation as far the health hazards of asbestos were concerned. As the largest of the world's asbestos companies, with both huge mines and numerous manufacturing facilities in North America, J-M had "gotten religion" big time. While not at all convinced that Dr. Selikoff's insulation worker mortality rates were applicable to all elements of the industry, it had the money and manpower to both clean up all its operations to the limits of technical feasibility and to launch itself, or instigate through its numerous trade associations, any number of health studies to determine the extent of the problems.

Through the Quebec Asbestos Mining Association, a huge research project was initiated and funded at McGill University in Montreal to study the mortality of the Quebec asbestos miners. It would not be a repeat of the mid-1950s study that found "no problem," but would instead be as thorough and as probing an epidemiological study as any industry had ever funded against itself. More importantly, it would be the first major asbestos study to try to identify not only the extent of disease in a segment of the asbestos industry, but also the levels of exposure that resulted in that disease.

The fundamental strategy that J-M adopted to deal with the crisis involved conducting a wide range of both health and technical studies to determine the extent of the problem within its own operations and to develop the technologies necessary to bring the situation under control. To assist the company in evaluating the truly astounding volume of studies beginning to appear in the medical literature on asbestos, it hired as a practically full-time consultant Dr. George W. Wright of the Medical Research Department at St. Luke's Hospital in Cleveland, who was himself a well-known asbestos researcher. It began a major outreach program of assistance and cooperation to government and private scientists worldwide, including Dr. Selikoff, who were seeking remedies to the emerging problem. It established particularly close links with the asbestos industry in Great Britain, where the problem had reached the acute stage years earlier and where much of the most valuable asbestos-health research was being conducted, a good deal of it being funded or at a minimum being cooperated in by the various English asbestos companies.

It always struck me as unique to the British system that a spirit of cooperation and joint purpose existed between the asbestos industry in the U.K. and Her Majesty's Factory Inspectorate, the regulatory group charged with policing industrial health in policies in that country. It was a far cry from the adversarial situation that would shortly develop in the United States with the establishment, both in 1970, of the EPA and the Occupational Safety and Health Administration (OSHA).

To manage the issue, J-M established an internal asbestos-health management committee, chaired by then-president Clint Burnett. It met at least monthly and included Solon, representing public relations, and Dr. Wright as outside medical consultant. Apart from the upper management committee, a separate public relations committee was formed consisting of Solon, Raines, and myself. Through Solon, and eventually on our own, Raines and I had access to Dr. Wright and to J-M's two top environmental control experts, Ed Fenner and Cliff Sheckler, for their assistance in developing responses to questions raised in the media regarding either the health side of the issue or Manville's own efforts at bringing the problem under control. At the none-too-subtle prodding of our English industry cousins, who believed the communications side of the issue in the U.S. was being mishandled if it was being handled at all, J-M retained the PR firm of Hill and Knowlton as outside consultants. H&K, which had recently passed Carl Byoir and Associates to become the largest PR firm in the world, had been on retainer to the British industry for a number of years. The account was placed in H&K's recently established Environmental Health Unit, the first division in any PR firm dedicated solely to assisting clients in responding to health and safety issues. Together with the H&K staff, it was our job to bring the communications side of the problem under control.

Building a Communications Team

It was a fundamental tenet of our approach that good science should dictate public policy on health issues. It was therefore essential that policy makers, as well as the general public, know what science told us.

Suave Dr. Selikoff Essentially the only side of the issue being reported in the press at that time was Dr. Selikoff's, who had over the years developed excellent media relationships. He had perfected the two essentials necessary to becoming an effective spokesperson for his cause: he always provided interesting, frequently controversial copy and he was always accessible. There was never any: "Let me think that over and I'll get back to you." He was always ready with an answer or an opinion. He understood deadlines and what constituted a "good" story, and was always patient, never condescending, to reporters who were having difficulty understanding his interpretation of the science. He perfected almost to an art form a technique that I now refer to as the "white coat approach." Whenever he appeared on television or was entertaining reporters at Mount Sinai, he never failed to appear in a white lab coat, as if he had just emerged from examining a patient or performing some experiment. While a standard technique today for conveying scientific credibility, in the late 1960s it was new and fresh and never failed to impress. As his staff at Mount Sinai grew, he taught them his techniques so that in time he had an entire cadre of scientists at his disposal who were also adept in media relations. And he possessed that most critical of all assets: since he had no apparent "cause" other than the health of asbestos industry workers around the world, he was exceedingly credible — a sort of Walter Cronkite of the scientific community. It was a tough act to handle.

Two things he did always drove us crazy. He always referred to the insulation workers as "asbestos workers," which was nearly always reported as meaning people who worked in asbestos mines and mills, which they, of course, did not. In later years, when J-M was involved in a joint program at Mount Sinai to develop new methodologies for reducing the asbestos exposure of the insulation workers, he was continually urged to change the misleading terminology when referring to the insulation workers. He promised many times to do so, but never did. I believe it served his purposes better to continue using a term that implies he represented the interests of a far larger segment of the industry than he actually did and that the problem was universal in the asbestos industry, which it was not.

The other thing he did that gave us fits was his insistence on extrapolating the health experience of the insulation workers, which was admittedly terrible, to any and all asbestos workers everywhere, regardless of their level of exposure. As the number of workers grew who were discovered to have had some, often trivial, exposure to asbestos in their working lifetime, the number of deaths he predicted grew by leaps and bounds. To be fair, he would preface each calculation with the words: "If our numbers are correct, we can predict...." but the disclaimer was seldom if ever picked up by the media, nor was its import understood.

Even when he tried to clarify for the media what he meant, it was often ignored in favor of the more dramatic. For example, in late 1972, CBS News contacted me for a response to a statement Dr. Selikoff had made at a congressional hearing. This was at a time when controversy raged over the fate of workers in U.S. shipyards during World War II, some of whom had substantial exposure to asbestos insulations used aboard navy ships. The reporter said Dr. Selikoff had predicted that 2 million former shipyard workers would die of asbestos-related diseases before the end of the century. I explained that he had misunderstood what was said. Since Dr. Selikoff had made the same prediction many times, I was able to quote him almost verbatim: "If our numbers are correct, of the 2 million workers employed in U.S. shipyards during the Second World War, 40 percent will die of asbestos-related diseases before the end of the century." I put him in contact with Dr. Selikoff, who confirmed to the reporter that he had gotten the prediction wrong. Relieved, I then proceeded to explain to the reporter why we considered the prediction totally off base. That evening, towards the end of the broadcast, Walter Cronkite solemnly intoned, "Noted asbestos researcher Irving J. Selikoff today predicted that 2 million American shipyard workers would die of asbestos-related disease before the end of the century. A spokesman for the asbestos industry said the number was too high." The next morning I called the reporter at CBS back to complain about the spot. Hadn't they talked to Dr. Selikoff? Hadn't he told them they had it wrong? He answered yes to both questions but said, "We used what we *thought* he said at the hearing because it made a better story."

We continued on track with our efforts. We developed and distributed a series of media background papers on the various aspects of the asbestos issue. Of particular concern was mesothelioma, because it was the only asbestos-related disease known to occur outside of the industrial setting. If so-called "neighborhood" and "household" cases were showing up with increasing frequency in Great Britain and South Africa, how soon would it be before they began occurring here, and with what level of public outcry?

Science-Based Communications

Fortunately, the scientific evidence was mounting that nearly all cases of mesothelioma could be traced to exposure to either of the two amphibole varieties of asbestos — crocidolite and amosite — or to mixtures of either of these and chrysotile, but essentially never to chrysotile alone. At J-M's huge plant complex in Manville, New Jersey, some 50 cases of mesothelioma would be identified by the mid-1970s, with all but one occurring among workers in the asbestos cement pipe plant, where in the 1940s and 1950s crocidolite and chrysotile had been commonly mixed together with pitch forks on the plant floor before being made into pipe. Amosite was also heavily used in the manufacture of the types of insulations used by the workers studied by Dr. Selikoff. In fact, the common type of wrap insulation used for many applications was called an "amosite blanket."

Asbestos concerns continue today, as workers in protective gear wash down buildings in New York City after a pipeline blast contaminated the area with asbestos.

All our efforts to communicate this new scientific evidence on mesothelioma were opposed strenuously in the media by Dr. Selikoff and his associates at Mount Sinai. He discounted the new research and asserted that we were trying to whitewash chrysotile, which was the mainstay of J-M's product line and the only type of asbestos mined by the company. He conveniently forgot or chose to ignore the fact that when faced with the same evidence, the British — whose approaches he normally admired — began moving rapidly toward setting stricter standards on crocidolite and amosite than on chrysotile and would eventually end up banning both varieties. To Dr. Selikoff, asbestos was asbestos, and he would accept no evidence that contradicted that view.

By late 1968 Manville and Dr. Selikoff were in close, almost daily, contact. While we continued to fight it out in the media over many issues, there was one on which we could both agree: the insulation workers had a horrible health record and something needed to be done to address their working conditions. J-M agreed to fund an effort at Mount Sinai that came to be called the Industrial Insulation Health Research Program (IIHRP). Its primary purpose was to develop environmental control practices for reducing the asbestos exposure of the insulation workers to safe levels. A board of directors was created to oversee the project. It included government health officials, J-M's vice-presidents of manufacturing and R&D, Dr. Wright, Dr. Selikoff, and a number of others. J-M bought Mount Sinai a state of the art electron microscope and assigned a top-notch industrial hygienist to work in residence with the Mount Sinai staff. Communications support was to be provided by Hill and Knowlton with Carl Thompson, an H&K executive vice-president and head of the firm's Environmental Health Unit, which handled the J-M account, becoming the defect head of PR for the IIHRP.

From a communications standpoint the joint effort worked fine. The venture was launched with considerable public fanfare with a press conference at Mount Sinai — Dr. Selikoff turned the media out in droves — and lots of smiles, hand-shakes, and pledges of eternal cooperation. Thompson wrote and produced the program's periodic newsletter, sent out press releases on various program accomplishments, and even ghostwrote an article for Dr. Selikoff for an occupational hygiene journal. Clearly, Manville's image was enhanced by its involvement in the IIHRP effort, but it continued to be the only asbestos company in the U.S. speaking out in defense of the industry when it came under attack. That was soon to change.

Industry Umbrella Opened

For years H&K had been urging that J-M set up a trade association in the United States to handle the communications aspects of the asbestos issue. The firm's London office had set up such a group, called the Asbestos Information Council, for the British asbestos industry, and H&K argued that a U.S. counterpart would provide the same two major benefits to Manville. First, by establishing an umbrella group to handle communications, it would reduce J-M's own individual media exposure; and second, it would create a voice that would speak for the entire U.S. industry and not just for one company.

The reasoning was persuasive, and in late 1970, a meeting of seven or eight of the major U.S. asbestos companies was convened in J-M's headquarters. Manville was viewed with some suspicion by the industry because of its close association with Dr. Selikoff, whom they totally distrusted in the IIHRP program, but when the president of the world's largest asbestos company called a meeting of his peers, they came. Solon asked me to write a slide presentation, which he would give after Burnett welcomed our guests. He asked me to pull no punches in the presentation and to lay out in no uncertain terms the seriousness of the problems facing the industry. I sat in on the meeting and was surprised to discover that many of the participants considered many of Dr. Selikoff's charges so outrageous that they had discounted them entirely. Many seemed unaware of the research coming out of the U.K. and South Africa that indicated the health threat was far wider in scope that they had been lead to believe.

Agreement as reached, after much discussion, to form a trade association that came to be called the Asbestos Information Association/North America (AIA/NA), with J-M providing both staff and funding for the first year of operation. If, at the end of that time, the member companies found the Association was providing a useful service, a mechanism would be developed for sharing the costs on an equitable basis. Raines became defect executive director with me as chief of staff. Clearly, at least to me, the deciding factor in inducing those in the room to join up was our warning that the two new regulatory agencies created by Congress that year — OSHA and EPA — were both eyeing asbestos as their first problem to tackle.

The responsibilities of the AIA/NA would go far beyond normal public relations, at least as it was commonly practiced in 1971. The operative word in the name of the Association was "information." The Association would not just deal with the media, but would create a technical information arm to advise industry members on the appropriate ways to control asbestos exposures in the workplace; a regulatory information arm to work with government agencies on the development of reasonable workplace and environmental standards; and, in the future, a legal arm to assist the industry as a whole in defending itself against liability claims. The latter would, in time, swallow the entire trade association, but in 1971, the liability issue did not even show up on the screen and would not do so for years to come.

Risk Comes Home   We had all been dreading the inevitable discovery of the first "neighborhood" or "household" case of mesothelioma in the United States. When it did happen, the shock was incredible because it had truly occurred in our own household. The victim was the wife of Cliff Sheckler, who was one of J-M's two top industrial hygiene officers and a member of the Environmental Control Committee of the AIA/NA. Since the Shecklers had never lived close to any Manville plant during his long career with the company, it was a true household case; she had developed the disease from inhaling the asbestos dust he brought home on his clothes from work. More than any other development, the death of Sheckler's wife forced the entire industry to face up to the realities of the asbestos threat, something it had seemed reluctant to do previously. Ed Fenner, the other top J-M industrial hygiene officer and, like Sheckler, a member of the Association's environmental committee, would himself die from mesothelioma in 1984. Both men had spent their early years at J-M as plant engineers, at a time when dust controls in industry plants and mills were rudimentary, if they existed at all.

As a matter of principle and good public relations, the Association steadfastly maintained that asbestos should not be used for "inappropriate purposes" and that any use of asbestos in its "free" form should be controlled to reduce employee and general public exposure to the extent technically feasible.

For decades, the steel girders of high-rise buildings in most American cities were fireproofed by a process called "asbestos spraying." Raw asbestos fiber was mixed with water in a tank and shot out of a nozzle at the girders from a far as 20 feet away. Despite the presence of water in the concoction, the process was notoriously dusty. In order to contain the dust within the construction site, tarpaulins were generally hung from the outside of the floor being sprayed. At this time in New York City, a number of high-rise buildings, including the World Trade Center, were under construction. On windy days, the tarpaulins would frequently buckle, particularly on the higher floors, allowing a shower of dried asbestos spray to cascade down on the heads of pedestrians below. Dr. Selikoff's people at Mount Sinai claimed that asbestos spraying was the cause of the "asbestos bodies" being routinely found at autopsy in the lungs of New Yorkers not occupationally exposed to asbestos and predicted an epidemic of asbestos-related disease in the general public.

Three Asbestos Curiosities

The head of the local asbestos sprayers trade group came to us for assistance. We studied his data and the precautions being taken to control the dust, and put it on the agenda for the next full meeting of the Association. It was not an economic consideration for mining members of the AIA since the volume of asbestos used for spray applications was infinitesimal. The discussion therefore centered solely on whether it was a controllable use of asbestos, and, if it wasn't, what should we do about it. During a break in the meeting, I strolled over to a nearby window and looked out. The meeting was being held in the Engineers Club, which was on 40th Street in New York City overlooking Bryant Park. Across the park, on 42nd Street, the W.R. Grace building was under construction. From a tarpaulined floor about 10 stories up, a virtual snow shower of sprayed asbestos was slowly drifting down to the street below. It was a visual demonstration of the public relations nightmare that we would be facing if we lent our support to the asbestos sprayers. I called everyone to the window. "That," I said, pointing across the street, "is why we have to take a walk on those people." We quietly informed Dr. Selikoff, the city of New York, and the EPA — which was also looking into asbestos spraying — that while we wouldn't attack the practice and health grounds, neither would we defend it. The practice was shortly banned by the city and later by the EPA nationally, with our concurrence.

Sometimes the problems that came floating in over the transom were just plain weird. In late 1971 I received a phone call from Dr. Selikoff. He had a problem that he hoped I could help him with. He said this was one we could both agree needed fixing. The situation he described was so preposterous even I had trouble believing any businessperson anywhere could be so ignorant of the evidence regarding the health risks of asbestos, or so callous he didn't care.

The situation was this. Import duties on finished asbestos products imported into the United States were essentially zero. On the other hand, the duties on clothing manufactured abroad were quite stiff. An Italian businessperson thought he had found a clever way to beat the customs folks at their own game. He produced thousands of ladies winter coats using a small amount of asbestos fiber in their manufacture and then tried to import them into the United States as "asbestos products" rather than as clothing. The coats were not even woven, but were a pressed melton, a type of material similar to that used in navy pea coats. Dr. Selikoff told me you could actually release free asbestos fibers from the coats using a small clothes brush. He wanted me to talk to the importer, who had contacted Dr. Selikoff for his assistance in convincing customs officials that the coats were safe. Dr. Selikoff said that he had tried reasoning with the importer, but that he refused to understand the seriousness of the problem, and was intent on forcing the issue with customs. Perhaps, he said, he would believe it if somebody from the asbestos industry backed up his concerns. I offered to meet with the importer, and Dr. Selikoff promised, in return, not to go to the media with the story until I had a chance to sit down with the importer and explain the hopelessness of his position.

I met with the importer a few days later. He couldn't see what the problem was. Women don't brush their coats every day, he argued, and besides, the amount of asbestos in the coats was very small, only enough to meet the customs service's definition of an asbestos product. As a fellow businessperson, he hoped I would understand that if the coats were declared unsafe, he couldn't sell them anywhere, let alone in the United States, and would loose his entire investment. I patiently explained that while the actual risk might be very small, the AIA considered what he had done a totally inappropriate use of asbestos and that we would never support him. He left dejected, saying he would have to think over his options. I reported on the meeting to Dr. Selikoff, who thanked me for my efforts, but said that he would now have to take matters into his own hands. Sure enough, within a couple of days, the New York media was swamped with stories on the hazardous "asbestos coats" from Italy. The demonstration Dr. Selikoff cooked up for the media was a masterful piece of theater. He put one of the coats on a female mannequin in an enclosed laboratory at Mount Sinai, and while he lectured the assembled press corps on the hazards of asbestos, two of his staff, dressed in moon suits, eventually brushed fibers from the coat into plastic baggies, which they then sealed, as if they contained some horribly radioactive substance, and took away for analysis. It was very effective and very photogenic.

The importer, of course, never got his coats into the United States. I thought we had dodged yet another stupid bullet, but rumors about "asbestos coats" and other types of asbestos clothing being on the market kept popping up here and there for years, each of which required a couple of phone calls or a letter to set the record straight.

In the early fall we learned of yet another idiocy. Small, five-pound sacks of raw asbestos fiber were being purchased by some schools and YWCAs to be used as an inexpensive modeling compound to construct puppets or sculpt heads. We checked a number of hardware stores in various cities and, sure enough, the stuff was available almost everywhere. Besides writing the distributors that we were able to identify, in November we sent a precautionary letter on the subject to nearly 5,000 teachers associations, hobby and craft publications, state boards of education, boy and girl scout councils, YMCAs and YWCAs urging that "the use of asbestos for hobby purposes be eliminated immediately." We received many thank-you letters back. Most indicated they weren't aware that inhaling asbestos fibers could be a serious health hazard. That gap in their education was soon to be filled.

As predicted, by late 1971 the newly created regulatory agencies of EPA and OSHA were in hot pursuit of the asbestos industry. Fueled by incessant pounding from Mount Sinai and organized labor, OSHA on December 7 issued an Emergency Temporary Standard reducing permissible asbestos exposure levels in the workplace from 12 to 5 fibers per cubic centimeter of air, with a proposed further reduction to 2 fibers if the medical evidence supported it. Under the statue that created OSHA, the agency would have to come up with a permanent standard within six months. At around the same time, the EPA announced its intention to hold a series of public hearings across the United States for the purpose of developing an ambient air standard on asbestos to protect the general public from the threat of asbestos-related disease. Our plate was filling up fast.

EPA Hearings: Cakewalk

To complicate matters, Johns-Manville was in the midst of moving its corporate headquarters from New York City to Denver. I had already announced my decision not to go West with the company and would therefore be without a job in early 1972. Raines had already left to join Union Pacific as public relations director, so I was left alone to handle the affairs of the trade association as it was entering its most trying period. In late December I was asked to fly to Buffalo, New York, to meet with Al Fay of National Gypsum, who was then president of the AIA/NA, to discuss my taking over the reins as executive director, which I agreed to do, effective January 1.

The EPA hearings were physically grueling, but from a PR standpoint they were a piece of cake. The media was obsessed with the occupational health aspects of the asbestos issue, but had not yet latched onto the environmental implications. Media coverage of the first hearings, held in New York, was zero. The Manville folks held center stage but since the industry had already turned its back on the sprayed asbestos people there was little controversy to attract attention.

The next hearings were held in Los Angeles a week later. The Association was the primary testifier and the only opposition came from a local chapter of the Sierra Club, which tried desperately to build a case that the asbestos industry was damaging the California environment. It didn't make a lot of sense since the entire northern half of the state was a bed of low-grade asbestos ore. Clearly, the environmental community was waking up to the asbestos issue, but it would be a long time before they understood it sufficiently to present a coherent case for increased environmental controls.

Following the Los Angeles hearings, I flew to London to consult with our English colleagues "over breakfast" on the EPA proposals. I left that same evening reassured that our position on the environmental asbestos standards was scientifically sound. The final hearings held that same week in East St. Louis were a total no-show. Not a single individual or organization appeared to testify. The whole thing was over in 20 minutes and I flew home for a much-needed rest. The real fight, the OSHA hearings, was coming up shortly.

OSHA Hearings: Through the Wringer

Nothing in the PR textbooks helped us prepare for the OSHA public hearings that began in February 1972 in the Labor Department auditorium on Constitution Avenue in Washington, D.C. We were, as they say, making it up as we went along. The strategy was simple: J-M would address the health issue and the Association would discuss economic impact and the specific changes we wanted in the proposed standards. Tactically, we set up an AIA/NA Information Center in a suite in the Madison Hotel, a few blocks from where the hearings were being held. From there we stood ready to issue press releases; develop industry testimony; prepare summaries for the media of the day's proceedings; arrange for media interviews with industry witnesses; and, in general, establish ourselves as a scientific resource center for disseminating material from the medical and technical literature supporting the industry's position. It all worked reasonably well and the tactics we developed as a matter of logical necessity have since become standard for handling hearings of a controversial health-related nature.

The real fireworks, however, occurred in the hearing room itself, where representatives of J-M and the asbestos industry shot it out toe-to-toe with the Mount Sinai crowd and their top guns in organized labor. What those hearings taught me was that, from a media relations standpoint, nothing the PR professional can do to position such a proceeding as a logical discussion of the issues will ever compete against the sheer drama of two proponents of opposing positions ripping each other's guts out in a public forum.

Unfortunately, J. Corbett McDonald, M.D., the doctor from McGill University who had been chief investigator in the huge industry-sponsored study of the Quebec asbestos mining industry, was ill-prepared for the personal abuse he was to take from Dr. Selikoff's associates. They questioned not only his data, but his veracity, and indeed implied that he was nothing less than a paid lackey of the asbestos industry. His only problem was that he had produced evidence that the asbestos miners in Quebec were not dying at the same rate as Dr. Selikoff's insulation workers, and that their exposure had to be exceedingly heavy for any disease to show up at all. Without directly saying so, he was casting doubt on Dr. Selikoff's fundamental proposition that the mortality experience of the insulation workers was reflective of conditions throughout the asbestos industry. If the asbestos miners were an exception to the Selikoff rule, then perhaps other segments of the industry were exempt as well.

Dr. Wright, who had the audacity to call for stricter standards on crocidolite and amosite — the types of asbestos most closely linked with mesothelioma — than on chrysotile, received the same type of abuse. Dr. Wright, however, conducted himself with greater composure and gave as well as he took.

A fundamental principle of crisis public relations rooted itself in my brain: I would never again, if I had anything to say about it, allow a client or a representative of a client to enter into such a situation without extensive confrontational communications training. It would be unfair to the client and would, indeed, be destructive of his or her position. I have never waivered in that conviction and have, in fact, refused to work with clients who declined such training.

Compared to what the Manville folks endured, our testimony was like a walk in the park. Fay discussed the potential economic impact of lowering the standards too far and too fast, and I ran through the litany of changes we wanted made in the proposed regulations: no lowering of the standard from five to two fibers in less than four years in order to give the industry time to install the necessary added controls; no warning labels on products where the asbestos was "locked in" with cement, plastics, or other binders; and greater flexibility in the use of respirators to control dust exposure. There were few questions since we had submitted our detailed recommendations earlier, and were only summarizing them now.

We were followed to the witness table by organized labor representatives who supported an immediate lowering of the permissible exposure level to two fibers; some even suggested that it be reduced to zero six months after that.

Curiously, Dr. Selikoff personally never testified. I have always suspected that he did not want to subject himself to the hard questioning from industry doctors and scientists that might have occured. He preferred avoiding situations where he was not totally in control. Dr. William Nicholson, who would, when Dr. Selikoff retired, replace him as head of the Environmental Sciences Laboratory, was left to carry the Mount Sinai banner alone.

One additional aspect of the hearings needs to be addressed. We had learned a day or so before they began that one of the first people to testify would be a J-M employee who was dying of mesothelioma. It was, to my way of thinking, a blatant attempt to sensationalize what ought to be a sober presentation of facts and recommendations (the AFL/CIO, indeed, proved my point by holding a press conference the first day of the hearings to showcase this individual to the media). I instructed our legal council to see what he could do to prevent the man's appearance, which he did by publicly raising objections at a prehearing conference held to settle the ground rules for the hearings. It was a terrible mistake. I had with one intemperate move created a groundswell of sympathy for the man and his condition, and had handed our opponents on a silver platter an example of the insensitivity of the asbestos industry toward those it was killing, or so they positioned it. I would never countenance anything like that again, and have counseled clients ever since that expressions of sympathy and concern for injured parties are a necessary component of any positioning of a health and safety issue.

Established Regulations Favorable

Compared to the turmoil of the public hearing, the rest of the year was anticlimactic. We continued to pepper OSHA and the media with more facts and figures supporting our position, as did our opponents. When the permanent regulations were published in the *Federal Register* in early June, OSHA had accepted our recommendations practically to the letter, the most important being that the two-fiber standard would not go into effect for another four years. It was a big win. We issued a simple press release commending OSHA for its actions and assuring the public that the standards were sufficiently strict to protect the health of asbestos workers everywhere. We declined any broadcast interviews on the grounds that only OSHA could answer questions as to how and why the standards came out the way they did.

Dr. Selikoff, on the other hand, was everywhere, screaming that the agency had condemned another 50,000 asbestos workers to a premature death by delaying the imposition of the two-fiber standard. The AFL/CIO took OSHA to court in an effort to overturn the standards. It was, I believe, the only time that organized labor sued OSHA over a health standard; in all other instances, it was the affected industry that claimed it had been wronged.

By the spring of 1973, I was coming to the conclusion that the tasks I had set out **Aftermath** to accomplish when I signed on with the AIA/NA were nearing completion. We had recently finished five new booklets and a couple of pamphlets on various aspects of the health issue; a five-booklet OSHA technical compliance manual was scheduled for publication in midsummer; and an AIA/NA manual for employees to help them understand the new OSHA regulations had been made available to the member companies for distribution to their own workforce.

The industry itself seemed to be in fine shape. The organized labor challenge to the OSHA standards had been rejected by the court of appeals and it appeared unlikely that there would be any more challenges to the status quo for years to come. The EPA regulations had likewise come out favorable to the industry so we no longer had to worry about the continued use of asbestos in public buildings. Even the media seemed to be getting bored with the asbestos-health issue.

I felt it was time to move on. I had done nothing except asbestos and health for the last five years and I craved new challenges and experiences. I resigned from the AIA in August 1973 and accepted a position with Hill and Knowlton. Because of my background with OSHA, one of my first assignments was to work with the plastics industry, which had recently discovered that a basic chemical, vinyl chloride, used in the manufacture of PVC plastic resin caused a rare cancer of the liver called angiosarcoma. I had heard rumors that the Mount Sinai team had been called in to help prepare organized labor's case for the OSHA hearings scheduled to begin in June 1974, so it did not totally surprise me when I ran into Dr. Nicholson in the corridor at a hastily convened vinyl chloride medical symposium in Washington,

D.C. "What are *you* doing here?" he asked. I smiled and replied, "The same thing you are." He walked into the crowded auditorium and took a seat next to Dr. Selikoff, who turned to me and waved. It was starting all over again.

Matthew M. Swetonic is currently senior vice-president and director of environmental operations at the E. Bruce Harrison Company. Before joining EBH in 1991, he was vice-president and director of Hill and Knowlton's Division of Scientific, Technical, and Environmental Affairs (STEA), a position he held since 1986. While at Hill and Knowlton, Mr. Swetonic handled crisis communications and environmental health problems for clients in the chemical, mining, plastics, food, and cosmetics industries. After graduating from Columbia University's Graduate School of Journalism, he joined the public relations staff of the Johns-Manville Corporation. He was named director of environmental affairs in 1971. In 1972, he became the first full-time executive director of the Asbestos Information Association/North America, a trade association dealing with health and environmental problems in the industry.

Tragedy
at McDonald's

Richard G. Starmann
Senior Vice-President, McDonald's Corporation

On July 18, 1984, James Huberty left his apartment in San Ysidro, California (a **Overview**
small, heavily Hispanic-populated suburb south of San Diego), telling his wife
Edna that he was going out "to hunt humans." By dusk that evening, Huberty had
invaded a McDonald's restaurant two blocks from his home and shot 40 people,
killing 21 and wounding 19 before he was shot and killed from a nearby rooftop by
a member of the San Diego Police Department's SWAT team.

McDonald's had no specific crisis plan to deal with a bizarre incident involving a
crazed gunman and a senseless slaughter. While the media, for the most part,
showed their human side in taking the point of view that McDonald's too had been
victimized by this violent aberration, it was not uncommon to see a headline or a
television news promo scream, "Big Mac Attack in California."

While no special plan was in place, an underlying business philosophy characterized McDonald's response to the crisis. It was expressed by Don Horwitz, then
executive vice president and general counsel of the company, who the day after
the incident told a few of us who were responding to more than 1,000 media
calls, "I don't want you people to worry or care about the legal implications of
what you might say. We are going to do what's right for the survivors and families
of the victims, and we'll worry about lawsuits later." "We're going to do what's
right" became the "Horwitz Rule."

McDonald's took many actions that have never been covered by the media: paying hospital bills of the wounded, flying in relatives of victims for the funerals,
providing counseling for families of victims — actions that could have been taken

into a court of law at a later date and used as twisted evidence that McDonald's in some misconstrued manner was at fault for the tragic incident. Some of that did occur, but because of actions of our top management and communications involvement in that process we were able to both act quickly and speak clearly with one voice.

Three months after the tragic San Ysidro shooting, Capitol Broadcasting Company of Raleigh, North Carolina, ran an editorial that closed with: "Many in the news media unfairly dubbed this tragedy the 'McDonald's Massacre.' It was not the McDonald's Massacre. It was the Huberty massacre and McDonald's Restaurant was victimized along with the others. The McDonald's Corporation's response to that San Diego community is laudable and worthy of our respect and appreciation nationwide." We never could have written that about ourselves.

The News Breaks   On July 18, 1984, I had taken my wife, Kathy, to a birthday dinner at the Drake Hotel's International Club in downtown Chicago, when the maitre d' told me I had a phone call. It was my 13-year-old son, R. G., calling from home. "Dad," he said, "I'm sorry to bother you but there's been a special news report — there has been a shooting at a McDonald's in California and four people were killed."

"Don't be silly," I said. "You did the right thing. Thanks, and if anyone calls give them the number down here."

I had taken the call at the maitre d's desk to avoid the attention of the portable phone gapers. I called Chuck Rubner, who was my director of communications, told him there had been a shooting at one of our stores in California (I asked if he knew where San Ysidro was — he didn't), told him I was at a birthday dinner with my wife, and asked him to stay on top of the situation. I returned to my table, told Kathy what was going on, and five minutes later received the first of 11 phone calls over the next 45 minutes.

With each call, the death toll mounted. My wife dropped me at our office in the Chicago suburb of Oak Brook shortly thereafter. Now, radio news was talking about this possibly being the largest single "massacre" in American history. When I arrived a number of our people were already gathered in the office taking media calls.

Every media outlet wanted a statement, and the phones were ringing off the hook. We had to make some quick decisions, we needed accurate information, we needed to let top management know what was going on. I spoke with Mike Quinlan, president of McDonald's worldwide. We agreed on the need for a statement that should reflect what we felt — shock, sympathy, disbelief — and should reflect our commitment to help the victims. The last line of the statement reflected what all of us felt personally: "What more can we say?"

After Quinlan approved the statement, we responded first to the wire services, to give it the broadest possible distribution, before settling in to return media calls throughout that night. Reporters wanted as many specifics as we could provide, and we did not have a lot of them. The death toll was still rising, and we did not know how many had been wounded. Reporters wanted to know whether children, seniors, or McDonald's employees had been killed or injured — and we did not know that either. We referred those calls to the San Diego Police Department.

I had also spoken with Ed Rensi, president of McDonald's USA, who upon hearing the news earlier had left a message that I should get on the next plane to California. I told Ed I would of course do what he wanted, but that the media action and immediate need was in Oak Brook and that was where I would best serve the company. Ed agreed, and it was at this point that we caught a break.

Steve Leroy, one of our media relations people who had been on the Carter White House press staff before joining McDonald's, was on vacation in San Francisco at the Democratic National Convention. He happened to be in the ABC trailer at the convention when the news broke, and called the office to see if he was needed. I told him to get to San Diego as quickly as he could, not to be a spokesperson, but to be our eyes and ears on site because our San Diego regional people were inundated with calls from families of crew members and were referring all local media calls to us as well. So we had a cool and experienced media pro on site in San Diego, and that served us well in keeping us informed as to what was happening on an ongoing basis.

The second major decision made that night regarded our advertising. Paul Schrage, executive vice-president and chief marketing officer, called and said one of our agency people had suggested we think about pulling our TV commercials, which we found was standard operating procedure for some airlines after a crash. Paul asked my opinion and I told him we should do the same. He agreed. Since it was Wednesday, we thought it best to take our advertising off the air nationally through the weekend. It was a $22 million decision. The thought of upbeat "McDonald's and you" commercials airing following a news segment showing casualties and talking "body count" was just too much. Probably one of the most widely distributed photos of 1984 was that of 11-year-old Omar Torrez, lying in a pool of blood under his bicycle just outside the restaurant. While the media did react with sensitivity for the most part, "McMurder," "McMassacre," and "Big Mac Attack" were headlines in more than a few news outlets.

A San Diego police officer bends over shooting victim Omar Torrez, killed in James Huberty's massacre of 20 people at the San Ysidro McDonald's.

We did interviews that entire night, and for the next three days. From a corporate perspective, our charge was to cut our losses. We knew instinctively that what would cut those losses would be our actions, not just our words. We had our media and public relations teams taking calls; our agency helping us in every conceivable way; our customer relations representatives responding to customer inquiries; calls from our regional offices asking how to handle local media; and calls from franchisees and suppliers. We took them all.

Marathon Media Blitz

I remember leaving the office around five in the morning, showering and returning at about 6:00 A.M. That day, on Thursday, July 19, I conducted more than 70 interviews — for five minutes on the phone, as a talking head at the office — for local, network, national, and international outlets, including CNN, ABC, CBS, NBC, BBC, *USA Today*, Dow Jones, and more. Our media relations team did 1,400 interviews over five days, and that Thursday evening I remember lying on top of my desk at eight o'clock with a phone in my ear, saying the same things I had said so many, many times.

We had established a process for logging calls and making assignments for returning them. As calls came in they were logged on our standard news information request form, categorized by type of media, and stacked in the office next to mine. As the communications officer of McDonald's, I served as corporate spokesperson and, thus, handled networks, national newspapers and radio, and major market newspapers. Other media calls were assigned to two key people — Chuck Rubner in my department, or Chuck Gelman, executive vice-president from our national PR agency, Golin/Harris Communications. C and D markets were handled by other media relations staff members, as were tons of local radio stations.

I was surprised at the extent to which networks and affiliates did not want feeds from one another but needed their "own pictures," even though they were all basically the same, especially early the first evening. When a crew wanted to come out we accommodated them, but we let them know up front that all I would do was give them the statement on camera. So while we did our best to respond to the television media, it was often in a time-consuming and redundant manner. Television reporters would often say something like, "I'm really sorry this happened to McDonald's," expressing the kind of sympathy you might find from a friend who says, "I'm sorry this happened at your house."

There were some tough questions asked, and some unfair ones, too. The toughest questions were about security guards or guns — past and present. It was the last thing we wanted to talk about. We certainly did not want to see any stories that lead with, "McDonald's to hire armed guards," but we also did not want to come off as being flip or complacent as if nothing had happened. So we developed a standard answer and said, "We'll look into that, but if we talk about security procedures, they really aren't secure." We were trying to deal with this question in an environment in which customers were calling and saying things like, "My son just loves McDonald's and so do I, but now he's afraid to go after what happened. What can you do?"

The most "unfair" question we were asked was, "Do you think this will spawn any copycat incidents?" Gelman, who had been answering calls with us around the clock, nearly lost it by responding, "That question serves absolutely no useful purpose *@#!" and hung up. We forgave him!

While we never publicized or released the information, teams of McDonald's personnel and operations people were sent to San Diego to help survivors and families of the victims, assisting with funeral arrangements and guaranteeing payment of hospital bills. Our teams arranged for counseling and flying family relatives into San Ysidro from Mexico.

Then came the follow-up stories. As body counts were finalized, media attention focused on the perpetrator and on the handling of the incident by the San Diego Police Department. At first, Huberty was characterized as "a Vietnam veteran who had gone crazy with his M-16 rifle." Later, bizarre stories would emerge, from Huberty having been driven insane by fumes he inhaled working in an Ohio manufacturing plant to a variation on the "Twinky defense" that claimed Huberty suffered a hormonal imbalance from eating McDonald's Chicken McNuggets.

Survivor's Fund Decision

Late Thursday afternoon, July 19, I was doing an interview with an AP reporter who asked, "What's McDonald's involvement with the fund that's been started for the survivors?" I told him I didn't know about any fund. About 15 minutes after the interview, one of my people walked in and said, "I just got a question about a survivor's fund that Joan Kroc has started — do you know anything about it?"

Joan Kroc, the widow of McDonald's founder Ray Kroc, lives in San Diego and was deeply moved by the tragic San Ysidro incident. She contributed $100,000 of her own money to start a survivor's fund and suddenly, as the news of it broke across the country, we were being asked again and again, "What's McDonald's going to do?"

We called Quinlan and met later that day to discuss McDonald's options. The meeting included myself, Mike Quinlan, Ed Rensi, Paul Schrage, Don Horwitz, Chuck Gelman, and Al Golin, chairman and CEO of Golin/Harris. As in most McDonald's management meetings, there were some strong and varied opinions voiced regarding options.

From a PR perspective, I knew that we had a limited media window to send a clear signal and that it would be open that day for only a few more hours. The media were waiting to hear one thing: What were we going to do?

During a spirited exchange of ideas, Horwitz's voice rose above the racket and said, "Hey, did you all hear what he said?" pointing to Gelman, who was sitting quietly on his right. The group stopped, and Horwitz spoke. "Chuck said, Why don't we contribute $1 million to the survivors fund." "Why a million?" someone asked. "Because it's a nice round number and it feels right," was the response. After some discussion, Quinlan said, "Do it."

By about three in the afternoon, we had finalized a statement, had it approved by Quinlan, and were responding to the huge pile of news information requests that were asking what we're going to do. Headlines started running across the U.S., "McDonald's Contributes $1 Million to Survivor's Fund." So we made it through the media window by doing what was right and moving quickly, with a little push from and a big thank-you to Joan Kroc for getting us "jump started" in a proactive and positive direction.

Early Friday morning, July 20, during our first top management meeting that day, we found out that there would be a mass the next morning at the Catholic church in San Ysidro. Eleven victims were to be buried, and a mass would be said at Our Lady of Mount Carmel, which sat on a little hill overlooking San Ysidro and the Mexican border.

Funeral in San Ysidro

Once more, the question was not what to say, but what to do. I recommended that McDonald's be represented at the funeral. I said the president of McDonald's should be there, but I also felt it should be handled very quietly. If the media were to make something of it, fine, but let it be discovered, not proactively announced. Mike Quinlan and Ed Rensi agreed, as did Al Golin. Later that night the four of us flew to San Diego on a private plane. The San Diego Police Department's SWAT team, concerned that someone would try to blame this on McDonald's, met us in unmarked cars and provided us with security during our short stay.

On Saturday morning we met Kroc at the funeral. There were some 5,000 people packed on the hillside outside the little church, and about 1,500 inside. We were seated in the front row with Kroc, and in a pew not far from us was Edna Huberty, James Huberty's widow.

It must have been more than 100 degrees inside the church as 11 caskets of varying sizes were wheeled in, containing victims from small children to adults. Reporters from around the world were situated throughout the church, making notes and trying to identify people. Mourners were crying and fainting during the two-hour requiem mass. Of all the correspondents in attendance not one of them identified the McDonald's top executives ... to this day I wonder if we should have told the media they were there.

After the service we decided not to attend the burials that were in several different local cemeteries but to return to Chicago. The prior evening when we flew out to San Diego, there had been a heated discussion about whether or not to reopen the restaurant. While I truly could see both sides of the argument, I had strongly urged that we close the site — forever.

A Visit to the Restaurant

I had thought about a situation that had occurred four years earlier, when I had flown to Switzerland after one of our restaurants in Zurich had been firebombed and destroyed in the middle of the night. Upon returning, I urged the vice chairman of McDonald's to reopen at any cost, as long as our partner was willing. If we didn't reopen, then anyone who did not want us around only had to firebomb us again and poof! — no more McDonald's.

That Friday night my traveling companions reminded me of the Swiss situation. But this incident was different. It was a terrible, nightmarish tragedy evoking such human pain, emotion, and suffering that it could not, for me, be equated with the loss of property. It took place in a community that was so tightly knit, so terribly poor, and so proud; a community that was close to both its church and its religious beliefs. There was such pride and pain as some people walked out of the church barefoot and in tee shirts carrying the caskets — people who violently lost family members to sudden, unforseen tragedy.

As we stood in the church parking lot, I asked one member of the SWAT team how far away the restaurant was, and he said a couple of minutes. I asked Quinlan if he wanted to go see it. He said, "Oh, gee," and I said, "If we don't go now we might never have the opportunity again."

The police drove us down San Ysidro Boulevard to the massacre site. There were hundreds of people gathered outside the big stucco wall in front of the restaurant's playland — flowers everywhere, hundreds of candles — it looked like the shrine at Lourdes.

There were crucifixes and statues of the Blessed Mother and Jesus. There were groups of people marching and carrying placards — not necessarily for the victims but for the media attention — groups espousing peace, right to life, and gun control.

We were able to get in the back of the restaurant, and we spent 30 minutes inside. Everything was as it had been two days prior, with the obvious exception that the victims were gone. No one said much of anything. When we got in the car to go to the airport, and retraced our steps on San Ysidro Boulevard, Quinlan and Rensi looked at me and said, "We're going to close that store forever. Announce it to the media."

Now came an interesting media quandary. We were going to close the store forever, and we owed that information to the media. We had been up-front with all other decisions, why not with this one? Because I did not want to see a McDonald's golden arches being torn down on television screens and on pages of newspapers and magazines around the world.

Deep Public Reaction On Sunday morning, July 22, I called our San Diego regional manager, Steve Zdunek, and told him we were closing the restaurant permanently. I also told him to have the sign taken down, and to have it done at three in the morning so no one could photograph it. He said, "I won't tell anyone but the police."

As much as I was thankful for the cooperation of and fine work done by the San Diego Police Department, I said, "Don't tell the police. The biggest media leaks you can find are generally in hospitals and police stations. God bless them for their help, but they don't need to know the truck is going through their line at 3:00 A.M. to take the sign down until it happens." As it turned out, there was a film crew at the site at 3:00 A.M.; there were crews and photographers staking out that site for a good six weeks after the tragedy. The film crew did get a very fuzzy shot of the sign coming down but it was so dark that it never appeared. Later that Monday morning, we announced to the media that we were closing the restaurant once and for all.

Public reaction to the closing was incredible, with letters from all over the U.S. and the world being 99 percent positive regarding our decision. The depth of the reactions from the general public surprised me, for while I thought we had done the right thing, I had no idea that so many people across the country were watching so closely and could be so emotionally moved by our action.

Among the letters with the most impact came one from a California contractor who also served as a reserve deputy with his local sheriff's department. He said:

> *With responsibilities as a business owner and a law enforcement officer I tend to see things from two completely opposite sides of the fence ... I would like to thank you and your McDonald's Corporation for having the attitude that you have. It's true that your company is a money-making enterprise working in the free enterprise system, but I was so overwhelmed to hear the news that McDonald's was closing the restaurant. Being an owner I know the incredible expense it requires to maintain a place of business, whether large or small. To just shut down a store as profitable as a McDonald's because you care about the people and families who suffered a tragedy cannot go without some type of recognition. I have seen the other side of the fence as a deputy, the horror in violent death. It is a very honorable and human deed when a large company, such as yours, can help to soothe the pain of others and not let money but your feelings be your guide....*

It had been a hectic 96 hours. We had made a number of major decisions and communicated them to the media. We still faced problems, although from a media standpoint they were becoming more localized in nature. One remaining issue was the disposition of the property now that we had announced we would not rebuild on the site, and if and when we would open a new restaurant in San Ysidro.

Bulldozed into Sand

Because Mount Carmel Church was such an integral part of the fabric of the San Ysidro community, we sought the counsel and help of the church's pastor. He was a godsend. This was his community — these were his people. He felt we had done as much as possible, and warned that there were elements of the community that were being unfair and sought to take advantage of McDonald's. We considered offering the site to the church, but it was too far away to serve a useful purpose. We sought his counsel regarding the stucco wall out front which had been turned into a shrine, for it had to come down with the restaurant and we did not wish to alienate people in the community for whom it held such special significance.

The pastor saved us. He said, "You tell me the morning you want the wall to come down. I will come an hour beforehand. I will take down the flowers, the statues, the lights — I will say a little prayer, give a blessing, the bulldozers come, and everyone goes home."

And that's the way it was. We spoke with San Diego community leaders, politicians, community groups — we fought off people who wanted to build tourist attractions and make movies and money off that site. We bulldozed the store into sand to stop those who wanted to cut up bricks and pieces of the facility to sell as souvenirs.

Eventually, after so many meetings in San Diego that Golin and I felt like we lived there, that site began to weigh heavily on McDonald's. While the media were down to a trickle, the question of what we would do with the property still hung over our heads. Fred Turner, McDonald's chairman and CEO at the time, had the best suggestion: "Get rid of it ... now!"

So we gave the property to the community. We said, "It's yours. Use it in the best interest of your citizens." There were a couple of caveats, such as never using the site as a commercial establishment and never selling it to a developer. That was a big decision because we could have sold it for at least $1 million.

A New Beginning We chose another site, some three blocks away, on which to open a new restaurant. We opened it because the old one had been part of the San Ysidro community — its playland had been a community playland. But we opened it carefully, and with little fanfare, because we knew the reopening of a McDonald's in San Ysidro had the potential to turn into a media circus, and we certainly did not want that.

We wanted it to be a new beginning. So what followed was probably the only time in McDonald's history when communications, not operations, decided when a new restaurant would open. We knew it would be a local — but tried to keep it from being a national — media story.

We selected the Wednesday of the week prior to Easter in 1985 for the opening day. We did not make a media announcement. No calls, no press release. Gelman and I went to San Diego a few days beforehand and I called one of the newspaper reporters I had gotten to know during the crisis and invited her for a drink. During the course of our conversation, I said, "By the way, we're opening the new store in San Ysidro tomorrow. Just thought you'd want to know." After daily conversations with her for over three months since the shooting, I figured she "deserved a break that day" on the story. She got it!

Sure enough, at 6:55 the next morning, the reporter was there, and from that time on, San Diego print and broadcast media showed up and covered the opening. I served as the spokesperson, and the tone and feeling were "a friend is back in town." There were a lot of families there that day — the manager of the new restaurant, who had been shot and wounded by Huberty, and half of the crew people who had been employed at the original San Ysidro store. The pastor came by and blessed the new golden arches.

Aftermath

Approximately a week to 10 days after the San Ysidro incident, a group of media and agency people gathered to review what we had done — good, bad, and ugly. While we had no specific crisis plan in place when the tragedy occurred, we did have three things:

- A clear-cut top management directive to "do what was right."

- A communications area that was an integral part of the decision-making process — in other words, we were in the room, not outside of it.

- Instantaneous access to all personnel — from the president of McDonald's on down.

From a media standpoint, we came out as well as we might have hoped. Two images come to mind: first, an editorial in the *Philadelphia Inquirer* headlined, "McDonald's — A Class Act"; second, a wire photo that appeared in papers across the country showing a San Ysidro resident weeping at the restaurant, and two others putting up a sign that simply said, "Thank you, McDonald's."

In some instances, we were luckier than we were smart. The first break was having media relations pro Steve Leroy close to southern California at the time of the incident and being able to have him on site when media attention was at its peak. The second was meeting the pastor in San Ysidro, and having the benefit of his wisdom and counsel. But the big bonus was Joan Kroc, who was able to think proactively of what might be done to aid the survivors while we were in the midst of trying to "preserve and protect" our good name.

We were able to muster needed resources quickly and efficiently and put together a core team consisting of myself, Chuck Rubner, Al Golin, and Chuck Gelman to make media decisions and prepare needed statements quickly. We handled the high hard ones first, but we did not neglect any media outlets, no matter how small. If we made a mistake here, it was in being too generous with our time rather than giving the media what they needed in a more efficient manner.

We benefitted from the full support of top management ... Mike Quinlan, Ed Schmidt, Ed Rensi, Don Horwitz, and Paul Schrage.

While we certainly had not sought favorable press from this tragedy, it is what we received. Sales had been hurt — but not for long, and they came back strong. Sales were down most in San Diego, and then, in geographic proximity to southern California. Although no PR could ever build sales in such a tragic situation, it is probably fair to say that the positive perception of the golden arches and thus, sales, were saved.

If the legacy of San Ysidro can provide any advice and counsel to those who may be impacted by crisis, it would be: Hope like hell that you have someone in your organization who can frame a Horwitz "Do What's Right" Rule. Hope you have members of top management who make bold, gutsy decisions quickly without looking over their shoulders. Finally, hope that you are ready to run with the ball when you're given the freedom to do your communications job the way you know it should be done.

Richard G. Starmann was named senior vice-president of communications for McDonald's Corporation in 1988. He is responsible for managing McDonald's worldwide communications efforts, including media and public relations, customer relations, publications, financial communications, and education programs. In 1986, he served as an advisory director on McDonald's Corporation's Board of Directors.

Starmann is a former member of the Board of Directors of the San Diego Padres professional baseball team. He is a founding member of the Board of Trustees of Ronald McDonald Children's Charities, which was established in 1984 in memory of McDonald's Corporation's founder, Ray A. Kroc, and has been a director of the International Advisory Board for the Ronald McDonald House program since its inception in 1976. Starmann also served as a first lieutenant in the U.S. Army Special Forces in Vietnam from 1968 to 1970.

Massacre at My Lai

Winant Sidle
Major General, USA-Retired

My Lai! These words conjure up the worst image many Americans over 30 have
of the U.S. Army. They represent a totally unnecessary massacre committed by
the army in the Vietnam War, by far the worst atrocity committed by American
forces in that war. They also represent one of the most serious public relations
problems faced by the army and the Department of Defense during that war. Not
only did the army forces involved commit the massacre, but they made it much
worse by attempting to cover it up.

Overview

Two companies were involved. Company C, 1st Battalion, 20th Infantry, 11th
Infantry Brigade, 23d (American) Infantry Division, went mad. So did Company B,
4th Battalion, 3d Infantry, 11th Infantry Brigade, but to a lesser degree.

What Happened?

Both companies were attached to Task Force Barker, a temporary grouping of
American Division troops that had the mission of destroying the 48th Viet Cong
(VC) Local Force (LF) Battalion. A third infantry company was also part of the
task force but was not afflicted by the madness.

The offensive was a three-day tactical operation, beginning March 16, 1968, conducted in the Son My village area. This approximately 25–kilometer–square area
was located in Quang Ngai Province, the southernmost in the I Corps Tactical
Zone at the northern end of South Vietnam. The area was located about 75 miles
south of Da Nang and was on the South China Sea.

Son My village was the home area of the 48th VC Battalion and had been for
years. The 48th had been a very effective fighting force but had taken a beating

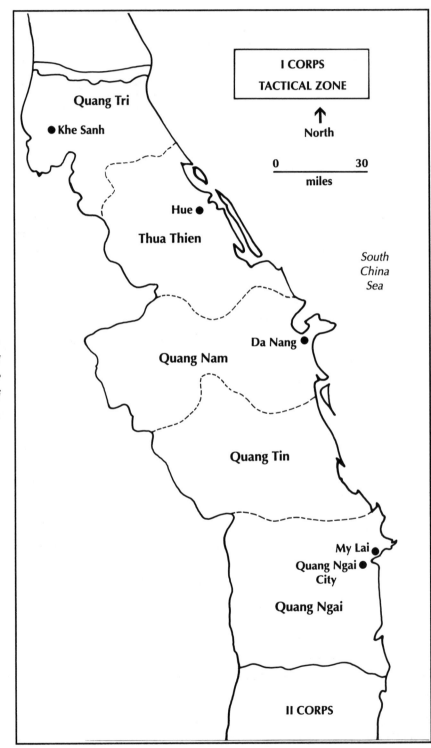

I Corps Tactical Zone, Vietnam, showing Quang Ngai Province and the My Lai hamlet area.

during the Tet offensive in early February and had returned to the Son My area for recruiting and retraining. The mission of Task Force Barker was to find and destroy the 48th before it could refurbish itself.

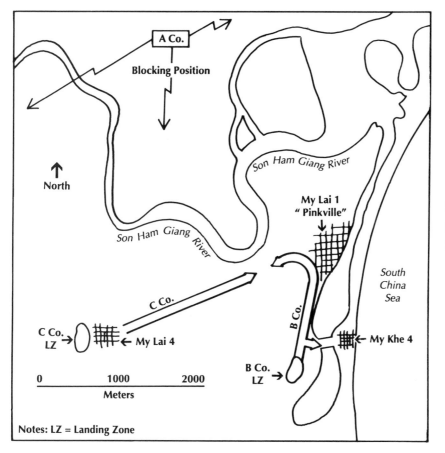

Son My operation attack plan, March 16, 1968.

As shown on the attack plan of the operation, C Company was to air assault the Son My village subhamlet of My Lai from the west. (An air assault is an attack by helicopter-borne troops. Preselected landing zones are cleared by fire, then troops land in these zones and attack from there.) Its mission was to sweep through the subhamlet and continue to the east to join up with Company B. (The My Lai incident was actually misnamed. The subhamlet where most of the action took place was shown on U.S. military maps as My Lai. The name used by the Vietnamese was Thuan Yen. The best name would have been the Son My incident. All of the military action occurred in the Son My village area.)

B Company was to air assault into a landing zone about 2,000 meters east of My Lai and south of My Khe and My Lai. The latter, an area loaded with VC, was commonly called "Pinkville" by the troops. The company was to sweep north and then west to meet up with C Company. The third company assumed blocking positions to the north.

Following an artillery preparation (barrage), some of which landed on the western edges of My Lai, C Company began its assault shortly before 8:00 A.M. on March 16.

The First Platoon, commanded by Lt. William L. Calley, moved through the southern half of the subhamlet. It met no resistance. Regardless, its soldiers proceeded to round up and kill many old men, women, and children and to destroy the housing. Villager roundup occurred both in and outside the subhamlet. No VC were seen.

The Second Platoon, moving through the north side of the subhamlet, met no resistance. They also swept a nearby subhamlet, Bin Tay, without resistance. They killed 60–70 old men, women, and children and raped some of the women.

The Third Platoon followed behind the other two and burned and destroyed the remaining dwellings, killed the remaining livestock, and killed a small group of women and children.

Later investigations showed that orders to stop the killing were issued two or three times during the morning. These apparently came from Col. Oran K. Henderson, the 11th Brigade commander. He had assumed command of the brigade one day prior to the assault. The Second Platoon received the order about 9:20 A.M. and complied. The First Platoon continued the killing until about 10:30 A.M. when the order was repeated. By this time it had completed its move through the subhamlet.

B Company's action also resulted in the deaths of a significant number of noncombatants. They, however, resulted primarily from a five-minute barrage fired indiscriminately into My Khe before B Company entered it. Although the soldiers met no resistance when they entered the hamlet, they fired and threw demolitions into the various huts and shelters without determining who was inside. Some casualties resulted from mines and booby traps during the action.

The atrocities committed by these two infantry companies were far and away the worst committed by U.S. troops at any time during the Vietnam War. They killed between 170 and 400 Vietnamese. They also created a huge public relations problem for the army and the Department of Defense (DoD) when the facts became known much later.

Not all of those killed were noncombatants. Three or four were later confirmed as *armed* Viet Cong. Undoubtedly a number of unarmed Viet Cong men, women, and probably children, as well as some VC supporters or sympathizers lived in the area. But, the indiscriminate killing of so many civilians, including babies, was a blatant war crime.

The massacre was a huge tragedy. The American Division made it much worse by its initially successful cover-up attempt. Committing and covering up war crimes violates the 1949 Geneva Convention, which the United States signed. The army also violated the rules and regulations put out by all U.S. commands in Vietnam, including the American Division and the 11th Brigade.

The Cover-Up and Army Investigations

The brigade's regulations were quite specific:

- Every possible safeguard short of endangering friendly lives will be used to avoid noncombatant casualties and indiscriminate destruction of private property when actions are being conducted in populated areas.

- Individuals who are attempting to escape may be frightened innocent civilians.

- Troops will be informed of the importance of minimizing noncombatant casualties and the destruction of property, including livestock.

- Detainees (suspected enemy) will be properly processed and will be considered detainees only until their status is "determined by a brigade interrogator."

- Spot (immediate) reports will be rendered without delay in the event of heavy civilian casualties occurring in a short period of time.

- Actual or suspected war crimes, including the killing of innocent civilians, will be reported by soldiers to their commanding officer who will forward the report up the chain of command.

C and B Companies either ignored or were not aware of these regulations. Instead, C Company reported 128 Viet Cong killed in action and three weapons captured. (The latter was suspicious in itself.) It also reported 20 noncombatants killed (later raised to 28) by artillery fire and by getting caught in crossfires during combat. Company C's casualties were one killed and ten wounded, all by mines and booby traps, plus one accidental self-inflicted wound.

For whatever reasons, the American Division never reported anything about the matter except that the operation was a victory and a significant number of Viet Cong were killed. This, of course, was false.

It is human nature to want to hide mistakes. But failing to admit them as soon as possible is a huge public relations minus. When an outsider, especially a reporter, finds out about a mistake and that you did not reveal it, you are in real trouble. And, someone always finds out, sooner or later.

Experience makes clear that you must "take credit" for your mistakes. This means that both leadership and public relations must get the facts straight and then reveal publicly that you "blew it." The revelation should include any good reasons for the mistake, if they exist. In other words admit your mistakes!

A mistake quickly and freely admitted usually results in a so-called one-day story. A mistake not admitted but discovered by a reporter becomes a many-day story, the number of days or months depending on the seriousness of the mistake.

Not admitting a mistake has another important drawback — opening your organization to the serious and valid charge of cover-up. Often, this charge will have a more adverse effect than the original mistake.

For some reason, many leaders in all aspects of American life fail to see the benefits in admitting a mistake. The Americal Division commander was one of these. He apparently felt, that if you don't admit it, the mistake will mysteriously go away.

WRONG!

Trying to cover up My Lai not only disgraced the army but also cost the commander, Maj. Gen. Samuel Koster, his career, a stiff price that he could have avoided had the massacre been properly reported. (Koster is best remembered for saying to cadets as he was being relieved: "Don't let the bastards grind you down!")

The army conducted two official investigations of the incident. The first was conducted by two different army agencies and began almost immediately after the army leadership was informed of the incident. This investigation resulted in war crimes being charged against several participants. The final investigation of the tragedy, the Peers Inquiry, named for its chief, Lt. Gen. William R. Peers, U.S.A., concluded that it was amazing that the facts remained hidden for so long. The first report of the incident was not received until April 1969 and that was received by the Pentagon, not U.S. headquarters in Vietnam. This was just a few days over a year from the day the massacre happened.

The original success of the cover-up is particularly surprising since large numbers of bodies of noncombatants were easily visible from the air, and the operation was supported by numerous helicopters and was overflown on several occasions by both the brigade and task force commanders.

In fact, one helicopter pilot, Warrant Officer Hugh Thompson, was so concerned at what he saw on the morning of March 16 that he landed his helicopter at My Lai several times.

The first time he complained strongly to a C Company officer about the killing of women and children. The second time, after he had seen 12–16 women and children and one or two old men hiding in a bunker, he landed between the bunker and the approaching American troops. He told his crew that, if the Americans fired on the bunker while he was getting the women and children out, to "fire back at them." Thompson got the civilians out of the bunker and they were rescued by another helicopter. On his third landing, Thompson evacuated a slightly wounded boy whom he found among a group of dead women and children.

Thompson then contacted his commanding officer and reported what he had seen and done. These reports were confirmed by other pilots and crewmen who had flown over the scene.

Late in the morning of March 16, Thompson's commander reported Thompson's allegations to the task force commander. The latter then left for his helicopter and took off. Thompson's commander, thinking that the task force commander would handle the matter, did nothing further at that time. Later, the task force commander told Thompson's commander that he could find nothing to substantiate the allegations. Thompson's commander did not believe this and late in the evening he informed his battalion commander of the allegations. Only Thompson's company was attached to the task force. Therefore, the battalion commander did not report to the task force.

The next morning the two reported the allegations to the assistant commander of the Americal Division, a brigadeer general. The report was watered down but did include the unnecessary killing of old men, women, and children as well as a confrontation between Thompson and the Company C troops.

The assistant division commander reported the matter to the division commander later on that day, March 17. Investigation has shown that this report was also watered down but did include some mention of indiscriminate killing of noncombatants.

The division commander was already aware of a possible problem. Brigade commander Colonel Henderson had reported to him on the 16th that he had observed a few noncombatant casualties. Also on that day, the task force commander had told Henderson that there were some noncombatant casualties. Late on the 16th, Henderson told the division commander there were about 20 such casualties.

Henderson must have been concerned. In the midafternoon of the 16th, he ordered the task force commander to send a company back to My Lai to investigate the number and types of casualties and causes of death.

The division commander heard this order on the radio and directly contacted the C Company commander. He was told by the latter that 20–28 noncombatants had been accidentally killed. At this point the division commander countermanded Henderson's order.

In any case, after receiving the version of the Thompson report on the 17th, the division commander directed that the incident should be considered "close hold" (for internal use only), a strange order under the circumstances. He also ordered Henderson to investigate it. No report was made to higher headquarters even though it was clearly required by regulations.

Henderson Report   Early on March 18, the assistant division commander met with Henderson, the task force commander, the aviation battalion commander, and Thompson's company commander. The latter repeated Thompson's allegations to the group. Henderson was then directed by the assistant division commander to conduct an investigation.

The Peers Inquiry concluded that at that point Henderson should have been fully aware of what really had happened.

However, his investigation was a sham.

Henderson had interviewed Thompson and his crew and the C Company commander. He then "interviewed" 30–40 C Company members in a group. His interview consisted of asking them as a group if they had seen any atrocities. The answer was negative. That ended his investigation except for a short flight over the My Lai area.

The Peers Inquiry concluded that Henderson's oral report to the division commander "deliberately misrepresented both the scope of the investigation and the information he had obtained." Henderson said that although "20 civilians had been killed" by artillery and/or gunships, there was no basis in fact to Thompson's allegations.

The division commander accepted the oral report. No report was made to higher headquarters even though even the "whitewashed" report should have been reported. The matter rested there until about mid-April when reports from the South Vietnamese began to come in.

The Son My village chief submitted a report to his district (roughly the equivalent of a county) chief that alleged mass killings had occurred in his village. The district chief then forwarded it on April 11 to his province chief (roughly the equivalent of a U.S. state). The report said that it had been alleged that a U.S. Army unit had "assembled and killed" more than 400 residents of My Lai and an additional 90 at My Khe.

Copies of this report were provided to the U.S. advisory teams at both district and province. Also, a copy was sent to Colonel Toan, commander of the Second ARVN (Army of the Republic of South Vietnam) Division. The Son My village was in the overall operating area of this division.

Then, at about the same time, the Viet Cong made a propaganda broadcast stating that U.S. forces had killed 500 people in the Son My village area. This broadcast became known to both Colonel Toan and the province chief of Quang Ngai province, Lt. Col. Khien.

The Peers investigation determined that both Colonel Henderson and the Americal Division commander "appeared" to have discussed the district chief's report with both Colonel Toan and Lt. Col. Khien. The report was also discussed with the U.S. Army deputy province advisor, a colonel.

The division commander reacted to this by ordering Colonel Henderson to put his oral report in writing. The written report made no mention of the Thompson allegations. It concluded that 20 noncombatants were inadvertently killed by artillery and cross fire between U.S. troops and the Viet Cong, no civilians were gathered together and shot, and the VC allegation was "obviously VC propaganda."

Henderson added two enclosures. First was an unsigned document apparently from the U.S. deputy senior province advisor that said the report of the Son My village chief was not considered important by his district chief. The second was a translation of the VC propaganda broadcast.

The Americal Division commander testified later that when he received Henderson's report he did not accept it and directed a formal investigation. The Peers investigation showed that no such formal investigation was ever made; at least no credible evidence of either was found.

This Henderson written report ended any Americal Division action on the matter — it was not forwarded to higher headquarters. No report was sent by any of the U.S. advisors who were aware of the South Vietnamese reports. Everyone except those who knew some or all of the facts dismissed the matter as VC propaganda.

This included the South Vietnamese. This was understandable. Viet Cong and North Vietnamese propagandists were constantly and falsely (until then) accusing U.S. forces of inhuman action against South Vietnamese civilians.

At least two other channels that might have reported the tragedy up the chain of command also failed.

Thompson contacted the Americal Division artillery chaplain when it appeared that his allegations were not going to bring any results. He told the chaplain the whole story. The chaplain passed it along to the division chaplain who was told that the matter was being investigated.

Public Affairs Failure The other special channel that failed was public affairs (then called information). Accompanying C Company on its March 16 attack were a reporter and a photographer from the division's public affairs office. These two saw and photographed the massacre, returning to division headquarters late in the morning.

The reporter wrote a misleading story that gave no indication of what really happened. The photographer kept his photos to himself. He was out of the army when the story became public, and he then sold his photos to the press.

There is no indication that the division public affairs officer was ever made aware of the massacre. This was unfortunate because he was one individual who should have realized that covering up the massacre was the most unwise course of action the division could take.

The Peers report states: "... at every command level from company to division, actions were taken or omitted which together effectively concealed the My Lai incident. Outside the division, U.S. Advisory Teams at Province, District, and possibly the Second ARVN Division also contributed to this end. Some of the acts and omissions were inadvertent while others constituted deliberate suppression or withholding of information."

When the My Lai debacle occurred on March 16, 1968, I was the chief of information, Military Assistance Command, Vietnam (MACV), the top U.S. command in Vietnam. In this position I received all reports of "bad" news as soon as possible after they arrived in the headquarters. I never heard a word about the My Lai massacre.

In March 1968 we had the largest number of news people in Vietnam than at any other time during the Vietnam War. These reporters and backup personnel were from many countries, but the majority were from the United States. About half of those accredited were actually reporters.

Normally about 30–40 reporters were in the field on any given day, but during the post-Tet operations in March many more were out with the troops. Apparently no reporter stumbled on to the story. This may have been due in part to the seige of Khe Sanh, a Marine Corps base located in the northern part of the I Corps Tactical Zone, the same zone in which My Lai was located. The press covered this seige heavily from the MACV press camp in Da Nang. In fact, we flew in about 30–35 reporters daily to Khe Sanh and returned them to Da Nang at night. It is also possible that any reporter who heard about the story dismissed it as VC propaganda. In any case, the MACV public affairs organization received no queries about My Lai.

I did not hear about My Lai until early November 1969, well over a year after the massacre occurred. I had been reassigned from Vietnam in late October 1969 to be the chief of information of the army (CINFO).

I had about one week of overlap with my predecessor and received many briefings about what was going on, but nothing about My Lai. Toward the end of the week, I was called to the office of the assistant secretary of defense, public affairs, and was told about My Lai.

Finally, Some Action

Defense and army officials had received a letter, dated March 29, 1969, from a former army enlisted man, Ron Ridenhour. Prior to going to Vietnam, Ridenhour had been a member of the 79th Infantry Detachment, part of the 11th Infantry Brigade in Hawaii.

His detachment was disbanded one week before the 11th Brigade left for Vietnam in December 1967. Its personnel were reassigned to other brigade units including the Company C that later took part in the My Lai massacre. Ridenhour was reassigned to the aviation section of brigade headquarters.

In April 1968, Ridenhour said "he first heard of 'Pinkville' from one of the enlisted men who had been assigned to C Company." He also said, "I received that first report with skepticism, but in the following months I was to hear similar stories from such a wide variety of people that it became impossible for me to disbelieve that something rather dark and bloody did indeed occur sometime in March 1968 in a village called 'Pinkville' in the Republic of South Vietnam."

Between April and November 1968, other members of C Company, including a sergeant, confirmed the story to Ridenhour in gory detail. He was discharged from the army a few weeks after his conversation with his final source and decided that something should be done concerning what he had heard. He quoted Winston Churchill: "A country without a soul is a country that cannot survive."

Ridenhour considered sending his letter to the news media, but felt that official action would be the "appropriate procedure." So, he sent copies of his letter to about 30 people, including Secretary of Defense Clark Clifford, Secretary of the Army Stanley R. Risor, some senior military, and some members of Congress.

He got action!

On April 18, 1969, Risor ordered a full investigation. Shortly thereafter, Ridenhour was visited by an army colonel seeking more information. On April 23, the chief of staff of the army, Gen. William C. Westmoreland, placed the investigation in the hands of the army inspector general. This phase of the investigation included interviews with 35 witnesses, some in the United States and some in Vietnam.

On August 4, the investigation was transferred to the army provost marshal general, whose responsibilities included the Criminal Investigation Division (CID). His investigators interviewed 75 more witnesses.

It quickly became clear that indeed a massive war crime had occurred.

Lt. William L. Calley, Jr., who had commanded C Company's First Platoon — the platoon that swept the southern half of My Lai — had played a major role in the catastrophe. He was about to be separated from the army but was held over and his separation deferred.

Calley was then charged with the murder of 109 noncombatant Vietnamese. This figure was later reduced to 102. He was the first participant to be charged.

Lt. William Calley, Jr., pictured during his court-martial at Ft. Benning, Ga., came to personify America's dilemma in the war in Indochina.

At this point, the top military officials involved were apparently unwilling to embrace the "admit your mistakes" principle. The tragedy was so monumental that even the experienced public relations civilians and military handling the public release of the story did not want to face it head-on.

Instead, the initial release was made on September 6, 1969, at Fort Benning, Georgia, where Calley was stationed. It said that Calley was being charged with killing a significant number of Vietnamese civilians. It did not indicate the enormity of what happened at My Lai.

When I was briefed on this news release in early November, just after I had become the CINFO, I voiced reservations about its light tone since I was a believer in mistake admitting. But, I went along with it.

Hersch Investigation

As anticipated, the release initially created little interest among the media. However, a free-lance reporter, Seymour Hersch, heard about the release and "smelled a rat."

Hersch began his own investigation, talked to Ridenhour and some C Company members, and realized he had a big story on his hands. I had worked with Hersch before on a previous Pentagon assignment. He called me after I became the CINFO to tell me he had a news bombshell about My Lai.

I reported this to my seniors at the Department of Defense. Looking back, I realize we should have at least discussed the pros and cons of making public more details of the story through a Pentagon news release.

We should have figured out a way at that time to communicate to the press the enormity of the story. This would have been complicated since some individual criminal investigations were ongoing and we still knew few of the details about the massive cover-up. Nonetheless, we knew quite a bit and might well have lessened the stigma of the cover-up. This would have reduced almost certainly the impact of Hersch's story when it broke.

Some did then and will still argue that we did not have enough information to make such a release at that time. Be that as it may, we simply hunkered down and awaited Hersch's action.

It came on November 13. Hersch's story broke in some 35 newspapers at the same time.

The problem was threefold: this terrible story was true, the Americal Division covered it up, and our action seemed to mask the massacre's enormity.

The story was carried by all media for days. President Richard Nixon commented that the massacre was not justified. President Nguyen Van Thieu of South Vietnam refused to admit that it had happened.

The public relations flap continued off and on for more than two years. It was refueled initially by a mass of other allegations of atrocities by U.S. troops. The great majority of these proved to be untrue after they were investigated, but they seemed to be true to those who knew little about combat. Furthermore, although many of these allegations received considerable publicity initially, very little was announced when the investigation proved them to be untrue.

The storm of unfavorable publicity that followed Hersch's release made the army and DoD realize that something had to be done. Also, the media were jumping on the fact that there must have been a major cover-up. We had to prove that there had been a cover-up, but that it had been limited to the Americal Division.

The result was the creation of the Peers Inquiry on November 26 by Secretary of the Army Risor and army chief of staff General Westmoreland. Its mission was to

Peers Inquiry Established

determine the adequacy of the ongoing army investigation and its subsequent reviews and reports within the chain of command, as well as the possible suppression or withholding of information by persons involved in the incident.

Lt. Gen. William R. Peers was selected to head the inquiry because he was a man of unimpeachable integrity, had successfully commanded a division in Vietnam, and was known by many, including a significant number of reporters, as completely objective and fair.

Announcement of the Peers investigation temporarily rekindled the publicity fire. But it was a good idea from a public relations view, especially when it became apparent that Peers was doing a most careful and thorough job. The press realized that, when he finished, all the facts would be available. Although it did not prevent stories from appearing in the interim, it did help take the heat off.

The Peers Inquiry interviewed 399 witnesses, amassed hundreds of documents, and put together a complete report by March 14, 1970. The Inquiry was headquartered in the Pentagon, but it also established an office in Saigon, and a large team was sent to Vietnam to interview appropriate individuals, gather documents, check the massacre site, and so forth.

The investigative team included experts of all types. At General Peer's suggestion, the army obtained as special counsel Robert MacCrate, Esq., a partner in a well-known New York City law firm. He was also a vice-president of both the New York State Bar Association and the Association of the Bar of the city of New York. Jerome K. Walsh, Jr., of the New York firm Walsh and Frisch, became associate special counsel.

To ensure that military law was fully covered, General Peers's deputy was Bland West, the assistant general counsel of the army.

The creation of the Peers Inquiry and the inclusion of the two special counsels were not moves made primarily for public relations reasons, but they did have a favorable impact on some of the media and the public.

The two special counsels proved to be most helpful to the Inquiry. They assisted considerably in determining the issues to be examined, information to be sought, and the thorough examination of witnesses. They also gave the Inquiry a stature it might not have had without them. Further, the final report, prepared with assistance and concurred with by them, has stood without challenge for over 20 years.

A Look Back Many mistakes, although bad, are not complicated enough to require a special investigation. Others may well merit such an investigation. When that is true, the

On January 9, 1970, a group of soldiers representing the Peers Inquiry probes an area in the hamlet of My Lai for evidence of the 1968 massacre.

special investigation should be conducted prior to admitting the mistake publicly. Then, you know your facts are straight.

When a special investigation is necessary, it should be both quick and thorough. At least some members of the investigatory team should be known to be reliable and some outsiders of stature should be included. The Peers Inquiry met these requirements (except for the timing) and it was most helpful.

With respect to timing, one of my associates said that the Peers Inquiry should have been established as soon as the original inspector general investigation revealed the scope of the My Lai incident and before anyone was court-martialed. A good thought, but such action requires considerable foresight.

The use of the two special counsels in the Peers investigation brings up another public relations principle. In today's legalistic world, public relations practitioners must work closely with their organization's lawyers.

This was particularly true in the My Lai case. There were many legal points involved, and these often dictated what you could say. In addition, the press, and probably the public expected, even demanded, that the perpetrators would be punished via the court-martial system.

This did not work out very well. Lieutenant Calley was convicted after a much-publicized trial, but his sentence was light in most people's eyes. His sentence was reduced on review by the U.S. Court of Military Appeals to 20 years' hard labor. President Nixon pardoned Calley after Calley served two years.

Charges were also brought against a number of others, but all escaped punishment thanks to various legal technicalities. Some were brought to trial but not convicted and in other cases charges were dropped, again due to legal technicalities.

As CINFO I considered this a blow. Public relations, the DoD, and army general counsel's offices had worked hard to make sure that the prosecutors had all the data they needed but to no avail.

The various court-martial and charge processing lasted many months and helped keep the My Lai case before the public. Eventually the media was forced to agree that not much could be done about the legal ramifications. The Peers Inquiry recommended that 28 individuals, not including Calley, be referred to the appropriate court-martial convening authorities for possible disciplinary or administrative action.

Even though they escaped court-martial discipline, many of these individuals did not escape punishment. The army was able to take serious administrative action against them.

For example, the American Division commander was reduced in grade from major general to brigadier general and was fired from his prestigious assignment as superintendant of the U.S. Military Academy. Others were denied promotion or otherwise found their military careers at an end for all practical purposes.

These punishments were most serious from the standpoint of those punished although they did not have the impact on the press or the public that court-martial punishment would have had. After much effort, we were able to convince a number of reporters that the punishments were indeed serious. This helped finally to put the My Lai case to bed.

Why Did the Massacre Occur?
One of the major items examined by the Peers Inquiry was why the My Lai tragedy had occurred. This was important from a public relations standpoint. There were a number of reasons, none of which excused the incident but were clearly mitigating circumstances. They did not receive as much publicity as they should have.

One of the main reasons for this inadequate publicity was that most of the reasons were uncovered by the Peers investigation. We did not know about them in time to make maximum use of them.

The initial army investigation did uncover at least one reason but public relations did not make much use of it. The problem was, I believe, that most of us were so shocked by the enormity of the war crimes that we felt that no excuses could hold up under scrutiny. So, we did not make a major effort to look for excuses.

This was a mistake. We did know that C Company was disturbed that they had suffered casualties from mines and booby traps in previous actions in the area without ever engaging the Viet Cong in combat. They were badly frustrated. This was told to the press but logically had minimal impact.

Too late I made a study of the possible reasons and found there were many factors which, when combined with the frustration, did provide a pretty good set of mitigating circumstances.

First, the Peers investigation discovered that there was very little rapport between the task force commander and his subordinates. The oral orders the commander gave his company commanders before the attack may have indicated that he wanted My Lai completely destroyed. It is clear that the orders relayed to the troops by the commanders of B and C Companies did indicate total destruction. The orders also failed to make any distinction between combatants and noncombatants.

My Lai was the base of some 48th VC Battalion members. It had been used in the past as a VC logistical and training center. In other words one could consider that everyone there was, at a minimum, a VC sympathizer. The task force commander at least hinted at total destruction. There is evidence that the company commanders gave the impression to the troops that everyone there should be killed, the houses burned, and the livestock destroyed.

Second, Americal Division at that time was not well organized. The creation of the task force took some key officers from the brigade staff to staff the task force. This left both headquarters understaffed. As a result there was inadequate supervision of the task force's plan preparation and the monitoring of execution of the attack.

The original plans had correctly estimated that there should be Viet Cong in My Lai. In fact there were 30–40 there until just prior to the attack. Due in part to understaffing, the troops were not aware of this departure.

In addition, the plans indicated that many of the inhabitants would be away from the subhamlet on the day of the attack. This was incorrect but not realized by the overworked staffs.

The troops, therefore, expected that the VC would be there in force and many of the civilians would be absent.

Third, C Company had a normal complement of draftees. These were mostly average citizens, but many had the idea that the Vietnamese were an inferior people. Most did not trust the Vietnamese. Although apparently friendly, most of the Vietnamese encountered before by C Company had failed to warn them about booby traps and mines. Seventeen members *were* killed or wounded between February 13 and March 16. These casualties occurred without any contact with actual VC forces. The company was frustrated and felt the attack was a chance to get even. Moreover, the VC was known to try to "melt into the population" when in trouble.

Fourth, the government of South Vietnam had considered the area under VC control for years and treated it as a free-fire zone. No prior coordination with government authorities was required when firing into the area.

Fifth, before it went to Vietnam, the 11th Brigade was training in Hawaii. It had a deployment date for Vietnam of January 1968. In October, this date was moved up to December 1967. This required condensing final training from eight weeks to four.

As a result, C Company, now scheduled to leave for Vietnam on December 1, received little training in the treatment of civilians and refugees and the responsibilities for reporting war crimes and atrocities. Further, there was input of over 50 percent new personnel into the company during the final training period. These factors seriously reduced the effectiveness of the training. B Company was similarly affected.

Finally, Communist forces in South Vietnam fully recognized U.S. reluctance to fight them in civilian populated areas due to concern over killing innocent civilians. The Communists took advantage of this throughout the war.

Moreover, there were many instances of VC women killing U.S. soldiers and children being booby trap specialists as well as potential and actual assassins.

Therefore, it was most important to distinguish between a combatant and a noncombatant — a difficult task. Sex or age were not always valid criteria for making this distinction. Babies, of course, were clearly noncombatants, but they didn't have to be very old before they were potentially dangerous.

Although these reasons cannot excuse the massacre, when they are combined they make a persuasive package of mitigating circumstances, at least for the enlisted men. They in no way excuse the cover-up.

Consider:

- The enlisted men received inadequate training about handling noncombatants and they were not very concerned about it.

- They were informed that My Lai contained VC soldiers and was a VC base so that its inhabitants had to be at least VC sypathizers.

- A number of civilians were supposed to be absent.

- The entire area was a free-fire zone (meaning it was under VC control).

- The Vietnamese civilians encountered previously in the area had failed to warn them about booby traps and mines. They were seriously frustrated by their losses to booby traps and mines, as well as by the lack of contact with VC troops on which they could have exacted some revenge.

- They found no obvious VC, but the latter were expert in "melting into the population."

- They were "egged on" by their superiors to destroy everything.

This is a pretty persuasive package. We made some attempts to use some of these reasons as we found out about them, but we never assembled them. There is no certainty that this would have helped, but it would have been worth the effort, even late in the game.

A point of caution. These mitigating circumstances were valid. Too often I have seen a public relations office attempt to excuse mistakes using invalid and/or not credible reasons. This is unwise. The reasons must be credible and valid.

Analysis

The My Lai incident is a good case study for public relations purposes. It covers a number of angles that public relations practitioners must consider when faced with a serious mistake.

The most important principle is to admit mistakes as soon as you know the facts about them. This is absolutely true regarding major mistakes. Always ask yourself: If an outsider, particularly a reporter, uncovers a mistake that you have made and not admitted, will this discovery impact adversely on your image? Invariably the answer is yes.

Another rule in admitting mistakes is to admit them fully. Be careful not to fall into the trap of trying to minimize the mistake through word-smithing.

I fell into this trap when working with General Peers on the press announcement of the results of his investigation. He had the word massacre in the announcement. I said we shouldn't use the word. He, quite rightly, insisted. It was a massacre and we should have called it that in the press announcement. Not saying so did not fool anyone and was not helpful from a credibility standpoint.

This principle relates closely to another — always tell the truth. If telling the truth will have a most serious effect, such as endangering national security, do not lie. Just say, "I cannot comment on this."

What Might Have Been

Various public affairs officers and I have often speculated on what would have happened if the Americal Division had reported *to higher headquarters* the 20–28 civilians killed that they knew about on the first day.

If they had, MACV headquarters would have known that something unfortunate had happened by March 17. This would have required that someone higher up go to the scene.

Such an individual arriving on the scene on March 18 or 19 would have easily found that the massacre had occurred. This would have quickly generated a full-scale investigation by either MACV or USARV (U.S. Army, Vietnam) senior headquarters.

Considering that all personnel, necessary reports, and other documentation involved would have been immediately available, the investigation should have been completed within a month.

At this point MACV would have released the story in Saigon. This would have been a really big flap. It would have been extended as charges were preferred against the individuals responsible for the tragedy, courts-martial held (with reporters invited), and so forth. However, the flap would have been comparatively short-lived — nothing like the two years that the actual My Lai case lasted.

Moreover, there would have been no recriminations for trying to cover up the incident, a most important consideration. In support of this speculation is MACV's policy to admit mistakes as soon as possible.

One final point. A public relations person must be credible in order to be really successful — credible to his or her boss and credible to the press. To be credible, he or she must insist on admitting mistakes.

Maj. Gen. Winant "Si" Sidle was in the U.S. Army for 35 years. An artilleryman who fought in three wars, his major assignments included: chief of information, Military Assistance Command, Vietnam; chief of information of the army; deputy commanding general, Fifth U.S. Army; and deputy assistant secretary of defense, public affairs. After retirement in 1975, he became director of public relations and the corporate director of ethics for Martin Marietta Corporation in Orlando, Florida. General Sidle re-retired in 1988 and moved to Pinehurst, North Carolina, with his wife, Anne.

United Airlines Prepares for the Worst

Robert A. Doughty
Former Manager of External Communications, United Airlines

While public relations has many challenging aspects, PR can be at its finest or at its worst when an organization finds itself dealing with a life and death situation. The distinguishing difference is how well an organization has prepared itself to handle a crisis.

Overview

Such was the case for us at United Airlines in 1989 when, after 10 years of operating without a fatal accident, we lost 121 people in two dramatic accidents. In the process, our newly revised crisis communications plan stood the test of international media attention two times in five months.

On February 24, 1989, United Airlines Flight 811, a Boeing 747 bound from Honolulu, Hawaii, to Sydney, Australia, with a stop in Auckland, New Zealand, experienced an explosive decompression of the cabin 18 minutes after departure from Honolulu.

Honolulu and Sioux City

The forward cargo door of the jumbo jet had opened suddenly in flight. Hinged at its top, the door tore loose from the aircraft taking with it a 10-by-20-foot section of the fuselage. Nine passengers swept out of their seats and through the hole were lost at sea.

Miraculously, Captain Dave Cronin and his crew were able to turn the aircraft carefully back to Honolulu and make a safe landing 30 minutes after the explosion. Thankfully, 354 people survived.

As if this disaster was not enough, on July 19, 1989, United Airlines Flight 232, a DC-10 bound from Denver to Philadelphia with an intermediate stop in Chicago, experienced a failure of the first stage compressor fan, the largest rotating part, in its number two engine, the center engine located on the tail of the aircraft.

In the event of an engine failure, the casing of a jet engine is designed to contain parts to be dispelled through the rear with the engine's exhaust. In Flight 232's case, the pieces were so large and were rotating at such fast speed that they actually pierced the engine casings and moved laterally from the engine.

As debris from the Flight 232 engine pierced the horizontal stabilizers, the small wings at the rear of the aircraft, it disabled all three of the aircraft's hydraulic systems. Without hydraulic pressure, the aircraft became virtually unflyable. Despite this severe handicap, Captain Al Haynes and his crew kept flying by using asymmetrical thrust of the two remaining engines to turn and lower the aircraft.

Forty-five minutes after the engine failure, Flight 232 crash landed at the Sioux City, Iowa, airport. One hundred and twelve people perished. Incredibly, 184 people survived.

The forward cargo door of this 747 jumbo jet tore loose, taking with it a 10-by-20-foot section of the fuselage.

Both of these accidents captured worldwide media attention not only because of the loss of life and the inherent interest the media and the world have in airline accidents, but also because both were viewed as aviation marvels. Never before had an aircraft the size of a Boeing 747 flown with such a large hole in its fuselage, and even the finest test pilots flying the most sophisticated flight simulators deemed it impossible to land a DC-10 without its hydraulic systems.

PR Preparations

As dramatic as these two events were, how we at United Airlines prepared for them is more useful information to share than the details of what happened. While I had always upheld the Boy Scout motto Be Prepared, it was in 1989 that the credo truly proved its worth in my professional life. Clearly, it is preparation that marks the difference between public relations at its finest and public relations that has failed. It was this preparation that prompted the *Chicago Tribune* to write following the Sioux City accident that United "reacted like a well-oiled machine."

When I arrived at United Airlines in 1986 as manager of international communications, I found a company well prepared to handle a major crisis. A detailed crisis manual, a dedicated crisis room opened only in the event of a major catastrophe, a corporation with incredible resources from a vast fleet of globe-skipping aircraft, a well-developed electronic communications system, a corporate culture that breathed safety — all equipped one of the world's largest airlines to handle a crisis. The company's own mission statement declared that providing safe air travel was its prime goal. Making a profit ranked number two.

In 1988, when I became manager of external communications, United Airlines was on a 10-year safety streak. The airline's last passenger fatality was the 1978 crash of a DC-8 in Portland, Oregon. This outstanding safety record, one of the finest in the industry, was a source of pride for the company and its employees. Yet it created an uneasiness for myself. While I shared the pride in United's safety record, I became increasingly concerned about the company's ability to respond to a major crisis in a professional manner.

I knew that the previous crisis preparedness worked partly because accidents earlier in the industry had occurred with such frequency that an airline and its employees tended to develop built-in competence. Employees who had handled particular aspects of previous accidents were summoned to assist with their expertise for the latest one.

My concern heightened when a competitive airline handled an accident rather poorly, demonstrating an apparent lack of preparedness. Following this accident, I looked at how it was handled and analyzed United's level of preparedness. After a brief discussion with senior management, I was ready for action. With commitment and great interest from the top and the legal department, I began dividing up assignments. I took a hard look at our crisis communications plan and not only made recommendations for any changes I deemed necessary, but also set a new standard in crisis communications. I wanted to make sure that United Airlines was seen as the safe, caring airline our corporate culture dictated.

A section of a DC-10 that crash landed at the Sioux City airport following engine failure.

Suddenly, I found myself with perhaps the biggest challenge of my career: take a crisis plan, which I already thought was the best I had seen, and make it even better. The process included:

- Audit similar incidents.

- Consult with other industries.

- Reexamine day-to-day operations.

- Learn governmental regulations and routines.

- Formulate a media plan: effective use of electronic and print outlets; press conferences; press releases.

- Honor the victims and the community.

- Handle smaller incidents effectively.

- Rehearse.

- Keep employees informed.

- Publicize positive efforts.

Initial Steps:
Collecting Data

I started by conducting an audit of a number of recent airline accidents, including the one that prompted us into action. I spoke with a number of industries outside of our own, including the nuclear power industry and the U.S. military. Jet engine maker Pratt & Whitney's willingness to share its plan and its experiences proved particularly helpful, partly because we were in the same industry but more importantly because, of all the companies we talked with, its crisis communications department was probably the best prepared.

I also reexamined our own handling of day-to-day operations. With more than 2,000 flights each day, United, as with any major airline, would have its share of minor incidents from time to time. While most of these incidents never reached national media attention, they could become big local or regional news stories. An aircraft developing a flat tire on landing in Omaha, for example, may not interest the New York media, but could become front page news in Nebraska.

Between these operational matters and the other national and international news generated by United and the airline industry in general (i.e. fare actions, new service, or the pressing need for additional airport facilities), public relations at a major airline is an intense business. With 100 media calls deemed a "light" work day, I often drew the analogy for my staff that we were the mirror image of the city desk of a major metropolitan newspaper. The amount of information we processed and the speed at which we had to work to meet reporters' deadlines from all over the world, gave our office the busy, controlled ambience of a major newsroom. With an operation this involved, I knew that we could learn from our own daily routine.

In the audit, I sought to include those ideas I thought made sense to our own possible situations and I looked for pitfalls to avoid. I used this process to set a goal: setting a continuum with the recent competitor's accident-handling at one end as a model of what we did not want to be. Rather than positioning ourselves in the center, I chose to place United at the far other end. The primary goal was to protect our image as a safe airline. In doing so, I set United as a symbol that would come to mean a new standard for crisis management.

For starters, the most recent competitor's accident held a number of pitfalls, in my view. First, the accident investigation was plagued by a *cause du jour* syndrome as each day the media proclaimed an entirely new probable cause. One day they assigned the blame to pilot error. The next day they blamed a failure of the engines, and so it went during the early days of the investigation.

The airline seemed ill-prepared to handle the media, especially in the early hours. Scenes of its local manager arguing with the media and putting his hand in front of the camera violated every public relations principle, every sense of better judgement, and did not portray an image of a caring airline.

Finally, the airline communications personnel chose not to release much, if any information, including the passenger manifest. This was the first time that a major airline had not released the passenger list following an accident. Although they proclaimed that they were protecting the families of the passengers, they created a highly charged adversarial atmosphere with the media. This atmosphere became disruptive to the investigation, to the media coverage, and, ultimately, to the airline's own image.

As United examined crisis plans, including its own, we realized that all of them were too mechanical, too logistical, to be really practical. All of them had the obligatory phone trees of who should call whom and when; pages of contacts and their phones numbers, and lists of actions to be taken.

While all of this information is critical to a good crisis plan, we all realized that an excellent, workable plan must have more flexibility. From our daily routine, we already knew quite well that no two accidents or incidents are alike. Each differs in time and place, the players involved, and its cause. Also, in the critical first few hours, when the threat of broadcasting unconfirmed information is at its greatest, we would be at our most vulnerable point as the people on the front line may not be prepared to deal with the flood of media calls and the demands for immediate information.

Flexibility Is Key

My objective was to develop a crisis plan that would help United manage the gray areas better and give us an instant framework to work against, especially in the pivotal early hours of a crisis. The most important question in those early hours must not include What do we do?

To bring greater control over the critical early hours and give focus to the following days, I prepared a philosophical statement as a communications framework of how we wished to be perceived throughout a crisis and its subsequent investigation. We realized that more important than phone numbers and the sequence of who calls whom when, was a statement of how we planned to work with the media, how open we would be with them, how we would treat information, how we would cooperate with government authorities and agencies and, ultimately, how we would maintain the image of a safe and caring airline that was so important to us, our shareholders, and our passengers.

Critical Areas I identified the following communications-related steps as critical to our success in a crisis:

- Cooperate with the media, which we defined as providing the media with *timely and accurate* information. We also made it policy to conduct a press conference or briefing as quickly following an accident as possible and to continue holding press conferences and briefings as required. All press conferences were to be conducted by a corporate officer.

- Position United Airlines as an airline that takes safety seriously and a company that is deeply concerned with making sure that the events that led to an accident are not repeated.

- Avoid speculation on any phase of the accident, especially factors related to the probable cause, and seek to reduce sensationalism.

- Take prompt action to correct erroneous reports or media statements.

- Cooperate with the investigating government agencies.

- Enable the United Airlines' accident team members to concentrate on their individual tasks.

- Maintain a record of all noncompany personnel who provide assistance to United and recognize them for their contributions.

- Release passenger and crew list to the media as quickly as possible, but only after notification of next of kin.

- Keep employees informed of the accident and the subsequent investigation.

Timely and Accurate Up until this point, I was responsible for revising United's crisis plan just in case an accident occurred. However, the company's preparedness certainly paid off once disaster struck with two accidents five months apart. If you were to ask me if there was one thing that I felt was handled particularly well, or one thing that was the key to the successful handling of these two accidents, I would have to say it was the releasing of timely and accurate information to the media. We placed timely and accurate on a par with one another. Giving equal priority to these two elements is critical to good day-to-day media relations. Maintaining this equilibrium during a crisis is the real challenge of crisis management and the hallmark of good communications under pressure.

In both the Honolulu and the Sioux City accidents, the only serious criticism I heard about our handling was that we were not timely in releasing the passenger manifest at Sioux City. This preordained communications philosophy with its *timely and accurate* caveat held us in good stead during that criticism and provided us with an answer we could share publicly.

In my view, prematurely releasing information about a passenger could create a new disaster for all. Imagine how devastating it could be for a family to be told one thing about the status of a loved one then later have the airline retract the statement. Additionally, such a retraction would seriously harm our own credibility at a time when we needed all the credibility we could muster.

The Truth about Passenger Manifests

At Sioux City, a *New York Times* reporter approached me about this issue, asking, "Why is it that United can not come up with the names of all of the passengers two days after the accident?" Rather than ducking the issue, I sat with the reporter for more than an hour and explained to him the complexity of the passenger manifest. I explained how there are actually three manifests created for every flight, one by the reservations office, one at check-in, and the third created from the "ticket lift" at the gate. I also explained that passengers do not always use their real names, or that they may be using someone else's ticket. Also, children under the age of two are not required to have a ticket in the United States and so they may not be listed on the manifests. For any of these reasons, you can see that simply releasing the manifest in the first few hours could be a huge mistake. The first problem to address, of course, would be which manifest to release. Regardless of which one you would choose, the names have not been confirmed as actual passengers, nor have the next of kin been notified.

Additionally, the increasing survival rate of air accidents has created the "walk away passenger" — people who literally walk out of an aircraft wreckage unharmed and leave the scene without seeking medical help or notifying authorities of their whereabouts or their conditions.

The reporter took our behind-the-scenes story and a few days after the accident the *New York Times* published a well-written account that answered why the seemingly easy question had a difficult answer. In the process, again United was portrayed as a caring company that was treating all of the aspects involved in the aftermath of the tragedy in a sensible and responsible manner.

**Court of
Public Opinion**

While working closely with our legal department we came to the agreement that crisis management must not be ruled by how the lawyers were going to argue lawsuits years after an accident. We recognized that the court of public opinion is an immediate process, while the court of law is slower and more deliberative. The public will formulate their opinions of an organization quickly as much, if not more, on how it responds to a crisis rather than on the cause itself. The court of law for cases in the future cannot be the driver in responding to the court of public opinion at the moment of the crisis.

In our preparations, we wanted to use the time before an accident to ask and answer the questions we might have to address during an accident. We felt that it would be more productive to deal with these issues outside of the pressures of a crisis. One of the issues we raised during our first planning session was the atmosphere that often developed following a crisis. The investigation phases of these accidents often tended to be characterized by an almost adversarial atmosphere between the company and the government officials.

NTSB Procedures

We felt that it would be important for all of our crisis team members to understand the crisis procedures of the various government agencies with which we would have to work during an air accident. In the airline industry, these would be the National Transportation Safety Board (NTSB) and the Federal Aviation Administration (FAA).

As a start, I contacted the public relations department of the NTSB, spending about 45 minutes on the phone with my counterpart, Drucella Anderson. Anderson patiently explained to me how the PR department functioned during the investigation of an air accident.

I learned that they are very open to the media and that they release information to the media as soon as that information is confirmed. Following the daily progress meeting (where each of the various investigating committees report on the progress made that day), the NTSB board member who has been assigned to that accident investigation holds a press briefing every evening that the investigation team is in the field. The airline is invited to send a PR person to the daily progress meeting as well as the daily press briefing.

I took copious notes during my phone discussion and at the end decided that we should include a section in our crisis plan on how the NTSB operates. I quickly typed my notes into a readable format and faxed them to Anderson who made a few comments and changes and sent them back to me. Within two hours, we had a very informative four-page addition to our plan. With this document in our crisis communications guide, we were prepared to work with the NTSB, further assuring ourselves that there would be no surprises.

This exercise and the document we produced from it proved to be so worthwhile that we carried it two steps further. First, we instructed other areas within the company to do the same for their operations — that is, get to know their governmental counterparts and learn more from them about what they do during an accident investigation.

Also, since United was spreading its wings internationally, we wanted to make sure that we could deal as well with a disaster outside of the United States. Sending the "How the NTSB Works" document to our regional public relations staff in Asia and the South Pacific, we asked them to contact the NTSB/FAA equivalent in the countries they represented and to prepare a similar document for each country.

Through the public relations committee of the Air Transport Association (ATA), I shared the description of the U.S. NTSB from our plan with my colleagues from other airlines. My rationale for sharing this information with our competitors was that airplane accidents affect the entire industry and that the image of the entire industry is at stake when any airline has an accident. The better prepared each airline is to handle an accident, the easier it is for the entire industry to weather a crisis within its ranks.

Covering Our Logo

Through my discussion, I also learned that the NTSB organizes at least one photo opportunity for the media at the accident site and that it notifies the airline in advance to allow the company to cover its logo on the fuselage of the accident aircraft if it so chooses. Knowing this fact in advance gave us the opportunity to debate the question among ourselves — Would we take the time to cover our logo? After a discussion, we decided that we would not attempt to cover our logo for several reasons.

Most importantly, covering the logo seemed to contradict the communications philosophy we had developed. Taking the time to cover the logo would, in our opinion, look as if we were hiding something.

Our thinking became even more firm when we studied the press coverage of previous accidents and saw time after time wire photos of the accident aircraft, sans its logo, carrying a caption reading something like, "The XYZ Airlines jet, with its logo covered up...."

This type of media attention would seem to violate our attempts to position United as a safe airline and one that is interested in making sure that type of accident does not happen again. It seemed to us that an airline that held safety as its number one objective would be more concerned with investigating the cause of the accident and rechecking its fleet than removing its logo from a wreckage.

Despite the care we took in thinking through this decision in the field, it was interpreted differently at our headquarters. In preparation for the press conference there, someone decided to throw a blanket over the large logo on the wall behind the lectern in our auditorium. All day long, when CNN aired its report of our press conference, there was the blanket, obviously hiding something, on the wall behind our corporate officer. The image was exactly what we wanted to avoid and proved the wisdom of our policy.

Supplier Input Similar to maintaining good working relationships with government authorities, we also saw the importance of maintaining good relationships with the communications staffs of our major suppliers. In United's case this included airframe manufacturers Boeing and McDonnell Douglas, jet engine makers Pratt & Whitney, and General Electric.

Pratt & Whitney senior public relations executives Curt Linke and Ed Cowles were particularly helpful to us as we prepared our crisis plan. Pratt & Whitney was savvy enough to make sure that it was ready to respond to any airline accident anywhere in the world. Regardless of the probable cause, its executives knew that speculation in the early hours inevitably would turn to the engines. They made sure that they could respond quickly.

As part of the overhaul of the United Airlines crisis communications plan, Linke and Cowles spent an entire day with our department talking about their experiences. In fact, Linke just happened to be passing through the airport at the time of the competitor airline's accident that prompted us into action. His recollection of what he witnessed in the first few hours gave us an excellent opportunity to reflect on our own course of action.

We, in turn, shared our thinking and concerns. The partnership proved to be a very healthy dialogue of two companies that shared the probability of a similar disaster.

CNN Impact Our discussion with Pratt & Whitney and the evaluations of recent airline accidents caused us to take an even harder look at the media environment at the time and how much that environment had changed since our last fatality in 1978. The most notable change was the tremendous influence that CNN has on the gathering and dissemination of information today, both in the United States and around the world.

Fortunately, we had identified the power of CNN before we had to deal with a crisis. We knew in 1988 and 1989 what the world would come to learn in the Gulf War of 1991 when CNN played the leading role in news reporting through "instant" coverage.

As we reviewed coverage of previous accidents, we saw CNN broadcasting live images of smoldering wreckage often within minutes, not hours, of a disaster. Our own Flight 232 accident became, perhaps, the first major airline accident to be captured on video as it happened. Unlike previous accidents where images of the wreckage became what the public remembered most, footage of the DC-10 cartwheeling down the runway and into the cornfield, aired over and over again, created one of the most compelling images the world has ever seen of a crisis in the making.

Over the years, we had come to respect CNN personnel a great deal in our daily media relations. They are a new breed of television journalists and they fully understand the importance of maintaining accuracy while they pursue speed in reporting. They are always willing to correct inaccurate or misleading information and the 24-hour format of their broadcasts allows them to respond and correct information much quicker and with much less debate than their competitors.

They are an aggressive group that is relentless in covering the news. Clearly, they have set a new standard. In Sioux City, for example, Captain Haynes became increasingly concerned about continuing media coverage that portrayed him as the hero. He was adamant that the entire crew acted as a team and he wanted the media to carry that message.

Working with the Air Line Pilot's Association (ALPA), the pilots' union, we arranged for a news conference on the morning Haynes was to be released from the hospital. When we informed the press pool of the pending news conference, a few days ahead of his release, not surprisingly CNN informed us immediately that it would carry the entire press conference live. The other national networks said that they would attend, but only to record for use later.

Just hours prior to the press conference, one by one, the national networks began informing us that they too would carry the conference live. Only one network chose not to go live because it would require breaking in to a popular soap opera.

The sudden reversal clearly demonstrated the pressure that CNN has now placed on the other networks. Even the local crews were surprised at the sudden change and several of them told me quite candidly that the reversal was due to the threat their New York headquarters saw in CNN.

The speed at which the media, particularly the electronic media, respond to a crisis situation of this magnitude is mind-boggling. Yet the mechanics of how reporters know of a newsworthy event are not mysterious. They simply monitor emergency broadcast channels.

Gary Brown, the emergency preparedness director of the Siouxland area, told me that Sioux City officials issued a request for additional help from as far away as Des Moines when they knew they were going to need more emergency vehicles. The media heard the message, too: One emergency vehicle racing up the interstate highway with lights flashing and siren blaring was passed by a television news van!

So fast is today's media, in fact, that in United's accidents, our first views of our own crises were the same ones that the world could see on their television sets.

Press Conference Positioning This changing media environment raised another critical issue for us: the press conference. Would we have one? Would we have more than one? When would we hold it? Where? Who would preside? After reflection, the answer came that, yes, we would hold a press conference from our Elk Grove Village, Illinois, headquarters, conducted by a corporate officer, as soon as we had some confirmed information and could assemble the press corps.

In 1989 we held press conferences in as little as three hours after these crises. In both cases, we provided as much information as was known at the time. We positioned United and its management as being very concerned and as a company taking action to learn what caused the accident and ready to take steps to correct any similar problems on the rest of its fleet. We wanted, and needed, to be seen as a safe airline.

In the early hours, there is little information that can be released. Basically, the only information we could confirm was the flight number, the type of aircraft, the routing of the plane, the location of the accident, and the number of passengers and crew believed to be aboard. Providing anything else at this point would have been pure speculation and we were not shy in reminding reporters of the dangers that speculating posed to their responsibility of fair and accurate reporting.

The lack of information, however, was no reason to hide from the media. We immediately set up banks of phones and staffed them with people from our consumer affairs and marketing departments to handle incoming calls. These calls were prioritized in three categories: the A list included the major national media and wire services; the B list was comprised of the local and regional media; and the C list included all other media.

In addition, we sent one or more members of our PR staff to the venue to handle the media there. I was the designated PR member of the "Go Team," which is comprised of representatives from a number of important disciplines from throughout the company — flight operations, in-flight services, public relations, legal, and customer service. As soon as possible, this team boards an aircraft and departs for the accident scene where team members set up a field station at an appropriate location.

Once at the scene, we immediately issued a media advisory on the PR Newswire and Business Wire to notify the media of our field location, listing the people staffing it and their phone numbers. I even provided the phone number for my hotel. While this may seem foolish, it did communicate that we were available and would be as helpful as possible. Only a few reporters called me in my room — possibly because I spent very little time there. Never did they abuse the invitation by calling me at an unreasonable hour.

Although we had little information in the early hours, we could still use the time effectively to work with the media. Apart from issuing the media advisory, I contacted my PR counterparts from the NTSB. I learned from them who was there from the media and the schedule of press events. They also alerted me to reporters who had asked them questions that would be better handled by the airline. I did not hide. I set out to find these reporters to see what I could do to help.

Twice in Honolulu I met junior reporters who were covering their first airline accident. They were a bit overwhelmed, not knowing what to expect or how to go about getting their stories. While Honolulu was my first airline accident as well, I had done my homework and could walk them through what I had learned to be the agenda. There was very little I could tell them about the disaster. Nevertheless, by helping them understand the sequence of events we became viewed as a reliable information source. The lack of information did not prevent us from developing a good working, nonadversarial relationship with the media. Our communications philosophy granted me the license to do this because I knew that cooperation was to be our hallmark. Reporters were very grateful and filed balanced and fair articles from the scene.

Press Releases: Basic Information Dissemination

We also used press releases to inform the traveling public, through the media, that one of our deepest concerns was making sure the events that caused these two accidents did not happen again. Even though in the early hours and days following an accident the cause is uncertain, United's management took steps to inspect its fleet for any similar concerns as quickly as possible.

Just one day after Flight 811, we issued a press release to announce our efforts to inspect the cargo doors of all of our 747s and immediately after Flight 232, we issued similar press releases explaining that we were inspecting all the fan disks on our DC-10 engines. As soon as these inspections were completed, we issued follow-up releases to announce their results. In both cases, we found nothing unusual in the cargo doors or the fan disks.

We also held several press briefings and press conferences in the field. With both Flight 811 and Flight 232, the media were quick to point out that techniques from our own Cockpit Leadership Resources (CLR) program were used by the crew and may have helped to reduce the number of fatalities.

CLR was a program United developed following the 1978 accident in Portland. Prior to that accident, a militaristic hierarchy tended to characterize the flight decks of most airlines; not a surprising phenomenon since most commercial pilots received their training in the military with its strict attention to rank. In the Portland accident, the crew went into a holding pattern while they determined the nature and severity of a light indicating that the landing gear was not locked. While circling over Portland, the captain did not pay attention to warnings from the second officer that the aircraft was low on fuel. The aircraft crashed a few miles from the airport. The cause was the lack of fuel.

Following that accident, United pioneered a new pilot training program, which sought to replace the former strict hierarchical atmosphere with a more cooperative one. Flight crews, especially captains, are taught to use all of the resources available to them, including the skills, knowledge, eyes, and ears of their flying partners.

Over the years, United had spent a great deal of time telling the media about this program. Detailed articles had appeared in several newspapers and magazines. So in 1989, when United crews demonstrated the value of the training, the media, digging into their databases, began feeding the story back to us. We cooperated with these stories by making our flight training staff and our chief flight officer available for backgrounders, briefings, and interviews. The effort resulted in several significant articles in such newspapers as the *Wall Street Journal* and the *New York Times* and helped to explain the heroic efforts of the two flight crews.

In Sioux City, when the issue of maintaining jet engines became a focal point, we again made executives from our maintenance base available to the media. We did not hold back and freely provided information on the maintenance history of that particular engine and the rationale for performing the types of testing that we performed on the fan disks.

This last point proved to be very useful when the media began to charge that we had not used the more sophisticated ultrasound testing of the fan disk in our procedures, claiming that we were attempting to cut costs. We quickly demonstrated to them that economics was not the issue. The issue was purely that a fan disk had never come apart in this manner and no one in the industry believed that ultrasonic testing for internal cracks was necessary after the inspections conducted during manufacturing. Presented with the facts, media interest in this incorrect story angle quickly moved to other issues.

Monitoring the media and correcting inaccurate media reports quickly are as critical to crisis management as any other aspects. In Sioux City, our monitoring of the news picked up a potentially devastating and disruptive news report on one of the major national networks. Combining pieces of unrelated sound bites, the network sensationalized its breaking story with the lead-in that "there is shocking new evidence that a mechanic's failure to close an engine cowling in Philadelphia *the night before* may have lead to the crash of Flight 232."

Correcting Media Error

With "evidence" in the form of disconnected sound bites from NTSB officials and "eyewitnesses," the network had attempted to perform its own investigation and tried to fix probable cause just three days after the accident. (The NTSB, by the way, takes almost a year of painstaking investigation before assigning probable cause.)

The story was ludicrous and we were appalled. As soon as I heard the report, I walked across the hall from our field station and reported the news to the NTSB public relations staff. We joined forces and approached network management. They retreated on their story and ceased perpetuating it. Two days later, they issued a retraction.

To their credit, the folks in Sioux City also reacted quickly to misleading media reports. What the world knows of Siouxlanders and their response to this crash is heroic. The emergency preparedness of this small community would put most metropolitan areas to shame.

Yet, in the precious first few minutes following the crash, a recently serviced fire truck with a faulty generator took seven minutes to reach the scene. Hearing of this problem, one reporter wasted little time in launching an almost stereotypical article along the lines of "a task too big for this small community."

One city official who had learned of the reporter's angle rapidly set the record straight by pointing out the tremendous job the emergency crews had done. The one problem with the fire truck proved to be only a small glitch in an otherwise superhuman response. The reporter changed his focus and the media coverage of the Sioux City response heaped well-deserved praise on the true heroes. President Bush later awarded Sioux City his Thousand Points of Light Award for the community's timely response.

Recognizing Community Effort

We reserved field press conferences to special news stories, especially those with a local slant. At the end of our hectic week in Honolulu, when we finally had a moment to sit back and think beyond the next 10 minutes, someone asked, "Have we forgotten anything?" Immediately, the thought ran through my head: We need to thank this community.

And so we did. Calling key media personnel together by this time required little or no effort. They knew who we were and where we were, and they were hungry for more information. At the press conference, we gave a heartfelt thank-you to a community that had truly extended the aloha spirit in an hour of need.

Again in Sioux City, we experienced unsurpassed cooperation from a community. The extraordinary effort of the people of Sioux City was captured accurately and deservedly in the ABC TV movie *The Crash of Flight 232*. A small community with the foresight to simulate the crash of a jumbo jet 18 months prior the Flight 232 (and on the same unused runway), a community that quickly lined up to give blood almost without being asked to do so, a community that cared about even the little things like doing our laundry in their own homes on a Sunday afternoon, deserved our gratitude. With equal admiration, we used our last day in Sioux City to thank the community via a press conference.

Responding to Non-Crash Crises

Do you really know when you have a crisis? Of course you have a crisis when a jumbo jet flies over the Pacific Ocean with a 10-by-20-foot hole in its side. Of course you have a crisis when a jetliner crashes in a fiery cartwheel. In some respects, these types of events are the easier ones to react to. What about the ones that aren't so easy to recognize, or that develop slowly? How do you establish the level of resources that should be set against a problem? Setting the right threshold for the implementation of a crisis plan is not always an obvious matter.

Aerial view of the Sioux Gateway Airport after the emergency landing of a DC-10.

In the midst of our preparation, we handled a minor incident that raised all of these questions for us. A Boeing 737 bound from Little Rock, Arkansas, to Chicago developed a contained turbine failure of one of its two engines on takeoff from Little Rock. Shrapnel from the engine failure in Little Rock punctured an oil line causing the oil to spray onto hot engine parts, which created a cloud of dense black smoke. Seeing this smoke, the tower reported it to the captain who aborted the takeoff and ordered an evacuation of the aircraft as a precaution.

While this incident may sound horrifying to the uninitiated, it was not a major concern for us. Contained turbine failures, while not a regular occurrence, are not rare. Neither was an aircraft evacuation; we averaged six per year, mostly as a precaution and most often without serious injury.

As compelling a story as this event sounds, it did not require us to initiate our crisis plan and most of the company was not affected by the incident. In the media relations department, we handled the media calls as a routine manner. The following day, however, we learned that our "incident" was in fact listed as an "accident" by the NTSB.

During the evacuation, it seems, a panicky male passenger pushed an elderly woman off the leading edge of the wing after exiting through one of the window exits. The woman landed on the concrete runway and broke her hip. A broken bone is one of the legal definitions of an accident according to the NTSB.

As we were in the process of evaluating our crisis plan anyway, the event caused us to reevaluate our threshold limits. Our new threshold became more flexible, allowing any group, especially media relations, to request that the crisis room be opened and that other appropriate departments send assistance. Again we saw the value of a flexible plan that was based on a communications philosophy rather than a rigid set of procedures.

Not all of the crisis team was needed to respond to a situation like Little Rock. Yet, some departments, such as ours, could do a better job with the resources of an operational crisis room. We needed to have the right people in the company paying attention at headquarters until we knew all was under control. We modified our plan to allow us to implement the parts we felt were needed to get the job done. Because no two accidents or incidents are alike, this method assured us that someone was paying attention and making sure that the right resources were deployed.

Practice Makes Prepared

In the next step of our preparation phase, we addressed the need to practice. Here again, we cast a new eye on an existing method. Previous accident simulations involved surprise calls at employees' homes, usually late at night on a weekend and often during foul weather. While that part could be quite realistic, the usefulness was questionable. After reviewing this practice, we realized that all we really accomplished was a test of the telephone lines and our ability to get the right people into the office at a moment's notice.

By now we trusted the phone company and decided that there had to be a more productive simulation. We chose, instead, to hold the simulations during working hours and to notify all of the important departments in advance of the date and time.

We did not stop there. We challenged each department to create its own simulation; to determine the two or three issues it would like to test. In corporate communications, we knew that we would have to gather people from outside of the media relations department to help us with the flood of calls. Since these people did not handle media calls on a routine basis, we wanted to make sure they were prepared. We also wanted to test our handling of the passenger manifest, one of the more important duties we would perform.

Debriefing Employees

The final element of our crisis program is that we debrief regularly. Naturally, we gathered to talk about our handling of the two major accidents. On an ongoing basis also, we constantly reevaluated our daily procedures and asked how we could make them better. A crisis plan can never be complete. It requires continual renewal.

We did make several changes in our plan as a result of these two accidents, including increasing the number of people staffing our PR field station. One person cannot possibly handle a large number of press inquiries. Once a media outlet has dispatched a reporter or group of reporters to a field location, it expects them to gather the bulk of the information. Our own media relations efforts needed to respond to that barrage by moving to where the action was. In Sioux City, we had as many as three members of our department there during the week our field station remained open.

We also learned the value of preparing behind-the-scenes information in advance for use in helping the media get information during those early hours and days when very little new data emerges. We prepared several prototype backgrounders that could be modified for each situation. These backgrounders dealt with the reconciliation of the passengers manifest, and the way we helped family members with their needs following an accident.

An organization should not think that implementing its crisis plan happens only concurrently with death and destruction. A good crisis plan should be ongoing in the form of building a good solid reputation. Educate the public on the safety aspects of your product or service. Talk about it — don't hide it!

Publicize Safety Efforts

United Airlines did just this, beginning in 1986. During the previous year, a number of fatal airline accidents all over the world began to capture the interest of the U.S. media, who were attempting to connect the rash of accidents to the deregulation of the airline industry. These two issues, of course, had little bearing on one another. The airline deregulation act of the U.S. government only removed government from the economics of running the airline industry by getting out of the fare setting and route assigning business. It did not deregulate air safety procedures.

When the television news program "20/20" approached United and other airlines for a story on aircraft maintenance, the initial reaction was the traditional, "We never talk about safety; we just do it." Yet, Kurt P. Stocker, who was senior vice president of corporate communications at the time, took the bold move of suggesting to Dick Ferris, United's chairman at the time, that we had nothing to lose and much to gain by telling our story. We were, after all, proud of our record. Our aircraft maintenance base in San Francisco stood as a model in the industry. Why not let them in?

We did. The resulting piece by newscaster Barbara Walters, for which only United cooperated, was a major turning point in the public discussion of airline safety. The program did wonders in reassuring an increasingly nervous public that air travel remained safe. The resulting positive public reaction flew in the face of the industry's unspoken credo that "we do not talk about safety." Today, airlines all over the world openly discuss safety and aircraft maintenance, even in their advertising, partially due to that one bold step United took in 1986.

Even though members of corporate communications at United Airlines are proud of the work performed in these two tragedies, it was United Airlines' reputation, built over six decades, that was the real key to PR success. A good crisis communications plan is not a red binder you place on the shelf and dust off when you think you need to do something. It must be a living, breathing, flexible, ever-changing set of principles supported by good business fundamentals and a regular and strategic communications program. Without the long-standing and well-known dedication to safety on the part of every United employee, our job would have been far more difficult.

Currently director of communications for The Gillette Company, Robert A. Doughty previously served as manager of external communications for United Airlines, where he was responsible for modifying the company's crisis communications plan. In 1989 United Airlines implemented this plan following two fatal accidents that occurred just five months apart. Mr. Doughty joined United Airlines in 1986 as manager of international corporate communications to coordinate the public relations aspects of United's acquisition of the Pacific Division of Pan American World Airways. Prior to joining United, Mr. Doughty held a number of public relations positions with Hill & Knowlton, Wilson Foods, and Hobart Brothers Company.

Union Carbide:
Disaster at Bhopal

Jackson B. Browning
Retired Vice President, Health, Safety, and Environmental Programs,
Union Carbide Corporation

Overview

In the early hours of Monday, December 3, 1984, a toxic cloud of methyl iso-cyanate (MIC) gas enveloped the hundreds of shanties and huts surrounding a pesticide plant in Bhopal, India. Later, as the deadly cloud slowly drifted in the cool night air through streets in surrounding sections, sleeping residents awoke, coughing, choking, and rubbing painfully stinging eyes. By the time the gas cleared at dawn, many were dead or injured. Four months after the tragedy, the Indian government reported to its parliament that 1,430 people had died. In 1991 the official Indian government panel charged with tabulating deaths and injuries updated the count to more than 3,800 dead and approximately 11,000 with disabilities.

Although it was not known at the time, the gas was formed when a disgruntled plant employee, apparently bent on spoiling a batch of methyl isocyanate, added water to a storage tank. The water caused a reaction that built up heat and pressure in the tank, quickly transforming the chemical compound into a lethal gas that escaped into the cool night air.

The plant was operated by Union Carbide India Limited (UCIL), just over 50 percent of which was owned by Union Carbide Corporation. The first report of the disaster reached Union Carbide executives in the United States more than 12 hours after the incident. By 6:00 A.M. in the U.S., executives were gathering with technical, legal, and communications staff at the company's Danbury, Connecticut, headquarters. Information was sparse but, as casualty estimates quickly climbed, the matter was soon recognized as a massive industrial disaster.

The first press inquiry came at 4:30 A.M. in the U.S., marking the beginning of a deluge that, at its peak, reached 500 calls a day for several weeks. The scope of the Bhopal tragedy made it "page one" material in the weeks and months that followed. And, as its legal, political, technological and — above all — human aspects were explored, it became a persistent headline into the 1990s.

Setting the Stage   In 1984 Union Carbide reported sales of $9.5 billion, reflecting its position as one of the largest industrial companies in the United States and the world. International operations represented nearly 30 percent of total sales that year. India was one of three dozen countries where the company had affiliates and business interests.

Divided by industry segments, sales encompassed petrochemicals (28 percent); technology, services, and specialty products (26 percent); consumer products such as batteries, automotive supplies, and plastic wraps and bags (20 percent); industrial gases (16 percent); and metals and carbon products (10 percent).

Financially, 1984 was a good year for Union Carbide. The company was pursuing ambitious commercial plans in the People's Republic of China. Twelve promising new high-performance specialty products were being marketed. A joint venture with Shell Chemical Company was moving forward. Union Carbide was keeping pace as the U.S. economy recovered from the persistent recession that had begun in 1981.

In 1984 Union Carbide India Limited was celebrating its 50th anniversary. UCIL had sales of about $200 million annually. It operated 14 plants, and was organized into five operating divisions with 9,000 employees. It was a diversified manufacturing concern. The shares of the Indian company, publicly traded on the Calcutta Stock Exchange, were held by more than 23,000 shareholders. About 24 percent of the shares were owned by government-run insurance companies. Union Carbide Corporation held 50.9 percent of the stock as part of a corporate global business strategy that evolved in the post–World War II era. By investing in companies abroad, Union Carbide expected to contribute to — and benefit from — growing national economies around the world.

Ironically, the plant at Bhopal had its origin in a humane goal: supplying pesticides to protect Indian agricultural production. The pesticides made at Bhopal were for the Indian market and contributed to the nation's ability to transform its agricultural sector into a modern activity capable of feeding one of the world's most heavily populated regions.

In the late 1960s, operations at Bhopal packaged the pesticide Sevin, then considered an environmentally preferred alternative to DDT, an insecticide now restricted by the EPA. Later, the Bhopal plant started handling methyl isocyanate shipped from the United States. The process, which reacted methyl isocyanate with another compound, was considered the leading technology for producing Sevin and another pesticide, Temik. The development was part of an active Indian government effort to achieve industrial self-sufficiency.

Ultimately, in the late 1970s those government objectives led to the construction of a plant for manufacturing methyl isocyanate at Bhopal. The plant was located on the outskirts of Bhopal on land leased to UCIL by the Indian state government of Madhya Pradesh.

In 1984 the entire work force at the Bhopal plant was Indian. In keeping with the government's interest in promoting self-sufficiency and local control, the last American employed at the site had left two years before. The Indian workers had years of experience working with methyl isocyanate, dating back to the mid-1970s. During the years since the plant first opened, a densely populated shanty town had grown up near the plant on land deeded by local officials. Its residents were the first and main victims of the poisonous gas.

Safety Emphasized

No balanced analysis of Union Carbide reaction to the Bhopal tragedy is possible without recognizing the considerable emphasis the company and its affiliates had placed on safe operations. It was a deeply ingrained commitment that involved every employee worldwide and had been spurred in the chemical business by stringent internal standards dating back to the 1930s. The development of toxicology, which studies the effects of poisonous substances, was spurred by industry efforts, led in part by joint Carbide and Carnegie-Mellon research in Pittsburgh. In the 1970s Carbide and other companies founded the Chemical Industry Institute of Toxicology. Because of such efforts, the company was well prepared to meet a surge of government environmental and safety regulations in the 1970s and 1980s.

Nonetheless, chemical companies, including Union Carbide, were a focus of both criticism and control. In 1976 Union Carbide was among the first corporations to respond to this tough regulatory climate. It established a corporate-level department to oversee activities that ranged from product safety and on-the-job safety to measuring the environmental impact of its operations and monitoring adherence to strict medical standards.

Commenting after the Bhopal incident was international management specialist Richard D. Robinson, a professor at the Massachusetts Institute of Technology:

> For those of us who follow the vicissitudes of the multinational corporation as part of our professional responsibilities it is particularly depressing that it was Union Carbide which was involved.
>
> For some years now, Union Carbide has maintained a sophisticated environmental monitoring system, backed by top management support, and has initiated joint health research with the U.S. National Institute of Occupational Safety and Health (NIOSH) which, at the time, was new for the industry.

Within the company, awareness of the depth and scope of the company's strict policies on safety made the news of the Bhopal tragedy astounding.

The Long Chain of Events

The chronology of the Bhopal incident is measured by both clock and calendar. It begins in the hours immediately following the incident, then tracks a series of connected developments that span years.

When the dreadful news reached Union Carbide in the United States, it was already afternoon in India, 10 and a half hours ahead of the company's Connecticut headquarters on standard time. Information direct from Bhopal was slow in arriving and fragmentary at best because the disaster had quickly overwhelmed the capacity of two telephone trunk lines serving the central Indian city of 750,000. In those early hours, company executives in Connecticut relied on telephone connections to New Delhi and Bombay, where BBC radio news reports were being taped and relayed.

I had received my first notice of the incident through a telephone call from a colleague at 2:30 A.M. on December 3. I was advised that there had been an "accident" at a plant in India, that no plant employees had been injured, but that there were fatalities — possibly 8 or 12 — in the nearby community. A meeting had been called for 6:00 A.M. in Danbury. On my way, I listened to news reports on my car radio as the death estimate rose to about 50. Later in the day, the number grew much larger.

Chairman Warren M. Anderson had received news about Bhopal in a telephone call from his office staff and from Alec Flamm, the corporation's president and chief operating officer. Anderson was returning from a business trip to Washington, suffering from a bad cold and a fever. We agreed that he would stay at home, relying on telephone reports to keep him updated. I was his media stand-in until he was able to come to the office the next day.

At 1:00 P.M. on December 3, we held our first press conference at the Danbury Hilton hotel. We chose a public site for the meeting because our offices had been transformed into a command center to gather information and mobilize resources. Since we were still not aware of what had taken place in Bhopal — or why — we were also concerned about security in Danbury and other company locations.

Responding to the Press

The first press conference was relatively short. We acknowledged that the disaster had occurred at a plant owned by Union Carbide India Limited, in which we had a 50.9 percent share. We explained that we were sending medical and technical experts to aid the people of Bhopal, to help dispose of the remaining methyl isocyanate at the plant, and to investigate the cause of the tragedy. We announced our plans to halt production at our only other methyl isocyanate plant in Institute, West Virginia, and to convert existing supplies into less volatile compounds. We explained that methyl isocyanate was not a common chemical and was not contained in products generally available to the public. We also pledged to share information with users of the chemical as we received it.

We didn't have a great deal of information to report and under no circumstance would we speculate. I went into the conference hoping to establish an important tone: one structured of frankness, credibility, and accessibility. I think the effort succeeded and formed a vital foundation for our relationship with the media and ultimately all the audiences we faced, including employees, shareholders, customers, suppliers, plant communities, government officials, and the general public. In the weeks and months that followed, we conducted a half dozen news conferences in Danbury, some attended by as many as 100 reporters. Elsewhere, we met with the media in briefings, editorial board discussions, and interviews.

In the first days, scheduled news conferences helped us deal with the hundreds of inquiries that poured in from around the world. There was no way we could respond to every individual call. But many of the frequently asked questions were considered when we prepared for daily briefings.

There was another benefit to the news conferences. They were public forums on which many key constituents, such as employees, shareholders, and customers, relied for information. They also demonstrated how the company would deal with the crisis as well as the demands of its ongoing businesses. We understood that above all we would have to demonstrate, as best we could, our integrity and competence. Additionally, I'm persuaded that the exceptional performance of Union Carbide employees throughout the world confirmed what we said. It also reassured all of us and our constituents that we would not hide or crumble in the face of adversity.

Press coverage was massive. At first, the story was a front page, general news disaster. In time, it became a complex legal drama. It also was an international detective story as our scientists and engineers sought to determine the cause of the disaster in a frustrating situation where they were denied cooperation, information, and access. Finally, it became a political story that focused on varied interpretations of the societal role of multinational corporations and crucial differences between Eastern and Western cultures.

In the first months alone, stories about Bhopal in the *New York Times* carried 25 different bylines. Bylines in the *Wall Street Journal* were shared by 16 writers. Even Connecticut's *Hartford Courant*, the nation's oldest newspaper (but one with a modest size staff and largely regional influence) had as many as a dozen different bylines on its Bhopal stories.

First Steps at Control   In those frustrating first days, as the dimensions of the tragedy gradually were learned, vital decisions were made:

- A Union Carbide facility in West Virginia was quickly closed because it manufactured methyl isocyanate. It remained closed until safety measures were reexamined and more light shed on the cause of the Bhopal tragedy.

- A management task force, headed by Anderson, was set up to deal with the crisis. President Flamm took over running the company's day-to-day business. That decision by Anderson permitted his Bhopal team to concentrate on the facts of the tragedy and its aftermath.

- Anderson, seeking to underscore our concern, decency, and humaneness in the face of the terrible tragedy, accepted moral responsibility for the incident at a December 4 news conference and announced that he would travel at once to India to offer relief to the victims, including an immediate aid offer of $1 million. UCIL also pledged the Indian equivalent of $840,000.

- A medical and technical team was dispatched to Bhopal within 24 hours of the disaster. Their tasks: to help arrange for immediate and long-term relief; to assist in the safe disposal of remaining methyl isocyanate supplies at the plant; and to investigate the incident.

These decisive early actions gave us an answer to the press question, "What is Carbide doing about this?" But we were still desperately short of information. We did not have answers to such basic questions as, "What caused the disaster?" or even, "What happened?" In this information vacuum, we reaffirmed a standing procedure — no speculation. (It took considerable effort on the first day to make even the simple determination that the tragedy did not involve an explosion or fire, as the media had reported in some instances.) It took courage to say, "We don't have the information. We'll have to get back on that," especially in face of the obvious question, "Why don't you know?"

Because of the obstacles placed in our way by Indian authorities, it would be March 1985 before we could point with certainty to the cause. In the interim, we took the heat.

Union Carbide had a contingency plan for emergencies. This plan provided a basic framework and some guidelines. In Bhopal, however, the unthinkable had happened and the terrible facts of the tragedy were overwhelming. However, the versatility of our staff, their stamina in the face of long, grueling hours, and a systematic approach to communications that had been in place for some time were significant assets.

Contingency Planning and Experience Help

Working to our strong advantage, also, were the quality and integrity of Union Carbide people. Trust, respect, and knowledge, developed over years of dealing with environmental and safety issues, helped us navigate the uncharted areas into which we had been swept. We shared with Anderson a special understanding — nurtured over 10 years in my case — that we worked for a responsible company. Colleagues recall me quoting, along the way, my mother's advice, "If you tell the truth, you'll never have to remember your lies." For me, that motto set an important tone that carried us through the crisis.

Other pluses were the diverse skills combined in the Bhopal crisis team. Many of the members were experienced in dealing with emergencies or unusual situations. We also had more than a decade of experience with methyl isocyanate without incident. Although, in light of the enormity of the event, it was difficult to persuade anyone of the significance or value of our considerable expertise.

Given that there was still methyl isocyanate in the Bhopal plant, we especially needed to convince Indian officials that our presence there was essential. Securing a substantial quantity of the remaining methyl isocyanate for analysis was a top priority for our technical team.

Team leader Ron Van Mynen overcame initial resistance through a patient, reasoned approach, stressing that safety was paramount. Government officials finally relented, agreeing that experts from Union Carbide, the Indian company, and the Indian government would convert the remaining methyl isocyanate into a less volatile compound. However, the effort, which Indian officials called "Operation Faith," sent a second shock wave through Bhopal resulting in a spontaneous exodus in the days leading up to the conversion.

In the end, the conversion came off without hitches, despite the distraction of water-laden Indian military airplanes flying overhead to dampen any cloud. During their three-week stay in Bhopal that December, team members were also able to recover residue from the tank directly involved in the gas leak as well as make detailed observations about the facility. The samples and information formed the basis of an intensive scientific investigation into the cause of the incident that took another two months.

Despite official assurances about safety, frightened residents queue to leave Bhopal.

In Danbury we put in 12- to 18-hour days working on various aspects of the aftermath. We simultaneously and alternately addressed concerns that cut across technical, humanitarian, legal, and business implications. Throughout we were constant in the assertion that the best approach was to be accessible to the media and to share reliable information as it became available. Occasionally, the media, with their voracious appetite for information, weren't satisfied and let us know. We persevered nonetheless.

We employed basic tools: news conferences, releases, videos, and interviews. Danbury was established as the single place to get reliable information. There was a continuing challenge to translate complex legal and technical data into accurate, understandable language quickly, especially in response to erroneous allegations. In our communications process, corporate jargon was also a very early casualty.

Keeping Vital Audiences Informed

While the press remained our most visible audience (and most important conduit to the public), we paid attention to other deeply interested parties. We reassured employees, suppliers, customers, and shareholders. We briefed the members of Congress and regulatory agencies. As early as December 14, Anderson and I testified before two subcommittees of the House Commerce and Energy Committee. Their question was one the press was already asking: "Can it happen here?"

We detailed the steps taken in closing our U.S. manufacturing facility for methyl isocyanate and the actions taken to return the product from France, which refused to accept a shipment that was en route by sea. We frankly admitted that we had not yet determined the cause of the tragedy, stressing our determination to limit any activity involving methyl isocyanate until we did know. We responded to questions about the company's safety practices, citing Union Carbide's top-of-the-industry performance in annual worker-safety reviews. We shared what information we had and stressed the company's determination to find the cause of the Bhopal tragedy and apply the lessons learned.

In Danbury, from the very first day, it was evident that communication resources had to be committed, on a high-priority basis, to informing our employees. On December 3 and the days following, our corporate offices were marked by individual and collective shock. As fatality estimates rose, many of our people were emotionally devastated. Some wept openly at their desks.

Great care was taken to include our employees in our overall communications effort. The policy of open and early release of factual information covered both internal and external communication. Employees received information at the same time as the press received it. Existing channels of communication — news bulletins, regular publications, and special videotapes in which senior executives appeared — were used to provide a consistent body of knowledge to all 90,000 employees.

In January, *UC World* magazine, which is mailed regularly to employees and retirees at their homes, dedicated its front page to coverage of the Bhopal incident. Later, the company videotape series, *What's Going On*, shown in cafeterias and at employee meetings, reviewed the Bhopal tragedy from the perspective of media coverage.

In early February, Anderson met with employees in Charleston, West Virginia, where the petrochemical business started in the 1920s, and not far from the company's only other methyl isocyanate-producing plant in Institute, West Virginia. He reassured them of the company's continuing commitment to employee and community safety and, specifically, to reaffirm the safety measures in place at their operation. The appearance was videotaped and highlights of the meeting were circulated to company and affiliated sites throughout the world. A measure of the personal concern and compassion of Union Carbide employees was their spontaneous establishment of a Carbide Employees Bhopal Relief Fund that collected more than $100,000 to aid the tragedy's victims.

By mid-December, Union Carbide's communications on the Bhopal incident were solidly in place. We had clearly identified Danbury as the contact point for the media — and so informed operating management in our plants, where managers had been besieged by press inquiries. Within the team, rotating assignments helped us cope with the problems of stress and fatigue generated by nonstop inquiries and the task of communicating simultaneously with our employees and others.

**Confrontation with
Local Authorities**

Despite our commitment and strategic approach to communications, we were still frustrated in our efforts to obtain information on the specifics of the incident. And a new element had entered the situation: confrontation.

It began with our relief efforts. When Anderson arrived in Bhopal, he was placed under house arrest by the local authorities and later released. Despite such a reception, at a December 10 press conference, he emphasized that he had been treated "with the utmost courtesy and consideration." Behind the scenes we were having difficulty finding an Indian agency or official who would channel more than $2 million in immediate aid Union Carbide, the Indian company, and others had pledged in response to the tragedy.

Within a week of the gas leak, we had recruited and dispatched an independent medical team, including internationally recognized pulmonary and ophthalmic specialists, to Bhopal. Within a few months, Union Carbide offered an additional $5 million in aid at the suggestion of the U.S. federal court judge hearing litigation which had been started in the U.S. When this was rejected by the Indian government, the $5 million was offered to Red Cross authorities working with Bhopal victims. Ultimately, the Indian Red Cross used a substantial portion of these funds.

Despite our repeated "no strings attached" assurance, the Indian government rejected relief that originated with the corporation. Even when we turned to third parties to aid the Bhopal victims, we were rebuffed. In the months following the tragedy, more than $2 million, for example, was designated for an Arizona State University project to build and operate a rehabilitation center in Bhopal. When it was learned that the funds had come from Union Carbide, the Indian government bulldozed the center. In 1987 CBS's "60 Minutes" depicted the episode as a disturbing example of Indian bureaucratic obstruction.

In communicating with the media, we made an intensive effort to provide facts and to avoid taking a confrontational stance with the Indian government. The latter became increasingly difficult as the Indian political climate changed and Prime Minister Rajiv Gandhi's administration came under fire on a number of political fronts.

At some risk of oversimplification, we can summarize the Indian political situation at the time of the Bhopal gas deaths. It was highly volatile. Just over a month earlier, Prime Minister Indira Gandhi had been assassinated. Communal violence followed, mostly based in religious differences. Rajiv Gandhi was the new prime minister, pledged to reform the government and ruling party. The press was afire with campaign-related political charges. And 350 million Indians were about to elect representatives to the Lok Sabha, the lower house of Parliament. These elections included the Indian state of Madhya Pradesh, whose capital is Bhopal.

In India, Union Carbide was a high-profile multinational company. A measure of that prominence was attributable to the role we and UCIL had played in the "Indianization" of industry in that country. We had been one of the first multinationals to invest in India, demonstrating our willingness to offer expertise, readiness to comply with Indian laws, and acceptance of a gradual approach to developing Indian consumer markets. Union Carbide's investment had gained us widespread good will — or so we thought.

Whatever our contributions to national industrialization goals, the current political arguments expediently recast us as an archetypal multinational villain, exploiting India's people and resources. As legal actions proceeded in the United States, it became evident to us that this caricature was designed to gain access to Union Carbide's financial resources.

Along the way it had become rather convenient for some Indian officials to ignore the goodwill and contributions that UCIL had made to India during more than a half century of doing business there. The government of India brought a suit against Union Carbide in the United States, even though the disaster occurred in India and the nation has a well-established court system based on the same legal principles as those in the United States. To resist efforts to send the case to India, the Indian Government's U.S. attorneys also invented a novel legal theory for the situation. They called it "multinational enterprise liability" which, in summary, places absolute responsibility on affiliated corporations if anything goes wrong for any reason at any affiliate. This was followed by a ruling in an unrelated case that made liability in India absolute where hazardous materials are involved, without exception, even for acts of God or third parties. It also said that the size and prosperity of the defendant should be considered in assessing damages. This novel approach effectively upended for India the basic legal principles of liability that have existed in common law countries for more than 100 years.

In the February 19, 1985 issue of the *Boston Globe*, MIT's Professor Robinson observed:

> *It would appear that some are condemning Union Carbide precisely because it was so responsive to Indian pressures and relinquished both a measure of ownership and control to Indians, as the Indian government desired. This is not to say that those culpable in the Indian tragedy by reason of negligence should not be held responsible, whomever that may be.*

> *But to destroy in the process a corporation distinguished by a management with a keen sense of public responsibility is likewise tragic. By doing so, we send the wrong message to all business, a*

message which says in essence: "Do not spend resources on trying to be a good citizen; it does not make any difference. Best to maximize profit, no matter what — whatever you can get away with."

Detective Story

The shock and the pressures of the early days of the Bhopal crisis were measured in hours. But then the horror story of the disaster began to develop along more specific lines: the cause of the tragedy, the continuing plight of the victims, and the legal consequences. These developments need to be tracked over months, even years.

Union Carbide's technical team, which ultimately was charged with the scientific investigation into the cause, assembled for the first time in India on December 6. Most of the members flew in from the United States. But team leader, Van Mynen, already in the Far East on routine safety inspections of facilities in that region, arrived a day earlier.

The group of seven engineers and scientists spent 24 days in India and, on return to the U.S., more than two additional months on analysis. It was hampered in its work by the Indian Central Bureau of Investigation, which had taken control of the plant. The team was barred from questioning employees at the plant and had access to only those documents they knew about and specifically requested. Team members were permitted only to examine the tank that had been the source of the leak at the plant and to take scientific samples.

Back in the United States, the team was obliged to pursue its investigation in a unique manner: first, analyze the composition of a gooey residue taken from the Bhopal storage tank where the chemical reaction had occurred; second, undertake a series of 500 experiments, working backward to define the cause. It was tough, detailed work similar to a National Transportation Safety Board (NTSB) effort of piecing an airplane together after a crash.

We were determined not to release information concerning the cause of the tragedy unless we were certain of our conclusions. However, because of the media's search for a quick and ready explanation for a major disaster, enormous public speculation occurred as to the cause. Every conceivable kind of explanation was published, from an Indian government scientist's contention that the reaction was touched off by a pint of water to a claim that an imaginary Sikh terrorist group named Black September was responsible. After a short time, some speculated that the tragedy was caused by a combination of management failures and the failure or shutdown of safety equipment. According to one popular story, the reaction was supposedly triggered by a water-washing of lines in another section of the plant, which allowed water to enter the system and, through a series of open valves, leak into the tank.

Ultimately, what actually occurred turned out to be something quite different. In March 1985, after three months of work, our technical team told the world that a substantial amount of water had entered the tank, that the water-washing hypothesis was improbable, and that they believed water had entered the tank directly.

It took us almost two more years before we could corroborate our scientific findings with interviews and documents because the Indian government prevented access to witnesses and records in India. It was only through court actions in the U.S. and in India that such information ultimately became available.

During the next year, the team was aided by the Indian government's reluctant release of some 70,000 pages of documentation. These records became available as a part of the discovery process as Bhopal court cases proceeded.

Late in 1986 Union Carbide filed a lengthy court document in India detailing the findings of its scientific and legal investigations: the cause of the disaster was undeniably sabotage. The evidence showed that an employee at the Bhopal plant had deliberately introduced water into a methyl isocyanate storage tank. The result was the cloud of poisonous gas. The episode is documented in a 17-minute videotape produced in 1988 by filmmaker Philip Gittelman, who was invited to undertake the documentary project by Union Carbide and its outside legal counsel, Kelley Drye and Warren of New York City. Also in 1988 an independent study of the incident by the prestigious international engineering consulting firm of Arthur D. Little supported the analysis by the Union Carbide team. Noting the obstacles placed in the team's path by the Indian government, the Little study said, "Had those constraints not been imposed, the actual cause of the incident would have been determined within several months."

The Indian government, to this day, has not taken a firm position on the tragedy's cause, leaving Carbide's findings as the only definitive conclusion on the subject. The government of India has apparently decided not to pursue an investigation into the charge of employee sabotage.

We released the report of the Union Carbide team and made our technical and legal investigators available to field inquiries from the press and other professional groups. Obviously, this fitted into our policy of open communication. But backing this rationale was our clear understanding that, whatever the cause, a disaster had occurred and we were obligated to help assure that it would not happen again.

Enter the Lawyers The legal dimensions of the Bhopal story began with what has been characterized as the "greatest ambulance chase in history" as American liability lawyers flocked to India within days of the tragedy and began signing up claimants. The first class action suit in the United States was filed a week after the disaster. Ultimately, 145 suits were filed in state and federal courts. An appalled public watched U.S. attorneys in India signing up local citizens indiscriminately.

A goat grazes near fresh graves with simple granite headstones that mark the final resting place for victims of the poison gas leak.

In 1985 the government of India filed a civil suit against Union Carbide in Federal District Court in New York City — after it had quickly enacted a law giving it the right to represent all Bhopal victims and the exclusive right to reach a settlement on their behalf. The Indian government had hired an American law firm, pursuing its strategy to try the case in U.S. courts where it presumably hoped for a higher award or settlement than could be expected in India. At one point in 1986, a settlement with attorneys in the U.S. seemed imminent but lawyers representing the government of India would not agree and the deal fell apart. Eventually the U.S.

courts established that India was the proper site for any Bhopal action and sent the litigation there for disposition.

The Indian government filed suit in India for an unspecified amount and later said claims would amount to $3 billion. In February 1989, four years after the tragedy, the Indian Supreme Court found itself confronted by activists in India who cared little for the victims and wanted the litigation to drag on for many years in order to "punish" a foreign multinational. Exercising great political courage in the face of that opposition, the Court directed a settlement of $470 million and nullified criminal charges. The Court described the settlement as "just, equitable, and agreeable." It was the largest settlement ever made in an Indian civil suit. The Court also instructed the Indian government to make relief payments to the victims of the tragedy.

Unfortunately, the $470 million, paid within ten days of the Court decision, sat untouched as Indian politicians, bureaucrats, and activist lawyers argued, speculated, and maneuvered. Then there was another election in India. V.P. Singh became the new prime minister and, within ten days, his government repudiated the Indian Supreme Court and rejected the $470 million settlement as "totally inadequate." His government announced its intention to return to the original $3 billion claim and to pursue criminal charges against Union Carbide executives. The Indian government had returned to square one. The Bhopal victims were ignored. Following a lengthy review by the Supreme Court, the original settlement was upheld and the criminal proceedings were reopened. Although the government of India has distributed a limited amount of its own funds, only small amounts of settlement money started trickling through in early 1993.

From a public relations standpoint, the story of Bhopal in the courts raised its own problems. Each news development brought a fresh retelling of the disaster. As the various legal events took place, there was a continuing requirement to tell the story in "plain language" and to try to trace the labyrinth of legal strategies and decisions.

I would be less than candid if I did not admit that many of us at Union Carbide were outraged by the Indian government's apparent indifference to the plight of the Bhopal victims. From the first day, we had been moved by compassion and sympathy. We believed that the company's position was responsible and fair. We could not understand why the government did not promptly distribute the relief funds to the real victims.

Myth versus Reality

Even years after the tragedy, it is difficult to measure the human cost of the disaster. Persistent myths conflict with reality. Political purpose and dramatic license have continually motivated some politicians and writers to inflate the fatality number. A very shaky basis for extrapolating casualty estimates has been the number of Indian claimants for damages — a number that has been as high as 500,000. Yet documents considered by the Supreme Court of India showed that approximately 75 percent of the claims were from areas that the government had not recognized as being gas-affected. And approximately 250,000 claimants elected not to respond to repeated requests to appear for physical examinations.

Television images right after the disaster showed many people with bandaged eyes, leading viewers to believe that many had been blinded. In point of fact, the escaping methyl isocyanate did not cause blindness and relatively few suffered any permanent eye damage at all.

Almost from the beginning, there have been horrendous speculations about the long-term impact of the disaster. But studies by India's Council of Medical Research report that serious injury to the lung is limited to a small percentage of the population and that there is no serious residual eye disease. There is no evidence that the disaster caused cancer, birth defects, or any other delayed effects. Further, Union Carbide, the U.S. National Institute of Health, and others conducted tests on methyl isocyanate and all concluded that no latent long-term problems were expected.

What Did We Learn? The contemporary Union Carbide Corporation is a different company from what it was at the time of the Bhopal incident in 1984. It is a smaller company. In 1992, its 75th anniversary year, the company spun off its industrial gases division to stockholders. The gases operation was the last tangible reflection of the giant conglomerate of the past. Gone are the metals, consumer products, and other diverse businesses. The restructured Union Carbide is a closely focused $5 billion basic chemical and plastics company with advanced process technologies and efficient, large-scale production facilities.

The company has kept pace with the accelerating changes of the times — changes in markets, economic patterns, and technologies. It has weathered a bitter and costly takeover attempt. It has tackled the basic problems of productivity and cost control that bedevil modern American businesses.

At the time of Bhopal, the company was rated among those manufacturers with the best worker safety records. To a degree, we were smug about our record. Bhopal put an end to that attitude. It spurred new cycles of process monitoring and a fresh look at risk management. In the months and years after Bhopal, Union Carbide focused a microscope on every operation. There was an unprecedented search for every risk, any risk. We discovered that there was still more that we could accomplish in maintaining safer operations. And money and staff were committed to those objectives.

The impact of Bhopal went well beyond Union Carbide. It changed views and practices among the entire U.S. chemical industry. It provided impetus to the development and enactment of federal laws requiring companies to notify government and the public about toxic substances they make or use. The EPA's Federal Superfund Reauthorization, spurred by the Bhopal tragedy, helped bring about a network of local emergency planning councils, in which corporate specialists work with their neighboring communities to safely deal with unthinkable environmental disasters.

The Chemical Manufacturers Association has established Community Action Emergency Response (CAER), a program to prevent or respond to industrial emergencies. Responsible Care is an industry initiative designed to establish basic standards for safe, healthy, and environmentally sound operations. It is being established in some 22 countries around the world. Union Carbide has been an active participant in these and other programs.

Aftermath

The sheer scope of the Bhopal incident made it an extremely complex public communications problem. Ron Wishart, summoned by Chairman Anderson from a government relations assignment in Washington to aid him in directing the Bhopal crisis team, put it very succinctly: "The problems raised by the tragedy spanned two companies, two governments, two continents, and two cultures." As our chief outside counsel put it, "There were three tragedies at Bhopal — the gas leak, the reaction to it by the Indian government, and the consequent inability to get relief to the genuine victims."

Union Carbide's approaches at the time of the Bhopal disaster were, I believe, correct ones. This is certainly true of the top-level decision to accept full moral responsibility. Just as logical was the decision to concentrate on relief for the victims.

Remaining accessible to and honest with the press — indeed, to and with all our audiences — was also a sound decision, though it placed severe pressures on our media relations people. Our adherence to fact and our unwillingness to deal in speculation were likewise appropriate, although not always popular with the press. With any breaking news story, each reporter attempts to get information that is new, different, and dramatic. These requirements were heightened in the Bhopal story because of its spectrum of consequences.

The Arthur D. Little report on Bhopal includes a commentary on the role of the press:

> *In the immediate aftermath of a large-magnitude incident, both nontechnical and technically trained reporters converge on the site, looking for quick "answers" to the question of what caused the event. Most reporters are responsible, restrained, and unbiased in their reporting. However, a fringe group usually appears on-site that is more interested in developing causation theories, which seem to have great public appeal, regardless of their veracity.*

When the Bhopal disaster occurred in 1984, Jackson B. Browning was responsible for Union Carbide Corporation's health, safety, and environmental programs. He and Chairman Warren M. Anderson were the company's chief spokespersons during the crisis. Browning also directed the teams that responded to and investigated the tragedy. Browning holds degrees in both chemical engineering and law. He joined Union Carbide as a patent attorney in 1948 and held positions of increasing management responsibility for research and operations until he became the company's first senior health, safety, and environmental affairs officer in 1976. He retired from the corporation in 1986 and remains active in his own business.

From the White House to Wall Street

Larry Speakes
Former Chief Spokesperson for President Ronald Reagan and
former Senior Vice-President, Communications, Merrill Lynch & Co.

During the last half of the 1980s, the national mood of the United States was shaken on two separate occasions by sudden and unexpected catastrophe. On January 28, 1986, the space shuttle *Challenger* exploded moments after its launch from Cape Canaveral, Florida, causing a fiery death for its crew, which included the first school teacher selected to fly in space. On October 19, 1987, the stock market plummeted more than 500 points, shaking the foundation of the world's financial system. Exploding with such swiftness, these crises — one in government, the other in the private sector — bore remarkable similarities.

Overview

News of both of the incidents instantly flashed around the world to a stunned and shocked global audience. Both institutions — the National Aeronautics and Space Administration (NASA) and Wall Street and its market system — maintained carefully cultivated, internationally respected images of strength and invulnerability. Yet they were threatened with unprecedented public relations disasters.

The crises required instant and precise responses to restore public confidence. And both provided the ultimate test for crisis communicators.

The U.S. space program, after three decades of triumph and achievement, had become the perfect blend of swashbuckling test pilot courage and high-tech wizardry. From the moment the original seven astronauts had been selected in the

Sir, the *Challenger* Has Exploded

late 1950s, NASA had carefully cultivated a nearly impeccable image of American ingenuity.

The "teacher in space" was a showcase example of NASA's public relations machine in action. For the first time, "an ordinary American" was going into space, and what better example than Christa McAuliffe, a high school teacher from Concord, New Hampshire.

That last Tuesday in January was never destined to be an ordinary day at the White House. Of course, few days were ever ordinary there, and this one was no exception. President Ronald Reagan was scheduled to deliver his State of the Union Address to Congress and the American people.

As his chief spokesperson, I had worked with our team in the Office of the Press Secretary, developing a communications plan to ensure that this important event was properly presented to the public. The initial step in this plan was unfolding in the Oval Office where a staff group was briefing the president for a luncheon meeting with the news anchors and reporters from ABC, CBS, CNN, and NBC.

A few steps away in the Roosevelt Room, the anchors — familiar faces to almost every American — were making small talk while awaiting the president's arrival. Our meeting in the Oval Office was relaxed, but it was clear that the president's mind was on the finishing touches he planned to add to his speech for that evening.

The President Receives Tragic News

As we posed mock questions, the door to the office cracked open, and the president's secretary motioned for me to step outside. Before I could respond, past her came Vice-President George Bush, quickly followed by National Security Director John Poindexter and Communications Director Pat Buchanan.

The president stopped in mid-answer. It was an unwritten rule that no one — even vice-presidents — entered the Oval Office without proper admission.

"There's been a serious incident with the space shuttle," the vice-president blurted.

Buchanan put it more bluntly. "Sir, the space shuttle exploded."

We sat in stunned silence. The president was visibly shaken. "Oh, no," he said, in a voice barely above a whisper.

The antique clock against the wall in the Oval Office ticked away seconds as the leadership of the United States government sought to grasp the reality of the moment. The time was 11:38 A.M.

For Ronald Reagan, it was an intimate, personal tragedy. He had proposed the idea of sending a teacher into space as a symbol to the nation's children. NASA had received more than 11,000 applications, and, a few weeks later, Christa McAuliffe had been introduced in the Roosevelt Room, where anchors Peter Jennings and Tom Brokaw, and their colleagues, were about to sit down to lunch.

In a very public way, the *Challenger* was meant to signal a new initiative by NASA and the Administration. The flight of the *Challenger* was to be followed by a record number of bolder expeditions. At the beginning of the year, NASA Administrator James M. Beggs had stated that 1986 "will probably be the most important year of our space program, and the most important year since the space age began."

As we silently sat in the Oval Office, we knew the worst of all horrors, the unthinkable, had turned a triumphant day into tragedy. It was the president who spoke first, suggesting we move into his tiny study next to the Oval Office where he kept a television set. As the videotaped image flickered on the screen, we watched the scene as the huge rocket slowly, powerfully lifted the *Challenger* upward, and we cringed as the explosion shattered the bright blue sky.

I watched Reagan's face as the White House photographer snapped a picture that captured an expression of such horror and disbelief that later I refused to release it to the press.

There was little doubt we were watching a disaster — a crisis — without precedent. My mind raced back to March 30, 1981, the day an assassin tried to take the president's life and almost succeeded. I had replayed that scene in my mind a thousand times, and, again and again, I weighed our performance and found it was not what it should have been.

This time, it was clear what must be done in this moment of new national tragedy.

Communication, Reassurance

My first instinct was to go to the White House press room to let the American people know that President Reagan was aware of the incident and to extend his condolences to the families of the seven astronauts. I told the president and, as I started toward the door, he touched my arm. "These people were dedicated to this program," he said. "We couldn't do more to honor them than to go forward. Tell them what we will do is fix it and we will keep it going."

With those words, Ronald Reagan had done what he does best. He had simply, yet firmly articulated our message. Sorrow. Shock. The space program will continue.

These people had not given their lives in vain. His words set the tone for the crisis communications plan we were to follow in the days and weeks to come.

A bare 17 minutes after the explosion — at 11:55 A.M. — I was on live, national television articulating the message the president had laid out. "I just want to come in for a second and relay to you that the president is deeply concerned and shocked at what he has just seen replayed on television concerning the shuttle launch. We do not have any more information than is being provided to the public at this time." Then I added: The accident "will not affect the United States' determination to continue the exploration of space...."

By immediately stepping forward, we had taken the first steps to reassure the nation. I had echoed the words the president had spoken to me moments before, and this became the single, unifying message that was to drive our crisis communications.

Speaking With One Voice While I had spoken to the press, we knew it was important that Reagan speak directly to the American people. We asked for television time to make an Oval Office address to the nation. As the networks swung into motion, it was evident that a series of actions must be taken.

First, our press office established contact with NASA public relations staff. We initiated an important part of a crisis communications plan that had been worked out two years before in the confusion that followed the American invasion of the Caribbean island of Grenada. Then, we had been hampered by a lack of accurate information as a clamoring press and an anxious nation waited.

We decided that in the future whenever crisis struck, we would dispatch a staff member from the White House to the government agency, and the agency, in turn, would provide us with a person from its staff. NASA did just that, and Mark Hess, a veteran space program public relations official with nine years' experience at Cape Canaveral, arrived to join my staff, providing his expertise until the crisis ended.

This decision provided a near-fail-safe system of information exchange between NASA and the White House. It provided one other key element of crisis communications — that we speak with one voice.

Another decision the president faced was the State of the Union Address — should he proceed with his speech? Usually, in times of crisis, a president is counseled to keep to his planned schedule because a disruption would add to the feeling of uncertainty.

But this was different. As communicators we knew it would not work to give a speech that dealt with the nitty gritty issues of governing, while pausing only momentarily to acknowledge the sacrifice of the *Challenger* crew and its effect on the nation. The president's decision was made on simpler terms. In his heart, he knew it was not the right thing to do.

At 1:55 P.M., I was back before cameras in the White House briefing room, ready to announce a series of presidential actions. Reagan had conferred with congressional leaders and would cancel his State of the Union Address that evening, rescheduling it for the following week.

The Need for Direct Communication

After meeting with Vice-President Bush and NASA's new Acting Director William Graham, he directed them to fly immediately to Cape Canaveral. They went directly from the Oval Office to Andrews Air Force Base. The assignment: "Begin the effort to find out the cause of this tragedy" and to return with a firsthand report.

Again, I hammered home the theme of the public message: "The vice-president will carry with him the president's personal concern for those courageous Americans who were aboard the space shuttle. We could do no more to honor them than to go forward with this program."

Meanwhile, throughout the White House, the job of crisis communications moved forward. Speechwriter Peggy Noonan was asked to draft the president's remarks. Camera crews invaded the Oval Office, rearranging furniture, draping a cover over the rug, carefully placing lights, cameras, and Teleprompters.

Promptly at 5:00 P.M., the president sat down behind his desk and delivered the most eloquent speech of his presidency. As Reagan looked into the camera, he looked into the living rooms of a grieving nation. His words flowed evenly, smoothly. It was a simple message, delivered with extraordinary grace, strength, and compassion.

Speaking Directly to the People

"Today is a day for mourning and remembering," the president began. "Nancy and I are pained to the core by the tragedy of the shuttle *Challenger*. We know that we share this pain with all of the people of our country. This is truly a national loss."

The president talked of the courage of the seven heroes who died in the explosion, expressing sympathy to their families. He had a special message for the nation's school children, many of whom watched the launch on television. "I know it's hard to understand that painful things like this sometimes happen."

And through it all, the president articulated the message of continuity he had first spoken to us moments after the tragedy. "The future doesn't belong to the faint-hearted. It belongs to the brave. We will continue our quest in space."

Then, with emotion, he quoted from the poem written nearly a half-century before by a World War II airman. The astronauts, he said, had "slipped the surly bonds of earth ... to touch the face of God."

Hours before, as he first heard of the *Challenger* tragedy, the president had been the average American citizen. He had the same emotions — shock, concern, sympathy, determination. And, like most Americans, he was watching it on television. Now he had spoken. He was the national leader. He articulated the same concerns. And he promised our space program would go forward.

To the cynical, it might seem that the White House handlers had stage-managed a crisis. That we had transformed Reagan from citizen to leader in a matter of hours. That we played on tragedy, manipulating a grieving nation. We had, however, done what communicators do. We conveyed the president's words and actions to the public quickly, accurately, and completely. This was crisis communications.

Answering the Public's Questions

But the communications plan could not end there. As the national mourning continued, the public began to seek answers to the tragedy. The president moved quickly to determine the cause of the accident. As each decision was made, it was our job to promptly and visibly communicate these steps to the public.

The next morning, Vice-President Bush, back from his whirlwind trip to the Cape, was the first appointment on the president's schedule. Bush reported his findings and described the somber mood of the people at NASA.

In the morning press briefing, I announced an interim Board of Inquiry, a group of NASA experts that would make an immediate, initial investigation into the cause of the accident.

Two days later, the president flew aboard *Air Force One* to the Johnson Space Center in Houston. There he met quietly with families of the astronauts and then led a memorial service. As a military band played hymns, he personally went into the audience to console the emotionally wrought families.

Within days, the president appointed a blue-ribbon panel of experts to investigate the cause of the crash. In a public ceremony, 13 prominent experts were assembled to pursue an in-depth investigation of the disaster. The panel was headed by

During memorial services, Nancy Reagan comforts the mother of astronaut Ellison Onizuka, while President Reagan shakes the hand of Steve McAuliffe.

former Secretary of State William Rogers; others included Neil Armstrong, the first astronaut to walk on the moon; Sally Ride, the first woman in space; and Chuck Yeager, the flamboyant test pilot and space-age pioneer.

To keep our lines of communications clear, a member of our White House press staff joined the commission as spokesperson. Assistant Press Secretary Mark Weinberg moved into the commission offices and remained there, keeping in close touch with the White House until the group reported its findings in a matter of weeks.

The Market Is Dropping like a Stone

For me, "Black Monday" began in the warm rays of Arizona sunshine. My flight had just touched down in Tucson where I was to attend the "Merrill Lynch Shoot-Out," a pre-tournament round of golf where the pros compete for low scores and big bucks. It was October 19, 1987, and this was my first junket since I had left the White House to join Merrill Lynch back in February.

Mindful that the stock market had taken a 108-point tumble before closing for the weekend, I asked the driver to flip on the radio. "Here's the news from Wall Street," the announcer said. "The market, following the pattern set at the close last Friday, is down 300 points in heavy trading."

The worst was yet to come. By day's end, the market had spiraled downward 508 points, losing nearly a quarter of its value in a free fall that was far greater than

Black Monday is memorialized in this front page story.

the turbulent days preceding the Depression. And before it was all over, this was to become known as "The Crash of 1987."

Through the 1980s, Manhattan's financial district had been a "boom town." Day after day, the market had climbed to new records in the high octane world where stockbrokers still in their 20s became instant millionaires and brokerage firms rode the bull market to unprecedented profits.

Proper Preparation for the Worst

There seemed to be no end in sight. Yet, mindful of the boom-and-bust cycles of the past, Burson-Marsteller, our public relations firm, and Bozell Jacobs, who handled our advertising, had wisely counselled us to prepare for a day we thought would never come. Earlier in the year, we had taken a few days away from the office to huddle with Harold Burson, the PR pioneer whose expertise we highly valued, and Chuck Peebler, the advertising expert who headed Bozell.

What do we want Merrill Lynch to look like when the economy goes sour and the bull market gives way to the bears of Wall Street? we asked ourselves. Our "war games" led us to craft a comprehensive communications plan that would deal with a scenario of an economic downturn and declining stock market prices.

Little did we know that we would be hurdled headlong into an unprecedented public relations fire storm before year's end. That was exactly what we faced as I arrived at the Vantana Canyon Resort in the Arizona desert.

Charlie Mangano, my advertising director, jerked open the car door as we pulled into the hotel driveway. "The market has gone to hell," Mangano said.

I was quickly on the phone back to New York, where Paul Critchlow, Merrill Lynch's deputy communications chief, said, "It's dropping like a stone."

By morning I was back in New York greeted by headlines that summed up Monday's market in a single word: Crash. Our communications staff assembled for a 7:00 A.M. meeting, and we quickly hammered out a crisis communications plan. My instinct was to bring into play many of the same tactics I had used during my years in politics.

"Communications in its simplest form is getting the message from you to your audience," I had often said. "The difficulty is to develop the right message, identify the right audience, and take it from Point A to Point B."

Planning and Communicating the Message

As the sun seeped into the canyons on Wall Street on that "morning after," an uneasiness bordering on panic was settling in. Overnight, the free-fall of the New York Stock Exchange had rippled around the globe, with Tokyo, London, Paris, and Brussels reporting chaotic market performances.

The high command of Merrill Lynch had assembled in a 32d-floor conference room that overlooked New York harbor. As senior executives of the nation's largest financial firm braced for what lay ahead, the first order of business was our communications plan.

It included a string of recommendations from advertising to internal communications. The centerpiece called for ditching our advertising campaign and canceling the commercials scheduled to run during the World Series that night. In its place, we recommended placing the firm's Chairman, William A. Schreyer, on television. This would be breaking new ground for Merrill Lynch. Never had the firm had an executive appear in its commercials; the bull had always been our representative.

By midafternoon, Bill Schreyer was in our studio, looking into the lens of a television camera. "I'm here for some straight talk about the stock market," Schreyer began. For the next 22 seconds, he talked about faith in the economy and the need for clear thinking. "Emotions can run high during market turbulence … just when reason should prevail."

He concluded with our key message. "America's economy is the strongest in the world … with great ability to bounce back." Then the punch line: "Merrill Lynch is *still* bullish on America." That was crisis communications in its purest form. No music. No graphics. Straight. Clean. One person speaking directly to the audience.

"Bullish on America" was a variation of Merrill's theme line from the early 1980s, which remained one of the most widely recalled campaigns in advertising history. The market crisis had given us an opportunity to reintroduce it. The tight confines of a 30-second television commercial had forced us to boil our message down to its simplest form: confidence.

**Hammering Down
the Message**
We debuted the new commercials on the World Series Thursday night, and, as the seesaw battle between the Cardinals and the Twins extended the championship to seven games, we bought more time and stayed on the air.

On Wednesday, we had expanded our advertising into print, buying full pages in the *Wall Street Journal* and ten other major market newspapers. The headline: "After October 19: A Perspective." In this ad, we enlarged on our central message, providing a more detailed analysis of the market downturn and a look toward the future. The ad copy ended with a clear statement of our philosophy. "We urge you to take a long-term view…. We see ahead a fundamentally sound economy." There it was again: confidence.

On Friday, we ran another full-page ad in major market newspapers. The headline looked forward: "Now, What About Next Week?" The ad also announced that Merrill's 450 offices around the world would extend their hours and brokers would be available for consultations with customers over the weekend.

While Schreyer was taping his television commercials on Tuesday, our media team was busy setting up interviews for the chairman. On Thursday, he appeared live from the floor of the New York Stock Exchange talking with Peter Jennings on ABC's "Evening News." Over the weekend, Schreyer and other Merrill Lynch officials appeared on many major news programs, including "Wall Street Week" and "NBC Nightly News."

At midweek, we had issued a series of press releases that provided an in-depth analysis of current market activity and recommended an investment strategy. A press kit had been mailed to writers in the 100 largest cities across the country.

We knew our employees were a key audience. I'd always said, "We've got 50,000 employees around the world. If we keep them informed, we've got 50,000 public relations spokespeople to carry our message."

Keeping Employees Involved and Informed

We kept Merrill's "B Wire," the electronic link with our brokers, and the "squawk box," an audio link with every office, humming with the company's message. It carried senior management's words to the troops, voicing our confidence in the long-term stability of the company and the economy. It also kept our employee team alert to our advertising strategy and the appearances of our spokespeople on television.

We had another medium to speak directly to employees — our own television network. Back in the 1970s, Merrill had pioneered the use of direct television broadcasts for business communications. We now had a sophisticated television studio and production unit that was linked by satellite to every office.

The television commercials that ran during the World Series had been produced there, and we were broadcasting daily live programming throughout the network. The company's president, Dan Tully, and senior research analysts had been on the air every day since Tuesday with our message of confidence.

By week's end, posters were up in the lobbies of our home office facilities, saying "Thanks — for a job well done in the toughest of times." A personal letter from the chairman was in the mail. We published a special issue of our employee magazine, *We the People*, highlighting the work of Merrill employees during the crisis week. And to top it off, Schreyer decreed that an extra day would be added to the vacation schedules of all employees.

As the crisis faded and Wall Street slowly dug out from the debris of Black Monday, the Wall Street we faced was quite different from the one that had set the records of the 1980s. And our task of communicating was just as different.

Continuing Communication After the Crisis

Our "Straight Talk" commercials were expanded to include our own employees talking about market conditions. The format was the same — one person talking directly to the audience. But the message of confidence was reinforced with specifics on market opportunities.

Three months later, we launched our new television ad campaign to the vast audience watching the 1988 Winter Olympics at Calgary. Coupled with a print campaign, it stressed the company's long tradition of leadership, trust, and stability. The line "... bullish on America" was once again retired and replaced with "Merrill Lynch ... a tradition of trust." The company today still uses it in all its advertising.

Schreyer, now a confident television performer, continued his appearances on television business shows, and company spokespeople kept a busy schedule of print interviews.

We were able to measure our success. A computer search showed that Merrill Lynch was mentioned over 500 times in print articles during the month following the crash. And our advertising campaign was praised in *Advertising Age* and *Forbes*. More important, it paid off at the bottom line. Merrill Lynch opened new accounts at a rate 40 percent higher than normal and increased our market share by 1.5 percent.

Two Crises: What Could Have Been, but What Was

The *Challenger* explosion and the Crash of 1987 threatened two venerable institutions — one, a highly visible government agency; the other, a pillar of the business world. When crisis occurred, both NASA and Wall Street faced the distinct possibility that their reputations would be permanently damaged.

They faced the hot light of public attention as the lightning struck their well-ordered world. They were confronted by the withering fire of press asking questions to which they had no answers. They were forced to improvise, create, and tap dance through an unexplored mine field of public relations problems.

Had they failed to successfully navigate the treacherous waters of crisis, it could have meant the end of these institutions. Yet, they not only survived, but out of disaster became stronger, more secure institutions.

The reasons for this are complex, yet simple. NASA and Wall Street communicated, and they did so effectively. They trusted the people with the truth and, in time, the people trusted them. When you lay them side by side, the similarities between the crisis communications efforts of Wall Street and NASA are striking. This fact underscores that communicating in crisis is the same — whether on Wall Street or at 1600 Pennsylvania Avenue.

Aftermath: Crisis Communication Principles

Looking back, I can sum up key principles of crisis communications:

Tell as much as you can as quickly as you can. Speed is critical. When crisis occurs, a momentary vacuum develops. Step in immediately with the facts — or rumors and inaccuracies take over and never can be fully corrected. When you don't know, say so. The public will understand if you can't immediately get the facts.

In the *Challenger* tragedy, within minutes, I was in the press briefing room live on national television. Four hours later, President Reagan spoke directly to the American people. And in the Crash of 1987, we moved immediately with a press release statement, and then, like Reagan, Merrill Lynch Chairman William Schreyer turned to television to convey his message. In both cases, we told the public what we knew and what we didn't know. And we followed this practice until the crisis ended.

Simplify your message. The first step in communications — development of the message — takes on added importance in crisis. Boil the message down to its simplest form, identify the audience, and take it to them.

When President Reagan said, "Tell the press we will fix the space program and keep it going," he articulated a message of concern, courage, and continuity. On Wall Street, as we developed the content of the "Straight Talk" commercials for television, our theme was summed up in a word: confidence. In both crises, we quickly decided what the message would be, and that's what we stuck with from start to finish.

Speak with the single voice. Mistakes will occur. The pressure cooker of crisis multiplies the chance of a slip. Missteps are magnified because they occur under the glare of national attention. By designating one spokesperson, a single channel to communicate with the public, chances of a serious mistake are greatly reduced.

Every word during the *Challenger* incident was spoken from the White House. NASA shared its information, but let the White House do the talking. And in the Wall Street crisis, we kept to a minimum the company officials who were authorized to speak, and we carefully selected the opportunities for public statements.

There is no substitute for honesty. Level with the people. Shoot straight. Fudging the facts spells trouble in the end. Credibility is your only currency. Spend it wisely. Wall Street, NASA, anywhere — this is the golden rule.

Larry M. Speakes is vice-president, communications, Northern Telecom Ltd. Prior to joining Northern Telecom in 1991, Mr. Speakes was a public relations consultant in Washington, D.C., and lecturer on politics and the press for academic and business audiences throughout the United States. He served as Senior vice-president, communications, for Merrill Lynch & Co., New York, from February 1987 to April 1988. There, he directed the company's communications and advertising program, including its response to the stock market Crash of 1987, which won the Silver Anvil Award presented by the Public Relations Society of America. He was chief spokesperson for the president of the United States, Ronald Reagan, from 1981 to 1987. Previously he had served in the White House under President Gerald R. Ford and President Richard M. Nixon. He is author of the best-selling autobiography, Speaking Out.

Planning

for Crisis

Douglas G. Hearle
Former Vice-Chairman, Hill and Knowlton

You must know what the real crisis is or you cannot deal with it. By extension, **Overview**
you must know what *potential crises* you are vulnerable to or you cannot prepare
for them. Let there be no mistake — you can prepare for a crisis.

In business, a crisis is a situation that, left unaddressed, will jeopardize the organization's ability to do business normally. The term is used frequently to describe
everything from a nagging problem to a busy day. Let's examine what a crisis
really is, who's involved with a crisis from the start, and who — on the outside —
gets involved afterward.

Crises usually evolve. The earlier they are caught during their evolution, the bet- **Recognizing Signals**
ter the chance to resolve them. Unfortunately, unless you are *looking for signals*
you might not see the crisis evolving until it is affecting your business. Often, signals are generic. Something happens outside the company and by interpolation a
signal might be discerned.

Medical science determined that high levels of cholesterol were bad for people.
That was clearly a signal to the egg industry that it was in for trouble. But it was
also a signal to manufacturers of egg cartons; to distributors of chicken feed; to
manufacturers of electronic components of incubator heaters. The cholesterol
finding was a signal to all those industries and others — it eventually caused a
shift in their markets and affected the way in which they did normal business —
but the news wasn't seen as such a threat to any of them at the time with the
exception of the egg producers.

The first step toward preparing for a crisis is the mind-set. You must begin to look for signals. You must begin to think in terms of what if? In most cases, attempts to manage a crisis begin after the situation has already set in and damage is being done to the organization.

The key word is *normal*. Businesses do best when they are running in the normal mode. Anything abnormal results in decisions that managers are not used to making. When business managers attempt to limit damage and still run the business while resolving the crisis at hand, they are operating abnormally. Trying to do all of those jobs guarantees that none of them gets done correctly. Decisions affecting the operation of the business start to get confused with decisions concerning damage control. Damage control gets confused with crisis resolution. Normalcy, the most comfortable environment, vaporizes and is replaced with chaos.

The Crisis Team A good first step in crisis preparedness is to assemble, on paper, a team that will be in charge of handling a crisis — whatever that crisis may be — while the organization continues to be managed normally by others. The team needs to be small, capable of moving fast, and able to make decisions. It has to have clout within the organization.

Since crises come in different forms, the crisis team needs to have members who are different from one another. The plan should provide for a core group — common to any crisis — and others who are strong in the area of specific forms of crisis. The core group may include the CEO or the CFO, the senior communications officer, and the general counsel or chief lawyer.

Since we're talking about a genuine crisis threatening the normalcy of the company, ego-rubbing should not be involved. The fact is that some CEOs are wonderful in a crisis and others are not. Some chief executives simply do not belong on a crisis team. They would make a far greater contribution doing what they do best — running the company.

There's another good reason for leaving the CEO off the team. The crisis team must drop everything, instantly, and deal only with the crisis. That may not be practical for the CEO. The company, now more than ever, needs to continue to do business as usual. Everyone except the crisis team should be dedicated to that and the CEO is often the one individual who can keep normalcy in focus.

Just as the crisis team deals only with the crisis, the rest of the organization stays out of the crisis and keeps running normally.

The next step is to consider the resources available. Depending on the nature of each potential crisis, what people would be most knowledgeable and helpful? List them. They will be your key players when the crisis hits the fan. This can be done by generically identifying potential crisis types. Usually a business crisis falls into one of these categories:

- Financial (profit failure, investment failure, takeover)

- Reputation (failed product, corruption, mismanagement)

- Outside Forces (boycott, labor problems, consumer shifts, regulatory or legislative action)

Now you match your worst-case scenarios with your resource list and have some idea of who will wrestle with what.

If you're really savvy, you should contact the names on your resource list and ask each person to identify at least two other people in whom he or she has confidence. That action alone will treble the number of arrows you'll have in your quiver. Remember, in every company there are two organizations — the formal and the informal. The formal organization is what you see on the Organization Chart. The informal organization is that group of people who really make things happen. The plant superintendent is the fellow whose name appears on the chart but he knows that Joe, the foreman in the boiler room, knows every pipe and valve in the plant and what pressures they are capable of handling. Joe is not on the chart but he's a key person in the informal organization. Joe should be on the resource list.

The Spokesperson

If ever anything demanded early, complete, and continual communication, it is a crisis. And an organization in crisis must speak in a single voice. So a spokesperson needs to be selected, trained for the job, and be kept thoroughly informed. A spokesperson for one type of crisis isn't necessarily the right one for another type, so several should be on the resource list. If the crisis turns out to be a legal one, a lawyer — probably the general counsel — should speak for the company. Who else is better qualified? If it's a health issue, a doctor should handle the role. A financial crisis requires the chief financial officer.

If the crisis is of sufficient magnitude, the CEO may be the only credible person to handle the job. Union Carbide's Bhopal, Dow's Agent Orange, and Johnson & Johnson's Tylenol crises required up-front roles by Messrs. Anderson, Orefice, and Burke. The magnitude of each crisis demanded that no lesser spokesperson would be acceptable. Exxon's Chairman Lawrence Rawl chose not to speak for the company in the *Exxon Valdez* spillage and some feel that decision prolonged and intensified the crisis enormously.

Tylenol capsules were removed from shelves following deaths caused by tamperings.

Media Preparation

Finally, in the general preparation stage, the logistics can be and must be planned for in advance. Key to this is the communications function and the vehicle is the media. Too often this crucial aspect is assumed. The media are considered that "necessary evil" that must be informed in some sort of controlled way. I'm certain that crisis plans filed away in hundreds of desks and cabinets carry the statement: "The media will be notified." This approach will be addressed further on, but at this point it's enough to say that such a provision isn't enough.

> *Every newspaper in your plan should be identified; every TV station should be identified; every wire service; every radio station. They should be identified along with every address. Every contact at each should be identified and updated every three months. Every telephone number should be listed. Every night number. Every home number. Every fax number.*

Every resource you have identified should have a telephone number alongside his or her name along with a home number, a weekend number, a mobile phone number if the contact has one, and a close relative's phone number. You're going to need resources and you didn't go to the trouble of identifying them in advance only to spend precious time trying to figure out how to contact them while the barn is burning. Obviously, the same goes for the authorities: the police, the fire department, the SEC, the EPA, the FDA, OSHA, and others.

So far, so good. You now have a basic crisis team. You have your resources lined up. You've identified appropriate "single voices" for the broad categories your worst-case scenarios dreamed up. You have stitched together as many logistics as you could conjure — and you still haven't got a crisis. How lucky can you get?

Looking for Trouble

What's next?

Now, you go hunting and your organization is your happy hunting ground. You go looking for trouble. You figure out from where inside your company your crises might come.

In preparing for his book, *Crisis Management*, author Steven Fink undertook a survey of Fortune 500 chief executives and came up with some fascinating results. The companies involved in Fink's survey all responded that they were at least somewhat vulnerable to the following types of crisis:

- Industrial accidents

- Environmental problems

- Union problems/strikes

- Product recalls

- Investor relations

- Hostile takeovers

- Proxy fights

- Rumors/media leaks

- Government regulatory problems

- Acts of terrorism

- Embezzlement

It's interesting to note that all of these real vulnerabilities as identified by real CEOs fall into the three broad "potential crisis" categories identified earlier: financial, reputation, and outside forces.

As you prepare to go hunting through your organization, you should prepare a list of questions designed to probe for the tender spots in the company. If it's a small organization or a highly centralized one, a series of interviews with senior management is required, followed by a series with middle management. Every department head should be involved and you'll find that vulnerabilities surface in direct relationship with the point of view of the department involved.

If the company is decentralized, each unit, subsidiary or division management should be interviewed. Plant superintendents should be included from their particular perspectives.

The purpose of these interviews is sixfold:

> • To set priorities with regard to preparedness. In effect, the data you gather will establish the company's Vulnerability Index. Worst-case scenarios that pop up more frequently in the interviews should get higher priority in preparing than those which only surface occasionally.
>
> • To determine the relative level of crisis preparedness that currently exists (both perceived and in fact).
>
> • To review management decision-making policies and procedures for issues that could either help or hinder crisis preparedness.
>
> • To assess communications systems within the company and particularly among units of the organization.
>
> • To review and critique past crises that may have occurred in the company's history.
>
> • To identify the most useful information for use in the plan.

In constructing a questionnaire to guide the interview process, you might consider these questions, taken from an actual interview format conducted for a Fortune 500 global pharmaceutical company:

1. What are the worst things you can imagine happening to the company? Why?

2. What are the *most likely* crises that could occur at the company in each of the following areas:

   a. Prescription and over-the-counter products?

b. Plants and equipment?

c. Financial?

d. Employee relations?

e. Management?

f. Government and regulatory affairs?

g. Protests/espionage/terrorism?

3. If a crisis were to occur today, what are the procedures, as you understand them, to deal with:

a. Authorities/emergency services/disaster relief?

b. Government officials?

c. Regulatory agencies?

d. The media?

e. The community surrounding a facility of the company?

f. The medical community/other customers?

g. Consumers?

h. Employees?

4. Is the company (the managers) prepared to respond to each of these constituencies?

5. What are the company's policies (written or stated) for dealing with these constituencies in a crisis?

6. What is the biggest crisis you have personally dealt with in the last few years?

a. How did you first learn of the crisis?

b. What actions did you take?

c. Was a crisis team established?

d. Who handled the media, employees, etc.?

e. How did customers and other audiences respond?

f. How would you rate the company's response?

g. Have any changes been made in procedures as a result?

7. In that crisis, did you refer to a crisis management manual, if one existed? If so:

a. For what information?

b. Was it there?

c. Was the manual useful overall?

d. How could the manual have been easier to use?

8. If you did not refer to the manual, why not?

9. If a serious crisis were to occur today, who are the five people within the company who are best equipped to handle it? Why?

10. What industry issues or trends most concern you?

These interview guidelines resulted in a wealth of data. In shorthand, the company involved was able to construct a Vulnerability Index that established priorities on such potential crises as:

- Product recall

- Health and safety issues

- Unplanned chemical release

- Product tampering

The study also uncovered the fact that while a crisis manual existed, it was filed away, outdated, unwieldy to use, and was of virtually no use in a real crisis situation. It had been constructed several years earlier, had never been updated, consisted of page after page of ponderous policies written in "legalese," and required burdensome layers of approval for any decisions or actions taken. As a result of the study, the company now has crisis procedures in its computer data banks and a current, simplified, categorized plan can be accessed with a touch of a button.

Prepare for Media Attention It would be nice if a company — if it had to have a crisis — could have it quietly. It would be nice if you could privately go in and out of a crisis without your customers knowing about it. It would be nice if your stockholders were unaware; if your competition had no idea; if your employees were totally ignorant of your plight; if the investment community went on investing in your organization in spite of your problem because they hadn't heard about it.

In fact, that kind of a crisis wouldn't even qualify as a crisis. In the real world a crisis is a *public happening* and it's public because of the media. News organizations thrive on bad news. If you are a source of bad news, you can be sure you'll get media attention in direct proportion to the degree of badness involved.

So dealing with the media is a critical component in crisis preparedness. Public communication through the media is the most compelling tool you have. In a very real sense the media can kill or cure you.

The time to work with the media is when things are running normally. What you need more than anything, going into a crisis situation, are high credibility, a good reputation, and an abundance of good will. None of these attributes can be generated during a crisis. They need to exist in advance.

Recently, I was called into a situation in which a company's very existence was threatened because of the activities of its principal owner. The company had taken on some of the personality of the man, who tended to be a loner, self-sufficient, successful, and very, very private. Reflecting this, the company had never made any effort to establish a sound and positive relationship with the news media. No access had ever been provided, no interviews ever suggested, and none ever granted. When the crisis hit, the relationship between the company and the media was instantly adversarial. Why not? There was nothing to build on, no good will to draw on, absolutely no linkage. What now existed was a company with *bad news* and a media feeding frenzy ensued.

As in the case of the study undertaken by the pharmaceutical company, any crisis preparedness plan should include an evaluation of media relationships and if they are not sound, steps need to be taken immediately to establish them. Then, as you seek out the potential crises suggested by your Vulnerability Index, you should ask yourself this question next to each: What do we need to be prepared to talk about?

If your potential crisis relates to an industrial accident, for example, you should be prepared to talk about industrial safety. You, therefore, need to have data available that cites your organization's safety record, the success of your OSHA inspections, etc. This should be updated every three months.

Your job as a communicator, as always, is to make the job of the news media easier. Your ability to begin communicating early with data and information supports your interest in keeping them, if not warm and friendly, at least objective and not openly hostile.

Think the way reporters think. They love bad news. Their questions reflect that. Anticipate the kinds of questions they would ask and prepare background materials that you can provide early in the crisis. What you are trying to achieve is a comfort level for yourself as the situation develops. If the news media with which you must deal comes at you like an enemy force, you're not going to be very comfortable. If, on the other hand, a few preparations can provide you with a reasonable comfort level, by all means, make them. Keep in mind that you must not overlook the fact that if you do not provide information — especially during the first twelve hours of the crisis — someone else will. That's not in your best interest. If you are providing information, your odds are better that the story will be balanced. Your participation in the process dramatically improves the chances of correcting false information.

And remember, "No comment" is always translated into two messages:

1. "We're guilty as charged."

2. "Screw you."

Douglas G. Hearle, one of the leading professionals in the public relations industry, is the former president and chief executive officer of Carl Byoir & Associates, Inc. He's acted as a key strategist in such well-known cases as the government attempt to ban saccharin and the dioxin/Agent Orange issue, as well as several product boycott campaigns and labor/management actions. He directed programs involving the communication aspects of product liability litigation and product recall. Hearle counseled the plastics industry for years, dealing with such issues as combustibility, waste disposal, and product safety.

From 1966 to 1986, he was with Hill and Knowlton, where he headed the Marketing Division, the American International Division, and was director of human resources worldwide. Hearle left Hill and Knowlton in 1986 and founded Douglas G. Hearle & Associates, specializing in litigation public relations and other crisis work. The business of DGH&A was acquired by Hill and Knowlton in January 1989, at which time Hearle rejoined Hill and Knowlton as vice-chairman.

APPENDIX

The Ultimate
Crisis Plan

Clarke L. Caywood
Professor of Business Communications, Northwestern University

Kurt P. Stocker
Chief Corporate Relations Officer, Continental Bank Corporation

It is nearly impossible to consider a contemporary business or organizational leader not expecting that someone in the firm had given time and energy to thinking about the effects of the 1993 family leave act, the actions of a competitor, or any number of management problems including: **Overview**

- a valued customer facing financial ruin.

- a price drop occurring overnight in valuable raw materials.

- insurance in the event of a serious accident or death of a business partner.

- a new product that is not accepted by the market due to a pricing blunder.

- a top sales manager leaving to join a competitor.

Each of these events are logically anticipated in most businesses through a process of planning, government affairs, financial planning, risk management, marketing, and human resource management. Each activity is managed with careful planning, execution, and control by the managers with responsibilities in those areas. None of the events would usually be labeled a crisis, but may be considered a serious management problem that can be rectified with careful planning.

As an example, the valued customer can be replaced if dependency was not too great or a joint financial venture to carry the customer through difficulty may be profitable to both firms. A line of credit, if arranged in advance, can be used to purchase the materials. A carefully planned executive insurance program would help an ownership transition. Marketing research and well-developed relationships with vendors would permit a rapid price change or repositioning of the product. Finally, a well-oiled human resources program would have the next sales manager quickly identified or have established headhunters on the job.

What is Crisis Management? We define a management crisis as an immediately unexpected event or action that threatens the lives of stakeholders and the ability of the organization to survive. While many forms of crises (an airplane crash, for example) can be statistically expected, its immediate happening is not, and constitutes a crisis. Loss of life or threat to life should certainly be considered a crisis when the lives of employees, customers, members of the community, and others who have a relationship with the organization and stake in its actions are threatened. Events that threaten the survival of a firm include product failures and plant explosions. Some events, such as weather storms or volcano eruptions, are uncontrollable, but other crises are deliberate, accidental, and irrational acts of those involved with the organization. As managers and students of management it is our contention that all crises can be planned for, even if no specific crisis can be precisely predicted or prevented.

Crisis management has a dual meaning. First, it means the management of operations during the actual crisis in the midst of the event — be it fire, evacuation, plant shutdown, or product recall — to the degree that the events can be managed. For example, many aspects of a crisis cannot be fully "managed" when events are out of control of human ability to respond, as in the case of a raging fire, a continuing loss of life from chemicals, or an airplane that "falls from the sky."

However, crisis management can also mean the management of the corporation before, during, and after the crisis. The existence of a crisis plan and system can be managed. The creation of a crisis room with communications equipment, phone numbers, emergency supplies, and a well-trained crisis team can be managed. The corporation's first statement to the victims, their families, and the public can be managed. And, among other actions, the organization's actions toward those affected by the crisis can be managed.

This dual management concept recognizes the importance of a well-structured operations program to be executed in the midst of a crisis in order to reduce the effects of the crisis and the importance of planning all aspects of a corporate response to a crisis. Crises must, then, be managed from the outside-in and the inside-out by a modern management team.

Crisis management can include the management by the organization of the perception of a crisis. While an operations plan might not anticipate a "perceived" crisis (for example, reputed glass in Gerber baby food), a fully developed crisis plan would include the corporate response to rumors, false or misleading media information, or misunderstood information. A fully developed crisis plan would manage the corporation's response immediately so that the perceived crisis does not threaten the survival of a firm. Crisis management is not a mechanistic action of rules, procedures and physical action by a firm. It consists of a full range of thoughtful processes and steps that anticipate the complex nature of crisis real and perceived.

A professional manager would not normally leave these events to chance because they all come under the areas of responsibility of management functions in accounting, finance, risk, marketing, and human resources. Also, the definition of management includes the "planning, implementation, and control" of activities and events in these areas of responsibilities. Although there is no management of an area of business activity that may occur less frequently, when it does, it occurs with sometimes fatal and disastrous results. The *management* of a crisis, when it occurs, is just as much a part of modern management as the more traditional functions noted above.

The key to management of any areas of importance to a firm is the deliberate effort to plan, execute, and then evaluate the events and activities connected with the function. In the case of crisis management, we can expect an organization to have given prior thought to developing a plan with a team of mangers expected to carry out the plan and then to evaluate their performance during the crisis. Even if this particular management activity only occurs once a year, once every three years, or once in a company's lifetime, the existence and the execution of the crisis plan can be just as important, or more so, to the survival of the organization as the marketing, financial, production, or human resources plans and management.

Here we offer a suggested approach to crisis planning. This plan was developed by the faculty and students of a new crisis management class taught during fall 1992 at Northwestern University in Evanston, Illinois. The director of the graduate program in Corporate Public Relations (CPR) polled his students to test their interest in a number of course subjects that could be offered to them during their last quarter in the five quarter graduate program. The students expressed a near unanimous interest in a course on crisis management that they would complete after

An Approach to Crisis Planning

their summer professional residencies with many of America's top corporations in corporate communications, public relations, and marketing public relations.

In the tradition of the CPR program and the Medill School of Journalism, the course was co-taught by a senior expert in the field, Kurt Stocker, and a full-time faculty member with a Ph.D. and professional experience, Clarke Caywood. The 13 graduate students brought up to seven years of business and organizational experience to the class, including graduate consulting experience and knowledge of investor relations, marketing public relations, research, employee communications, media relations, and a range of core management subjects from accounting to marketing and management. Their approach to crisis planning and analysis was built on a foundation of knowledge and experience in corporate communications, but they were qualified to sit at the management table to analyze the crisis from financial, human resource, marketing, and broad business dimensions.

From the simulation of 13 crisis cases, from a general reading on crisis planning, and from their knowledge of business and communications, the students and faculty conceived and built what was called for motivation and encouragement the "ultimate crisis management plan." Having planned and completed the course, we recognize that the plan will be reexamined each year for its weaknesses and strengths. The plan is presented here to at least provide the basis of a framework for managers to use as they develop a plan useful to them. As with most management thinking, it is tempered with experience and judgment. The objective of the plan is to stimulate managers in organizations to begin the management process as it is applied to one of their most important functions — the management of crisis.

The "Ultimate Crisis Plan" The following outline and brief discussions frame the basis of the "ultimate crisis plan." The title obviously begs for indulgence of our "puffery." The authors, including the students in the seminar, merely want to bring as quickly and vividly as possible the importance of crisis planning to the attention of managers . We recognize that this is not yet the ultimate plan — but we start with the assumption that managers can take our ingredients and create their own plan that may be closer to the ultimate plan in their own organization. At the end of this chapter we ask for the reader's contribution to some day making this truly the "ultimate crisis plan."

I. Mission/Approach

A. Company's Mission Statement

A brief version of the company's mission statement will provide a solid framework from which to construct the crisis plan. By restating the company's main goals and objectives here, employees will better understand how the substance of the plan is in keeping with these goals and why the plan is a necessity for the company.

B. Company's Philosophy/Behavior Standards

This section reveals the unwritten insights about additional company philosophies and accepted codes of conduct. This is also the corporate conscience section — the place to mention a company's devotion to recycling efforts or its declaration to never compare itself to a particular competitor in public. By including this information up front, employees will be able to view the plan in the context of these unwritten, generally accepted insights that form the basis for the corporate culture of the organization.

C. Key Overriding Messages (not crisis-related)

The company's most important messages — to all its stakeholders — are explained here. This is the section in which the company broadcasts its commitment to "value the thoughts and opinion of our diversified body of shareholders and employees above all else," for example. The company should use this space to its maximum advantage — to explain why it is a "more caring company" with the best interests of its publics always at heart.

D. Objectives

1. Hierarchy of what's important

This section will outline what the crisis plan hopes to achieve and prevent. When faced with a crisis situation, some things take precedence over others and must be given higher priority; these items are identified here so as to prevent any potential confusion over what should be attended to first.

2. What/who are we protecting?

Again, this section allows the company to give priority to certain items — tangible or not — that the plan is aiming to protect. Whether it is the company's good name, its customers's safety, its suppliers's interests, its product's quality, its chairman's life, or its shareholders's return on investment (ROI), the company's top several protection priorities should be identified to prevent any misunderstandings. If there is one place to *spell it all out*, it's right here.

E. Performance Standards & Benchmarks

In this section, the explanation covers the benchmarks against which employees's performance during a crisis will be measured. This part will identify whether employees will be compared to each other, to employees of other companies who faced similar crises, or to their own personal potential for handling crisis situations. After reading this portion of the plan, employees will have a clear picture of how they and their colleagues will be judged by management.

F. Rationale for This Plan

1. Need for crisis team

The crisis team's mission will be outlined so that all employees will be familiar with the team's important function in managing a crisis. The members of the team will be identified later, so this section merely defends the team's existence.

2. Need for walk-through and evaluation

Since some employees might regard a walk-through simulation of a crisis and the subsequent evaluation of that activity as futile or a waste of time, this section will explain why both segments are vital to crisis training and why they appear in the plan.

3. Brief list of past crises

Without providing a full history of past crises, this section will briefly mention a few key crises to inform employees of the ease and frequency with which crises can occur. If employees have been skeptical about the likelihood of a crisis affecting their company, this section will eliminate those doubts.

II. History of Crises and Potential Crises

A. History of Crises

An important first step in the crisis planning is reviewing and critiquing past crises that occurred in the company's history. Describing the past crises confirms the need for the crisis plan. This account also provides perspective by showing the effect of the crises had on the firm. In addition, depicting how competitors and companies in related industries have handled crises gives insight into how to prepare for and manage potential crises.

B. Potential Crises

Another crucial element of crisis planning is identifying areas in which the company is vulnerable to a crisis. Once management identifies these areas, they can either work to correct the issues or prepare to manage when the inevitable crisis occurs. If caught in time, some potential crises can be averted by a proactive company. This list of potential crises should be categorized by preventable/non-preventable and internal/external. An inventory of a company's vulnerabilities serves two purposes. First, it identifies potential trouble spots and affected audiences, and second, it provides the information needed to build a comprehensive system to manage crisis communications internally and externally.

C. Survey Results

The company should conduct an audit of corporate vulnerabilities to determine where crises might erupt and the kind of response systems that currently exist. The audit can consist of a series of interviews with senior management and a questionnaire of middle managers. The questions should focus on discovering weak links in the company's structure, products, and policies. The soft-soundings and surveys should include executives from financial, operations, human resources, and other important departments.

The company may consider hiring an outside consultant to perform the audit. Consultants tend to have a more objective view of the situation, which helps them detect the company's weaknesses more easily. The issues manger should be able to help identify impending legislation or communication action to which the company may be vulnerable. If the company does not have an issues manager, there would be some kind of process to keep track of changes outside the company.

D. Definition of Crisis and Different Levels of Reaction

The crisis team should agree on a definition of a crisis. Characterizing a crisis will assist in differentiating a serious crisis from a headache. The crisis audit will help the team prioritize potential crises. It is a good idea to rank the crises according to types, vulnerability, priority, and reaction intensity. Ranking crisis according to their probability and potential impact reveals which issues need immediate action and the most preparation. It is helpful to use past events to forecast future events and make an estimate of probability of occurrence.

E. Crisis Stages

Since crises usually evolve, it is important to identify them early in their evolution so management will have a better chance of resolving them. Crises usually follow a similar pattern of development and take time to surface. Therefore, early warning signals of impending crises should be identified so employees can be trained to look for and report such signals.

The stages include:

1. Pre-crisis: Warning signs/acknowledgement/resolve
2. Crisis: Climax/assessment/action
3. Post-Crisis: Rebuilding/recovery/reform

Describing how crises might escalate will provide insight on how to plan for particular crises.

III. First Steps

A. Notify Internal (and some External) Publics That Crisis Exists

1. Notify crisis leaders/team members
2. Inform board of directors, CEO, CFO

B. Crisis Team

1. When to pull team in
   After the crisis leaders have briefly defined the problem, the crisis team should be pulled in.

2. Responsibilities of all members
   a. one gatekeeper is established to oversee all incoming and outgoing materials
   b. all members previously have been informed of their duties and been provided an organizational chart describing their duties

3. Furnishing a crisis room
   a. sufficient electrical outlets
   b. computers with modems that access company files and online system; laser printer
   c. portable computers with modems
   d. fax machine, blast fax, fax cover sheets
   e. pre-programmed telephones with a separate line for each member of the crisis team and voice mail and call interrupt

f. cellular phone with listed numbers and voice mail and call interrupt connections

g. telephone directories for all organizational sites

h. organization chart

i. diagram of a "phone tree" for calling

j. media directories, governmental directories, business and professional directories

k. televisions with cable to receive CNN, C-SPAN, and multiple networks

l. radios including shortwave

m. photocopier

n. VCR and audio tape play back and copying ability

o. risk area maps in hard copy or software

p. body bags in the event of crisis-related deaths

q. legal pads, pens, pencils, paper clips, staplers/staples

r. corporation stationery, envelopes (some pre-labelled with employee or other names)

s. extra stick-on labels for mailing to stakeholders

t. Federal Express or other rapid delivery materials

u. lists (see IV. Audiences)

v. tables and chairs

w. trash receptacles

x. clocks

y. restrooms/shower facilities nearby

z. refreshments

4. Stocking a crisis kit

   a. cash

   b. lists

   c. portable phone

   d. portable computer

   e. still and video cameras

   f. tape recorder and extra tape cassettes

   g. beeper

h. corporate credit card

i. fax machine/blast fax

j. laminated wallet size listing of all phone numbers for crisis team and top management

5. When and how to pull in outside advisors or experts

Experts should be used for third party endorsement (for example, the FDA during the Gerber baby food tampering scare)

6. References to other departments' operational plans

a. descriptions of how other departments function

b. organizational structure of the company

C. Establishing a Media Center

A media briefing room should include:

1. general press kits: background of safety record, fact sheet

2. refreshments

3. telephones

4. podium, microphone, and portable PA system

5. chairs, tables, desks

6. computers, modems, printers

7. photocopiers

D. Collect a Plethora of Information on the Crisis

1. go to the scene of the crisis

2. listen to the radio, TV

3. wire services

4. call police, government, hospitals

IV. Audiences

A. Define & Identify Audiences

1. Comprehensive list of key stakeholders. This differs for each company, but may include:

a. board of directors

b. community and civic leaders

    c. media

    d. customers

    e. shareholders

    f. clients

    g. neighbors

    h. financial partners

    i. government agencies

    j. regulatory agencies

    k. vendors

    l. suppliers

    m. certain competitors

    n. family members

    o. analysts

    p. legal groups

    q. media

    r. subsidiary heads

    s. employees

    t. plant managers

    u. union officials

    v. retirees

    w. pension holders

    x. sales/marketing personnel

    y. agencies

  2. Prioritize list of key stakeholders for contact order under several scenarios

B. Identify Mechanisms to Reach Audiences

  1. Determine appropriate channels of communication for each audience

    a. press releases

    b. letter

    c. personal visits

    d. telephone call

e. general meetings

f. video conference

g. advertising

h. video news release (VNR)

i. internal publications

j. news conferences

k. interoffice memos

l. faxes/blast fax for pre-programmed multiple sending ability

m. telegrams and telexes

n. electronic mail

o. overnight mail

2. Determine who is responsible to reach each audience and through what means

3. Prioritize communication channels, based upon several scenarios

4. Have the facilities and the abilities to use various channels

5. Ensure two-way communication (make sure that audiences have a way to communicate back with you)

6. Establish a mechanism to collect information from audiences

C. Know the Audiences

1. Track stakeholders before the crisis hits — know your friends and those who might criticize you

2. Be sensitive to the needs of each audience

3. Know the key contacts in each stakeholder group and assign a member of the crisis team or organization member to maintain contacts during non-crisis times

D. Know and Follow any Governmental Rules, Regulations and Laws Segmented by type of crisis

V. Media

A. Identify Corporate Media Policy

This section should state the importance of being open, honest, and pro-active with the media in crisis situations. Its purpose is to set the tone for specific procedures that involve the media throughout the crisis plan.

B. Identify Spokespeople

1. Level and type of crisis dictate spokespeople

The spokespeople should be determined based upon the nature and extent of the crisis. For example, it may not be appropriate for the CEO to act as spokesperson for a minor company crisis. Rather, his or her leadership is more needed in higher level crises that warrant high visibility and public scrutiny. Spokespeople should further be determined based upon their expertise in certain areas, their speaking abilities and their ability to think quickly on their feet. A short list of trained and appropriate spokespeople for the different crises should be on hand prior to the crisis. Periodic retraining for print and broadcast interview techniques would be required.

2. Gatekeeper's responsibility to identify them

Since the gatekeeper will act as the main source between the media and the corporation, his or her judgement is most appropriate in identifying the key spokespeople.

C. Gatekeeper's Function

1. Centralize and control the flow of information

Make sure all information is accurate and valid. By managing the information flow, the gatekeeper must ensure the right information reaches the appropriate target in a timely manner.

2. Select the appropriate spokespeople and provide media training as necessary

3. Monitor the flow of all internal and external communication to ensure a consistent message with one voice. The gatekeeper and communications staff should provide the media with the information they need — without information, speculation abounds. Be open with the media; try to serve their needs and let them serve your company's needs.

4. Must always be accessible for good news and bad

D. Media Database

1. Media deadlines

Always accommodate the media as much as possible. The gatekeeper and communication staff should know media deadlines, policies, etc. Following the media's "rules" — especially during a crisis — presents a key opportunity to strengthen your company's relationship with various media contacts.

2. Priority of contact

Time is precious, therefore it should be predetermined which media should be contacted first, as well as which department within that newspaper, magazine, station, or agency should be contacted.

3. Updating database

A company's media contact lists should be updated on a regular basis in order to expedite the contact process during a crisis situation; phone numbers and addresses change periodically, and editors change even faster. The most current media directories should be available and updated.

4. Refer to crisis kit as needed for lists, maps, and other pertinent information

See above for crisis kit information

E. Third Party Sources

The company should continually develop and update a list of people to whom the media can refer for detailed, analytical information during a crisis. These contacts should be credible, reliable, trusted sources who are often quoted in the media (for example, industry experts, financial analysts, scientists). The company should also maintain contact with these people during non-crisis times in order to establish mutually trusting relationships, thereby increasing the chances that they will be balanced in their statements about your company during crisis situations.

F. Rules and Regulations

1. Specific procedures

2. Disclosure rules

In order to prevent liability and ensure accurate and consistent communications, it is essential that the gatekeeper is made solely responsible for information released to the media. The rest of the staff should be made aware of the media disclosure rules and forbidden to release any information, unless otherwise told by the gatekeeper.

G. How to Handle Media Inquiries

A system should be developed to handle the abundance of media inquiries that will come in following a crisis. The system should designate staff to answer the calls and include procedures for response. For example the following questions should be answered when developing the media: How will the calls be recorded? Who will the calls be forwarded to? How will they be prioritized when answered? How will they be answered (i.e. fax or phone)? A short briefing period should be held to go over these procedures before and during the crisis.

H. Establish Fact-Checking Process

A tracking process should be established in order to check the validity and accuracy of the stories being printed and/or broadcast in the media. Ideally, one person will coordinate this effort; however, depending on the magnitude of the crisis, it will probably take a team of people to make the effort worthwhile.

VI. Walk-through

A simulation that requires the crisis team members to use and test elements of the crisis plan and material should be practiced.

VII. Evaluation

When the crisis has been resolved, it is critical that all elements of the plan are analyzed to determine the effectiveness of each in resolving the situation while keeping media portrayals of the company in the best possible light. This evaluation must begin immediately after the crisis has been resolved, although some parts will utilize information gathered during the crisis. The crisis should also be analyzed at the end of the first three months following the completion of the crisis, again at the end of six months, and yet again at the end of one year. Anniversary dates of the crisis (five years, ten years) and similar crises in other firms will often produce more publicity, and evaluation procedures should be carried out at those times.

A. Conduct Interviews/Soft Soundings with External Publics

This is an informal method of determining how people outside of the company viewed the company's actions during the crisis. It requires calling important stakeholders and asking what they thought of how the company reacted and how the reactions can be improved for future situations. Some of the external publics may include vendors, consumer organizations, and even government agencies. It may be useful to conduct face-to-face interviews with these stakeholders to gain further insights based on their physical reactions to questions. This step will not only allow the company to gather important information, but it will also show stakeholders that the company is concerned about keeping them informed during a crisis and that the company values their opinions.

B. Survey Internal Publics

Each crisis team member should take responsibility for evaluating one section of the plan as it pertains to internal publics. For example, one person can find out how well the phone tree worked and if employees were well-informed during the crisis. Another can examine how effective employees were in pulling together information for the media, both proactively and reactively, and whether the media were dealt with in the manner predetermined by the crisis plan. A questionnaire should be developed and distributed that allows employees to voice their opinions of how well the crisis was handled by the crisis team. The survey technique previously utilized in the evaluation of the drill can be expanded and used in the step after an actual crisis has occurred.

C. Survey Media to Determine How Well Informed They Were

The same type of questionnaire used to obtain information from employees can also be used to discover whether or not the appropriate information was getting through to the media during the crisis. Members of the crisis team should contact key members of the media and ask them if they received information they needed and consistently and quickly, if the media center was organized in a useful way, if the company was sensitive to media deadlines, and so on, until a clear picture of the company's effectiveness with the media can be developed. This will show that the company is interested in keeping the media informed and helping them to perform their jobs in a crisis situation. It will also strengthen the media ties that were created during the crisis.

D. Conduct a Content Analysis of Clippings

In addition to contacting key members of the media to obtain personal accounts of how the situation, one person — usually from the crisis team — should be appointed to collect and analyze media clippings to determine if the media portrayals are in line with what the media actually said to the company. It may be useful for the company to contract the services of an external agency to gather this information, especially since the crisis team will be deeply involved in the crisis and may miss crucial articles or broadcasts.

E. Analyze the Crisis's Impact on the Bottom Line

The financial department should be consulted for this step. Lost sales, expenditures for disseminating information, and staff hours spent on the crisis are just some of the elements that must be looked at to determine how cost-effective the crisis plan was. If the crisis was handled extremely well, the company may actually see an increase in sales.

F. Appreciation

The company should send thank-you notes to those individuals who are not affiliated with the company (i.e. are not employed by or on retainer with the company), but who nonetheless helped out during the crisis. Example: The company next door loans the use of its phones to employees who are frantically making calls to local publics. Sending out thank-you notes may seem like a small touch, but it is also an inexpensive way for the company to show its appreciation to people or organizations that the company may very well deal with or depend on in the future.

G. Evaluate Crisis Management Against Benchmark

Benchmarks can be a variety of things, from the way a similar crisis was handled at a similar company to the most perfect handling of a crisis according to some academic standard. The Tylenol case may be considered to be a benchmark case in crisis communications history.

The company should decide beforehand what benchmark it will measure the handling of a company crisis against. Outside consultants, academics, and experts within the organization can all help to formulate this benchmark. The company may not be able to choose the benchmark until the crisis occurs. It may prove to be easier to measure various aspect of the crisis' handling against benchmarks, rather than measure the crisis as a whole. These components also should be decided beforehand.

H. Modify the Plan

After a crisis has occurred, modifications should be make to the crisis plan in those areas where improvements are needed. While aspects of the plan may sound good in theory, in the clutch they may not work. These areas can be determined through surveys, soft-sounding, and interviews conducted following the crisis. After the modifications are made, the plan should be redistributed, and practiced, with the changes.

I. Develop a Case Study

A written case study about a crisis that has happened at your company can prove invaluable for several reasons. First, it can be used as a training tool for company employees. Second, it can serve to reinforce the importance of crisis training. Third, it can point out the important roles that everyone must play to manage the crisis effectively. Finally, it can allow the company to sep back and observe the crisis from an objective viewpoint, which will allow company employees to determine for themselves if they have done a good job.

J. Distribute "Extra Mile" Awards to Employees

These awards can serve to reinforce employee morale as they reward employees for actions that were truly important to the company. IF a crisis occurs in the future, employees will remember that they were recognized before, and will be again, if they perform above the call of duty.

Top management should give out these awards, helping to reinforce the importance of employee action.

The Incomplete Plan A plan is always incomplete. It is a "work-in-progress" for managers who face unique situations every day. If, however, some form of a plan is not in position, practiced, and reexamined frequently, it will be no more useful than a manger's visceral reaction to a more garden variety management problem. The "ultimate crisis plan" attempts to overcome the gut reaction, knee jerk, shoot from the hip, off the top of the head, and other anatomical reactions of managers. By beginning a comprehensive planning process, the ultimate crisis plan attempts to place some of the most difficult problems that managers will ever face in their careers more directly in control through true management by planning, executing, and controlling actions that many have thought to be uncontrollable.

This plan illustrates a number of steps and actions that managers can take to position their organization to be prepared for the eventuality of a crisis. The development and maintenance of a complete management crisis plan should be the responsibility of several managers in a firm. Their career progress should be measured in part by the work they put into the development and refinement of a plan. In addition, their careers should be rewarded for attention to the important detail of a crisis plan. We would propose that a cross-functional team of managers from communications and public relations, marketing, production, operations or services, human resources, legal, and finance or accounting be included.

Outside Counsel? Outside counsel should be considered in many firms. Retained counsel may not be necessary, but an outside advisory board of knowledgeable and experienced men and women could be very valuable. A number of professional firms specialize in assisting firms during a crisis. While there is great value in having another experienced professional at the table during a crisis, our objective, in part, has been to persuade readers that they can and must begin the planning process. No one could possibly manage a crisis better than the firm experiencing the crisis.

The planning process or even partial elements of the process should stimulate inventive thinking. The authors request comments from the readers of *Crisis Response* and this chapter to help them refine and develop the plan for future generations of communications and general managers. Readers can send their written comments to the chapter authors at the Corporate Public Relations Program, Department of Integrated Marketing Communications, 1835 Hinman Avenue, Evanston, Illinois.

Aftermath

Readers interested in more refined versions of this chapter as it develops over time should also write the authors.

Finally, our objective was to develop a new generation of communications-educated and trained men and women with management knowledge and skills to manage crisis and manage an organization's response to a crisis — in the hope that their actions would save lives, mediate the physical and emotional effects of crisis, and save the organization from the repercussions of a crisis that might threaten its existence.

Clarke L. Caywood is director of Northwestern University's graduate program in Corporate Public Relations in the Department of Integrated Advertising/Marketing Communications. The program counts among its corporate associates firms such as Amoco, Shell, AT&T, Ford, Kodak, Sara Lee, First Chicago Bank, Citibank, and many other corporations. Professor Caywood teaches the program's graduate class in Corporate Public Affairs/Issues Management as well as graduate classes in management and marketing. Prior to coming to Northwestern, he taught in the marketing department of the Graduate School of Business of the University of Wisconsin at Madison. Caywood has published on political advertising and political marketing as well as done research on values in contemporary advertising and integrated marketing communications.

Caywood is a marketing business consultant to IBM Corporation and other firms on integrated marketing communications, and has worked in politics. He holds a joint doctorate in Business and Communications from the University of Wisconsin at Madison and a graduate degree in Public Affairs from the University of Texas at Austin. Professor Caywood is a member of the American Academy of Advertising, the American Marketing Association, and the Public Relations Society of America (PRSA).

Index

My Lai, as base for Viet Cong, 339
My Lai massacre, 323–42
    Army press and, 332
    chronicle of, 323, 326
    companies involved in, 323
    cover-up of, chronicle of, 327, 329, 330, 331
    inadequate training of companies involved in, 339, 340
    media coverage of, 334, 335
    participants in, punishment of, 338
    Peers Inquiry investigation of, 328, 331, 332, 335, 336
    reasons for, 338–41
    reports of, 329
    South Vietnamese reports of, 330
    Thompson report of, 329
    U.S. Army investigations of, 327, 328, 333, 339
    Viet Cong reports of, 331

N

NASA. *See* National Aeronautics and Space Administration (NASA)
National Academy of Sciences (NAS), 168
National Aeronautics and Space Administration (NASA), 383, 394
    Board of Inquiry, 388, 389
    "teacher in space" program, 384
    and White House, information exchange between, 386
National Broiler Council, 161
    and alleged chicken contamination crisis, 160
    news bureau for, 165
    PR effort of, 159
    role of, in media campaign, 166
National Consumers League, 167, 171
National Enquirer, 225, 226
National Gypsum, 289, 304
National Highway Traffic Safety Administration, 128
National Institute of Health (NIH), 143
    cuts UCLA study funding, 149
    secret condom tests, 146
National Institute of Occupational Safety and Health (NIOSH), 368
National Joint Council of Meat and Poultry Inspection Locals, 167
National News Council, 39
National Town Meetings, 40, 41
National Transportation Safety Board (NTSB), 198, 264, 267, 352
    and Calnev pipeline fire investigation, 271
    crisis procedures of, 352
Natural Resources Defense Council (NRDC), 186
    and Alar scare, 235, 236, 246
"NBC Nightly News," 24, 392
Nelson, George, 194
Nelson, James, 19
New Republic, 86
New York Police Department, 55
New York Society of Security Analysts, 180
New York Times, 5, 6, 85–7, 107, 145, 178
    and dioxin reassessment, 233
    coverage by, of Phillips's Bravo, 69
    on Mobil Oil Corporation, 34, 44

T